JEWRIES AT THE FRONTIER

JEWRIES AT THE FRONTIER

Accommodation

Identity

Conflict

Edited by

Sander L. Gilman
and Milton Shain

UNIVERSITY OF ILLINOIS PRESS

URBANA AND CHICAGO

Publication of this book was supported by a grant from the Isaac and Jessie Kaplan Centre for Jewish Studies and Research, University of Cape Town

Manufactured in the United States of America
1 2 3 4 5 C P 5 4 3 2 1

∞ This book is printed on acid-free paper.

Library of Congress Cataloging-in-Publication Data
Jewries at the frontier: accommodation, identity, conflict /
edited by Sander L. Gilman and Milton Shain.
p. cm.
Includes bibliographical references and index.
ISBN 0-252-02409-5 (cloth: alk. paper)
ISBN 0-252-06792-4 (pbk.: alk. paper)
1. Jewish diaspora.
2. Jews—Identity.
3. Jews—History—1789-1945.
4. Jews—History—1945-
5. Jews—Civilization.
I. Gilman, Sander L.
II. Shain, Milton.
DS134.J47 1999
909'.04924—dc21 98-58094
CIP

CONTENTS

Introduction: The Frontier as a Model for Jewish History

SANDER L. GILMAN

According to Amos Elon in a talk given in the spring of 1996 at the University of Chicago, we stand at the beginning of the post-Zionist era.[1] What that means for the writing of Jewish history is profound. Let me share an epiphany with you. Like many of you, I found myself one day at the Museum of the Diaspora in Israel, the Bet-Ha-Tefutzot, a space devoted to the documentation of the cultural achievement of the Diaspora, a counterweight to Yad Va-shem, which documents the victimization of Diaspora Jews. Inscribed at its entrance, as Arnold Eisen, in *Galut: Modern Reflections on Homelessness and Homecoming,* imagines, is the unwritten admonition: "Remember where you stand. Only the Land around you is real. The rest is not. If you come from a Diaspora of the present, know that sooner than you think, your community too will be part of our past, a room in our museum."[2] When I first experienced this, my sense was that the foundation of the state of Israel had made the life of Diasporic Jews somehow simpler if more stressful. Today this epiphany of a Diaspora Jew reading such a statement in what was claimed to be a non-Diasporic, Zionist space brings home to me that the overarching model for Jewish history has been that of the center or core and the periphery. This model had been reinforced by the role that Israel and Zionist historians have had in reshaping the narrative of Jewish history. It was (and remains) the model of "you" and "us." It is the imagined center which defines me as being on the periphery. "Israel," the lost Garden of Eden, the City on the Hill, is its center; all the rest of Jewish experience is on the periphery. Today, such a model no longer seems adequate for the writing of any aspect of Jewish history, including that of Zionism and of the State of Israel.

The complexities of the models for Jewish identity and historiography rest in part on the link between knowing who you are (identity) and knowing how you came to be who you are (history). The linkage between questions of identity/identification and history/historiography rests on the construction of organizational categories by the authors and readers of texts. We inscribe who we believe ourselves to be and where we believe ourselves to have come from in these texts we call "history." Identity is what you imagine yourself and the Other to be; history/historiography is the writing of the narratives of that difference.

Since the post-Egyptian biblical narrative, the reader finds the center defined as the God-given space of the Jews speaking the authentic language of the Jews; all other Jewish experience lies "beyond." But "beyond" is a space poisoned by the very notion of the center. The competing notions of the "Diaspora" and the "Galut" which structure Jewish historiography predispose a model of center and periphery and condemn the periphery to remain "marginal."

One of the great problems of Jews and non-Jews since the founding of the State of Israel is to understand the very meaning of Jewish life beyond Israel or the Holy Land as a valid life experience to be expressed authentically in a language and/or discourse adequate to the message. For a millennium this had been the distance from an imagined, textually based center—Torah as the symbolic topography of the missing center. Following the founding of the State of Israel, "exile" has meant exile from a real, geographically bounded place, while the act of returning, endlessly postponed, is now a possibility. The traditional center/periphery models of the meaning of the "exile" experience for Jews still provide good ways to understand this Jewish experience.

The contradictory yet overlapping models of a Jewish "Diaspora" as opposed to a Jewish "Galut" have formed the Jewish self-understanding of what "exile" means. The voluntary dispersion of the Jews ("Galut" or "Golah") is articulated as inherently different from the involuntary exile of the Jews ("Diaspora"). These two models exist simultaneously in Jewish history in the image of the uprooted and powerless Jews on the one hand, and rooted and empowered Jews on the other. It is possible to have a firm, meaningful cultural experience as a Jew in the Diaspora or to feel alone and abandoned in the Galut (as well as vice versa)—two people can live in the same space and time and can experience that space and time in antithetical ways. Indeed, the same person can find his or her existence bounded conceptually by these two models at different times and in different contexts.

The notion of a dispersion of the Jews is inscribed in the Torah in a specific manner with negative, punishing overtones. This dispersion represents punishment for the transgression of specific boundaries. The idea of a textual model for the Diaspora rooted in the Torah and reflected in other writings is important to any comprehension of a Jewish articulation of the meaning of "exile." But the very assumption of the Diaspora is ambiguous and contradictory even though it carries the force of divine revelation incorporated in texts. The Galut, on the other hand, is often understood as the experienced reality of being in exile, structured, however, by the internalization of the textual notion of the Diaspora tempered by the daily experience (good or bad) of life in the world. The Jew experiences the daily life of "exile" through the mirror of the biblical model of the expulsion—whether it be the expulsion from the Garden of Eden or the captivity in Egypt. If these two experiences are parallel—if life in the Galut is harsh and painful (as it often was)—it seems a further proof of the validity of the model of the Diaspora. The South African Jewish writer Sandra Braude has stated this succinctly: "But Jews tend to forget that there is only one promised land, and that they seldom are permitted to remain in any one place for longer than three generations."[3] It is the "land" that shapes the center/periphery model. Historians such as Jacob Neusner, in *Self-fulfilling Prophecy: Exile and Return in the History of Judaism,* have argued for a material understanding of this notion of Diaspora.[4] For Neusner it is the model of wilderness and land, the dialectic between tent and house, nomadism and agriculture, wilderness and Canaan, wandering and settlement, Diaspora and State. W. D. Davies has argued, in *The Territorial Dimension in Judaism,* that this dichotomy only seems to be balanced, that for every quote praising wilderness as the decisive factor in Judaism, there could be found a counterpart praising the Land of Zion.[5]

Such a model has different readings from different positions. Certainly a gendered reading of the center/periphery would and does provide quite different inflections of the model. But the domination of the model even levels the implication of gender for the writing of a history of Jewish culture and life.[6] For center/periphery models demand a specific type of hegemonic orientation. In the writing of women's history the core becomes the family and the periphery the world. Such models in the writing of the history of Jewish women tend to recapitulate the complexities of the role which the center/periphery has for the writing of all aspects of Jewish history. No place is this more clearly evident than in the writing of the history of the Jews after the Shoah.

If there is a postmodern reading of the center/periphery model which dominates the writing of "Diaspora" Jewish history in the 1990s it is the translation of the center from that of "Jerusalem" to that of the "Holocaust."

Such a reading of the "Shoah," "Holocaust," "Churban" as the new center of Jewish history and historiography makes all of the rest of Jewish history into a new periphery. Thus more and more it becomes necessary to define Jewish history either teleologically or metaphorically in terms of this new translation of the center. Readings of Jewish history from the Middle Ages to the 1920s become preparatory for the Holocaust. Studies of anti-Semitism as a European phenomenon come to make sense only in terms of its relationship to the new center, the Holocaust. Indeed, even studies of the origin and meaning of the State of Israel in all of its forms are read in terms of the Holocaust. Given the power in the writing of Jewish history which understands the center/periphery model to be normative, its translation into a "Holocaust-centered" model with its intimations of meaning and punishment seems frighteningly logical.

Thus Daniel Goldhagen's *Hitler's Willing Executioners* postulates a relatively straight path from medieval Jew-hatred to the Holocaust.[7] The center of Jewish history becomes the Holocaust and all Jewish experience comes to prefigure it. Unlike Goldhagen, I understand that there is a complicated history of anti-Semitism (for me a blanket term for Jew-hatred) in the Christian West which is different than simple ubiquitous xenophobia. I see this as stemming from the very origins of Christianity and its constant need to distance itself from Judaism and the Jews. What Goldhagen views as eliminationist anti-Semitism is present in the early Church. Yet given the specificity of the self-conscious construction of a *Staatsnation* (in the sense of Friedrich Meinecke) in the place of a *Kulturnation,* and the movement from the status and power of religious anti-Semitism to the new status of scientific racism at the close of the nineteenth century, the function of anti-Semitism in Germany is different from that in France or Austria. The *Sonderweg* debate—whether Germany and "the Germans," however defined, were different in their specificity at the end of the nineteenth and beginning of the twentieth centuries, whether in their understanding of colonialism or the "Jewish Question"—is not resolved. Indeed, comparative studies are beginning to pinpoint specifically the function of such stereotypes in understanding "German" culture in contrast with other self-consciously constructed national and local cultures in Central Europe. This is not to say that nineteenth- and early twentieth-century "German" culture in its construction of "Germanness," the "Germans," and the "Jews," was better or worse than in other national cultures, only that it fulfilled a different function. All of this means that, in my reading, the presence of what Goldhagen labels "eliminationist" (rather than exclusionist) anti-Semitism in Germany was necessary, but not sufficient for the Shoah to take place. Such a reading of the experience of the

Jews at the "German" frontier would eliminate the seeming centrality of the Holocaust for an understanding of Jew-hatred and would allow for a new reading of anti-Semitism as endemic rather than as teleologically resulting in the Shoah.

But the center/periphery model is in truth a symbolic structure of the understanding of the impossibility of a Diasporic life within this model of center and periphery. Such a definition demands the existence of a "real" center and thus defines the Jews in terms of their relationship to that center. An alternative model would be that of Jonathan Boyarin, who comments that "postmodern sensibilities allow us to recuperate the alternative (and in this sense traditional) resource of identifying with Jews as a collective through continuity (coextension in time) at least as much as through contiguity (coextension in space)."[8] This rejection of "land" means that "Jews can only constitute themselves as such in relation to others who are both like and unlike them" (128). In spite of his insight into the redefinition of the "Jews" as a temporal rather than as a topographic category, Boyarin himself falls into an attenuated center/periphery model seeing in his suggestion "a postmodern ideal of Diaspora" (124). I would see this as transcending rather than inscribing the center/periphery model. The center/periphery model cannot be/can be "postmodern" in any way.

If Jewish experience is contradictory to the expectations of the Diaspora model, as in the "Golden Age" of the Jews in Spain or the "exile" of Jews in the United States, the meaning of the models becomes muddled. This is certainly the case in the late twentieth century. Today, the pervasiveness of the center/periphery model (Diaspora, borderlands, margins and the like) for a conceptualization of Jewish history is thus fraught with new difficulties. We experience the simple reversal of the condemnation of the periphery as the place of failure and punishment. The margin becomes either the space of alienation from *Yiddishkeit* (as the fantasy inscription at the Diaspora Museum notes) or it becomes the pure site of radicality, creativity, and intellectual empowerment. Today we have seen a radical transvaluation of the meaning ascribed to the periphery. "Diasporic" has come to mean deterritorialized, homeless, rootless, displaced, dispersed, nomadic, discontinuous, hybrid, plural, incommensurable, interstitial, and minor. All of these terms have permeated the critical and historical appropriation of the center/periphery model. They have come to mark the desirability of life at the margin rather than its failure.

Both such readings are inherent to the center/periphery model and both point up its problem—it is a problem of authenticity. One reading sees the authentic at the center and only in terms of the center; the other sees the flight from the center as the hallmark of the authentic. What is striking in understanding the complexity of this model is that one marker seems to be central to its articulation and that is language—whether it is Hebrew (as the center) and the false, base Diasporic languages of the Jews, or Yiddish (as the center) and the false lapse into languages of acculturation or assimilation, or German/Magyar/English (as the center) and the peripheral and false languages of victimhood (Yiddish/German), our center/periphery is always articulated in terms of the struggle for language.

In holding the conference in Cape Town in 1996 during which early drafts of these essays (and a number of other contributions) were presented, the very idea of looking at Jewries at the frontier was embodied. For South Africa was and is again a frontier society for the construction of Jewish identity. South Africa in the past hundred years presents a complex case study for the notion of Jewries at the frontier. Popular wisdom stresses (and stressed) the homogeneity of South African Jewish culture, its Lithuanian and orthodox origin, its simultaneous rise to status and its relationship to other groups (the English, Afrikaners, and indigenous peoples) in South Africa. And yet that narrative was structured by the very understanding of the frontier experience by Jews in South Africa. Gideon Shimoni's study of the politics of immigration in Lithuania and South Africa sets the stage for an understanding of the bases for the image of a homogeneous South African Jewry before 1939, while John Simon shows how the "official" Jewish community needed that notion of homogeneity of culture, language and religion as part of its normalization in post–World War II South Africa. Marcia Leveson's study of the representations of the Jew in Jewish and non-Jewish writing in Anglophone South Africa replicates the desire of homogeneity and the true rupture sensed in the image of the Jew suspended between materialist and aesthete. The question of the representation and self-representation of the Jew on the real and the imagined frontier is the stuff of fiction from Leveson's survey of Jewish writing in South Africa to, as Heidi Grunebaum-Ralph shows us in her close reading of Albert Memmi's autobiography, an account of the author as a Northern African Jew. The African frontier, indeed, but seen from the perspective of northern Africa read from the southern tip of Africa.

How such conflicts demanded levels of accommodation even (or especially) in the prime self-defining aspect of South African Jewry, religious expression, can be grasped in Claudia Braude's reading of the conflicts revealed in religious pronouncements under the apartheid system. Milton Shain's discussion of the parallels and differences between South African Jewish history and that of the Jews of North America highlights the complexity hidden beneath the surface. All of these essays look at South African Jewry in the light of a self-proclaimed autonomous status, one claimed for the community by itself as well as imposed on it by anti-Semitic rhetoric. Yet, as Sally Frankental shows, there are other "Jews" in South Africa, such as the Israelis, whose identity as sojourners presents a crazy-house mirror to this notion of homogeneity. Recently, the welcoming home of Jews, such as the late Joe Slovo, former head of the Communist Party of South Africa, at least posthumously back into the fold of the "Jews" of South Africa (by having a Rabbi speak at his funeral) shows how even groups excoriated and ignored have come to be reintegrated into the new Jew at the South African Frontier. The complex notion of living at the margins (of a society and of a continent) shaped and shape the need for specific forms of self-representation in South Africa.

LANGUAGE AS ONE OF THE KEYS TO THIS PROBLEM

"Next Year in Jerusalem?" asks the Jewish/Israeli/American philosopher Richard Shusterman, in his paean (the paean of a *bal-tsuvot* in exile in America) to the formative power of the center/periphery model for creating an authentic Jewish identity only in relationship to a mythic center.[9] Having "returned" to the United States (also a real and a mythic space), he finds himself

> no longer one of the redeemed ascenders to full Jewish national identity (*olim*) but one of the fallen (*yordim*) who lives in what is termed "exile" (Galut). However, I'm not yet sure whether I should be written off as a *yored*. For not merely do I maintain a love for Israel, whose experience and way of life have structured so much of my own that it is an inalienable part of me; but I have not renounced the option of going back to resettle there and thus to reenact the myth of return, that, I argue, is quintessential to Jewish identity. But such a return, in contrast to my official *aliyah*, will indeed be an actual return as well as a mythic one, for I will have already been there before. (295)

And Shusterman tags his Jewish identity in his American text by interpolating the authentic language and/or discourse of the center/periphery model (Hebrew) into his parenthetic model, saying, in effect, "I write in English, the language of cultural hegemony, but within me resides the true Jew, whose language is quintessential to Jewish identity." Language is a primary marker of the center/periphery model in the understanding of Jewish identity and the writing of Jewish history.[10]

In the same volume of philosophical discussions of Jewish identity in which Shusterman's essay appeared, Gabriel Josipovici, quite a different Jew in his own definition ("not circumcised, have not taken my bar mitzvah, do not attend synagogue or celebrate any of the feasts" [309] and, one might add, living in England, not Israel) bemoans the problem of the meaning of language by evoking his models on the margins, such as that of Kafka's diary entry "in which he examines why the German language, which is the only one he really knows, is incapable of expressing in the word *Mutter* his own (Jewish) sense of his mother; or Proust's description of Marcel's despair at not being able to express his sense of joy at the way the sunlight strikes the river and being reduced to banging his umbrella on the ground and crying 'Zut zut zut'" (314).[11] Here Josipovici interpolates Kafka's "Jewish" response to his German into his English, for him, now a language which can only approximate his exilic condition; yet Proust's inarticulate sounds are not at all labeled as Jewish. Who is more "Jewish"? The writer who reflects on the inability of his language to carry meaning (while showing that it does) or the one reduced to describing the inarticulate banging of the umbrella. Yet both are, of course, merely conventional enactments of modernist concerns about language. Proust's language is certainly as expressive as that of Kafka in stating its inexpressiveness. As Josipovici himself notes, all writers doubt the power of their own language and/or discourse to express the world which they imagine. But for the Jew (self-defined and defined temporally as the Other—whether Kafka or Proust or Josipovici), language on the margin becomes the testing place for the notion of an authentic language of the Jews—even the language that one does possess is drawn into question.

The language politics of the eastern marches of the Austro-Hungarian Empire can be seen as being the line of demarcation between those groups (such as the Poles and Ruthenians) who demanded some degree of acknowledgment of their "national" languages and the Jews, who actively abandoned Yiddish while developing both pro- and antimonarchical positions. Certainly the language politics of early Zionism was a continuity of the dismissal of Yiddish and the insistence on "real" national languages in Herzl's imaginary construction of a future state. In their essay in this volume on the differences among the various regions of the eastern marches, Albert Lichtblau and Michael John illustrate the complex relationship between the "frontier" mentality of those on the fringes of empire and the need for a "real" (read "not Jewish") mode of expressing that sense of belonging.

Where the authentic lies in our understanding of the center/periphery model in Jewish history is tied to the notion of language. It is clear that such a symbolic model has structured the writing of Jewish history or perhaps better, the history of the Jews, from at least Flavius Josephus. Even insightful historiographers, such as Arnaldo Momigliano, share the center/periphery model while being quite clear in their understanding of its limitation.[12] It is striking, however, that the hidden litmus test for the center/periphery model is a quality of the Jewish experience which is ambiguous in its very nature. It is the function of language and/or discourse as a marker of Jewish identity. Thus Momigliano writes that modern ideas of the Diaspora, such as those held by the historian Pierre Vidal-Naquet, overlap with that of Flavius Josephus: "Flavius Josephus, the historian of the war of 70 A.D., is a Jew who speaks Aramaic and writes first in Aramaic. It is only after he has acquired Roman citizenship and settled in Rome that he begins, with some difficulty, to write in Greek. By adopting Greek patterns of thought Flavius signified his distance from Palestinian Jews, but at the same time wrote an apology of Judaism" (69). "Flavius Josephus is far from secularizing his categories of judgment" (75). For Momigliano the key to his reading of Flavius is the fact that Flavius ignores the "synagogue" and the tradition of the apocalypse. Both are linked in the notion of the center of the Jewish experience as Jerusalem but also to "Hebrew" as the liturgical language of the Jews. Since Flavius is on the margins—in both historical and geographic terms—of the Roman empire, his sensibilities come to represent the Diasporic tradition for Momigliano. Rome (or Paris or Chicago) can be understood as the periphery, if the Diasporic is taken only in relationship to the unarticulated center (Jerusalem). And that center must be timeless, unlike the world of the Diaspora, which is defined as temporally bound.

But Flavius is also a prime example of problems perceived by those Jews who live at the symbolic margin. It is not that all Jews became Hellenistic critics of Maccabee power, not all Jews so overidentify with "Rome" (while writing in Greek), but the line between the poles—between the religious fanaticism of Masada and total acculturation—became a permanent marker of the Jews in the Diaspora. Flavius's position, according to Momigliano, came to be marked by a need to repress the center/periphery model and its language in his conceptualization of the historical process of the Jews and to replace it with a new center, the language of Greco-Roman historiography.

For Momigliano, Pierre Vidal-Naquet's French patterns of thought and his use of French come to represent the "good" Jew using the languages of the Diaspora to reveal rather than disguise his Jewishness. Vidal-Naquet represents in Momigliano's estimation the positive values of a Jewish historiography on the periphery, one which is conscious of its Jewishness. But there is still a specter which haunts Momigliano's notion of the authentic Jewish historian—it is the distance from the center, a center now "real," existing in Israel, rather than symbolic, existing in the Jewish (read "Hebrew") texts which uniquely formed his Jewish-Italian identity as a child. In a complicated way, Momigliano uses Flavius as the negative image of acculturation and Vidal-Naquet as the positive one. Vidal-Naquet represents the world of Romanic Judaism which Momigliano identifies as his own:

> Vidal-Naquet has not forgotten and will not forget that he is Jewish, one of the Jews from the Arba' Kehillot, from the "four communities" of the Contado Venassino, whose center is in Carpentras; ever since the Middle Ages, generations of rabbis and doctors, and more recently musicians, politicians, writers, and scientists, have come from Carpentras in very high proportions compared to their small numbers. Both Vidal-Naquet's father, who participated in the Resistance in 1940, and his mother, were deported and killed at Auschwitz by the Nazis. (68)

This is a biography which echoes the autobiographical account of Momigliano's youth and upbringing which prefaces the volume of his Jewish essays (xxv–xxviii).

Momigliano's Caraglio is a space for Jews and his Jewishness is that of text, including the Zohar. He is raised in a religious orthodoxy unusual among his peers and he remains conscious, unlike Flavius, of synagogue and language. His "father and mother were among the victims" of the Nazis (xxvii). Momigliano comes to represent the problems of the Diasporic model which seem to end in the Shoah, the ultimate condemnation of the periphery, and yet, as in his work and that of Vidal-Naquet, continue at the margins after the Shoah. Flavius's Greek, Vidal-Naquet's French, and Momigliano's Italian all come to represent languages and cultural traditions on the periphery rather than the new site of cultural contestation. And yet, in Momigliano's words, there is the desire for the traditions of Diaspora Jews to be unbounded in terms of time. His genealogies are provided to show continuity of Jewish life before and (in his own work) after the Shoah. It is the dream of a new center on the periphery.

Recent non-Jewish critiques on the use of the Diaspora model, such as that by the Irish-American anthropologist Benedict Anderson, point to the need for an alternative manner of imagining the historical movement of people.[13] "Today's long-distance nationalism," the globalization of national identity, is seen by Anderson as a reflex of "capitalism's remorseless, accelerating transformation of all human societies" (327). Yet he too sees the process of national identity as a process of interaction on the margins. He comments that the construction of the "native" is a white-on-black negative. "The nativeness of natives is always unmoored, its real significance hybrid and oxymoronic. It appears when Moors, heathens, Mohammedans, savages, Hindoos, and so forth are becoming obsolete, that is not only when, in the proximity of real print-encounter, substantial numbers of Vietnamese read, write, and perhaps speak French but also when Czechs do the same with German and Jews with Hungarian. Nationalism's purities (and thus also cleansings) are set to emerge from exactly with hybridity" (316). The collapse of the Diaspora model in the contemporary world (in contrast to Momigliano's romanticization of its tenacity) is the result of the ability to shift language. Momigliano makes Hebrew and the synagogue, the touchstone of identity, the true center, replaced, following the accepted model of the Alliance Israélite Universelle, by French as the cultural equivalent of Hebrew, or the Hilfsverein der deutschen Juden, who saw German as the cultural center for Diasporic German Jews in the nineteenth century. This language hegemony extended into the United States, as Michael Meyer has shown.[14] Remember German and French were the language of the schools founded by them to westernize the Jews of the Orient, and turn them into Western Jews. It is the mobility of language (for Anderson tied to modern technology and print) that now defines hybridity—and it is of course an older, and more ideologically suspect, marker than even he gives credit. Anderson is thus answering to a degree James Clifford's image of all of those exiles, migrants, displaced peoples caught up in a margin of nonmovement within a tyrant economy of movement.[15] Clifford's vision of the periphery, unlike those of Momigliano or Anderson is totally disempowering. He is aware that the romanticization of the periphery creates but a new center and perpetuates the model of the marginal. It is language which marks all of these readings of "exodus" and the "periphery." It is language which can also provide a key to an alternative model for viewing Jewish history, the model of the frontier.

THE FRONTIER AS THE ALTERNATIVE ANSWER TO THE PROBLEM

Let us imagine a new Jewish history written as the history of the Jews at the frontier, a history with no center; a history marked by the dynamics of change, confrontation, and accommodation; a history which focuses on the present and in which all participants are given voice. It is the place of the "migrant culture of the in-between" as both a transitional and translational phenomenon, one that "dramatizes the activity of culture's untranslatability," according to Homi Bhabha.[16] It is clear that the "frontier" is a modern, if not a postmodern, concept. The word itself is not to be found in the King James translation of the Bible. And yet by the Revised Standard Version the concept of the frontier begins to infiltrate an English reading of the text.[17]

The passages in the Revised Standard Version reflect a postcolonial English reading of the sense of place, a place not defined by a center and a periphery but by a constant sense of confrontation at the margin. The Jews go out and confront "Others" at the margins—where they too become marginal. Is it war, avoidance, intermarriage, accommodation, or acculturation which can result on the frontier? All of course are possible when the inhabitants of Israel meet the Jewish "Others," "the Reubenites and the Gadites and the half-tribe of Manas'seh," or the non-Jewish Others, "the Moabites," or even the sons of Lot at the frontier. It is the focus on this space, a rupture of the frontier from the center, which can provide the space not only of confrontation but also of accommodation. (Both concepts have a negative and positive valance.)

The frontier is a colonial and a postcolonial concept which is applicable in complex ways to the writing of a new Jewish history. Today we should move from the King James Version of the Bible, with its missing "frontier" and its evocation of London as the new Jerusalem, to the New English Bible, not because it is aesthetically superior, but because it reinscribes a series of colonial and postcolonial images onto the language of the Hebrew Bible which may well clarify a new reading of Jewish history. If language, even the language of the "Bibles," can be viewed as a litmus test of the formation of a "Jewish" identity, however defined, the submerged model for the writing of Jewish history, which also is present in Tanach, is that of the frontier.

I am quite attuned to the problems of symbolic representations of the Jew as an abstract figure beyond history. Daniel and Jonathan Boyarin were right to call our attention to the political challenge implied in Jean-François Lyotard's act of allegorizing the Jew.[18] Yet it is equally false to separate the internal and external definitions of the Jew. It is the center/periphery model which enables this separation to seem "natural." Once the center/periphery model is suspended, the frontier becomes the space where the complex interaction of the definitions of self and Other are able to be constructed. Once we understand that the bipolar structure of center and periphery maintains the separation between "real" and "symbolic" definitions of the Jew, the model of the frontier can lead to a new reading of Jewish history of the modern era in which the symbolic becomes a meaningful function of both internal and external identity as an extension of the network of meaning into all aspects of our understanding of the "Jews."

The frontier in biblical terms is also marked by a specific relationship with the inhabitants. Initially hostile and yet willing to join with them or confront them. The land/space/topology that God gave to the Jews is thus Moses's frontier as it was Abraham's. In the King James Version of Genesis 17:5: "Neither shall thy name any more be called Abram, but thy name shall be Abraham; for a father of many nations have I made thee." Abraham's is a tale of the frontier for he "journeyed from thence toward the south country, and dwelled between Kadesh and Shur, and sojourned in Gerar" (21:1). Abraham, caught between Sarah (whom he disguises as his sister for Abimelech, the king of Gerar) and his "bondwoman" Hagar the Egyptian, is typical of the experiences on the frontier, experiences in which language, culture, and even sexuality, are the markers of the frontier experience. These two women represent two quite different modes of living on the frontier. Sexual conflicts and accommodations on the frontier mirror cultural ones. These nations are nations in conflict and change, are nations ever shifting in their cultural definition and space. The tale of Abraham is the tale of the frontier, a frontier still without a true center. It is, as all biblical narratives are, repeated with variations through the Bible, each variation proving the truth of the original model. Just as the center/periphery model begins with the tale of the expulsion from Eden, so too the model of the frontier begins with Abraham and his confrontations at the frontier. Both models (like those of Diaspora and Galut) exist simultaneously in the symbolic space of the Bible, and yet each can be seen to have a separate function in providing different narratives for the history of the Jews. As in Talmud, it is not necessary to fix one single model or meaning as the authentic one. Rather it is from the competition of multiple models that some sense of a pattern can be found.

What if we heuristically assume the existence of this submerged biblical model of the frontier and apply it to "modern" Jewish history? Always at a frontier, often a material frontier, the Jews (however defined) understood this material frontier symbolically. Indeed, it becomes the space in which the "Jews" are defined and define themselves. Here we must move from Flavius Josephus, the Greco-Roman Jewish historian, to the Roman historian of the German frontier, Tacitus (who did not like the Jews very much), to examine both sides of the image. Modern Jewish history can be understood as the existence of the Jews on a permanent symbolic frontier. From Roman Germany through medieval Poland through to nineteenth-century United States and South Africa, Jews have always functioned on the frontier. Israel itself was and remains a frontier state, and can so be read outside of a center/periphery model. The very creation of modern Jewish identity within a center/periphery model demanded a frontier sensibility at its core.

The model of the frontier I imagine is not Frederick Jackson Turner's model with its reliance on "real" frontiers, an analogy to the stress on the materiality of the land that Jacob Neusner understands as the basis of the center/periphery model of Jewish history. One must think of the very concept of "frontier" as a structure of communal fantasy, as a model of imagining oneself in the world. There is no better example of such an imagining than in the "New Western History," that new model of understanding the American frontier. Stephen Aron notes that the "New Western History" began with Patricia Limerick's casting off of Turner's notion of the frontier as an "unsubtle concept for a subtle world." But, Aron argues quite correctly, the frontier is the very center of a New Western History: "Rather than banishing the word for past offenses, western historians need to make the most of the frontier. Reconfigured as the lands where separate polities converged and competed, and where distinct cultures collided and occasionally coincided, the frontier unfolds the history of the Great West in ways that Turner never imagined."[19] Turner, who used the idea of the frontier to define his understanding of America, would not have recognized the notion of the frontier today. For North American historians it is the new "'F' word," according to Kerwin Lee Klein, and one which may have problems in constructing a new regionalism at the expense of a national identity.[20] However, it is the ability to balance the moment of the frontier experience with the general sense of an integrative history of peoples which makes the frontier a useful category for the writing of the new Jewish history.

The frontier is, to use a poetic evocation of a Jewish "borderland," as the German-language poet Hilde Domin did in an interview in the 1970s, a way of seeing oneself as a Jew as a "border dweller" and Jewish history as a *Grenzfall,* a case on the and at the margins: "It is true," she said, "that I see the fate of the Jews as only the extremist case of the general. The specific, the marginal case (*Grenzfall*) is sublimated into fate, especially by the poets."[21] But it is at the real and at the imagined frontier that the shaping of Jewish identity does take place. Such a sense of the frontier as a space of contestation rather than as a border between constructed identities runs counter to Homi Bhabha's claim about the Jews as the force of cultural translation (in Walter Benjamin's terms and analogous to Zygmunt Bauman's argument). The Jews are seen as one of the "wandering people who will not be contained within the *Heim* of the national culture and its unisonant discourse" (164). Instead, such peoples "are themselves the marks of a shifting boundary that alienates the frontiers of the modern nation . . . . They articulate the death-in-life of the idea of the 'imagined community' of the nation; the worn-out metaphors of the resplendent national life now circulate in another narrative of entry-permits and passports and work-permits that at once preserve and proliferate, bind and breach the human rights of nation" (164). Bhabha's notion of the frontier is suddenly no longer imagined but concrete. It is the border which is maintained as the illusionary mark of difference, rather than the frontier as the site of contestation and accommodation. It is a "real" border rather than an imagined frontier. But, on the other hand, recent discussions of the imagined border, as we have mentioned, such as that by Gloria Anzaldúa in her *Borderlands/La Frontera: The New Mestiza,* have tended to romanticize the border as the ideal space of meeting and merging.[22]

The border can also be the frontier where competition can lead to destruction and to death, to the commission of abominable acts in the eyes of all parties. Terrible things can happen at the frontier—massacres, banishments, rapes, and murders. The destruction of the Amalechites, of the Jews of England, of the Native Americans in the *pays d'en haut,* can all occur at the frontier. But it is in this liminal space that all parties are forced to understand and define themselves in the light of their experience of the Other. It is not a space in which liminality is always rewarded by the approval of the marginal, by its movement to a new center with the forces of power now at the periphery.

Richard White's writing on the frontier can serve as a model for how such a history can be undertaken. White's greatest historical work is *The Middle Ground.*[23] This work began as a rather straight rewriting of North American Native American history in the *pays d'en haut.* White, too, was surprised when he found the frontier a useful concept. In his detailed, often horrific, often fascinating account of the long eighteenth century in lower Canada and the adjacent British colonies to the South, the idea of a space of contestation and accommodation is developed. His idea of the frontier as the "middle ground," as the space of compromise, is helpful in shaping a new vision of Jewish history.

The middle ground in North American history is, of course, different from the numerous middle grounds of Jewish history. But the potential values and horrors of the compromise position, of the position in which the confrontation between cultures and peoples and among cultures and peoples provides a new multivocal account of the histories of a people, is useful. The frontier as imagined by White is not a pure space, an absolute answer to the center/periphery model of history. White's model is an attenuated center/periphery model which focuses on the distance from the presumptive center as a factor in the ability of the "middle ground" to serve as that place of accommodation and confrontation. Yet the center (London or Paris in White's account of the Great Lakes Region from 1650 to 1815) truly vanishes in his account, while the real markers of the middle ground in his narrative are the languages spoken. Certainly English and French are the contesting languages, but it is the wide range of Native American tongues which dominate his account. Indeed, his marker of the mediator is the "hybrid," which White defines in terms of the offspring of Europeans and Native Americans. Stories which replicate those of Abraham, Sarah, Abimelech, and Hagar constantly reappear in White's narrative of the frontier. In point of fact, the true "hybrids," to use the term most favored in postcolonial theory, are those who can negotiate between languages. Language, as much as sexuality, is the marker of hybridity as well as the source of conflict. This is the true marker of the frontier in White's account.

On certain colonial and postcolonial frontiers, the very appearance of colonial settlements which carried the weight of the home culture meant that Jews were only ambiguously understood as belonging "marginally" to a majority culture. In colonial Australia the problem of the stigmatization of a specific group of early settlers (the "convicts") is, as Paul Bartrop shows in his contribution on Christians, Jews, and Aborigines, a means of creating a great space for (and antagonism against) those perceived as different. Jews on the colonial frontier come to be seen both as part of an "in" group but also as part of a hierarchy of social values and cultural esteem. If Bartrop illustrates the problems of identity formation in a world defined by class and race, Jon Stratton's view of the latter history of the idea of the Jew in Australia raises the specter that Jews in Australia (like those in South Africa) may have struggled with the notion of their own whiteness in a society defined by images of race. In examining the contemporary antipodal scene in New Zealand, Livia Wittmann shows how this lien of race continues to haunt the images of Jewish women in the postcolonial world. In this context the move from accommodation to conflict to a new identity formation crosses historical and gender boundaries. In complex ways these are all the "same story," but the particular shift which each author takes in examining specific moments provides very different narratives of the Jewries at this frontier.

I know that the "middle ground" is a controversial term and that my linking of it with language already will evoke a critical response. This Aristotelian term comes to play a central role in the construction of ideas of liminality. Thus it is a term which shows up within Bruno Latour's work as the object of one of his critiques of the "modern."[24] The middle ground is one of his answers to the "illusion" of the "totalitarian center" and its reflex, the "ridiculous" claims for the margins (124). He too understands the preoccupation with the hybrid as a fault of such a conceptualization of the center/periphery model: "The less the moderns think they are blended, the more they blend" (43). And one assumes the reverse is also true. Here too the center/periphery model disguises its intent. Those constructing the modern, according to Latour, could, as one strategy, "seize the middle ground, whose dimensions were continuing to expand. Instead of concentrating on the extremes of the work of purification, this strategy concentrated on one of its mediations, language" (62). For Latour, such a strategy loses the networked complexity of his understanding of how material and symbolic structures interact. He, however, misjudges how language and/or discourse reflects the problems of identity formation, enabling each of us to construct multiple worlds of words. Even Latour's critique of the "middle ground" and its appropriation of language is clothed in a language of confrontation rather than accommodation. It too holds the "middle ground."

If there is a "Jewish" pendant to Latour's anxiety about the function of language and/or discourse as a contested space, it is Zygmunt Bauman's claim that the very culture of modernity is "a 'project' of postmodernity in a prodromal stage,"[25] which is represented by Jewish art as the essential representation of the modern. (This is Bauman's reading of the function of the Jews as a pariah nation, a catalyst for change or a measure of change, in the related terms of Max Weber and Hannah Arendt [71–77].) Thus the "Jewish struggle with modernity" (in answer to earlier claims of Cuddihy) are merely by-products of "modernity's struggle with itself" (154). Thus the language of the frontier, of the confrontation of the Jew and the Other, comes to constitute "the seminal contribution of the obstreperous, critical and rebellious culture of modernity" (195). There is no Jewish particularism; it is all a function of the strains and claims of the modern. (This is very much in line with Gabriel Josipovici's desire to see the alienated language of the modern, European Jew as a sign of the modern condition). This is the romanticized version of the frontier which assumes that each groups confrontation will be creative within the model of an avant-garde. But what if it is not Freud and Simmel and Kafka that one takes as one's witnesses but Oppenheimer and Gundolf and Rathenau, the conservatives at the frontier, whose confrontation resulted in accommodation, or Hirsch and Scholem and Heschel, whose modernism is to be found within traditional religious forms of argument and language. It is not only "metonymic, iterative temporality" that is the counternarrative of the nation, as Homi Bhabha claims (55). Are these other voices not also representatives of this prodromal stage of postmodernity, are they not hybrids of a not very exotic type? In her *Displacements: Cultural Identities in Question,* Angelika Bammer has noted that the Diasporic experience may be one of mobility, plurality, alterity, but eventually also one of fixation, of the need to settle down upon certain symbols, of assimilation.[26]

It is vital to understand that the middle ground is not equivalent to the nomadic, seen by Gilles Deleuze and Félix Guattari as the definition of the modern Jewish experience. They sketch the process of identity-formation in their description of "becoming-Jewish." They wrote in *A Thousand Plateaus:*

> Jews . . . may constitute minorities under certain conditions, but that in itself does not make them becomings. . . . Even Jews must become-Jewish (it certainly takes more than a state). But if this is the case, then becoming-Jewish necessarily affects the non-Jew as much as the Jew. Becoming-woman necessarily affects men as much as women. Conversely, if Jews themselves must become-Jewish . . . , it is because only a minority is capable of serving as the active medium of becoming, but under such conditions that it ceases to be a definable aggregate in relation to the majority. . . . Becoming-Jewish . . . therefore implies simultaneous movements, one by which a term (the subject) is withdrawn from the majority, and another by which a term (the medium or agent) rises up from the minority.[27]

This merging of the identity of the majority which defines and the minority which is defined and thus redefines the majority is a process of constant construction and reconstruction of identity.[28] Now such identity transformations have been understood as being internal, purely psychological in their representation. "Becoming-Jewish," in the sense of Gilles Deleuze and Félix Guattari, is understood as a process of identity formation. And yet this too presents a problem, the problem of the loss of specificity in time.

Frontiers attract different social and psychological "types": they can be the site of the reconstruction of complex social groups (such as in South Africa) or they can be the site of flight from such groups (such as Alaska). The very notion of the frontier provides both the potential for community or the escape from community. Bernard Reisman shows in his illuminating contribution how the Alaskan community is potentially in transition from one model to the other, or at least is developing the potential for concepts of community and a common set of self-definitions. Out of many, one—a concept which may be inherently "American" (it is present on all currency), but which flies in the face of the experience of the "loner" fleeing to the frontier which marks that space where the one can function alone. The construction of a "Jewry" on the Alaskan frontier shows how the very notion of a collective (no matter how defined) can be the structure against which the individual reacts. Seth Wolitz's contribution shows how such a transition can take place in popular culture. The notion of the "loner" as defining the Texan comes to merge with the sense of community (under siege) which is the present-day mirror image of the Jew on the new southwestern frontier. The "Jew" sees him- or herself as part of a specific community—that of Texas Jewry—which provides him or her with intertwined and self-reinforcing definitions.

In all of these critics, the struggle with the "modern" comes to evoke and use the Jews and the problem of a Jewish historiographic model as the touchstone for the specific problems of the modern or the illusion of modernity.

"The Jews" in each case are defined ahistorically rather then temporally. It is in this move where the error lies, for it is in the radical temporality of Jewish existence that one can find the answer to the atemporality and ahistorical nature of the center/periphery model. Who are the Jews? Those who understood themselves as Jews at specific moments in time. Does this definition change? It is constantly shifting and constantly challenged, which is why absolute boundaries *must* be constructed for the "Jews" within and without Jewish cultural and ritual. The less possible a definition is, the more rigid it appears. This is true in Felix Theilhaber's and Bernard Wasserstein's complaints about the vanishing Jews of Europe[29] (one substantially before, the other substantially after the Shoah); this is true within debates in Germany and Israel today about who are "real" Jews. Over and over, one side of the debate comes to be defined as the "authentic Jews."

On the frontier as defined by specific moments in time, it is vital to hear all of the voices—both those voices defined and self-defined as Jewish and those understood by the Jews as "Other." R. Po-chia Hsia has shown how vital it is in the history of the Jews in early Modern Germany to understand both sides of the history,[30] and any understanding of the Haskala or modern Israel needs both sides too. The "sides" are marked by the languages of the protagonists. And this language actually marks the frontier. It is the middle ground, the space in which contestations take place—and by the way, if White's balanced account is any indicator, true horrors as well as accommodations take place on both sides. Horrors, because motivations are not comprehended; noble actions because the very fabric of the culture observed is never quite comprehended. Language serves as the marker. Why do Jews in Central and Eastern Europe speak Yiddish as their "Jewish" secular language (as opposed to the liturgical language of Hebrew or the language of the population among whom they lived)? They speak Yiddish because in the Rhineland before ghettoization they spoke the German dialect of the area. They moved from whatever language they had brought with them from the south—whether Latin or Greek or Aramaic—to German because they were on the Roman frontier, a frontier marked by its distance from Rome. They spoke the language of their neighbors. When they moved to Poland and the East, they continued to speak German (or now proto-Yiddish) because it was a language of hegemonic value given the role of the German knights in the East. This identification of Yiddish with German reappeared during World War I when German politicians wished to win Jews in Russia to their cause and again after 1989 when the claim was made that Yiddish-speaking Jews were indeed displaced Germans who should be able to claim German citizenship under the German parallel to the "Law of Return."

This is also the pattern of the history of the Jews. The Jews are to be understood as a multiple yet single entity: multiple because of the cultures manifested under that label, yet unitary because of the common archaeology or cultural identity they believed themselves to share, even with those who are never self-consciously part of the Jews. This is not to say that the center/periphery model is wrong or even incomplete given its power. It is only to say that, within the constitution of models for Jewish history, the frontier model, with language as its central marker, can have powerful heuristic value. It is clear that neither model is found in a "pure" state. The center/periphery model can be read as a frontier model and the frontier can be understood as "merely" an isolated aspect of a center/periphery model. But it is the tension which is of real interest.

It is not the "real" frontier, the actual land which concerns the "New Western" historians, but rather the fantasy topography of the frontier which Turner actually constructed. It is the frontier as that contested space beyond the world of the self, inhabited by those who both belong there and those who inhabit the frontier before the newcomers arrive and must be dealt with in one way or another. It is a frontier of fantasy. But it replaces a notion of the frontier (as Francis Parkman's *History of the Conspiracy of Pontiac* shows) in which one imagines oneself teleologically as the center and end of history and in which one understands one's own physical position in the world as that cutting edge of (divine) history. It is clear Parkman created his Pontiac as the Native American whom he needed for his dramatic confrontation between "world historical personalities," rather than charting the *mentalité* of the construction of meeting and interaction of peoples. But Jewish history in the center/periphery model tends to provide such concrete figures in much the same manner. Sigmund Freud's Moses, in his *Moses and Monotheism,* becomes much the same type of surrogate for the Jews as a collective as is Parkman's Pontiac. Such acts of concretization seem to be needed as long as one imagines a center, even the author's self as center.

To answer this move to the concrete, one must therefore imagine the frontier as a constructed, psychological space. It is the structure that underlies all of colonial expansion, whether cultural expansion from China into Japan; or the mercantile expansion of British might into Africa, North America and India; or the political/cultural hegemony of America in the contemporary world. In each case a frontier, populated by indigenous people, must be confronted in order to establish the identity of the group entering into the established order—and that established order can be "primitive," as in Francis Galton's Hottentots, or can be "cultured," as in Marco Polo's Moguls. Such a frontier is seen, however, from only one perspective. My sense of the frontier is one in which all voices can be articulated. Language as the medium and the stuff of dynamic interaction needs to be seen from both sides—the speakers of different languages, idiolects, and discourses come together and therefore all sets of texts become imperative in understanding the contact between and among groups.[31]

Zhou Xun's groundbreaking paper on the representations and realities of the Jews in late nineteenth- and early twentieth-century China illustrates how differentiated one must be when one speaks of the "Jews." No single marker defines both image and experienced reality except their location at the frontier of "China," itself a constructed space. The "Jews" of China in their language, culture, status, and imaginary as well as real existence are different one from the other in virtually every way. What is striking is that they exist and are understood as part of a coherent Jewry—and therefore provide a normative measure of the validity or falsity of the stereotypes of the Jew in the complex culture which is modern China.

Such linguistic and cultural interaction and conflict take place within the psyches of those crossing the frontier. It is the notion of violation and transcendence of boundaries that is inherent to such a construction of the frontier. No frontier exists unless this notion of violation is present. Thus the notion of the frontier is that it seems to be inscribed on the land but is actually a narrative tradition superimposed on a landscape. It is defined by the very notion of violation and this notion can be read as positive or negative. It is a means of organizing the world, rather than the world itself. It creates the markers even if the markers rely on phenomena of the world. Thus language is a constant marker for the frontier. Some at the frontier are understood to speak a language perceived as crude and deceptive; it is the language which marks difference. But it can be equally true that those at the frontier are imagined to speak a tongue understood as complex and revealing. The language of the Other is not the language of the self.

The Jewish experience as imagined on such a frontier is thus complex; indeed more complex than most. It is not the colonial or postcolonial experience as understood by contemporary theory but it is certainly impacted by the notion of the frontier which haunts postcolonial theory. The borderlands are where the Jews, like all people, perpetually live. Indeed, the margin is defined by the presence of those who identify themselves as "Jews" or where "Jews" are imagined to dwell. Jews may accompany or create colonial expansion, whether cultural, as in Hellenistic or Roman culture, or mercantile, as with the European expansion, or cultural-political, as with the globalization of American popular culture, such as films, shaped by a Jewry at the American frontier—California.[32] America as the frontier is a space where various languages and discourses meet and match and transcend, as Marc Shell has commented.[33]

Jews confront and are confronted by the inhabitants of each land, from medieval Britain to Poland to China to India to Palestine. The options open to them are defined in terms of the experience of the frontier, including imagining that the frontier no longer exists. The frontier can be either the guldene medina or the place of torment. It is a place of perpetual contact at the margins.

This is the Jewish construction of the frontier. It is to be found in models such as the "land without people for a people without land." Here is the notion of the frontier without conflict which marked the fantasy of the Jewish desire for a space different than the frontier experiences in Europe. Such a notion of the frontier of the Middle East marks the transgression of another frontier by Jews from another frontier—Europe, North America, South Africa—who imagine the frontier space of the Middle East as without the conflicts that marked their own frontier experiences. Here the Zionist fantasy of Israel as the frontier is tied to language in a most powerful manner. Theodore Herzl's Israel in his *Der Judenstaat* was to be a linguistic Switzerland: a compromise without conflict at the borders of his fantasy. All languages would be welcome there and all cultures from the other frontiers preserved with the sole exception of Yiddish. Yiddish was for Herzl the mark of the failure of the Jews at the frontier. It was not German; it was the linguistic marker of the failure of the Jews at the frontier to create a "real" cultural space. Thus Jews who moved into the imagined space of Israel with the first and second *aliyah* clearly could not identify with the language of the majority (Arabic) or with the colonial forces occupying the land (Turkish or English) but with the language of a present minority, the Hebrew-speaking Jews. Hebrew becomes the identifying marker of Jewish particularity at the frontier. It is a language which is given virtually miraculous powers as the sign of Jewish cultural resurgence at the frontier. Yet it is clear that Hebrew and Jewish identity are not interchangeable even at this frontier. With the rise of a Hebrew-speaking and -writing Arabic minority the age of post-Zionism begins. For the magic nature of Hebrew as the new language of a new people gives way to the more utilitarian understanding of Hebrew as a language of a frontier experience, which produces boundary-crossers of a most complex nature. The construction of Dugri speech as the language of the Sabra, a language which was to capture the new psychology of the tough Jew at the frontier now admits others than Jews into its pantheon of language use. Hebrew in a post-Zionist world has become a "normal" language, a language at the frontier, a space of accommodation and conflict, as Benjamin Harshav has recently noted.[34]

The model of accommodation and conflict at the frontier can be found in the acculturation of Jews into the Middle East today as well as in the Rhine valley in the High Middle Ages and modern North America. Such a conceptualization shows how language becomes a marker for the movement across the frontier and the establishment of a complex relationship with the inhabitants. Such movement across the frontier does not have to integrate the Jews into frontier society. It can result in a self-conscious distancing of the Jews into rigidly defined communities at the frontier, defined by self-interest as well as overt hostility. It can also result in the destruction of the Jews or, if one evokes certain biblical moments, of those peoples with whom the Jews come into conflict at the frontier.

The problem of language and culture as markers of identity which transcend the empirical expression of such "realities" can be seen the history of the province of Quebec, reflected in Régine Robin's paper, and in the very different world of Jeffrey Lesser's Brazil. No matter how "French" the Jews of Quebec become they can never become French enough; the Jews of Brazil maintain their difference while becoming part of the general culture as Jews. Two sides to the same coin, yet with very different implications for the identity of the Jews on each of these frontiers.

The temporal frontier as the topography of Jewish history has, as does the center/periphery model, a biblical model, if the model of the frontier is applied to a reading of biblical history from Abraham to Moses to the expansion of the Kingdoms of Judah and Israel into the frontier. Before the construction of "Jerusalem" there is no center and therefore no periphery. Israel exists only in the narrative of the Bible retrospectively as the center superimposed on the Abrahamic search for God. For it was "Abraham [who] planted a grove in Beersheba, and called there on the name of the LORD, the everlasting God. And Abraham sojourned in the Philistines' land many days" (Genesis 21:33). As do we all.

Notes

1. Steven Kepnes, ed., *Interpreting Judaism in a Postmodern Age* (New York: New York University Press, 1996).

2. Arnold M. Eisen, *Galut: Modern Jewish Reflection on Homelessness and Homecoming* (Bloomington: Indiana University Press, 1986), 43.

3. Sandra Braude, *Windswept Plains* (Cape Town: Buchu Books, 1991), 79.

4. Jacob Neusner, *Self-Fulfilling Prophecy: Exile and Return in the History of Judaism* (1987; rpt., Atlanta: Scholars Press, 1990).

5. W. D. Davies, *The Territorial Dimension in Judaism* (1982; rpt., Minneapolis: Fortress Press, 1991).

6. See, specifically, Deborah Bernstein, *The Struggle for Equality: Urban Women Workers in Prestate Israeli Society* (New York: Praeger, 1987), and Vicki Caron, *Between France and Germany: The Jews of Alsace-Lorraine, 1871–1918* (Stanford: Stanford University Press, 1988). The central text to rethink history in gendered terms remains Joan Wallach Scott, *Gender and the Politics of History* (New York: Columbia University Press, 1988).

7. Daniel Goldhagen, *Hitler's Willing Executioners: Ordinary Germans and the Holocaust* (New York: Knopf, 1996).

8. Jonathan Boyarin, *Storm after Paradise* (Minneapolis: University of Minnesota Press, 1992), xvii.

9. Richard Schusterman, "Next Year in Jerusalem?" in *Jewish Identity,* ed. David Theo Goldberg and Michael Krausz (Philadelphia: Temple University Press, 1993), 291–308.

10. On the history and background of Jewish attitudes toward language, the languages of the Jews, and the image of the Jews' language, see Sander L. Gilman, *Jewish Self Hatred: Anti-Semitism and the Hidden Language of the Jews* (Baltimore: Johns Hopkins University Press, 1986).

11. Gabriel Josipovici, "Going and Resting," in *Jewish Identity,* ed. David Theo Goldberg and Michael Krausz (Philadelphia: Temple University Press, 1993), 309–21.

12. Arnaldo Momigliano, "What Flavius Did Not See," in *Essays on Ancient and Modern Judaism,* ed. Silvia Berti, trans. Maura Masella-Gayley (Chicago: University of Chicago Press, 1994), 67–78.

13. Benedict Anderson, "Exodus," *Critical Inquiry* 20 (1994): 314–27.

14. Michael A. Meyer, "German-Jewish Identity in Nineteenth-Century America," in *The American Jewish Experience,* ed. Jonathan D. Sarna (New York: Holmes and Meier, 1986), 45–59.

15. James Clifford, "Traveling Cultures," in *Cultural Studies,* ed. Lawrence Grossberg, Cary Nelson, and Paula Treichler (New York: Routledge, 1992), 96–112. See also the discussion following Clifford's essay on pp. 112–16.

16. Homi Bhabha, *The Location of Culture* (London: Routledge, 1994), 224.

17. The following verses come to reflect the sense of boundaries, borders, and frontiers. In the major postcolonial version of the English Bible, *The New Standard Version,* there are a series of evocations of the frontier:

Deuteronomy 2:19 states, "and when you approach the frontier of the sons of Ammon, do not harass them or contend with them, for I will not give you any of the land of the sons of Ammon as a possession, because I have given it to the sons of Lot for a possession."

In Joshua 22:11: "And the people of Israel heard say, 'Behold, the Reubenites and the Gadites and the half-tribe of Manas'seh have built an altar at the frontier of the land of Canaan, in the region about the Jordan, on the side that belongs to the people of Israel.'"

In 2 Kings 3:21: "When all the Moabites heard that the kings had come up to fight against them, all who were able to put on armor, from the youngest to the oldest, were called out, and were drawn up at the frontier."

In Ezekiel 25:9: "Therefore I will lay open the flank of Moab from the cities on its frontier, the glory of the country, Beth-jesh'imoth, Ba'al-me'on, and Kiriatha'im."

18. Daniel and Jonathan Boyarin, "Diaspora: Generation and the Ground of Jewish Identity," *Critical Inquiry* 19 (1993): 693–725.

19. Stephen Aron, "Lessons in Conquest: Towards a Greater Western History," *Pacific Historical Review* 63 (1991): 128.

20. Kerwin Lee Klein, "Reclaiming the 'F' Word; or, Being and Becoming Postwestern," *Pacific Historical Review* 65 (1996): 179–215.

21. Hilde Domin quoted in Hans Jürgen Schultz, ed., *Mein Judentum* (Stuttgart: Kreuz-Verlag, 1978), 98.

22. Gloria Anzaldúa, *Borderlands/La Frontera: The New Mestiza* (San Francisco: Spinsters/Aunt Lute, 1987), 79–81.

23. Richard White, *The Middle Ground: Indians, Empires, and Republics in the Great Lakes Region, 1650–1815* (Cambridge: Cambridge University Press, 1991).

24. Bruno Latour, *We Have Never Been Modern,* trans. Catherine Porter (Cambridge, Mass.: Harvard University Press, 1993).

25. Zygmunt Bauman, *Modernity and Ambivalence* (Cambridge: Polity Press, 1991), 5.

26. Angelika Bammer, *Displacements: Cultural Identities in Question* (Bloomington: Indiana University Press, 1994).

27. Gilles Deleuze and Félix Guattari, *A Thousand Plateaus: Capitalism and Schizophrenia,* trans. Brian Massumi (Minneapolis: University of Minnesota Press, 1987), 291–92.

28. Yael Zerubavel, *Recovered Roots: Collective Memory and the Making of Israeli National Tradition* (Chicago: University of Chicago Press, 1995).

29. Felix A. Theilhaber, *Der Untergang der deutschen Juden: Eine volkswirtschaftliche Studie* (Munich: E. Reinhardt, 1911); Bernard Wasserstein, *Vanishing Diaspora: The Jews in Europe since 1945* (Cambridge, Mass.: Harvard University Press, 1996); Mitchell Bryan Hart, "Social Science and National Identity: A History of Jewish Statistics, 1880–1930" (Ph.D. diss., University of California at Los Angeles, 1994).

30. R. Po-chia Hsia, *The Myth of Ritual Murder: Jews and Magic in Reformation Germany* (New Haven, Conn.: Yale University Press, 1988); idem, *Trent 1475: Stories of a Ritual Murder Trial* (New Haven, Conn.: Yale University Press, in cooperation with Yeshiva University Library, 1992); idem, *In and Out of the Ghetto: Jewish-Gentile Relations in Late Medieval and Early Modern Germany* (Washington, D.C.: German Historical Institute, 1995).

31. This is an extension of the idea of a "contact zone," developed in Mary Louise Pratt, *Imperial Eyes: Travel Writing and Transculturation* (London: Routledge, 1992).

32. According to Billy Wilder, on his ninetieth birthday, California was a smart place to be as a Jew—certainly smarter than being in Hitler's Berlin. *Frankfurter Rundschau* 22 June 1996: 9.

33. Marc Shell, "Babel in America; or, The Politics of Language Diversity in the U.S.," *Critical Inquiry* 20 (1993): 103–27.

34. Benjamin Harshav, *Language in Time of Revolution* (Berkeley: University of California Press, 1993).

PART I Accommodation

1 Jewries in Galicia and Bukovina, in Lemberg and Czernowitz: Two Divergent Examples of Jewish Communities in the Far East of the Austro-Hungarian Monarchy

ALBERT LICHTBLAU AND MICHAEL JOHN

Galicia and Bukovina were strategically important provinces on the extreme eastern edge of the Hapsburg Empire. They bordered Russia, Prussia (respectively, the German Reich), and—after an internal boundary had been drawn separating the cisleithan (western) and transleithan (eastern) halves of the Empire—Hungary as well. Galicia was absorbed by the Hapsburg Monarchy in 1772 as a result of the partition of Poland; in 1775, the Viennese Imperial Court could add the formerly Turkish-ruled region of Bukovina to its possessions. Bukovina was under military rule until 1786; up to 1849, it was a part of Galicia; then, the status of a separate crown land was conferred upon the region. In 1867, both crown lands were permanently established as a part of the Austrian half of the Empire and retained this position until the dissolution of the Monarchy in 1918. Galicia then became a part of the Republic of Poland and Bukovina came under Rumanian rule.[1] Although both crown lands were situated on the easternmost edge of the Monarchy, often displaying a similar historical pattern, and each constituted a region in which, over several decades, the Jews—or at least a segment of the Jewish population—assumed the function of a quasi-colonial cultural and economic elite closely allied with the Hapsburg state in which German-speakers still played the dominant role, the Jewish communities of Galicia and Bukovina developed in distinctly different directions.

Jewish life in the two crown lands displayed numerous contrasts, some of which persisted over a long term. We will now go about describing and investigating these differences. In doing so, we will draw upon evidence of linguistic behavior, mentality, and cultural orientation as indicators. The comparison of the two crown lands themselves follows a broadly outlined and by no means rigid schema. This process will include a detailed and comprehensive examination of their respective capitals, Lemberg/Lwów/Lviv and Czernowitz/Cernauti/Chernowtsy/Cernivci.[2] Our investigation will focus on the second half of the nineteenth and early twentieth centuries up to the interwar period. One of the ways in which divergent developmental directions manifested themselves was in the relative strength of the tendency toward a "modern," "secular" orientation upon German *Kultur.* And this could be observed, above all, in Czernowitz, in the extreme east, hundreds of kilometers away from the urban centers of Galicia located far to the west of Czernowitz. As a broad generalization, notwithstanding regional differences as well as the existence of countervailing tendencies, in this distant eastern protrusion of the Monarchy, we discover a Jewry whose majority was oriented toward modernity and "western" values, whereas more traditional patterns of behavior and assimilation into the society of the Polish majority dominated regions geographically situated much further to the west.

What needs to be explained is why this orientation upon German *Kultur* is also to be found in regions situated so far to the east and, moreover, among population groups which were often regarded skeptically in societies with German-speaking majorities. To come straight to the point: in our opinion, the point of origin of this orientation upon German *Kultur,* this adulation of and inclination toward the imperial capital Vienna and the Hapsburg Dynasty as a whole is, in this case, connected to what we have previously termed—in a rather vague formulation—the "quasi-colonial" function assumed by segments of the Jewish population in the Monarchy's extreme eastern, non-German-speaking regions.[3]

Can the term "colonialism" be applied to Galicia and Bukovina? Certainly not in the classical sense, even if there certainly had been talk of "colonization" in connection with Galicia within Austrian circles in eighteenth-century Vienna.[4] The concept of "internal colonialism," however, can be properly applied to Galicia and Bukovina. For example, the surplus by which the Hapsburg state's tax receipts and other revenues transferred from Galicia exceeded its expense outlays for that crown land ran, year after year, into the tens of millions. The term "internal colonialism" was originally coined to describe the form of dependence of underdeveloped regions of the Third World following their formal political independence. The territory of such an underdeveloped region is not a colony in the political-administrative sense; in its economic relationship to a center within a national framework, though, it certainly is. The concept was subsequently broadened to include developed or developing industrial nations—referring here to the dependent development and growing economic inequality of peripheral regions vis-à-vis a dominant economic center. Furthermore, the concept of "internal colonialism" has also been employed in the area of cultural relations, an aspect that will prove to be particularly applicable in this essay.

GALICIA AND LEMBERG/LWÓW/LVIV

"If Lemberg has enjoyed times of prosperity and well-being," ran the description in a widely read travel guide published at the turn of the century, "then these were also times of affluence and good fortune for the Empire. But when troubled times came for the Empire, then Lemberg was the first gate at which the foe came knocking. If the Empire was a foremost bulwark of western culture and values, then Lemberg was its most advanced bastion which had to absorb and withstand the initial impact of the wild, hostile hordes. And a mighty defense it was against the raging turbulence of the east, though at the same time a bridge linking Europe and the Orient." [5] The affiliation with "western culture" can be viewed as a paradigmatic principle of a segment of the Jewish population of Galicia, and Lemberg in particular, a claim which at least partially characterized the behavior of this group over a period of decades. In Galicia as well as in Lemberg over the entire period under consideration here, a considerable portion of the Jewish population remained true to Orthodoxy and under the sway of Chassidism. Aside from this, however, we can distinguish three chief phases in the history of Jewish acculturation within the geographical area of Galicia: (1) the epoch from 1772 until the end of the 1860s; (2) from circa 1870 to the reestablishment of the Polish state in 1918; (3) the period of the Second Polish Republic from 1918 to 1939.[6]

From 1772 to 1867: The Phase of Germanization

The Austrian occupation and settlement began with "colonization" in the truest sense of the word. The first point on the Austrian agenda was to precisely survey and map its newest possession; more than a thousand surveyors, cartographers and their assistants were involved in this effort in Galicia during this period. Even as early as the eighteenth century, several measures were put in place directed toward the emancipation of and the provision of equal rights for Galicia's Jewish population, and it was the "policies of tolerance" followed by Kaiser Joseph II during the 1780s which encouraged a pro-Austrian attitude on the part of the majority of the Jews. In 1788, regulations allowing for the enlistment of Jews into military service were put in force in Galicia. This form of integration was then accepted by both sides—the military and the Jews. Thus, an officer stationed in Galicia wrote in his report dated 1788:

> We have just been assigned 18 Hebrews who were recently drafted as surveyors' assistants. These are nice-looking young men, conducting themselves well and, since they speak German, are coming along better than the Poles. They have shaved off their beards. They have been granted permission . . . to celebrate Shabbes. . . . After the rabbis had explained everything clearly to them and impressed them with the fact that a lot of other boys were in the same position they are, they were soon able to regain their good spirits and are now shaping up quite nicely, as if they had already been soldiers for years.[7]

The Polish writer Stanislaw Wasylewski, who reported on the Austrian occupation with deep resentment, commented in a derogatory way on the subject of collaboration during the first decades: "The Jews were won with privileges . . . the nobility with titles."[8] Actually, the "General Ordinance Governing All Jewry of the Kingdom of Galicia and Lodomeria" issued in 1776 during the reign of Empress Maria Theresa was intended to formally grant the Jewish population civil rights which must be regarded as extraordinarily wide-ranging. Jewish communities were both cultural and political communities and, as such, enjoyed a certain degree of autonomy. On the other hand, the oppressive taxation policy pursued during the era of Maria Theresa and Joseph II must also be mentioned, along with the requirement instituted under Kaiser Franz II in 1810 requiring Jews who wished to marry to undergo a religious examination given in German—thus resorting even to repressive means to insure loyalty to the Hapsburg Empire and to the language of its elites.[9]

A trend is clear in this phase of development: those Jews for whom "out of the ghetto" was the solution, whose goal was the modernization of the Jewish sphere of life in Galicia and who included above all the middle classes, threw in their lot with the Austrian colonializing elites of the Hapsburg State and strove to assume a German-Austrian identity at this time. There were two reasons explaining the strong influence exerted by German *Kultur.* First, forces advancing the cause of the modern reform of Judaism emerged almost exclusively from those circles of educated Jews for whom German was the primary language of culture. Second, the vast majority of all Galician Jews spoke Yiddish, which was at that time considered a German dialect to which German would presumably provide a natural correspondence as a literary language.[10] In the 1820s and 1830s, Jewish children in Galicia increasingly attended German elementary schools and German high schools, and many began studying at the university level. Over the course of the 1830s, Jewish university graduates, for the most part physicians and lawyers, began to appear in Lemberg and other Galician towns. It was precisely in this group of educated Jews that a process of cultural convergence could be especially clearly recognized. "One secretly read Schiller and Lessing, hidden behind Talmud folios," wrote the Jewish-Galician historian Majer Balaban.[11] The reform synagogue erected in Lemberg in 1846 bore the name Deutsch-Israelitisches Bethaus (German-Israelite House of Prayer). Following the suppression of the Revolution of 1848, which also displayed Polish nationalist traits in Galicia, the Jewish communities there were the first to pay homage to the young Hapsburg, Franz Joseph—by no means a matter to be completely taken for granted, since Jewish intellectuals had been among the leading forces of revolution in Vienna. Until the 1860s, thousands of Jewish children attended Jewish-German elementary schools.

For example, in his description of the Jewish population as the author of the volume on Galicia in the deluxe commemorative series "The Austro-Hungarian Monarchy in Words and Pictures," issued on the occasion of the fifty-year jubilee of the reign of Kaiser Franz Joseph, Leo Herzberg-Fränkl summarized the period from the 1840s to the 1860s as follows:

> Nowhere are there so many autodidacts to be found as among this particular group of Polish Jews. . . . Naturally, it is by no means a systematic, scholarly body of knowledge that these . . . people acquire; hardly able to read, they take up Schiller and are delighted by his melodious pathos, or study the philosophical writings of Mendelsohn or even Kant's *Critique of Pure Reason*. But the sons of these men are already permitted to attend school and enjoy proper instruction. The first book for which an autodidact reaches is, without exception, a German one because his Jewish-German idiom certainly makes this language more accessible to him; furthermore, for him, German embodies everything European—culture, art and progress.[12]

From the *Ausgleich* to the Outbreak of World War I

Autonomy and Polonization This trend toward Germanization came to an end in the late 1860s, as new reforms came into force establishing Galicia's new autonomous status within the Hapsburg Monarchy. From this point on, it was Poles who above all assumed the key positions in the provincial government. The educational and judicial systems were oriented toward Polish traditions and culture, and the Polish nobility could strengthen its position of power. This process also had effects upon linguistic hegemony. In 1871, the Polonization of the University of Lemberg was completed;[13] in 1872, the German-language theater Deutsche Schaubühne was forced to close its doors.[14] This trend toward Polonization was likewise evident within the Jewish population. The German-Jewish poet Alfred Nossig provides a literary illustration in this connection. In his 1892 novel *Prophet Johannes,* published in Lemberg and set there in the year 1880, the biographically-drawn protagonist depicts a group strolling along the Lemberg Promenade: the adults walk at the head of the group, among them the narrator who "hears only chitchat in German all around him." The young people follow slightly behind, "conversing among themselves in splendid Polish."[15]

Leo Herzberg-Fränkl maintains that, in the 1880s and 1890s, it was "the younger generation, particularly in the larger cities, which first began to assimilate Polish culture, though without completely distancing themselves from German language and education."[16] This generalization is consistent with figures from the University of Lemberg. At the School of Law, the percentage of Jewish students dropped by about two-thirds from 1863–64 (instruction in German) to 1873–74 (Polish), at which point it slowly began to climb again, though it was only in 1893–94 that the percentage again equaled that of the 1860s. In the Department of Philosophy as well, it was not until the 1890s that a higher proportion of Jewish students was reached.[17] In 1880 in Lemberg—the survey asked only for the respondent's language of everyday use—8.3 percent of the local population spoke German; by 1910, the figure had sunk to 2.8 percent. Even taking into account the persistent underreporting of minority groups in national censuses, the proportion of Galician Jews who specified German as their language of everyday use in 1910 was a mere 2.9 percent. In contrast, 92.7 percent of Galician Jews specified Polish as their language of everyday use. The Deutsch-Israelitisches Bethaus received a new Polish name after the turn of the century. The percentage of Jews who gave German as their language of everyday use dropped particularly in the decade 1900–1910; according to a survey taken at the turn of the century in which respondents could name only one language, this group had still made up 15.3 percent of the total.[18] In spite of the fact that enormous pressure was frequently placed upon Jews to report Polish to the census takers,[19] we can nevertheless work under the assumption that there was a massive tendency toward Polonization among Galician Jews.

The socialist movement opened a specific way to Polonization in the second half of the 1880s. The Polish socialists advocated equal rights for Jews and called for their linguistic and cultural assimilation. Like most European socialists, they also regarded the Jewish religion as a collection of superstitions and a symptom of backwardness. Their tolerance was accorded to Jews as individuals but not to Judaism. Jewish socialists in Galicia were in some cases themselves radical proponents of Polonization—Hermann Diamand, one of the movement's leaders in Lemberg, was a prominent example.[20] Zionistic points of view had also become widespread beginning in the 1880s within a small circle of Jewish socialist intellectuals and "progressive" thinkers. The first Zionist newspaper in Lemberg was published in Polish. Majer Balaban and the young Martin Buber are examples of Zionists who tended to assimilate Polish culture during this phase. Buber was born in Vienna and raised by his grandfather in Lemberg where he attended the Polish high school; it was during this time that he attempted to translate Friedrich Nietzsche into Polish.[21]

In considering data available regarding the social and economic situation of the Jewish population and comparing it with that of the non-Jewish population, it becomes clear that these statistics at least do not contradict the hypothesis which has been advanced thus far. The 1910 census offers the opportunity for a comparison of the social and economic situation of the Jewish and the non-Jewish population. Here it is evident that, on the level of aggregate data, there doubtlessly were differences in social stratification between the Jewish and non-Jewish populations. Self-employment was much higher than average among Jews. It is interesting to note, however, that laborers were not underrepresented, a fact that becomes clear upon comparison with, for instance, data from Vienna. Calculating an Index of Disparity (analogous to the Index of Dissimilarity)[22] on the basis of social-statistical difference, the value for Galicia comes to 26.7 (Difference/2); this means that 26.7 percent of the Jewish or non-Jewish population would have had to change professions in order to display the same distribution percentages as the other group. The corresponding Disparity Index calculated for Vienna in 1910 is clearly higher: 35. The value for Galicia lies closer to that of Budapest (23.4), a city well known for its social climate favoring integration in the years before the outbreak of World War I (see table 1.1).[23]

The differences become even clearer in the case of the distribution of Jews and non-Jews according to employment by economic sector, whereby the Index of Disparity calculated for 1910 came to 70.7. This can be traced back to the enormous overrepresentation of the non-Jewish workforce in agriculture where Jews were strongly underrepresented, whereas Jews were overrepresented in commerce and transportation. Nevertheless, in Galicia we find a broad class of low-income Jews comprised of approximately 80,000 laborers (day laborers and apprentices) and 80,000 unskilled hands. This demonstrates the existence of a large underclass (about 50 percent of the population). The Jewish population thus by no means constituted a small economic elite. For this reason, the chances of integration by means of Polonization do not appear completely unrealistic at this point in time. In any case, a de-

Table 1.1. Occupational Breakdown of the Jewish and Non-Jewish Workforce in Galicia, 1910

	Jews	(%)	Non-Jews	(%)	Proportion of Jews	Difference
Self-employed	168,151	(49.1)	1,380,043	(33.2)	10.9	15.9
Leaseholders	3,546	(1.0)	3,550	(0.1)	50.0	0.9
Employees	18,535	(5.4)	72,174	(1.7)	20.5	3.7
Laborers	52,979	(15.5)	467,249	(11.2)	11.2	4.3
Apprentices	8,665	(2.5)	24,419	(0.6)	26.2	1.9
Day laborers	10,779	(3.1)	215,691	(5.2)	4.8	2.1
Employed in family business and farming	80,087	(23.4)	1,998,033	(48.0)	3.9	24.6
	342,742		4,161,159		7.6	(53.4)

Source: Österreichische Statistik, Neue Folge, 3:10 (Vienna, 1916), 225.

gree of social inequality dividing Jews and non-Jews, such as that which then existed in Vienna or Czernowitz (Bukovina), did not seem to be present (see table 1.2).

In view of the Polish hegemony, those who viewed the strong Polonization with skepticism had not many opportunities to form alternative cultures or countercultures. After all, massive anti-Semitism was highly prevalent among non-Jewish elites. Some pogroms took place in West Galician cities in 1898 and 1903 and there arose a powerful "League for the Polonization of Our Cities," which tried to organize a boycott of Jewish businessmen and to keep Jews out of certain professions.[24]

One alternative to Polonization was migration. Many emigrated to North America, motivated above all by economic factors: of 281,150 Jewish emigrants during the period 1881–1910, 85 percent came from Galicia. Decade after decade beginning in the 1870s, 20,000–30,000 migrated to Vienna and

Table 1.2. Jewish and Non-Jewish Population in Galicia by Economic Sector, 1910

	Total	Jews	(%)	Non-Jews	(%)	Proportion of Jews	Difference
Agriculture	3,545,042	46,066	(13.4)	3,498,976	(84.1)	1.3	70.7
Industry and crafts	304,827	78,691	(23.0)	226,136	(5.4)	25.8	17.6
Commerce and transportation	288,591	174,711	(51.0)	113,880	(2.8)	60.5	48.2
Public servants and professionals	365,441	43,274	(12.6)	322,167	(7.7)	11.8	4.9
	4,503,901	342,742		4,161,159		7.6	(141.4)

Source: Österreichische Statistik, Neue Folge, 3:10 (Vienna, 1916), 225.

Lower Austria as well. The proportion of Galicians among the Jews of Vienna rose continuously. From approximately 11 percent in 1880, this figure rose to about 20 percent by the outbreak of World War I. In 1910, 42,695 individuals residing in Vienna had been born in Galicia;[25] of whom not all were Jews. As to their motives, it may be assumed that the cultural element played a role alongside many other motives and there is, in fact, good reason to suspect that other migrational movements, such as the one to the United States of America and to New York in particular, were more strongly determined by purely economic motives.[26] Following the wave of refugees during the years 1914–19, the number of Galician Jews in Vienna climbed even further.[27] Those intellectuals and writers who migrated to Vienna such as Joseph Roth or Manes Sperber subsequently turned completely to the German language.[28] For this group, the question of hegemonies had been decided once and for all by means of migration.

Contradictions and Countertendencies The tendency toward Polonization beginning in the late 1860s and continuing up until the outbreak of World War I is uncontested. In concrete terms, however, this process played itself out in a much more complex and contradictory fashion than the "smooth" trend would suggest. Thus, in the 1860s, Moritz/Maurycy Rappoport, an influential representative of the Jewish community, composed a poem which can be regarded as a Polish Nationalist ode. Indeed, the original version had been written in German, the language Rappoport preferred to use since his mastery of Polish was far from perfect.

> From Orient, the Fantasy,
> In the breast, a Slavic fire,
> How my young soul was inflamed,
> Songs flowed from the golden lyre,
> How melancholy filled my heart
> From Sarmatians' bitter wails,
> How my soul rose heavenward
> At my father's wondrous tales,
> How lustrous in the twilight's gleam
> Ancient ruins in pallid glow;
> To be a Pole as well as Jew,
> Is the double crown of woe. [29]

The contradiction inherent in Moritz/Maurycy Rappoport's assertion regarding his nationality ("to be a Pole") and his cultural background or identity (German language) is by no means a unique phenomenon. The idea of the ethnically and linguistically homogenous national state, the idea of the nineteenth century, contradicted the fundamental principle of the Hapsburg Dynasty and the imperial-dynastic conception. In Austria, a state comprised of numerous nationalities, this led to deep-seated conflicts which ultimately contributed decisively to the dissolution of the Hapsburg Empire. Neither the spirit of the age nor individual sensibilities admitted multiple loyalties; instead, they steered a course in the direction of either/or. Contradictions emerged in great numbers and often in one and the same person. Jewish intellectuals often ran the danger of getting caught in the crossfire between nationalist fronts. Particularly in regions such as Bohemia, Moravia and Galicia, anti-Semitic elements among the "smaller" national groups (Czechs, Hungarians, Poles, Ukrainians) employed as their leading anti-Jewish argument the fact that the Jews regarded themselves as Germans and, since they were on the side of the German-speakers, were a threat to the nationalist movements in their own countries, or that they were indeed not "Germans" but rather loyal Hapsburg subjects devoid of nationalist loyalties. Those confronted by this were placed under massive pressure to conform, not only in the 1860s and 1870s but in later decades as well.[30]

There were also several instances in which Jewish communities successfully resisted Polonization. This was the case, for instance, in Brody, an East Galician town 70 kilometers away from Lemberg on the Russian border. In 1880, Brody had 20,000 inhabitants of whom 76.3 percent were Jews, and thus displayed the highest proportion of Jewish population of all Galician cities. Of the three public elementary schools in Brody at that time, one offered instruction in German and two in Polish. The School Board of the Province of Galicia then approved the construction of two additional elementary schools but rejected the demand of the Brody municipal authorities that the language of instruction in both of them be German rather than Polish. As a consequence, the city filed a complaint in 1880 with the K.K. Reichsgericht (Royal Supreme Court) in Vienna. Brody argued its case as follows: "Four fifths of the population profess the Mosaic Confession; at the same time, because they employ the German language as their mother tongue, they consider themselves to be members of the German nationality." They regarded the decision of the provincial school board as a violation of their national rights. The court found in favor of the City of Brody, allowing that German schools might be built in Galicia even in the year 1880.[31] Brody also had a German high school, which would later become a national bone of contention reaching as far as the Imperial Parliament. Along with anti-Semitism, this affair once again had to do with the massive pressure of Polonization exerted upon the Jewish students at this school.[32]

POLAND IN THE INTERWAR PERIOD

When the Hapsburg Empire collapsed in November 1918, fighting between Polish and Ukrainian troops began immediately. The Jewish population claimed to be neutral during this period of conflict. After the end of the fighting and as a result of the Polish victory, some of the Polish soldiers and the civilian population started a pogrom against the Jewish inhabitants. Polish soldiers maintained that the Jews had sympathized with the Ukrainian position during the conflicts. Plundering and insults were the results, and many Jewish houses were set on fire. According to Polish statistics which perhaps underestimate the extent of the progrom, 72 persons were killed during these days (November 22–23), 433 Jews were injured, 38 houses were burned down. During the whole period of this military operation (November 1–24, 1918) 262 Jewish victims were said to have been killed in connection with the conflicts following the breakdown of the Austro-Hungarian Monarchy.[33] Jewish authors said that these figures clearly underestimate the true extent of the Lemberg pogrom.[34] These events gained international recognitiòn, newspapers in the United States, Great Britain and France reported them, and diplomatic interventions followed.

After the clarification of the political situation in Lemberg, Polish was solidly established as the language of political power and culture. Lemberg, now known as Lwów, became the capital of Malopolsk (Little Poland), and the name Galicia was no longer used. On the linguistic level, Polish influence was amplified even further. The now mandatory use of the Polish language in government, the educational system, and the military, furthered this development. Throughout Poland in 1925–26, the network of minority schools which had existed until then was replaced by institutions of learning marked by a Polish nationalist character. From this time forth, a strict policy of Polonization was pursued.[35] A number of Jewish intellectuals resettled in other parts of Poland: the historian Majer Balaban as well as writers Jozef Wittlin, Filip Friedmann and Raphael Mahler moved to Warsaw or to Lodz. A segment of the assimilated Jews underwent conversion, thus completing the final step to full assimilation and Polonization.

If we now compare Lemberg with Czernowitz during this phase, we notice the surprising fact that, with respect to culture and identity, out-of-the-way Czernowitz presented a much more "western" image than Lemberg which actually lies 300 kilometers further to the northwest. In Czernowitz, the economic and cultural elites, including many Jewish citizens, continued even into the 1920s to cast their eyes toward Vienna and could thus write a new chapter of their quasi-colonial history; in Lemberg, on the other hand, the new Polish state and the traditional Polish elites permitted only the path to linguistic Polonization to remain open. The 1931 census showed that the proportion of German speakers among Lemberg's 99,600 Jews (35.1 percent of the population) was under 1 percent. A quite significant German-language literary output and cultural scene casts some doubt upon this figure.[36] It is also interesting to note that there was an increasing concentration of the Jewish population in the highly tense atmosphere of the interwar period. The pace at which urbanization took place was far higher among the Jewish population than among non-Jews. This can be concretely illustrated using the example of Lemberg: in 1910, 6.6 percent of all Jews in the Crown Land of Galicia lived in Lemberg, whereas in 1931, 12.6 percent of the Jews living in the administrative districts corresponding to the former Galicia lived in Lemberg/Lwów.[37]

As to the question of the identity of the Jews of Lemberg and Galicia, Jewish national consciousness and self-confidence had gained increasing influence. This had its roots in the highly problematic relations between Jews and Poles, whose strongest manifestation was the Lemberg pogrom. And this had not been the end of efforts undertaken against Jewish citizens.[38] In the face of this massive anti-Semitism with which the Galician Jews in the Polish state were confronted, ranging from the introduction of restrictive university admissions policies aimed particularly at Jews all the way to the staging of pogroms, a majority of Jews oriented themselves toward those outlooks in which their own national identity played an increasingly prominent role. To a certain extent, however, religious orthodoxy and Chassidism along with the rejection of Zionism continued to dominate rural Jewish communities.[39] This can also be seen in the results of the 1921 Polish census, which polled not only religious confession but also affiliation with a "Jewish nationality." In Lemberg/Lwów 76,783 individuals professed a Jewish religious affiliation, of whom an overwhelming majority (60,417 persons, representing 78.7 percent of the total population) acknowledged a Jewish nationality as well. The contrast to the Jewish communities in the small towns and outlying villages in the District of Lemberg/Lwów is striking indeed: out of 11,568 Jews professing no religious affiliation, a mere 5,440 (47 percent) acknowledged a Jewish nationality.[40]

We can characterize the period from the 1870s to the 1930s in Galicia as a phase of growing—and, ultimately, established—Polish autonomy and/or sovereignty, as illustrated by the following developments: (1) the Jewish minority as a former segment of the German-speaking minority reacted to the new situation by slowly adopting the new hegemonic language and the new hegemonic culture; (2) migration by many of those who did not want to accept the new hegemonic language and culture; (3) increasing concentration of the minority in urban centers (centralization); (4) as a specific reaction of the Jewish minority, an increased effort to redefine its conception of itself as a separate nationality (the triumphant advance of Zionism in the metropolises of Europe during the interwar period was, to be sure, a widespread phenomenon; in Lemberg, however, this form of self-definition quickly attracted strong and lasting allegiance most likely as a result of increasingly virulent anti-Semitism and massive Polonization);[41] (5) A "Zionization" of Jews originally from Galicia also took place in Vienna, home to a community numbering 10,000.[42] A massive remigration movement on the part of individuals who had previously migrated to Vienna and Lower Austria could be observed in most of the Monarchy's successor states during the interwar period. Not so in (former) Galicia; here, the number of emigrants remained steady. In many cases, the absence of desire to return was connected to the pogroms conducted by Poles in Lemberg and other Galician towns following the disintegration of the Hapsburg Monarchy.

BUKOVINA AND CZERNOWITZ/CERNAUTI/CZERNOWTSY/CHERNIVTSI

> *. . . because we are followers of the gigantic German culture.*
> —Benno Straucher

When the Austrians assumed dominion over Bukovina, it was a territory that had been depopulated by war, and its future capital Czernowitz was an insignificant backwater.[43] The new rulers were by no means favorably disposed to Jews, keeping them in line rather by means of expulsions.[44] It was only in the wake of the annexation to Galicia in 1785 with the implementation of Joseph II's policies of tolerance that the Jews experienced some relief. In the following section, we will concentrate on the historical phase after 1849 during which Bukovina was a separate crown land.

Bukovina comprised a mere 10,500 kilometers. Prior to World War I, it bordered on Romania and Russia, as well as on the Hungarian half of the Hapsburg Empire. Since it was a land in which the coexistence of various ethnic groups unfolded in a seemingly peaceful manner, and since it is a land that no longer exists today but has rather become a synonym for wasted chances for the peaceful coexistence of different peoples in one land, various mythologies have been retrospectively woven around this part of Eastern Europe. For example, it has been labeled as "Europa Minor" and has been characterized as a "microcosm" of the Monarchy, the Hapsburg Empire in miniature—a juxtaposition of various ethnic and religious groups. During the final decades of the Hapsburg Monarchy, the Jews of Bukovina were an important pillar supporting the "German" character of Bukovina.[45]

Karl Emil Franzos was born in the eastern Galician town of Czortków in 1848. His grandfather and father were followers of the Enlightenment and utterly rejected Orthodoxy and Chassidism. Religion retained little significance in his family, whereas the feeling of attachment to German *Kultur* was paramount: "The German national feeling that comes over me, which I have also actively pursued my entire life, has been instilled in me since my early childhood. When I was just a lad, my father said to me: 'Your nationality is not Polish, not Ruthenian, nor Jewish—you are a German.' But just as often, he said to me: 'As to your religion, you are a Jew.'"[46]

Raised as a "German by choice" and a "Jew by obligation," Franzos and his family moved to Czernowitz following the death of his father in 1859 and he attended high school there as had been specified in his father's will. The city and the school offered an environment for upbringing and education in which he felt at home: "Here, I was no longer an outsider, but rather a German among Germans."[47]

The results of the Austrian censuses begun in 1880 provide an idea of the relative dimensions of the various ethnic groups based upon statistics gathered regarding language of everyday use: to the north along the border to Galicia, the demographically largest linguistic group, the Ruthenians, dominated; the Romanians were strongest in the south. The German-speakers were the third most populous group. Then, far behind, came the smaller linguistic groups, the Poles and "Magyars" (see table 1.3)

Whereas only one or two languages were dominant in most of the other crown lands, Bukovina as an administrative district with three relevant linguistic groups personified a multicultural ethnic mixture.[48] Upon closer examination of the situation in Czernowitz, it becomes evident that the linguistic mix there included four relevant groups: German speakers dominated with nearly half of the total, followed by the most widespread regional language, Ruthenian, and thereafter the Polish and Romanian language groups, which displayed an unusually high share in comparison to the rest of the province—more than one third of all Polish-speakers in Bukovina lived in Czernowitz (see table 1.4).

These statistics of language of everyday use were of enormous importance in the multiethnic Hapsburg state since they served as a measure of the "nationalist standard of living" and were incorporated as a standard in a wide variety of legislation. Following the *Ausgleich* (settlement) with Hungary in 1867, the Hapsburg Monarchy functioned according to the principle of na-

Table 1.3. Language of Everyday Use among Resident Population in Bukovina Holding Austrian Citizenship, 1880–1910[a]

	1880		1890		1900		1910	
Ruthenian (Ukrainian)	239,690	(42.16%)	268,367	(41.77%)	297,798	(41.16)	305,101	(38.38)
Romanian	190,005	(33.43)	208,301	(32.42)	229,018	(31.65)	273,254	34.38)
German	108,820	(19.14)	133,501	(20.78)	159,486	(22.04)	168,851	(21.24)
Yiddish	—		—		—		—	
Polish	18,251	(3.21)	23,604	(3.68)	26,857	(3.71)	36,210	(4.56)
Hungarian	9,887	(1.74)	8,139	(1.27)	9,516	(1.32)	10,391	(1.31)
Bohemian-Moravian-Slovakian	1,738	(0.31)	536	(0.08)	596	(0.08)	1,005	(0.12)
Slovenian	38	(0.01)	28		108	(0.02)	80	(0.01)
Italian-Ladin	24		18		119	(0.02)	36	
Serbo-Croatian	0		1		6		1	
	568,453		642,495		723,504		794,929	

Source: Emil Brix, *Die Umgangssprachen in Altösterreich zwischen Agitation und Assimilation* (Vienna, 1982), 449; *Enciclopedia Romaniei,* 1 (Bucharest, 1938), 152.

a. By 1930 the resident population totaled 854,000.

Table 1.4. Language of Everyday Use among Population of Cernowitz Holding Austrian Citizenship, 1910

	Number	Percentage
German	41,360	48.4
Ruthenian	15,254	17.9
Polish	14,893	17.4
Romanian	13,440	15.7
Bohemian-Moravian-Slovakian	411	0.5
Hungarian	57	—
Slovenian	29	—
Italian-Ladin	13	—
Serbo-Croatian	1	—
	85,458	100.0

Source: Die Ergebnisse der Volks- und Viehzählung vom 31. Dezember 1910 im Herzogtume Bukowina nach den Angaben der k.k. statistischen Zentral-Kommission in Wien, *Mitteilungen des statistischen Landesamtes des Herzogtums Bukowina,* vol. 17 (Czernowitz, 1913), 54ff., 80ff.

tionality. No longer was German the unifying official language of the state; rather, the languages which were customarily used in individual provinces assumed preeminence in political and administrative dealings. Whereas in Galicia this development gave the green light to the process of Polonization, German could retain its hegemonic predominance in Bukovina.

We have consciously chosen to use the term "German-speaking" since this linguistic group was divided into two segments: Jews who designated German as their language of everyday use and the so-called speakers of Buchenlanddeutsch who, under Austrian rule, were settled into the easternmost provinces of the Hapsburg Empire. "Buchenland" was the German name for Bukovina. The principle of nationality which was accepted in the Austrian half of the Empire recognized the Jews only as a religion and not as a nationality. The consequence of this view was that the Yiddish language was not taken into account in censuses since this would have disrupted demographic polling according to the principle of nationality. It was not until the late nineteenth century and particularly following the turn of the century that the Jewish nationalist and Zionist movements drew attention to this shortcoming and demanded the right to designate Yiddish. The Austrian bureaucracy reacted with repression, punishing those who insisted upon their right to enter Yiddish on official state census forms.[49]

The Jews of Bukovina were a substantial force in support of German since, even in the last census in 1910, 95.6 percent cited German as their language of everyday use, and 54.4 percent of all German-speakers were members of the Jewish religious community. How large the proportion of Yiddish-speakers had actually been remains a matter of speculation. The census conducted under the Romanian government in 1930 can provide at best a reference value: according to these results, 75 percent of the Jews in Bukovina spoke Yiddish.[50] In attempting to apply this figure to prior circumstances under Hapsburg rule, it must be taken into account that intervening events may well have accounted for a large increase after 1918. In the wake of Austria-Hungary's collapse, thousands of Jews had left Bukovina; a disproportionately high number of them were those who felt a close attachment to the sphere of German culture and set off to find a new homeland in Vienna or in Germany. In contrast to Austrian polling, the Romanian statistics were based on mother tongue. Furthermore, a wave of immigration of Yiddish-speaking Jews from the east, above all from Bessarabia, has taken place in the meantime.

The Jewish population of Bukovina was thus by no means as homogenous as the census statistics based upon language of everyday use would suggest. They were also sharply divided in their attitudes toward the Jewish religion and Enlightenment ideas—into "blacks" and "whites" as the reformed Jews put it. These designations, often used by secular Jews, refer to the dark clothing worn by Chassidim, while those with a worldlier orientation indulged in the elegance of fashion. In Sadagura, where the dynasty of Rabbi Israel Friedman resided amid splendor after having fled from Russia in 1842, in Bojan and in the Carpathian Mountains in Wischnitz, where Rabbi

Mendel Hager of Kossov settled in 1850, Bukovina was the headquarters of significant Chassidic communities, whose circle of followers extended far beyond the province's borders. The accuracy of the claim that a quarter of all Jews in Bukovina were Chassidim is a matter that has yet to be subjected to more thorough investigation.[51]

Thus, a significant amendment must be made to the impression left by statistics suggesting that three or four languages dominated among the populations of, respectively, Bukovina and Czernowitz—both figures must be increased by one to include Yiddish. For Czernowitz, this means that German would have to give up a portion of its leading share in favor of Yiddish. The statistics, used to force implementation of proportional national standards, fail to take into account the reality of multilingual life which characterized Bukovina to a very high extent. And this was particularly true for Jews, since relationships in everyday life as well as matters of business demanded of both sides a knowledge of one another's language.[52]

The Special Status

Nevertheless, the census responses of the Jews of Bukovina were so overwhelming for the German language that the figures are comparable only to those from the dominant German-speaking regions in the western half of the Monarchy. In the following section, we will go into the causal factors to which this development can be traced.

In Bukovina in the final days of the Hapsburg Monarchy, the proportion of Jews in the total population reached 12.9 percent, the highest figure for any Austrian crown land, followed by Galicia with 10.9 percent; the proportion for the entire Austrian half of the Empire amounted to a mere 4.6 percent in 1910. The Jews of Bukovina were thus second only to the Greek Orthodox religious community and were numerically stronger than the Catholics. In Czernowitz, the center of political and cultural affairs, the Jews, considered as a religious group, comprised a third of the population and were thus the largest religious group (see table 1.5).

But this was not the only factor which characterized this special status. Measured by the prerequisites of a modern industrializing society, a considerable segment of the Jewish population of Bukovina belonged to the social elite. This can be documented through a number of indicators. Bukovina (along with Galicia and Dalmatia) was among the most backward regions of the Austrian half of the Empire; that is to say, they were only in the initial stage of the modernization process. We would like to illustrate this phenomenon as well as the elite status of the Jews using the example of two indicators.

Table 1.5. Religions in Bukovina (1910, 1930) and Czernowitz (1910)

	Bukovina (1910)		Czernowitz (city, 1910)		Bukovina (1930)
Greek Orthodox	547,603	(69.4%)	20,615	(23.7%)	71.9%
"Israelites"	102,919	(12.9)	28,613	(32.8)	10.9
Roman Catholic	98,565	(12.3)	23,474	(27.0)	11.5
Greek Catholic	26,182	(3.3)	9,588	(11.0)	2.3
Augsburg Confession	20,029	(2.5)	4,294	(4.9)	2.4
Lippowans	3,232	(0.4)	84	(0.1)	
Armenian Catholic	657	(0.1)	311	(0.4)	0.4
Helvetian Confession	484	(0.1)	75	(0.1)	
Armenian Orthodox	341		31		
Old Catholic	14		14		
Islam	8		2		
Anglican	1		1		
Mennonite	1		1		
No religious affiliation	62		25		0.1
	800,098		87,128		(99.5%)[a]

Source: Die Ergebnisse der Volks- und Viehzählung vom 31. Dezember 1910 im Herzogtume Bukowina nach den Angaben der k.k. statistischen Zentral-Kommission in Wien, *Mitteilungen des statistischen Landesamtes des Herzogtums Bukowina,* vol. 17 (Czernowitz, 1913), 54ff., 80 ff.; *Enciclopedia Romaniei,* vol. 1 (Bucharest, 1938), 154.

a. The source gave only percentages; total $N = 854{,}000$. The remaining 0.5 percent consists of 0.1 percent Adventists, 0.1 percent Baptists, and other small groups with shares below 0.1 percent.

Education In the 1871 school year, only 10.9 percent of all school-aged children in Bukovina attended a public elementary school. By the outbreak of World War I, however, this deficiency had been remedied. In the 1913–14 school year, a mere 3 percent of all school-aged children were not receiving instruction, and these were mostly the children of Huzuls (Hootsool) in the remote villages of the Carpathians, the mountain range in the southern and western portions of Bukovina.[53] As a result of this structural weakness in the area of education, illiteracy was still widespread among Romanians (60.39 percent) and Ruthenians (61.03 percent) in the Austrian half of the Empire as late as 1910.[54]

With the founding of the University of Czernowitz in 1875, German efforts to achieve social hegemony had created a key bastion in the extreme eastern reaches of the Monarchy, which assumed even greater significance following the Polonization of the University of Lemberg. And the Jews of Bukovina took advantage of the German-language educational opportunities offered there to a far greater extent than any other group. At no other Austrian university did the percentage of Jewish students comprise a higher proportion of the total than in Czernowitz (see table 1.6).[55]

Table 1.6. Percentage of Students Enrolled in Selected Colleges or Departments of Austrian Universities, by Religion

	School of Law			School of Medicine			Department of Philosophy			Total		
	C	J	O	C	J	O	C	J	O	C	J	O
Czernowitz												
1883-84	31.9	36.2	31.9	—	—	—	34.9	33.3	31.8	24.0	25.8	50.2
1893-94	29.6	40.8	29.6	—	—	—	34.7	30.6	34.7	25.7	33.0	41.3
1902-3	22.6	52.4	25.0	—	—	—	38.0	27.5	34.5	24.9	40.5	34.6
1913-14	23.3	45.3	26.4	—	—	—	29.8	42.3	27.9	24.2	36.9	38.9
Lemberg												
1883-84	82.1	17.3	0.6	—	—	—	88.4	11.6	—	89.0	10.7	0.3
1893-94	73.8	25.3	0.9	—	—	—	78.0	21.0	1.0	81.0	18.3	0.7
1903-4	70.4	29.4	0.2	62.6	35.5	1.9	84.6	14.2	1.2	78.5	21.0	0.5
1913-14	70.4	29.1	0.5	52.3	46.5	1.2	75.5	23.3	1.2	70.9	28.4	0.7
All Austrian Universities												
1863-64	88.1	8.8	3.1	60.9	29.5	9.6	86.1	4.8	9.1	83.6	11.2	5.2
1873-74	80.7	15.0	4.3	64.5	23.4	12.1	92.9	2.6	4.5	81.9	12.4	5.7
1883-84	79.9	16.1	4.0	52.3	38.7	9.0	81.7	8.5	9.8	73.6	19.9	6.5
1893-94	78.6	16.0	5.4	62.9	28.1	9.0	79.7	11.1	9.2	74.4	18.5	7.1
1903-4	76.1	18.0	5.5	58.6	27.6	13.8	79.5	12.4	8.1	76.2	16.4	7.4
1913-14	74.5	20.2	5.3	61.2	28.6	10.2	76.2	14.6	9.2	72.6	19.5	7.9

Key: C = Catholic; J = Jewish; O = other

Source: Ernst Pliwa, *Österreichs Universitäten 1863/4-1902/3. Statistisch-Graphische Studie* (Vienna, 1908), 28; Statistik der Unterrichtsanstalten in Österreich für das Jahr 1913/1914, *Österreichische Statistik,* NF, 17:3 (Vienna, 1919), 4ff.

Jews were particularly interested in receiving education in German since this seemed to offer the greatest promise for advancement within the Monarchy. This intensive interest in German-language educational opportunities is shown, for example, by the trend in the number of Jewish students attending the German high school in Czernowitz, where Jews ultimately accounted for three quarters of the student body. One indication of this readiness to participate in the process of modernization, which seemed to be almost an exclusive trait of Jews in Bukovina, is the extraordinarily high proportion of Jewish girls in the middle (high school) level of the educational system in Bukovina in comparison to other crown lands.[56]

Despite the fact that, to a great extent of course, the Jews of Bukovina continued to speak Yiddish, the German language exerted a strong attraction upon the younger generation as a sort of status symbol. Prive Friedjung, a butcher's daughter born in Zadowa in 1902, still recalls this fact: "The children of the Jewish inhabitants attended the German-language school. The mother tongue, Yiddish, was taught and learned through private instruction in the *cheder.* In school we probably also spoke Yiddish among ourselves, but German as well. Of course we wanted to speak German; after all, it was 'finer.' The German-speakers were the 'better people.'"[57] Here as well, we can see the hegemonic forces at work, implemented by means of the educational system.

Social Stratification The "elite thesis" can also be observed from a second indicator—occupational structure of the population of Bukovina. Among members of Bukovina's two largest linguistic groups, the Ruthenians and the Romanians, the agricultural sector was dominant, accounting for nearly 90 percent of each group!

However, after 1860, when it was legally permitted for Jews to own land, they also played an important role in agriculture and forestry. In the law regulating elections for the provincial legislature in Bukovina, which took effect following the so-called *Ausgleich* in 1911 and was set up according to complicated national and social criteria, Jewish candidates were automatically awarded two legislative seats representing the electoral class of large landowners.[58]

Although considerable numbers of Jews in Bukovina as well as in Galicia were involved in agriculture, we would like to focus our attention on those sectors which were essential to the process of modernization of the economy. In trade and transportation, Jews made up almost two thirds of all employed persons, and the proportion in trade would be even higher if the figure had been separated from that for transportation. In industry and crafts, Jews comprised almost one third of the workforce and were, along with the Germans, the most numerous and most important group.

The Disparity Index of 70.6 between Jews and non-Jews with regard to economic classes was nearly the same as that in Galicia and thus extraordinarily high. This is above all attributable to the dominance of the agricultural sector by the non-Jewish workforce.[59] Applied to occupational groups, the Disparity Index, with a value of 39.1, was higher than in Galicia and the Austrian half of the Empire as a whole (see tables 1.7 and 1.8).[60]

The society of Bukovina continued to be based upon the division of labor by ethnic classes; that is to say, the separation of social functions according to ethnicity. Since social mobility had not yet begun to take effect within the large groups of Romanians and Ruthenians, the process of modernization had not yet created the potential for a climate of tension among the various ethnic groups.

This elite position can be further illustrated by a few examples, such as one taken from the previously mentioned educational sector: of the 44 faculty chairmen elected at the University of Czernowitz between 1875 and 1919,

Table 1.7. Employed Persons in Bukovina by Economic Sector and Nationality, 1910

	Jews	Germans[a]	Ruthenians	Romanians	Poles	Jews as Percentage of All Employed Persons
Agriculture and	5,361	14,607	156,989	139,831	5,610	
forestry	(13.3%)	(48.2%)	(89.6%)	(89.7%)	(35.5%)	1.6
Industry and crafts	9,827	7,344	5,346	4,289	4,683	30.7
	(24.3)	(24.2)	(3.0)	(2.8)	(29.7)	
Commerce and	16,818	1,957	4,001	2,328	2,075	62.3
transportation	(41.7)	(6.5)	(2.3)	(1.5)	(13.1)	
Public and military	8,360	6,411	9,504	9,431	3,420	21.1
service, professions	(20.7)	(21.1)	(5.4)	(6.0)	(21.7)	
(law, medicine, etc.),						
other	40,366	30,319	175,840	155,879	15,788	9.5

Source: Österreichische Statistik, NF, 3:10 (Vienna, 1916), 226ff.

a. Calculated according to census data specifying language of everyday use, according to which 95.6 percent of all Jews specified German. The corresponding portion of "German-speaking Jews" was in each case analogously subtracted from those listed under "German."

Table 1.8. Occupational Breakdown of the Jewish and Non-Jewish Workforce in Bukovina, 1910

	Jews (%)		Non-Jews (%)		Proportion of Jews	Difference
Self-employed	20,790	(51.5)	124,559	(32.3)	14.3	19.2
Leaseholders	616	(1.5)	408	(0.1)	60.2	1.4
Employees	3,920	(9.7)	7,065	(1.8)	35.7	7.9
Laborers	7,420	(18.4)	41,382	(10.8)	15.2	7.6
Apprentices	1,433	(3.6)	2,276	(0.6)	38.6	3.0
Day laborers	1,170	(2.9)	72,725	(18.9)	1.6	16.0
Employed in family business and farming	5,017	(12.4)	136,772	(35.5)	3.5	23.1
	40,366		385,187		9.5	(78.2)

Source: Österreichische Statistik, NF, 3:10 (Vienna, 1916), 226ff.

there were 22 Germans, 11 Romanians, 9 Jews and 2 Ukrainians.[61] This elite position is also evident in the sphere of politics. Since the Jewish city council members controlled approximately 20 of the 50 seats in that body, they twice succeeded in advancing a member of their ranks to the position of mayor of the capital city: Dr. Edmund Reiss (1905–8) and Dr. Salo Weisselberger (1913–14) who, as a result of his conduct during the period of Russian occupation during World War I, was subsequently raised to the nobility.[62] Moreover, according to figures cited by Benno Straucher, Jews paid more than 75 percent of all taxes in the City of Czernowitz and almost half of all direct taxes in Bukovina.[63]

It would, of course, be a highly incomplete picture of Jewish society in Bukovina to portray their position as limited to the elite. Their social composition was quite heterogeneous—reminiscences recall all too often only the laborers, innkeepers, artisans and those living on the verge of poverty.[64] What we have attempted to show here is that the Jews in Bukovina constituted a segment of the social elite and played a significant role especially in the—admittedly not very highly developed—modern sectors of the economy. Since, in contrast to the Polish large landowners in Galicia, there was no traditionally established, non-German elite to speak of in Bukovina, and the hegemonic powers of German-Austrian domination in the areas of education and administration still played a leading role, the Jews of Bukovina oriented themselves in this direction. The positions of power of the two large national groups, the Romanians and the Ruthenians, were still too weak to cause a shift in this orientation on the part of the Jews. In their situation as a people living in a Diaspora, the Jews were forced to rely on the protection of the hegemonic powers and this seemed, as before, to emanate from Vienna.

Between German and Jewish Identity or Nationality: The Problematic German-Jewish Symbiosis

"Into the fourth decade of the 19th century, the Chassidim had the upper hand. It was only after 1848, as freedom spread across the land, that their influence began to recede and Jewish lifestyle outwardly adapted itself to the spirit of the age, such as moving out of the Jewish Quarter, European clothing, German as the language of everyday use and a diminishment in the observance of all the traditional commandments."[65] Much later than in Central Europe, namely in the aftermath of 1848, the ideas of the Enlightenment found great resonance among the Jews of Bukovina, and they saw their future political course in the Liberalism of the Germans, whom they seemingly had to thank for their newly-acquired rights. The attractiveness of the Germans did not stop short of religious life: in 1855, the German-Israelite School was opened and, from 1872 on, sermons in the main Czernowitz synagogue were preached in German.[66]

This also marked the beginning of the phase in which the German hegemonic culture set up institutions in order to solidly establish its influence.

These were primarily institutions of *Kultur* and education such as the university and the new municipal theater. German influence was enormous, particularly in the school system, since Yiddish, the actual language of most of the Jews of Bukovina, was disavowed and ignored while the other languages of the province exerted only a modest attraction upon Jewish students.

The previously cited quote from Karl Emil Franzos could speak for an entire generation of enlightened and/or already secularized Jews who wished to give up their old ways and fully assimilate into German-Austrian society. The Jewish religion seemed to be a matter of little importance; above all, one was conscious of being a citizen and, after 1867, a citizen with equal rights. As was also true in the west of the Monarchy in the 1860s, Germans and Jews worked closely together in Bukovina. For example, in 1861 in the elections for the first session of the provincial legislature in Bukovina, the Jewish vice-mayor of Czernowitz, the German-Liberal Dr. Josef Fechner, was elected together with the Germans.[67] The historian Martin Broszat, however, came to the conclusion that this was not a matter of adaptation toward the culture of the Germans of Bukovina, since, with respect to social or civilizational level, this group was by no means superior to the Jews. This process of acculturation was much more strongly oriented toward *Kulturdeutschtum* as this was hegemonically transmitted by the Austrian state through its government officials, army officers and teachers.[68]

Although the process of separation of this German-Jewish symbiosis did not proceed as brutally as it did in regions of the Monarchy which were poisoned by anti-Semitism, segregation according to so-called nationalities did not stop short of Bukovina. Here, at the very latest, the meager extent to which the provisions of law were anchored in the attitudes of citizens became amply evident, such that the Jews were regarded merely as a religious community. The rest of the population, including the Germans of Bukovina, continued to view Jews as a nationality, as "others."

Prior to the final end of the Hapsburg Monarchy, the most important political representative of the Jews of Bukovina was the attorney Dr. Benno Straucher, born in 1854 in Rohozna near Sadagura.[69] From 1897, he was a delegate to the Austrian Imperial Parliament, where he was a spokesman for an unusual mixture of German Liberalism and Jewish Nationalism—a sort of half-hearted Zionism. His chief innovation was to break with German Liberalism and, in the 1890s, to refuse further cooperation with the Germans. He then pursued his own independent course, a declared policy advancing Jewish interests. He joined none of the parliamentary fractions, though he was later chairman of the short-lived "Jewish Club."[70] As a parliamentary representative and, from 1903, as president of the Jewish Community of Czernowitz, he dominated Jewish political life in Bukovina for several decades until after World War I.[71] In Parliament, Straucher was immediately confronted with massive and verbally aggressive anti-Semitism, which reached its high point with the stand he took on the Hilsner Affair—the supposed ritual murder of Polna. Similar to the efforts of Rabbi Josef Samuel Bloch who had previously represented legislative districts in Galicia, Benno Straucher attempted to employ argumentation in the fight against anti-Semitism.[72]

Those who have written about Bukovina are quite fond of depicting it as a region in which there was peaceful coexistence; nevertheless, Bukovina can not be separated and viewed in isolation from the context of the Empire as a whole. Naturally, those secular Jews—whose acculturation had been a modern one, for whom religion and tradition retained little significance and for whom German *Kultur* had assumed almost mythological stature as a substitute for the traditional culture they had given up—were shocked by the rise of German Nationalist anti-Semitism in the western provinces of the Monarchy, since it endangered their perspective of their own identity. The extent to which the sense of security in this German identity was undermined among Jews beginning in the 1890s can be vividly illustrated with a quote taken from a heated exchange of words in which Benno Straucher was involved in Parliament—an example taken from a budget debate:

> The Jews have made enemies with many other peoples because of the Germans and have been, and to some extent remain so today, loyal party supporters of the Germans, but the Germans have only wished to kick the Jews around in return! Do not treat the Jews so contemptuously, do not abuse and deride the Jews. Why, then, are the Germans engaged in an economic and political war against the Jews? I as well have been raised and educated only as a German. Why am I inferior? (*Representative Dr. Lemisch: No!*) But you are expelling us from your midst! (*Representative Dr. Lemisch: You have said yourself that you are a Jew and not a German!*) . . . We are drawing the obvious conclusion! And nevertheless we remain friends of the German people because we are admirers of the prodigious German culture. We as a people want to be loyal friends of the German people and of other peoples, if and to the extent that they acknowledge our equal rights and equal worth![73]

The disassociation from the Germans on the political level thus had no similar effect on the cultural level—and Straucher had put forth the opinion of the majority of politically active Jews in Bukovina. This striving to hold fast to values of German *Kultur,* which seems so defensive and helpless here, elevated the sense of connectedness to German culture to a mythologized and deeply emotional level. The extreme infrequency of conflicts among nationalities within Bukovina would later contribute to the effort to mythologize and transfigure the time of the Hapsburg Monarchy, but this cannot obscure the fact that the entire state had become a dangerous powder keg.

The gradual dissolution of the German-Jewish symbiosis was advanced in Bukovina by segregationist developments on both sides. As in Vienna, the first symptom appeared among German students who founded German Nationalist and/or exclusively Christian fraternities in Czernowitz as early as the 1880s. As a countermove, Jewish students at the University of Czernowitz—among them, Mayer Ebner, the future leader of the Bukovina Zionists—reacted with the founding of the Jewish Nationalist fraternity Hasmonäa in 1891; more were to follow.[74] The influence of nationalism among the German populace also made its presence felt on the general political level with the emergence, after some delay, of a nationalist political wing. For instance, both German parliamentary representatives, Arthur Skedl and Michael Kipper, joined the "Society of Christian Germans in Bukovina" which was founded in 1897.[75] This society and the German Nationalist fraternities were behind the establishment of the Deutsches Haus in the Herrengasse, a prominent address in Czernowitz.

Along with the supporters of Straucher, the development of Zionism brought forth a second wing of Jewish Nationalism which would take on historical weight as a result of its subsequent significance. Mayer Ebner, born in 1872 in Czernowitz, was the leading Zionist activist in Czernowitz and embodied the new mood of skepticism toward the potential for integration. This attitude characterized his speech at the First Zionist Congress: "The Jews have felt themselves to be German and have remained loyal to the Germans. . . . After the German Liberal Party collapsed, the Society of Christian Germans in Bukovina came into being. That was the thanks we got! That was the reward for the decades of chauvinistic emphasis on all things German on the part of the Jews."[76] For reasons of realpolitik, Zionists who were aligned with Mayer Ebner initially supported Benno Straucher in the parliamentary elections of 1901 and founded with him the Jewish-nationalistic Jüdischer Volksverein in Czernowitz. Zionism in Bukovina, however, suffered as a result of the highly emotionally charged quarrels between those who advocated a course of realpolitik and the Herzl-Zionists who completely rejected a Jewish national policy in the Diaspora.

A Final Hegemonic Attempt to Construct a German-Jewish Symbiosis: The Bukovina Settlement

Although the separation of Jewish and German interests was a fait accompli following the turn of the century, hegemonic energies displayed resurgent power in the so-called Bukovina *Ausgleich* (settlement) of 1910–11 which had to do with electoral reform of the Bukovina Provincial Legislature. As in the case of the electoral reform in Moravia and in accordance with the wishes of Ruthenian, Romanian and Jewish political leaders in Bukovina, legislative districting were to be revamped to take national criteria into account. In view of the heterogeneous population of various groups living commingled with one another, this was an extraordinarily complicated undertaking. At the suggestion of provincial politicians, electoral constituencies specifically allocated for national groups were created. For the very first time, Jewish voting blocs were demanded. However, the government formally rejected the creation of Jewish constituencies since this would have meant the recognition of the Jews as a nationality. On one hand, they thereby acted in accordance with the wishes of the powerful, non-nationalist Jewish groupings such as the Austrian-Israelite Union. On the other hand, they did not want to give in to the efforts of the anti-Semites who called for the segregation of the Jews in all spheres of society. The central argument, however, was that the Jews, in the future as in the past, should not be recognized as a separate people and would thereby not be accorded the special rights due to such nationalities.[77] In a compromise plan, though, a few separate Jewish electoral districts were created; formally, Jews continued to be grouped together with the Germans for electoral purposes.[78] Despite protest assemblies and widespread disappointment, this solution had to be accepted. This was the final hegemonic demarcation point of the Hapsburg Monarchy which linked together the Jews of Bukovina and the Germans.

The first elections for the provincial legislature conducted according to nationality criteria took place in 1911. However, the Germans (both German Liberals and German Nationalists) as well as the Jews were deeply split. On the Jewish side, the powerful group of the Nationalist Party headed by Benno Straucher ran against the less successful Zionists of the People's Council Party of Leon Kellner and Mayer Ebner. Instead of the nine Jewish representatives as foreseen in secret government projections, they succeeded in winning ten, an indication of the unreliability of nationality-based electoral constituencies.[79]

Belonging and Exclusion: The Imaginary West in the East

The acceptance and adoption of German *Kultur* by the Jews of Bukovina had to do with the hegemonic concepts of the multiethnic Hapsburg state. The internalization of this culture was deeply rooted in the attitudes of human beings and this could be traced back primarily to the fact that many of the Jews of Bukovina were quite sympathetically disposed toward this hegemonic power. The quotes attesting to the Bukovina Jews' patriotism and loyalty to the Kaiser are endless: "The Jews' allegiance to the state is nothing less than proverbial," stated Benno Straucher during one of his speeches in Parliament.[80] Lydia Harnik, born in 1909 in Sereth and still living in Czernowitz to this day, still feels deep ties to the spirit of old Austria. She wrote in her reminiscences: "My father was a bank executive, my mother an elementary school teacher. Although a Jew, I was raised in the German spirit, in the spirit of German and Austrian classical poetry, [I] grew up in an atmosphere of fervent Austrian patriotism, passionate love of my homeland, and ardent admiration and reverence for our beloved emperor who had become a living legend and a figure of mythic proportions—Kaiser Franz Josef."[81] It was to the Kaiser's great credit that, during his last visit to Czernowitz in 1880, he paid a visit to the synagogue on the Day of Atonement.

The history of the Jews can certainly not be treated by focusing solely on the deeply rooted German hegemonic culture. It is imperative to not lose sight of the cleft which divided the Jewish population into "blacks" and "whites"—that is, the religious traditionalists and the various groups of Chassidim, and those whose acculturation was based on modernism and secularism. From the investigative perspective we have chosen, the orthodox and Chassidic Jews are hardly apparent since they hardly participated in political life. In other perspectives of the day, it was precisely this group which was the prime object of attention—depending upon the motivation of the observer, to offer a literary taste of their exotic nature or in order to portray all Jews as "the others." For example, a festschrift published in 1899 in Czernowitz celebrating the jubilee of the reign of the Kaiser exclusively depicted orthodox Jews: "On Shabbes or on the High Holidays, they wear long sabbath robes (Igitze), sabbath caps trimmed with fur (Stramel), short breeches, white knee socks and slippers."[82] Anthropology, then still in its infancy, also turned its attention to the Jews of Bukovina, advancing, for example, the following bold theory: "Most noticeable in their faces, aside from the large nose and mouth, is the relatively limited height of the lower structures."[83]

Of course, the secularly acculturated Jews of Czernowitz saw themselves as completely different and wanted to avoid any connection with these exotic portrayals and stigmatizations. They were fond of referring to "their" city as "Little Vienna" in proud reference to its cultural life, its *Kaffeehauskultur,* its architecture and layout, and its newspapers. The German cultural orientation was likewise meant to sever it from its Eastern European, backward, "semi-Asiatic" framework.[84] The effort to distance themselves from the "backward" East—incriminated as it was by negative images—had a very real background motivation for the Jews of the Hapsburg Monarchy: even as late as the census of 1846, they were categorized, along with the Magyars, Gypsies and Armenians, among the "Asiatic tribes."[85] In the late nineteenth century, it was solely the orientation upon German hegemonic culture which seemed to offer the possibility of integration into the "western" (Western European) and thus the modern world, and the experience with emancipation seemed to offer empirical confirmation of this.

In the nineteenth century, a new form of stigmatization became attached to the German language—the concept of the "Ostjude" (Eastern European Jew), which took on various connotations according to the context in which it was used. To an impartial observer, this term was linked to images of orthodox, poor, religious, Yiddish-speaking Jews; for secularized, nationalistic Jews, it evoked romanticized conceptions of a still-genuine Jewish life; for the anti-Semites, however, it brought to mind images which were chiefly aimed at continuing to portray the Jews as "strangers," as migrants, as elements which did not fit in, to stigmatize them as "Asiatics" or as "Orientals."[86] If Bukovina Jews whose acculturation had been a process of immersion in German *Kultur* would have been asked if they felt themselves to be "Ostjuden," the questioner could well have expected to receive indignant reactions.[87]

The Search for Secular Elements of Identity: Language

As the destabilizing effects of the German host culture on their own identity became obvious in the wake of the mutually agreed-upon segregation, secularly acculturated Jews of Bukovina sought a new mainstay on which to base their Jewish nationality. Aside from Zionism, they discovered "Yiddishkeit" as a core element. The language itself did not force them into a retreat to traditional religion, but rather seemed to them an argument in support of their demands for Jewish national autonomy in the Austrian multiethnic state.

In the history of the Yiddish language, the first Yiddish Linguistic Conference which took place in Czernowitz from August 31 to September 3, 1908, marked a key turning point. For the first time, the effort was made to acknowledge Yiddish as a language of culture and not to disparagingly discredit it as a "jargon," as a "language of lesser value," as a "corrupt form of German" or as the language of the ghetto.[88] In the Zionist movement, the conflict took on a new twist, pitting the Yiddishists against the Hebraists.[89] It is highly characteristic that the coorganizers of the Yiddish Linguistic Conference, Nathan Birnbaum, an early Zionist from Vienna, and Max Diamant, an attorney active in the struggle to achieve recognition for the Jews as a nationality, regarded their efforts as an "ideological" involvement in the Jewish Nationalist cause, since neither had grown up in the Yiddish linguistic culture.[90] With regard to the political balance of power which then prevailed in Bukovina, it was highly significant that Benno Straucher, the unchallenged dominant force within the Jewish communities of Czernowitz, was forbidden to hold this conference in the Jüdisches Haus; the participants met instead in the concert hall of the Music Society and in the Ukrainian National House.[91] Despite the highly diverse stimulus provided from outside, Yiddish cultural life reached its full bloom only after the end of the Hapsburg Monarchy as Bukovina became the homeland of significant Yiddish writers. An examination of the newspapers and books published by and for the Jews of Bukovina during the final decades of the Hapsburg Monarchy clearly illustrates this trend; in contrast to developments in Galicia, the press in Bukovina turned away from its original Yiddish and toward the German language.[92]

Outlook

The strength of German-language *Kultur* and the depth of its roots among the Jews of Bukovina can be seen in the period of the collapse of the Monarchy and the annexation of Bukovina by Romania. A new hegemonic, Romanian alignment was imparted to all key institutions of education, culture and official language. The school system was Romanized as was, in 1920, the University of Czernowitz; the German Municipal Theater became a Romanian one.

The allegiance to the Hapsburg Monarchy displayed by the Jews of Bukovina was associated with their recognition of the fact that they enjoyed a much better social position in comparison to the adjacent areas of Russia and Romania. Life on the border of countries whose governments were notoriously hostile to Jews engendered, as its mental consequence, an attitude of rejection of their cultures. On numerous occasions in speeches before the Austrian Parliament, Benno Straucher addressed the persecution of Jews in these countries, as well as intervening on behalf of the persecuted Jews and Armenians in Turkey.

No wonder that the new rulers were greeted with cool distance on the part of the Jews. The poet Alfred Gong, born in Czernowitz in 1920, described this in a poem about his father.

> My father couldn't stomach the new masters,
> *"Zigeuner"* he reviled them and dreamed
> of the coming Reich of Otto von Habsburg.
> He piously preserved his Imperial & Royal belt
> and beat me with it, then ordered me to kiss the leather.[93]

Despite the policy of Romanization, the Germanness of the Bukovina Jews was not so quickly expunged. "The language which could still be heard downtown was German, so to speak, 'Viennese,'" Lily Glanz, who was born in Czernowitz in 1913, wrote in her reminiscences.[94] Pearl Fichman, born in 1920 in Czernowitz, confirms this: "In our house and all around me people spoke German, read German books and the daily local German newspapers."[95] As long as the performances continued to be presented at the famous theaters of Czernowitz, the illusion remained intact: "I remember it as an Austrian way of life."[96]

German linguistic culture experienced one final and long-lasting creative impulse in Czernowitz. One of the most creative lyricists of the German language was the Czernowitz native Paul Celan; he enrolled in the city's Romanian State High School in 1930, later transferring to the Ukrainian counterpart. He coined one of the most frequently-cited expressions referring to Bukovina: "It was a place in which the human beings and the books were alive."[97] German *Kultur,* above all literature and language, continued to be almost venerated by a segment of the Jews in Czernowitz and Bukovina. The link to the geographical region in which German is spoken was finally severed by borders: "Amidst all the losses, only this remained accessible, near and not lost: the language."[98]

EPILOGUE

Many Eastern European Jews cultivated a mythic concept of "that which was German," wishing to regard German *Kultur* as the supreme embodiment of a highly developed form of culture. This and the identification with "the West" proved to be long-lived phenomena and were expressions of the powerful attraction exerted by "culturally imperialistic," quasi-colonial paradigms. The political borders had long since been redrawn; in the minds of the people, though, something remained of the former alignment. This myth, approaching almost a religious dimension, found its end only in the confrontation with events that were barely comprehensible: the reality of the genocide which emerged from Germany. "After all, how could a people as 'civilized' as the Germans follow such a madman [Hitler]?" Pearl Fichman asks herself in her reminiscences.[99]

During the interwar period, the myth of German *Kultur* undoubtedly remained present for segments of the Jewish population. For example, Salomea Genin, in her autobiography subtitled "From Lemberg to Berlin," looks back on the 1920s and describes the decision to emigrate from the former capital of Galicia to Germany: "First we go to Berlin. A good life is possible there too. . . . The Germans are industrious, thorough and highly disciplined. In a newspaper, I read that high-quality German workmanship is prized throughout the world. . . . What they don't have are anti-Semitic laws. In Germany, the Jews have long been citizens with equal rights. . . . Naturally, we don't have to stay there long. But, in the meantime, maybe the children will learn a thing or two about cleanliness and order, which is something we don't have here. After all, it's a civilized land of poets and thinkers; here, we're stuck in a state of barbarism."[100]

This myth had life-threatening consequences in the years 1939–41 and the fact of the Holocaust makes the myth appear bizarre in retrospect. There is no doubt that the Jewish populations of Galicia and Lemberg were terribly shocked by Hitler's invasion of Poland. This was also linked to fears. The Soviet occupation which had been carried out in the meantime in the wake of the Hitler-Stalin Pact had all the qualities of a brutal dictatorship. This in turn nourished hopes of less barbaric treatment at the hands of the German forces. Simon Wiesenthal, born in 1908 in Buczaz, recalls:

> German was spoken and read in my parents' home. Mostly German classics stood on our bookshelves. If my mother wanted to explain something especially precisely to me, she often did it with quotations which she had looked up in the works of Goethe, Schiller, Heine or Lessing. We held the Kaiser in the highest esteem and regarded him as out protector. We were fervent Hapsburg-Austrian patriots. . . . On September 17, 1939, Soviet soldiers occupied Lemberg. They were followed by the Soviet secret police, whose actions decided the fate of the population—particularly the Poles and the Jews. In a wave of arrests, all persons who were suspicious or were members of the "capitalist class" were imprisoned. The same with the intelligentsia. . . . Circumstances such as these make it understandable that, following two years of Soviet rule, there were people in Lemberg who greeted the German troops with open arms.[101]

Lemberg native Benedikt Friedmann recalls how his father, like so many other Jewish citizens, "was devoted to German culture and Austrian patriotism. Even on the very eve of the German invasion (1941), they said 'The Germans are pursuing an anti-Semitic course now. They are harassing the Jews there and they'll do the same here. But I was an Austrian soldier. . . . I met Germans on the Eastern Front. They were good comrades-in-arms. . . . They won't do anything bad to us.'"[102]

Josef Burg, a writer from Czernowitz, has similar memories: "In this critical hour, my uncle lived about 50 km west of Czernowitz. He said: 'The Germans with their magnificent culture—I'm not afraid of them. They won't do anything to me. I'm more afraid of the Russians, the Ukrainians and the Romanians.'"[103]

Old anti-Russian resentments and the form taken by the Soviet dictatorship, in which it was impossible to carry on a business or occupation of one's own choosing, led in May 1940 to a virtually incredible series of events. As a result of the Hitler-Stalin Pact, a German resettlement commission came to Lemberg in May. Thousands of Jewish residents of Lemberg and even refugees who had fled from the areas of Poland then occupied by the Nazis actually applied to this commission for resettlement to the *Generalgouvernement* portion of Poland. These registration lists were employed by the Soviet authorities to solve this problem in their own fashion in June 1940. In an operation lasting several days, they deported all persons whose names appeared on this list to Siberia and Kazakhstan. Through one of the small ironies of history, it was only in this way that they were able to escape the Holocaust.[104]

Notes

We wish to express our thanks to Mr. Hallabrin of the Bukovina Institute in Augsburg for his valuable advice and assistance; to Mel Greenwald for his English translation; to our colleagues Helga Embacher and Gerald Sprengnagel; and to our interview partners—in Czernowitz: Josef Burg, Lydia Harnik and Rosa Roth-Zuckermann; in New York: Pearl Fichman, Jonas Gottesmann, Beyle Schächter-Gottesmann, Rachel Hersonsky; and in Vienna: Helene Schapira.

1. In 1939, the German Wehrmacht took over West Galicia. East Galicia was then occupied by the Soviet Union until 1941, when German troops moved in and occupied this area as well (Generalgouvernement, District of Galicia). Following liberation from Nazi rule, West Galicia became Polish once again; the former East Galicia was annexed by the Soviet Union, as was the former North Bukovina including the former provincial capital, Czernowitz; southern Bukovina was retained by the Rumanians. At present, East Galicia as well as North Bukovina are a part of the Ukraine, one of the states emerging from the breakup of the Soviet Union.

2. To make for enhanced readability, we will henceforth use only the German-language forms of place names.

3. See Jochen Blaschke, "Nationalstaatsbildung und interner Kolonialismus als Entwicklungsimpulse regionaler Entwicklungen in Westeuropa," in *Krise ländlicher Lebenswelten: Analysen, Erklärungsansätze und Länderperspektiven*, ed. Klaus Schmals and Rüdiger Voigt (Frankfurt: Campus, 1986), 49–90.

4. Horst Glassl, *Das österreichische Einrichtungswerk in Galizien 1772 bis 1790* (Wiesbaden: Harassowitz, 1975), 5–8.

5. Adolf von Szysko-Bohusz, "Lemberg," in Josef Piotrowski, *Lemberg und Umgebung: Handbuch für Kunstliebhaber und Reisende* (Leipzig: Altenberg, Seyfarth, Wende, 1916), 1.

6. This scheme has been taken from Jerzy Holzer, "Vom Orient die Phantasie, und in der Brust der Slawen Feuer: Jüdisches Leben und Akkulturation im Lemberg des 19. und 20. Jahrhunderts," in *Lemberg–Lwów–Lviv: Eine Stadt im Schnittpunkt europäischer Kulturen*, ed. Peter Fässler, Thomas Held, and Dirk Sawitzki (Cologne: Böhlau, 1995), 77.

7. *Brünner Zeitung* (June 20, 1788), quoted in Wolfgang Häusler, *Das galizisches Judentum in der Hamburgermonarchie: Im Lichte der zeitgenössichen Publizistik und Reiseliteratur von 1772–1848* (Vienna: Verlag für Geschichte und Politik, 1979), 40.

8. Quoted in Maria Klanska, "Lemberg: Die 'Stadt der verwischten Grenzen,'" in *Lemberg/L'viv 1772–1918: Wiederbegegnung mit einer Landeshauptstadt der Donaumonarchie* (Vienna: Museen der Stadt Wien, 1993), 10–16.

9. See Leo Rosenberg, "Galizien," *Neue Jüdische Monatshefte. Zeitschrift für Politik, Wirtschaft und Literatur in Ost und West* 2.9–10 (Feb. 1918): 199–201.

10. See Gerald Stourzh, "Galten die Juden als Nationalität Altösterreichs?" *Studia Judaica* 10 (1984): 88–91.

11. See Holzer, "Jüdisches Leben," 80.

12. Leo Herzberg-Fränkl, "Die Juden," in *Die österreichisch-ungarische Monarchie in Wort und Bild: Galizien* (Vienna: Kaiserlich-königliche Hof- und Staatsdruckerei, 1898), 478.

13. See Marian Dabrowa, "Die Kultur in Galizien 1867–1914," in *Polen-Österreich: Aus der Geschichte einer Nachbarschaft*, ed. Walter Leitsch and Maria Wawrykowa (Vienna: Öster. Bundesverlag, 1988), 223.

14. See Klanska, "Lemberg," 12.

15. See Alfred Nossig, *Jan Prorok: Opowiesc na tle galicyjskim z 1880r* (Lemberg: Nakl. Funduszu Konkurswego im. H. Wawelberga, 1892), 108.

16. Herzberg-Fränkl, "Die Juden," 478ff.

17. Ernst Pliwa, *Österreichs Universitäten 1863/4–1902/3* (Vienna: F. Rempsky, 1908), 29.

18. See *Zeitschrift für Demographie und Statistik der Juden* 12 (1916): 3.

19. See *Stenographische Protokolle über die Sitzungen des Hauses der Abgeordneten des österreichischen Reichsrates,* 21st session (Vienna: Kaiserlich-königliche Hof- und Staatsdruckerei, 1911), 5183.

20. See Holzer, "Jüdisches Leben," 84.

21. See Israel M. Biderman, *Mayer Balaban, Historian of Polish Jewry: His Influence on the Younger Generation of Jewish Historians* (New York: Israel M. Biderman Book Com-

mittee, 1976), 77; and John Bunzl, *Klassenkampf in der Diaspora: Zur Geschichte der jüdischen Arbeiterbewegung* (Vienna: Europa-Verlag, 1975), 119–31.

22. This Index of Disparity is based on the Occupational Breakdown of the Jewish and Non-Jewish workforce and it is an analogue index to the Index of Segregation, which has been brought into empirical research by Otis Duncan and Beverly Duncan. The Index of Dissimilarity measures the proportion of one population which would have to move to achieve similarity of residential distribution with another population. The scale runs from 0 to 100, with 0 indicating complete integration and 100 complete segregation ("ghetto-situation"). The index is discussed in Otis D. Duncan and Beverly Duncan, "A Methodological Analysis of Segregation Indexes," *American Sociological Review* 20 (1955): 210–17. See also Albert Lichtblau, *Antisemitismus und soziale Spannung in Berlin und Wien 1867–1914* (Berlin: Metropol, 1994), 26–38.

23. See Michael John, "Die jüdische Bevölkerung in Wirtschaft und Gesellschaft Österreich-Ungarns 1867–1918: Bestandsaufnahme, Überblick und Thesen unter besonderer Berücksichtigung der Süd-Ostregion," in *Juden im Grenzraum: Wissenschaftliche Arbeiten aus dem Burgenland,* ed. Rudolf Kropf (Eisenstadt: Burgenländisches Landesmuseum, 1994), 202–11.

24. See Rosenberg, "Galizien," 204.

25. *Statistisches Jahrbuch der Stadt Wien für das Jahr 1912* (Vienna: Wiener Magistrat, 1914), 898.

26. See Klaus Hödl, *"Vom Shtetl an die Lower East Side": Galizische Juden in New York* (Vienna: Böhlau, 1991), 41ff.

27. See Beatrix Hoffmann-Holter, *"Abreisendmachung": Jüdische Kriegsflüchtlinge in Vienna 1914 bis 1923* (Vienna: Böhlau, 1995), 141–68.

28. See Jerzy Holzer, "Zur Frage der Akkulturation der Juden in Galizien im 19. und 20. Jahrhundert," *Jahrbücher für die Geschichte Osteuropas,* n.s., 37.2 (1989): 222–23.

29. See Holzer, "Jüdische Leben," 83.

30. See Michael John, "Migration und Multikulturalität in Österreich: Kontinuitäten und Brüche im 19. und 20. Jahrhundert," in *Österreichischer Zeitgeschichte-Tag 1993. Tagungsband,* ed. Ingrid Böhler and Rolf Steininger (Innsbruck: Studien-Verlag, 1995), 197–208.

31. See Stourzh, "Juden als Nationalität," 74–79.

32. See *Stenographische Protokolle,* 17th session (Vienna: Kaiserlich-königliche Hof- und Staatsdruckerei, 1906), 3682–85.

33. See Frank Golczewski, *Polnisch-Jüdische Beziehungen 1881–1922: Eine Studie zur Geschichte des Antisemitismus in Osteuropa* (Wiesbaden: Steiner-Verlag, 1981), 198–203.

34. See *Neue Freie Presse,* Nov. 27, 1918, 1–2; Samuel Gewürz, *Lemberg: Eine kritische Betrachtung des Judenpogroms vom 21. bis 23. November 1918* (Berlin: Louis Lamm, 1919), 3–13.

35. See Hans Roos, *Geschichte der Polnischen Nation 1918–1978: Von der Staatsgründung im Ersten Weltkrieg bis zur Gegenwart* (Cologne: Kohlhammer, 1979), 136ff.

36. See *Maly Rocznik Statystyczny 1939* (Warsaw: Nakl. Glownego urzedu Statystycznego, 1939), 24.

37. Evyatar Friesel, *Atlas of Modern Jewish History* (New York: Oxford University Press, 1990), 92–93; *Österreichische Statistik,* n.s., 1.1 (1912): 80–81.

38. See Golczewski, *Polnisch-Jüdische Beziehungen,* 204.

39. See Holzer, "Jüdisches Leben," 86–87.

40. Jonas Kreppel, *Juden und Judentum heute* (Zurich: Amalthea-Verlag, 1925), 315.

41. Holzer, "Jüdisches Leben," 85–88.

42. See Klaus Hödl, *Als Bettler in die Leopoldstadt: Galizische Juden auf dem Weg nach Wien* (Vienna: Böhlau, 1994), 290–94.

43. See Hermann Sternberg, "Zur Geschichte der Juden in Czernowitz," in Hugo Gold, *Geschichte der Juden in der Bukowina*, 2 vols. (Tel Aviv: Olamenu, 1962), 2:27–47.

44. Joseph Karniel, *Die Toleranzpolitik Kaiser Josephs II* (Gerlingen: Bleicher, 1985), 437–38.

45. See Gold, *Geschichte der Juden*, 2:153: "And nevertheless, this 'German' character of Bukovina could only be artificially maintained with the help of the Jews, because they gave their mother tongue [this was actually language of everyday use] as 'German.'"

46. Taken from a handwritten outline from the Estate of Karl Emil Franzos in the Manuscript Department of the Library of the City and Province of Vienna; cited in Ernest Wichner and Herbert Wiesner, eds., *In der Sprache der Mörder: Eine Literatur aus Czernowitz, Bukowina* (Berlin: Literaturhaus Berlin, 1993), 31. "Ruthenian" was the accepted designation for "Ukrainian" in the Hapsburg Monarchy; after 1918, the concept survived to refer to Ukrainians who were favorably disposed to the Hapsburgs.

47. Karl Emil Franzos, *Die Geschichte des Erstlingswerkes. Selbstbiographische Aufsätz* (Leipzig: Titze, 1894), 230. See also Monika Mayer, "Galizische und bukowinische Juden in Wien: Migration und Akkulturation: Das Leben im 'Shtetl' und in der neuen 'Heimat' im Spiegel lebensgeschichtlicher Aufzeichnungen" (diss., Dipl.Arb., Salzburg, 1995), 37.

48. Only Silesia with German, Polish, and Bohemian-Moravian-Slovakian, as well as Istria with Serbo-Croatian, Italian-Ladin, and Slovenian had a tripartite linguistic configuration similar to Bukovina.

49. Emil Brix, *Die Umgangssprachen in Altösterreich zwischen Agitation und Assimilation* (Vienna: Böhlau, 1982), 382ff.

50. See *Anuarul statstic al Romaniei 1930* (Bucharest: Directia Centrala de Statistica, 1932).

51. Adolf Armbruster, ed., *Vom Moldauwappen zum Doppeladler. Ausgewählte Beiträge zur Geschichte der Bukowina*, vol. 2: *Festschrift zum 75. Geburtstag von Frau Dr. Paula Tiefenthaler* (Augsburg: Hofmann, 1993), 86.

52. The Yiddish poet Josef Burg, born in 1912 in Wischnitz, recounts that, from his earliest childhood, he grew up speaking five languages. From an interview conducted in Salzburg, February 15, 1996, by Albert Lichtblau.

53. Hannelore Burger, "Mehrsprachigkeit und Unterrichtswesen in der Bukowina 1869–1918," in *Die Bukowina: Vergangenheit und Gegenwart*, ed. Ilona Slawinski and Joseph P. Strelka (Bern: Lang, 1995), 99.

54. Adam Wandruszka and Peter Urbanitsch, eds., *Die Habsburgermonarchie 1848–1918*, vol. 3: *Die Völker des Reiches* (Vienna: Verlag der öster. Akademie der Wissenschaften, 1980), 77.

55. See also Berthold Windt, "Die Juden an den Mittel- und Hochschulen Oesterreichs seit 1850," *Statistische Monatsschrift* (1881), 442–57; Jakob Thon, "Anteil der Juden am Hochschulstudium in Oesterreich seit dem Jahre 1851," *Zeitschrift für Demographie und Statistik der Juden* (Mar. 1907), 33ff.

56. Also in the lyceums for girls which were then increasingly popular in Bukovina,

51.6 percent (707) of the students were Jewish. This was, once again, the highest proportion of all crown lands. See *Österreichische Statistik,* n.s., 17.3 (1919): 60ff.

57. Albert Lichtblau and Sabine Jahn, eds., *Prive Friedjung: "Wir wollten nur das Paradies auf Erden": Die Erinnerungen einer jüdischen Kommunistin aus der Bukowina* (Vienna: Böhlau, 1995), 67.

58. John Leslie, "Der Ausgleich in der Bukowina von 1910: Zur österreichischen Nationalitätenpolitik vor dem Ersten Weltkrieg," in *Geschichte zwischen Freiheit und Ordnung: Gerald Stourzh zum 60. Geburtstag,* ed. Emil Brix, Thomas Froeschl, and Josef Leidenfrost (Graz: Styria, 1991), 129.

59. For the Austrian half of the Monarchy, the Disparity Index of Jews and non-Jews with respect to economic classes according to the census of 1910 was 45.05.

60. For the Austrian half of the Monarchy, the Disparity Index of Jews and non-Jews with respect to occupational groups according to the census of 1910 was 28.05.

61. Wichner and Wiesner, *In der Sprache der Mörder,* 51.

62. See, for instance, Gold, *Geschichte der Juden,* 2:33.

63. *Stenographische Protokolle,* 17th session, meeting of March 13, 1906 (Vienna: Kaiserlich-königliche Hof- und Staatsdruckerei, 1906), 35112.

64. According to the 1910 census, 7,420 Jewish members of the workforce representing 18.4 percent of all Jews employed were laborers. The percentage in Galicia was 15.5 percent and was slightly higher in the capital Vienna with 21.3 percent. See also Gold, *Geschichte der Juden,* 2:35–36.

65. Hugo Gold, *Geschichte der Juden in der Bukowina,* 2 vols. (Tel Aviv: Olamenu, 1958), 1:57.

66. Ibid., 1:51, 77ff.; Martin Broszat, "Von der Kulturnation zur Volksgruppe: Die nationale Stellung der Juden in der Bukowina im 19. und 20. Jahrhundert," *Historische Zeitschrift* 200 (1965): 583.

67. Gold, *Geschichte der Juden,* 1:59; Broszat, "Von der Kulturnation zur Volksgruppe," 548ff.

68. Broszat, "Von der Kulturnation zur Volksgruppe," 580.

69. See, for example, Gold, *Geschichte der Juden,* 1:60.

70. Adolf Gaisbauer, *Davidstern und Doppeladler: Zionismus und jüdischer Nationalismus in Österreich 1882–1918* (Vienna: Böhlau, 1988), 479ff.

71. Ibid., 511ff.

72. On the subject of Bloch, see, for instance, Robert S. Wistrich, *The Jews of Vienna in the Age of Franz Joseph* (Oxford: Oxford University Press, 1990), 270ff.

73. *Stenographische Protokolle,* 17th session, 35113.

74. See, for example, Harald Seewann, *Zirkel und Zionsstern. Bilder und Dokumente aus der versunkenen Welt des jüdisch-nationalen Kooperationsstudententums,* 5 vols. (Graz: Eigenverlag, 1990), 1:169ff.

75. Broszat, "Von der Kulturnation zur Volksgruppe," 591.

76. Leon Arie Schmelzer, "Geschichte des Zionismus in der Bukowina," in Gold, *Geschichte der Juden,* 1:93.

77. See the works of Gerald Stourzh.

78. See Leslie, "Der Ausgleich in der Bukowina," 129.

79. Ibid., 134ff.

80. *Stenographische Protokolle,* 17th session, 35113.

81. Lydia Harnik, "Erinnerungen an die Flucht vor der Russeninvasion nach Wien

im August 1914" (Czernowtsy, 1992), ms., Archive of the Institute for the History of the Jews in Austria, St. Pölten, 1–2.

82. *Die Bukowina: Eine allgemeine Heimatkunde verfaßt anläßlich des 50jährigen glorreichen Regierungsjubiläums seiner kaiserlichen und königlichen Apostolischen Majestät unseres Allergnädigsten Kaisers und Obersten Kriegsherrn durch die k.k. Landes-Gendarmarie-Commandos No. 13* (Czernowitz: Pardini, 1899), 183.

83. Johann Polek, "Statistik des Judenthums in der Bukowina," in *Statistische Monatsschrift* (Vienna: H. Pardini'sche Universitäts-Buchhandlung, 1881), 259.

84. A reference to Karl Emil Franzos, *Aus Halb-Asien.* Benno Straucher took issue with this label in a polemic in Parliament: "Certain semi-asiatic conditions are said to exist in Bukovina, but this is most unfair." *Stenographische Protokolle,* 17th session, 35107.

85. Brix, *Die Umgangssprachen,* 75.

86. Ludger Heid, "Der Ostjude," in *Antisemitismus: Vorurteile und Mythen,* ed. Julius H. Schoeps and Joachim Schlör (Munich: Piper, 1995), 241–51.

87. For example, an interview with Rosa Roth-Zuckermann conducted on June 11, 1996, in Vienna, for the Survivors of the Shoah project. Born in 1908 in Czernowitz, she grew up in an orthodox family—her grandfather was a follower of the Chassidic Rabbi of Sadagora—in which her education was oriented toward German culture. In response to the question of whether she considered herself an *Ostjüdin,* she responded with a clear "No."

88. *Die Bukowina,* 181. "This stunted and twisted jargon, this language of the ghetto which we now use, this is a habit that we will drop. These were forms of speech stolen by prisoners," Theodor Herzl wrote in *The Jewish State.* See Theodor Herzl, "Der Judenstaat," in *"Wenn ihr wollt, ist es kein Märchen": Altneuland/Der Judenstaat,* ed. Julius H. Schoeps (Königstein/Ts.: Athenäum, 1985), 244.

89. On the subject of the Hebrew language movement, see Gold, *Geschichte der Juden,* 2:163ff.

90. On the subject of Birnbaum, see, for example, Gaisbauer, *Davidstern,* 44–45, 362ff.; Wistrich, *Jews of Vienna,* 381ff. For a biographical account of Max Diamant, see Stourzh, "Juden als Nationalität," 81ff.

91. Gold, *Geschichte der Juden,* 2:34ff., 46.

92. Jacob Toury, *Die jüdische Presse im österreichischen Kaiserreich: Ein Beitrag zur Problematik der Akkulturation 1802–1918* (Tübingen: J. C. B. Morh [Paul Siebeck], 1983), 138–44.

93. From "Mein Vater," by Alfred Gong. Cited in Amy Colin and Alfred Kittner, eds., *Versunkene Dichtung der Bukowina: Eine Anthologie deutschsprachiger Lyrik,* (Munich: W. Fink, 1994), 294. *Zigeuner* (Gypsy) is considered an insult in German and is used primarily to refer to untrustworthy persons.

94. Lily Glanz, "About My Hometown Czernowitz" (Montreal, 1991), ms., Archive of the Institute for the History of the Jews in Austria, St. Pölten, 4.

95. Pearl Fichman, "Before Memories Fade: Memoirs" (New York, 1989), ms., Archive of the Institute for the History of the Jews in Austria, St. Pölten, 12.

96. Ibid., 5, about her early youth.

97. Paul Celan, "Ansprache anläßlich der Entgegennahme des Literaturpreises der freien Hansestadt Bremen," *Ausgewählte Gedichte: Zwei Reden* (Frankfurt am Main: Suhrkamp, 1968), 127.

98. Ibid.

99. Fichman, "Before Memories Fade," 45.

100. Salomea Genin, *Scheindl und Salomea. Von Lemberg nach Berlin* (Frankfurt: Fischer, 1972), 70.

101. Maria Sporrer and Herbert Steiner, eds, *Simon Wiesenthal: Ein unbequemer Zeitgenosse (Vienna: Orac, 1992), 16, 28–30.*

102. Benedikt Friedman, Zornige Erinnerungen eines jüdischen Österreichers (Vienna: Promedia, 1992), 6.

103. Author interview with Josef Burg (born 1912), transcript in author's files.

104. Thomas Held, "Vom Pogrom zum Massenmord: Die Vernichtung der jüdischen Bevölkerung Lembergs im Zweiten Weltkrieg," in *Lemberg-Lwów-Lviv,* ed. Fässler et al., 119–20.

2 At the Frontier: The South African Jewish Experience

JOHN SIMON

THE EXPANSION OF THE FRONTIER

The history of South Africa from the very earliest times is largely constituted by the so-called Boer-Brit-Black Axis. This is, of course, neat alliterative shorthand for the interrelationship between the English- and Afrikaans-speaking sections of the white population and the indigenous black people of Southern Africa.[1]

The Afrikaner, whether his origins were from Holland, France or Germany, never looked back to his European roots. Those of British descent, however, assiduously preserved and fostered their links with the homeland—the South African of English descent who would speak of "home," even in the third or fourth generation, frequently aroused the ire of the Afrikaner fellow citizen. The indigenous black tribes moving ever southward through the subcontinent viewed their roots through the prism of a form of ancestor worship, rather than in a geographical sense. Each therefore established a frontier of a distinctive character, and settled on a periphery whose center was different in time and place from that of the others.

The Jew found himself in an uneasy, sometimes perilous position in the various movements and countermovements which made up this kaleidoscope. He never forgot or lost contact with his geographical roots and still less with his religious and cultural background.

The first contact which the Jews had as settlers in the Cape was with the English establishment, and these particular Jews were largely of Anglo-Jewish origin. A generation or two in Great Britain had served to enable the Jews who came from Central and Eastern Europe to adapt largely to the Anglo-Saxon lifestyle. Those immigrants therefore who came to the eastern frontier with the 1820 Settlers, and those who made their way direct to the Cape Colony, did not feel themselves in an alien environment living under British colonial rule. In Cape Town and its environs they made common cause with their fellow colonists. They enjoyed full religious freedom, which they utilized in 1841 to establish the first Jewish Congregation in southern Africa.[2] They were part of the sometimes turbulent life of the colony and very much involved in such issues as the anti-convict agitation.[3] On the eastern frontier they were fully involved in the military actions which were part of the earliest confrontations between the English settlers and the indigenous blacks.[4] They would become farmers, merchants, traders and soldiers, as well as founders of the Grahamstown Jewish community and important stalwarts of the Cape Town Hebrew Congregation in its early years.[5]

The boundaries of the colony spread, or rather were pushed out by the Dutch settlers who moved firstly eastward, playing a somber game of leapfrog with the British government who tried to extend its authority from river to river as the Dutch trekkers moved eastward along the coastline.[6]

In the famous Great Trek from 1836 onward, the Dutch trekkers mainly from the eastern frontier moved northward and northwestward through the land, establishing their communities and later their republics in the territories which became known as Griqualand West, Orange Free State and the South African Republic (later Transvaal).[7]

There was some sprinkling of Jews amongst the early travelers who accompanied or followed the very early migrations in the Eastern Province, Natal and elsewhere.[8] Their stories are full of adventure and romance, but they are individual stories and cannot be regarded in any way as contact between any sort of Jewish community on the one hand and the settlers or indigenes on the other hand. Perhaps no such contact would ever have taken place were it not for those epochal and nation-building events, the discovery of diamonds in the Griqualand West area (later Kimberley) in 1869 and the discovery of gold on the Witwatersrand in the 1880s.

This period of expansion and development also saw the establishment and growth of South African Jewry.[9] In this sense the Jewish settlers (outside of the Cape Colony itself) were in a somewhat unique situation. Instead of arriving as newcomers in a settled country, and thus being vulnerable to the centuries-old taunt that the Jews invariably come and reap in prosperous comfort where others have sowed in travail, South African Jews were able to claim that they were in at the beginning and that their initiative, their enterprise, their toil and sweat had contributed equally with the non-Jew toward the creation and growth of a new settlement, a new community, indeed a new country.

JEWS OF ANGLO-JEWISH ORIGIN

Not only did these events bring about direct contact and confrontation between Jews and the various population groups of southern Africa, but it was a new type of Jew which would be involved principally in this confrontation. As has been pointed out, the first Jewish settlers were of Anglo-Jewish descent. Anglo Jewry was by the middle of the nineteenth century a community which combined strong (albeit voluntary) religious loyalty with a determined sense of identity, but which at the same time was subject to a considerable degree of social assimilation.[10]

This preoccupation with identity in a voluntary community is to be contrasted with the process which at all times affected Jews of Central and Eastern Europe. A Jew in the Greater Russian Empire confined to the Pale of Settlement, cocooned and constricted in the shtetl, never had the opportunity to assimilate, even if sufficient of a maverick to wish to do so. Even a Jew of the more enlightened German Confederation (or Empire as it later became) was always conscious of being a member of the *Gemeinde.*[11] By contrast, the Jew in Great Britain, living in a more open society, had perforce to cling to outward signs of religious observance to maintain his or her identity, and to observe "rites of passage" so as to keep contact with his or her roots and fellow Jews.[12] This pattern would largely prevail amongst South African Jews of Anglo Jewish descent.

In Cape Town a colonial atmosphere prevailed, heavily under the influence of England in social and political matters.[13] The small Jewish community was nurtured and flourished in this colonial atmosphere which spread to religious matters also. From the beginning the community looked to the Chief Rabbi of the United Kingdom for the appointment of its ministers and direction in matters spiritual and ritual. Both in the formal sense and in practical matters the Chief Rabbinate directed the community. No juridical step could be taken—a conversion, a divorce, the opening of a *mikvah,* the consecration of a burial ground, even the acquisition of a Torah scroll—without the specific authority of the Chief Rabbi.

JEWS FROM EASTERN EUROPE

Turning now to the contrasting background of the Jews who came from Eastern Europe, it is estimated that between 30,000 and 40,000 Jews came to

South Africa from Greater Russia between 1880 and 1914. By sheer force of numbers they therefore soon dominated the community. It is necessary to examine the background from which they came and the cultural and religious "baggage" which they brought with them in order to understand how they impacted on the community which they found and how they helped to shape South African Jewry.

For over three centuries the Jews of Eastern Europe had maintained an intensive religious life observing an intellectual and spiritual isolation which was not only imposed on them but self-imposed. The Haskalah (Enlightenment) Movement had permitted a certain infusion of secular learning and thought and had exposed Jews who did not reject it to wider cultural and intellectual horizons; but it did not bring with it any serious threat to the integrity of Jewish life, or religious observance. Social assimilation was neither available to, or sought by, the Jews who had lived under the dominion of the czar (notwithstanding efforts by the latter and some of his officials). In the words of Simon Dubnow, Russian civilization was "not worth the having."[14]

By and large the Jews who came to South Africa from Eastern Europe in the last two decades of the nineteenth and the first two decades of the twentieth centuries were seeking economic advancement and social acceptance, not religious freedom, which they had enjoyed to the full in their homeland. To visit far-off and remote farmsteads, to keep his shop open for fifteen hours a day seven days a week, to become accepted, was a more urgent need for the recent immigrant than the need to observe the Sabbath or keep Kosher.

Those who were not prepared to make these sacrifices stayed at home. Some of them found in changing circumstances in Greater Russia opportunities for new competition and confrontation with non-Jews. The large property owners, professionals, and wealthier classes generally stayed.[15] Only 5 percent of Jewish immigrants into the United States in the first decade of the twentieth century were over forty-five years of age[16] and there is no reason to believe that the percentage in South Africa was significantly different. Indeed, in 1936, over 75 percent of South African Jews under thirty years of age were South African born.[17]

We have interesting details of 1237 applicants for South African naturalization in 1904–6. They included 428 "general dealers and merchants" and 133 "tailors and outfitters." Applicants for naturalization could of course be expected to "upgrade" the description of their occupation.[18] Furthermore, it would only have been the hardy and adventurous spirits who would have ventured to a new and unknown land. Those who went to the United States had a great deal of information about the land they were choosing both for good and for ill. Although there had been some information coming through in increasing volume from South Africa it was by and large unknown territory.[19]

But even those who had achieved only a minimum education and who practiced a minimum of ritual observance themselves followed a tradition of respect for learning and piety. As a recent student of these Jews has observed: "Lithuanian Jews were well versed in traditional Jewish sources, rich in spirituality and sincerely respectful of knowledge in general and Jewish learning in particular."[20] The result was that whether the South African Jew lived in one of the large cities or a remote rural area he would as soon as circumstances permitted establish such religious and educational structures as were practicable.

The new immigrant lost no time in assuming the outward trappings necessary to establish himself in his new home but equally lost little time in establishing the essential institutions—the synagogue, the *cheder* (Hebrew school) and the burial ground—which would enable him to preserve his roots. This would play a large part in preserving the integrity and homogeneity of South African Jewry.

The *Cape Times,* in an editorial of July 1896, recognized these elements:

> The Russian exile who scarcely would call his soul his own in Europe rejoices to draw in the free air of the British Colony. . . . The man who stepped ashore in his long outlandish boots—which he slept in, perhaps close to the fo'c's'le coming over—and with a beard to his equally outlandish belt, suddenly one fine day emerges with the cut of a genteel Cape Colonist. He toils, he saves and as soon as he has saved a little, he calculates how many times that sum will enable him to send his son to college. . . . When he has made his fortune he is as a rule as unashamed of his beginnings as he is proud to rank among his own people.[21]

By the end of the century the majority of Cape Town Jews were of Eastern European origin. They were soon characterized by the cultural and religious luggage which they brought with them. Their mother tongue was Yiddish and only a small number had a smattering of English, if that; this soon changed and even though they may never have lost their accents, they soon learned to speak fluent and idiomatic English. They worked hard in trying to adapt to their circumstances, learning and observing from whatever opportunity presented itself—most became peddlers, petty traders or artisans. But they did not like what they saw of the way in which the Jewish religion was practiced and observed.

Writing of the Dutch settlers at the Cape in the seventeenth century, Noel Mostert noted that after just two or three generations in South Africa, the settlers scarcely retained a shadow of their European heritage. More than in any other colonial settlement the South African colonists "thoroughly and irrevocably [severed] themselves from the culture and civilization, the habits of thought and expression, the ritual institutional obedience and industry of their forefathers." There was no room in the imaginations of African colonials for what this author called "inherited nostalgia."[22]

This description differs so vastly from the experience of Jewish immigrants to South Africa that study of the community must endeavor to identify all the influences and characteristics leading to the community maintaining its "inherited nostalgia" and its "institutional obedience" while at the same time establishing itself as an integral and growing part of the new frontier society.

THE INFLUENCE OF THE CHIEF RABBINATE

Although both in the formal sense and in practical matters the Chief Rabbinate in London directed the community, it would not be long before the new infant began to assume some of the semblance of an *enfant terrible.* There was never any constitutional or formal component in the relationship, and the demographic changes which took place in the community led to changes in loyalties. The Chief Rabbi exercised a moral authority, but only over those who were voluntarily willing to submit themselves to such authority. So from the very beginning the Cape Town Hebrew Congregation, the mother congregation of South Africa, submitted itself to the authority of the Chief Rabbi, but it was not long before tensions arose in the tiny congregation and these related precisely to issues such as cemeteries and kashrut, upon which the malcontents would not accept the authority of the Chief Rabbi.

Given that the Chief Rabbinate was a typical English institution which was shot through and through with English customs and practices, one can understand how it was that the Jews of the Cape Colony adjusted without difficulty to this control from London. Yet we find that even in the robust and less polished atmosphere of the Transvaal the measured tones of Imperialism, even if expressed in the Jewish idiom, held sway. In fact, the Chief Rabbi's letterbooks and correspondence files reveal that by 1894 correspondence with Johannesburg had become much more frequent than with Cape Town.[23] The size of the growing Jewish community on the Witwatersrand in turn meant that new problems would be encountered with increasing frequency about such matters as divorce, conversion, funeral customs and the like. All this meant an increasing need for guidance from London, guidance which was needed just as much in the Transvaal Republic as in the Cape Colony.

THE INFLUENCE OF ZIONISM

One of the important spheres in which certain Rabbis exercised an influence on the South African community was in the important part that Zionism played in the community.[24] Zionism as an intellectual exercise, a program of action and an organizational activity, was taken up very early in South Africa.[25]

Zionism was part of the warp and weft of Jewish communal life in South Africa. The Rabbinate preached the Zionist message on all appropriate occasions, and the *Kolboiniks*,[26] in their halls and *cheder* rooms, always paid great attention to those festivals having a national theme. Posters illustrating the work of the Jewish National Fund and many other Zionist institutions and celebrations were the standard decorations of Jewish communal halls throughout South Africa.

THE INFLUENCE OF OVERSEAS "RESPONSA"

Not the least factor which has influenced the way in which the South African Jewish community developed was its far removal from the mainstream of Jewish life and the long distances within the country itself. Europe, America and Palestine were far away and it is only in recent decades that modern technology made it easier to communicate across the continents. There were long distances within the territory itself and the community developed no local *yeshivot* (Rabbinic academies) or other centers of Jewish learning. There was never a recognized central authority. Fully one quarter of South African Jews lived outside the two main cities. It was inevitable therefore that certain particular nuances or emphases would develop, and some of these have been recognized in *responsa* which were issued to questions addressed by South African Ministers to their overseas colleagues.[27]

On more than one occasion it was found possible to give lenient rulings for the stated reason that the local circumstances justified this. It is clear from at least one *responsum* that South African Jews were generally considered to be lax in their observance of religious precepts.

In 1922 the eminent scholar of Vilna, Rabbi Chaim Ozer Grodzinski (1863–1940), was asked whether the fact that the witnesses to a *get* (religious decree of divorce), one of whom was a shopkeeper and the other a tavern-keeper, publicly desecrated the Sabbath by keeping their respective establishments open on Saturdays, would invalidate the *get*. His ruling was that the *get* was valid and he gave the following explanation: "Since desecration of the Sabbath is so common in that place and virtually no one sees any prohibition in opening a business on the Sabbath, the witness is not disqualified since he is not aware that he has done an act which disqualifies him."[28]

Another *responsum* which has regard to the circumstances of the place is from Rabbi Waldenberg, who permitted boys under the age of thirteen who were being prepared for their bar mitzvah to be taught on the sabbath how to don *t'fillin* (phylacteries). He commented in 1964: "The teacher from Johannesburg may teach these youngsters who have no other opportunity to learn how to put on tephillin even on a Sabbath. . . . This ruling is made taking into consideration the special circumstances of the children in the diaspora who are forced by law to spend their week studying the curriculum of the public schools."[29]

Other rulings which have been affected by South African circumstances relate to permission being granted to deliver a *get* to a woman living far away in German South West Africa (present-day Namibia) by registered post because of the near impossibility of finding messengers to deliver it by hand;[30] and a fascinating case referred to in 1897 by Chief Rabbi Adler, but also referred to as a contemporary issue by Rabbi Mirvish, of permission being given to a happily married couple to become divorced. The husband was on his deathbed, they had no children, and he had brothers living in America and Russia from whom the widow would find it virtually impossible to obtain *chalitza* (the release which a childless widow must receive from her deceased husband's brother before she can marry again—see Leviticus 25:5–10) and she would therefore be compelled to live as an *agunah* (a woman who, although widowed or abandoned by her husband, may not marry again). In a lenient *Responsum,* Rav Kook stated that the preferred course was for the wife to be given a *get* so there would be no risk of her becoming an *agunah,* but he added that if the husband were to recover then he and his wife would have to be prudent and discreet about their future life together.[31]

It was not only in the synagogue where matters of ritual arose. Other occasions in life presented themselves where accommodation had to be allowed. The whole question of custom and ritual relating to death, burial, and mourning was one which often presented problems, as did repeated calls in the Jewish press and in the community generally for the updating and revision of synagogue services. Although this was a recurrent theme, this makes it all the more significant that those who were responsible for the synagogue administration and the way in which the services were conducted—the Rabbis, the Cantors and the lay leaders—by and large remained firm throughout the community against any substantial change,[32] and there was almost complete uniformity of religious services throughout South Africa.

SYNAGOGUE LIFE AND DIRECTION

There were fairly substantial variations in synagogue attendance from time to time and from place to place and from congregation to congregation. Ministers frequently complained of poor attendance at religious services other than on certain occasions. Those occasions upon which the synagogue was invariably crowded and a large congregation required overflow services were Yom Kippur, particularly Kol Nidre (the opening service) and Yiskor (the memorial service for deceased relatives) and Neilah (the concluding service); the first day of Rosh Hashana and to a lesser extent the first night of the so-called pilgrim festivals. Chanukah was popular as having a military significance, and in particular young people's groups, Jewish Boy Scout Groups and similar movements, would have parades and special services on Chanukah. Pesach, which celebrates the birth of Jewish nationhood, became more and more popular as the Zionist movement grew and Jewish nationalism came to the fore.

The centripetal affect of the synagogue ensured that South African Jews would on the whole be punctilious in the traditional observance of the rites of passage; do what they could to provide a modicum of Jewish education for their children; and maintain their religious institutions with dignity and their officiants with respect. But this did not make them rigorous or even particularly attentive in matters of religious observance. The lay leaders played a very important part in the development of South African Judaism, in ensuring the provision of all facilities required for the maintenance of religious life, synagogues, officiants, and religious necessities. Individual figures played their part in placing their stamp on their respective communities. But neither they nor their colleagues were versed in the Halacha (religious law) or the sources; so they may have played a part in determining what sort of architect would be engaged to design the synagogue or how to set about engaging a minister and determine his remuneration, but they had nothing to do with what prayers were recited or how to respond to the queries which led to the *responsa* mentioned earlier.

As far back as 1903, the *South African Jewish Chronicle,* in an editorial referring to a sermon delivered by Chief Rabbi Adler in which he criticized any attempt to reform the liturgy, made an extremely perceptive comment which remains valid today: "Even in South Africa there is a strong tendency to fit, or attempt to do so, our religion to the so-called exigencies of the time."[33]

JEWS ON THE DIAMOND FIELDS

The Jewish settlers who came to the diamond fields in the wake of the discovery of diamonds conformed by and large to the observation of Henry Lichtenstein that "It is seldom the most polished part of the population of any country that seek their fortunes by establishing themselves in newly founded colonies."[34] Some colorful Jewish personalities were involved from the time of the very first discoveries, and as soon as the diamond diggings were established along the banks of the Vaal River Jews were to be found there as diggers, traders and artisans. The famous duo of Isaac Lewis and Samuel Marks, the latter of whom particularly was to play so large a part in serving the Transvaal Republic,[35] made their first profits by travelling to the diamond fields with wagons loaded with essential goods required by the diggers.[36] Many names appeared, of English, German, and Russian origin, which would ultimately be etched deeply into the romantic story. The point to be made, however, is that these Jews were part of and not separate from the developing diamond world of Griqualand West. Whether as diggers, traders, or financiers and entrepreneurs, they met and mingled with their counterparts at every level of life in the diamond fields.

There is another very important observation to make about these Jewish pioneers on the diamond fields. Within less than five years after the discovery of diamonds, Jewish religious services were being held on the diggings and only a year later the foundation of a synagogue was laid. Speaking at the ceremony of the laying of the foundation stone the governor, Sir Henry Barkly, in the course of a most cordial address, made the following comment: "In Griqualand West, especially, it has so happened, from the first, that some of the most energetic and enterprising members of society have been Jews. The assemblage of today shows how important a part the Jewish congregations now form of the community."[37] Milton Shain has commented on the establishment in the diamond fields in 1876 of a branch of the Alliance Israélite Universelle, and the establishment in Cape Town in the 1880s of a branch of the Anglo-Jewish Association. He argues that the secular nature of these two bodies serves as "an indication that Jews were no longer looking to the synagogue alone for communal support."[38] This may be so; but the synagogue as the focal point of Jewish identity long survived the Alliance

Israélite Universelle in Kimberley and the Anglo-Jewish Association in Cape Town. Not even the establishment of the South African Zionist Federation in 1898 or the Board of Deputies in the Transvaal in 1903, the Cape in 1904, and the amalgamated body in 1912 seriously challenged this supremacy.

JEWS IN THE SOUTH AFRICAN REPUBLIC (TRANSVAAL)

The place of the Jew in the South African Republic was defined very largely by the issue of religion. The equally important issues of the franchise, political rights, and economic opportunity for Uitlanders (foreigners) and the sovereign status of the Republic derived ultimately from the religious issue. This was because the Republic under the leadership of its redoubtable President Paul Kruger withheld civil rights from all but the Protestant Afrikaner establishment. In 1887, a year after the founding of Johannesburg, the Jewish population was 100; by the following year it was estimated at upward of 500; by 1891, 4000 and within five years the Jews constituted some 10 percent of the total population.[39] The demographic division in the Transvaal Jewish community differed from that in the Cape. At first, Jews of Anglo-Jewish descent and Jews from Eastern Europe were roughly of equal numbers but the latter by reason of increased immigration soon predominated. Tensions developed between the patriarchal government of the South African Republic, directed by strong-minded Protestants, and the burgeoning Jewish community, which was determined to partake in what was hoped to be the prosperity of the goldfields while at the same time maintaining its identity.[40] Prominent figures such as Rabbi J. H. Hertz were much involved in the agitation for civil liberties and religious freedom for non-Protestants.[41] On the other hand, important politico-economic personalities, supreme amongst them Sammy Marks, not only maintained bridgeheads into the establishment across which Jews of acceptable opinions might cross, but became valued advisors to the government and to Kruger himself.[42] By and large, relations between the Boers and Jews at the social and personal level were good, but religious differences did occasionally spill over into the public sphere.

After England's victory in the Anglo-Boer War, Rabbi Hertz and other Jews who had left as refugees returned to the Witwatersrand in the wake of the victorious forces. Life proceeded, prosperity followed and the Jews would meet their counterparts in commerce, mining, industry, the professions, and academia.

In the Orange Free State the religious elements encountered in the Transvaal were largely missing.[43] President F. W. Reitz had a very different attitude toward the Jews from that of Kruger. There is on record a letter which he wrote to Reverend Joel Rabinowitz in 1880 expressing his support for the collection of funds in the Free State for distressed Russian Jewry.[44]

JEWS AND AFRIKANERS

This whole question of the Jewish relationship with Afrikaners assumed greater and greater importance as the twentieth century advanced. There were issues on which and locations where fairly close harmony existed. Particularly in the smaller country towns the Jews invariably had a warm and close personal relationship with their Afrikaans neighbors.[45] Invariably the Jew followed a trade or occupation which brought him close to a fairly large section of the general community, which was predominantly Afrikaans-speaking—he would be the hotel proprietor or the garage owner or the owner of a general dealer's store or perhaps a doctor or lawyer. He was thus well known and an important figure in the community. Those comparatively few Jews who actually became farmers themselves—they earned the complimentary soubriquet of "Boere Jode"—shared the tribulations and sometimes the prosperity of their Afrikaner neighbors.

But as the century advanced the tensions between Jew and Afrikaner increased. There was a sharp increase in the emigration of Eastern European Jews during the second half of the 1920s. By an unhappy chance this coincided with a period of unemployment in South Africa and the development of what became known as the "poor white issue," that is, dislocated recently urbanized Afrikaners. Almost inevitably these people compared their parlors situation with that of the upward mobility of the new immigrants and their children, who succeeded in business and in the industrial and professional spheres. Not only did this become an issue on its own of jealousy and resentment, but the perceived "theft" by the new immigrants and their children of the "birthright" of the Afrikaner became used by an emerging Afrikaner national movement as a useful plank in its political platform. As Milton Shain phrased it, "There was no question at this point of persecuting Jews but there was a definite sense that the alleged Jewish role in commerce could be used as a stalking horse to exploit growing national Afrikaner sentiment."[46]

Paradoxically, the immigrants were attacked on two diametrically opposed grounds. On the one hand, as pointed out, the new immigrants seemed to be forging ahead in commerce, industry and the professions, and thus were seen as a threat to the Afrikaner who could not meet him on these fields. On the other hand, however, the immigrant was described as poverty-stricken, morally degenerate, dishonest and unassimilable; there was no lack of politicians and political journalists who were more than willing to fish in these troubled waters as part of their struggle to establish Afrikaner nationalism within the framework of South African political discourse.[47]

The Greyshirt movement, therefore, with its vicious anti-Semitism which emerged in the 1930s, was largely made up of Afrikaners who derived their attitudes from the political rhetoric of the 1920s.[48] During the war, the substantial sections of the Afrikaner population which supported Nazi Germany may have done so more because of their hatred for England than their love of Germany, but this did not serve to make them any more friendly toward the Jews or to be seen by the Jews as other than enemies. The Nationalist party, which by and large embodied the political aspirations of the Afrikaners, if not openly anti-Semitic in its platform, barred Jews from membership in some of its most important branches. Jews by and large therefore strongly supported the mainly English-speaking United party in the 1948 general elections and there was much fear and apprehension when the Nationalist party came to power under Dr. D. F. Malan. The fact that Dr. Malan was one of the first world leaders to recognize the State of Israel allayed some of the fears, but by and large the Jew was antigovernment.

By this time, of course, a new dimension had taken its place in the South African political scene, namely the color issue.

JEWS IN THE APARTHEID ERA

The whole story of race relations in South Africa, the so-called Apartheid era, the liberation struggle and the dramatic transformation of South Africa into a democracy is of course beyond the scope of this paper. What is important for our purposes is to note that throughout this period Jews were to be found across the political spectrum. There were Jews closely involved in what the Apartheid government called "treasonable activities"; members of the Communist party, openly before its banning and clandestinely thereafter; and who figured prominently in the various Treason Trials and the other rigorous measures which the government took to suppress extra-Parliamentary opposition, such as detention without trial and house arrest.[49] There were Jews, on the other hand, who were closely identified with government policies, and there were some who in their private and business lives exemplified white domination in all its aspects. But most Jews occupied a position between these two polarities. If it were possible to graph the political opinions of individual Jews one would find that they were principally concentrated somewhat left of center. They were prominent in the "respectable" bodies and activities which opposed the government and often played leading roles in the struggle for civil liberties and the amelioration of the conditions of the nonwhite peoples of South Africa. It is impossible to justify this contention with any evidence at this stage. I believe that, insofar as the public lives and careers of South African Jews are concerned, this is a correct view of the matter. It would be wrong to ignore much evidence however that in their private lives Jews were fully involved in all activities by which white South Africans benefited from apartheid measures. They were often motivated by a feeling of insecurity instilled by the establishment's "swart gevaar" propaganda. ("Swart gevaar"—black peril; cf. yellow peril, red peril, etc.) A frequently encountered quip during the latter years of the Apartheid regime was that the Jew "thinks like a Prog, votes UP, and thanks God for the Nationalists."[50]

Nothing of course is static, least of all public opinion and political activity during the regime such as that which governed South Africa from 1948 to 1994. It is instructive to survey the published transactions and policies of the South African Jewish Board of Deputies[51] to see how its stance altered during at least the latter part of this period.

THE SOUTH AFRICAN JEWISH BOARD OF DEPUTIES

The Twenty-fourth National Congress of the Board of Deputies in 1965 restated the attitude of the board as it had been proclaimed and maintained at least since 1948.[52] The board, stated its report, had a twofold aim: On the one hand to safeguard the position of Jews as free and equal citizens of the Republic, and on the other hand to maintain and promote good relations and understanding between the Jewish community and all other sections of the population of the Republic. The community had been disturbed by editorials which had appeared in certain Afrikaans newspapers, supporters of the government, who had put pertinent questions as to what was the official Jewish standpoint to the fact that a high percentage of whites who were detained under the "90 day clause" of the General Law Amendment Act were Jews.[53] The board in its response to this sort of insinuation never at this time came out in support of Jews who were involved in anti-apartheid activities. They repeated their attitude that the board had no collective responsibility for the actions of individual Jews and proclaimed time and time again that the Jewish community was an established, loyal, and patriotic part of the South African population. The board's journal, *Jewish Affairs,* had written editorials in opposition to "violence and civil disorder," as antigovernment protests were termed by the establishment.

The resolution passed at this congress was reiterated frequently at subsequent congresses and is worth stating in full as being the official stance of the South African community until it became "fashionable" for official bodies openly to proclaim support for the struggle for human rights and civil liberty for all.

> Congress, recognising that the fundamental racial problems of South African concern members of the Jewish community as vitally as they do all other sections of the population, urges every Jewish citizen to make his individual contribution in accordance with the teachings and precepts of Judaism towards the pursuit of understanding, goodwill and co-operation between the various races, peoples and groups in South Africa and towards the achievement of a peaceful and secure future for all inhabitants of the country based on the principles of justice and the dignity of the individual.

The Twenty-sixth Congress of the board in 1970 saw fit to welcome a speech which Prime Minister B. J. Vorster had made before the recent general election, in which he announced that the Nationalist party was open to all white persons (previously Jews had been banned from membership of certain branches of the party). The board countered criticism which had been expressed by the minister of justice, S. L. Muller, of student antigovernment protests in which Jewish students had been prominent; the twin themes of "no collective responsibility" and being opposed to "illegal acts" were again stressed. By this time several international Jewish organizations had been openly calling upon South African Jewry to oppose apartheid and the board deprecated these attempts. The 1965 Resolution quoted above was repeated and the report contained five pages dealing with "The Jew as Citizen."

At the Twenty-seventh Congress in 1972 it was thought necessary to stress once more that the board could have no unified approach or policy toward South African racial policies because "Jews support every party." Great satisfaction was expressed at the launch of the board's Afrikaans journal *Buurman* (Neighbor) which, it was hoped, would enhance the standing of the Jewish community amongst the Afrikaans section of the population, predominantly, of course, the government.

One of the great failures of the Jewish community in general and its communal representatives in particular was that until a very late stage, indeed until it was almost too late, the community concentrated its outreach efforts entirely in the direction of white South Africans. Its contact with the black community was confined almost entirely to the domestic servant relationship, the retail trade, and to certain by no means unimportant social welfare programs in which some communal bodies, particularly those administered by Jewish women, were engaged. This did not go unnoticed amongst the black community. Already in the early years of the South African Republic the Jew would often be the concession store proprietor or general dealer whom the underprivileged black saw as an exploiter. This image was to continue, fairly or unfairly, when the Jew was seen as the secondhand motor dealer who sold dud vehicles or the rapacious secondhand furniture dealer who repossessed the furniture which the customer proved to be incapable of paying for. The fact that there is considerable evidence that these stereotypes were unjust and unfounded is irrelevant to this question of perception, save as it relates to the community's failure to take appropriate steps to project a favorable image amongst blacks as it did amongst whites. It is somewhat surprising therefore to note the surprise, alarm, and consternation which the community experienced when sociological investigation in the 1970s indicated that blacks had a very negative image of the Jew by and large. Negative perception of the Jew in his private life proved to form and influence black public opinion more than the public careers of those Jews who had rightly earned glowing tributes for their important work in the promotion of race relations.[54]

To revert to the 1972 Congress, the resolution which was passed was perhaps the first move toward a less insular approach toward South African affairs. It read as follows:

> Whilst recognising that in regard to the racial and political problems of the Republic there is a diversity of outlook in the Jewish city as there is among our fellow South Africans we share with all those who dwell in our country the great challenge and opportunity involved in establishing on ethical foundations a just stable and peaceful relationship between all races and groups in South Africa, whilst acknowledging the right of all to live in dignity and security, to maintain their group identity and distinctive culture and to exercise the opportunity to advance in all spheres.

The Twenty-eighth Congress of 1974 began to demonstrate a growing concern with the moral issues of South African life. As if to commence the mounting of a defense against its lack of involvement in the struggle, the board in its report dealt at length with the social welfare activities of many Jewish organizations and referred to an interprovincial conference of the regional committees of the board which had dealt specifically with calls on the Jewish community constantly to review its wages and employment policies so as to ensure that Jewish organizations and Jewish individuals were to the fore in improving the conditions of black employees.

The board urged individuals to act in political life to improve the South African situation and urged the Rabbinate in particular to lose no opportunity to proclaim Jewish teaching of these matters. The board illustrated its dilemma in getting involved in issues which, however moral they may have appeared on the surface, could have political implications; and the report quoted as follows from a pamphlet published in 1973 by its secretary general, Gustav Saron: "In the concrete South African situation, it is not possible to make a clear distinction in the field of race relationships between the moral and political aspects, or to decide where morals end and politics begin, since inter-relationships constitute the very core of the politics of the country."[55]

The 1976 Congress showed some considerable progress. For the first time the Congress report (these reports were always lavishly produced and usually entitled "Report to South African Jewry") contained a photograph of a black political leader being entertained by the board at a communal luncheon. Admittedly the dignitary concerned was the Prime Minister of Lebowa, one of the government-created "Bantustans,"[56] so he could hardly be regarded as a leader of the black liberation movement; this shows that the board was prepared to move forward in the field of intergroup relations, but only to the extent that this was already fashionable or respectable. The resolution reflects a small forward movement: "In the belief that the attainment of an equitable society necessitates changes in the existing political, social and economic conditions, Congress urges every member of our community to strive for peaceful change—in particular for the elimination of unjust discrimination—so that all regardless of race, creed or colour be permitted and encouraged to achieve the full potential of their capabilities and live in dignity and harmony." The 1980 Conference Report continued the forward movement. This time the black personality featured was not a government functionary, but a prominent black businessman. The report contained the following significant passage: "With significant and far reaching changes taking place in South Africa, the leadership of the Board of Deputies has begun to direct attention to issues beyond those which are of specific concern to the Jewish community. This is inevitable in view of what is happening both within the Republic and beyond its immediate borders." The Resolution went further than any previous Resolution and read as follows: "Congress urges the Jewish community to co-operate in securing the immediate amelioration and ultimate removal of all unjust discriminatory laws and practices based on race creed or colour. Only in this way can we hope to stem the widening gulf and dangerous polarisation between our different population groups and establish that common bond of trust and loyalty essential for a peaceful united and just society."

By the Thirty-fifth Congress in 1989 we find the board report referring to outright action taken by its Cape Committee who had joined in the public condemnation of the forced removal of squatters and detention without trial of those suspected of antigovernment activities. Under the rubric "Building Bridges" the board reported that its representative had met with the Soweto Council of Ten.[57] The report roundly condemned discriminatory actions and measures entrenched in the legislation and called for the abolition of "racially discriminatory measures and a positive and accelerated movement towards a western style democratic society."

It is hardly necessary to add that the 1995 report joined in the euphoria of national rejoicing and was entitled "The Beat of Africa."

The Board of Deputies was of course not the only Jewish voice speaking, or the only Jewish organization operating, and being seen to operate, during the Apartheid years. Nonetheless as the official voice of the community, its activities, as well as its perceived changes of stance as we have traced them, throw a significant light on what was going on in the community. The only other equivalent group whose public statements serve in part to chart the actions and thought processes of the community was the rabbinate—but that chart reflected an indistinct and inconsistent pattern. The rabbis were not silent—but it is very difficult to trace any common theme from their sermons, addresses and writings.

As in the case of individual Jews to which we have referred, there were two widely disparate poles defining the attitude of the rabbis, and most were to be found somewhere between these extremes. To make confusion worse confounded, the same rabbi would often strike a different chord at different times and in different places. There were those who spoke strongly, some thought intemperately, against the regime, basing their fulminations on what they saw as the true prophetic message as applicable to the South African situation. Some were recent arrivals from overseas, usually America, and were therefore vulnerable to ad hominem criticism—and in at least one case to deportation. There were others who argued—responsibly or pusillanimously, according to one's view of the matter—that their duty was to preach on scriptural matters, and religion in the wider sense, and so avoid placing their congregants at risk of attack by ill-intentioned persons who would seek to make anti-Semitic capital out of antigovernment activity if it was seen to emanate from the synagogue. Again, most were between these polarities, and often used what seemed to them appropriate occasions to point out that the suffering of the Jews at the hands of oppressors throughout their history made them, or should make them, particularly sensitive to the sufferings of others. Scriptural authority and historical precedent could be found for most points of view.[58]

CONCLUSION

Where does South African Jewry stand in relation to any postulated core or periphery in the subcontinent or in World Jewry? Can it be tested against any of the criteria which emerged during the conference at which this book has its origins?

There is no simplistic answer to these questions. South African Jews were never fully integrated into any of the competing elements of what I have called the Boer/Brit/Black axis. At different times they were indeed seen by the members of one or other of these groups as agents for, or unduly inclined toward, one or more of the other groups. It would certainly be difficult to identify any characteristic or condition of South Africa's multinational environment as the primary cause of the economic prosperity and cultural success attained by South African Jewry or of any other aspect of the life and development of the community.

The South African Jewish community never exceeded 120,000, 4.5 percent of the white population and 0.8 percent of the total population.[59] Such paucity of numbers can be a source of vulnerability and of strength. The community retained a remarkable homogeneity, and the rate of assimilation was extremely low. The Jews of South Africa also benefited from the manner in which, at least during the formative years of the community, they were spread throughout the length and breadth of the country. The principal concentration was of course in the main cities—about half in Johannesburg, and about a quarter in the Cape and its environs. But the Jews scattered in the smaller rural areas were an important part of the Jewish community at large. They maintained their identity, and they remained a recognizable and influential presence.

The Jews as a community played no part in any emergent nationalism in South Africa, but they were very much an influential and thrustful part of the English-speaking minority of the white minority. This is neither to criticize nor to apologize for the part which Jews played on the South African frontier. On the one hand Jews participated in abundant measure in the benefits of the Apartheid era; on the other hand, they played a part far beyond their numbers in the struggle which brought about a new South African society. Blacks, Colored, and Indians never focused specifically on the Jews when articulating their grievances and aspirations. Indeed, research thus far conducted by the Kaplan Centre for Jewish Studies at the University of Cape Town has revealed that the African-language press was almost entirely mute on any Jewish issue.

In physical and material terms, South Africa is no longer a frontier society, and South African Jewry is no longer a frontier community. But there are mental, psychological and even spiritual frontiers too. There the encounters continue between Boer, Black and Brit; and the Jew remains a somewhat enigmatic figure in between. These encounters continue—the three main elements are too close to disengage, and the Jew, for better or worse, is right there.

Notes

1. Suggested sources to be consulted on the history of South Africa are: M. Wilson and L. Thompson, eds., *The Oxford History of South Africa,* vols. 1–2 (Oxford: Clarendon Press, 1969 and 1971); C. W. de Kiewiet, *A History of Africa: Social and Economic* (London: Oxford University Press, 1957); L. Marquard, *The Peoples and Policies of South Africa* (Cape Town: Oxford University Press, 1960); L. Thompson and A. Prior, *South African Politics* (Cape Town: David Philip, 1982).

2. For a brief account of the establishment and early years of the Cape Town Hebrew Congregation, see John Simon, "The Cape Town Hebrew Congregation: The Early Years, 1841–1937," in *Cabo* 5.2 (1991). The minutes and early records of the congregation are in the Manuscripts and Archives Department, University of Cape Town.

3. For an account of this cause célèbre which arose as a result of the Colonial Government's attempt to establish a convict settlement at the Cape, see H. C. Botha, *John Fairbairn in South Africa* (Cape Town: Historical Publications Society, 1984).

4. For a full account of this, and the expansion of South Africa's frontiers generally, see Noel Mostert, *Frontiers: The Epic of South Africa's Creation and the Tragedy of the Xhosa People* (London: Jonathan Cape, 1992).

5. See A. Addleson, "In the Eastern Province," in *The Jews in South Africa: A History,* ed. G. Saron and L. Hotz (Cape Town: Oxford University Press, 1955).

6. Mostert, *Frontiers.*

7. Ibid.

8. The best known, and perhaps most typical, was Nathaniel Isaacs, whose adventurous story is told in L. Herrman, ed., *Travels and Adventures in Eastern Africa by Nathaniel Isaacs,* 2 vols. (Cape Town: Van Riebeeck Society, 1936–37).

9. For an overview of the principal published material available on South African Jewry, see John Simon, "Towards an Appraisal of South African Jewish Historiography," in *Festschrift in Honour of Frank R. Bradlow,* ed. P. E. Westra and B. Warner (Cape Town: Friends of the South African Library, 1993).

10. M. C. N. Salbstein, *The Emancipation of the Jews in Britain: The Question of Admission of the Jews to Parliament, 1828–1860* (London: Associated University Presses, 1982); Todd M. Endelman, "English Jewish History," *Modern Judaism* 11.1 (Feb. 1991); V. D. Lipman, *A History of the Jews in Britain since 1858* (Leicester: Leicester University Press, 1990).

11. David Sorkin, *The Transformation of German Jewry, 1780–1840* (New York: Oxford University Press, 1987).

12. For an account of Jewish religious practice in England in the nineteenth cen-

tury, see Stephen Sharot, "Religious Change in Native Orthodoxy in London, 1870–1914: The Synagogue Service," *Jewish Journal of Sociology* 15.1 (June 1973); and Steven Singer, "Orthodox Judaism in Early Victorian London 1840–1858" (Ph.D. diss., Yeshiva University, 1981). See also Todd M. Endelman, "Communal Solidarity among the Jewish Elite of Victorian London," *Victorian Studies* 29.3 (Spring 1985).

13. T. R. H. Davenport, "The Consolidation of a New Society," in *Oxford History of South Africa,* ed. Wilson and Thompson, vol. 1.

14. S. M. Dubnow, *History of the Jews in Russia and Poland from the Earliest Times to the Present Day,* trans. I. Friedlaender (Philadelphia: Jewish Publication Society, 1918).

15. C. Goldscheider and A. S. Zuckerman, *The Transformation of the Jews* (Chicago: University of Chicago Press, 1984).

16. Samuel Joseph, *Jewish Immigration to the United States from 1881 to 1910.* Columbia University Studies in the Social Sciences No. 145. (New York, 1914).

17. H. Sonnabend, "S.A. Jewry in Figures: Interesting Facts about Our Community," *Jewish Affairs* 1.6 (Dec. 1941); "The Social Role of the Jew in South Africa," *Jewish Affairs* 3.1 (Jan. 1948).

18. "Register of Jewish Residents Seeking Naturalization in the Cape Colony 1904–1906," Alexander Papers, University of Cape Town. This instructive body of material is analyzed in Louis Hotz, "Jews Who Arrived Here Sixty Years Ago," *Jewish Affairs* 18.2 (Feb. 1963).

19. Many articles and letters appeared in the Yiddish and Hebrew press in Eastern Europe, particularly *Ha-melitz, Ha-maggid,* and *Ha-tzfirah,* in which recent immigrants to South Africa reported on their experiences and impressions in their new homes. They are extensively quoted in M. P. Grossman, "A Study of the Trends and Tendencies of Hebrew and Yiddish Writings in South Africa since their Beginnings in the Early Nineties of the Last Century to 1930" (Ph.D. diss., University of the Witwatersrand, 1973). Two particularly vivid accounts by M. D. Hersch and N. D. Hoffmann, respectively, are quoted by G. Shimoni, *Jews and Zionism: The South African Experience, 1910–1967* (Cape Town: Oxford University Press, 1980).

20. M. Greenbaum, *The Jews of Lithuania* (Jerusalem: Gefen Publishing House, 1995).

21. Quoted in the *London Jewish Chronicle,* July 31, 1896.

22. Mostert, *Frontiers,* 163.

23. For details of this source, and a guide to the references used, see John Simon, "New Archival Material Relating to the Early Development of South Africa's Jewish Community," in *Waters Out of the Well,* ed. R. Musiker and J. Sherman (Johannesburg: Library of the University of the Witwatersrand, 1988).

24. In this regard see Shimoni, *Jews and Zionism.*

25. For the early development of the Zionist movement in South Africa, see Marcia Gitlin, *The Vision Amazing: The Story of South African Zionism* (Johannesburg: Menorah Book Club, 1950).

26. This homely expression is applied to the religious officiants, usually appointed to the smaller communities, who combined the functions of minister, cantor, teacher, shochet, and (usually) mohel, and generally ministered to all the religious needs of the community. From the Hebrew *"Kol bo"* (all-embracing).

27. A collection of such *Responsa* taken from the *Responsa* computer project of Bar-Ilan University is described, summarized, and analyzed in John Simon, "Responsa and

Rulings Reflecting Some South African Issues," *Jewish Journal of Sociology* 36.1 (June 1994).

28. *Ahiezer,* vol. 3 (Vilna, 1939), chap. 25.

29. *Tzitz Eliezer,* 2d ed., vol. 1 (Jerusalem: privately published, 1985), chap. 5.

30. M. C. Mirvish, *D'roshei ve-Shut ha-Ramach* (Cape Town: privately published, 1935).

31. Ibid.

32. The Anglo-Jewish world generally was experiencing at this time pressures and counterpressures regarding changes in the synagogue service. For an overall examination, although focused mainly in London, see Sharot, "Religious Change in Native Orthodoxy in London, 1870–1914." For an examination and comment on the South African situation, see a series of articles by "Morenu Rav" in the *South African Jewish Chronicle,* June–July 1907. For arguments for and against the "reform" of services in South Africa, which are typical of the debate, see articles and correspondence in ibid., Nov. 22, Nov. 29, Dec. 6, 1929.

33. *South African Jewish Chronicle,* Jan. 16, 1903.

34. M. H. K. Lichtenstein, *Travels in South Africa in the Years 1803, 1804, 1805, 1806.* 2 vols. (1812, 1815; rpt., Cape Town: Van Riebeeck Society, 1928), 1:443.

35. R. Mendelsohn, *Sammy Marks: "The Uncrowned King of the Transvaal"* (Cape Town: David Philip, 1991).

36. Jewish traders who traveled on foot or horseback or by horse-drawn cart to remote parts of South Africa played an important—some say a vital—part in expanding the frontier. They were often called *smouse* (singular *smous*). For some information about these interesting characters, see John Simon, s.v. "Tokhers, Shmoyzers or Travelling Pedlars," in L. Feldman, *Oudtshoorn, Jerusalem of Africa,* ed. J Sherman, trans. L Dubb and S Barkusky (Johannesburg: Friends of the Library, University of the Witwatersrand, 1989). See also Milton Shain, "'Vant to puy a Vaatch?': The Smous and Pioneer Trader in South African Jewish Historiography," *Jewish Affairs* 44.5 (Sept. 1989).

37. *London Jewish Chronicle* (n.d.) quoted by Eric Rosenthal, "On the Diamond Fields," in *The Jews in South Africa,* ed. Saron and Hortz.

38. M. Shain, *Jewry and Cape Society* (Cape Town: Historical Publication Society, 1983), 3.

39. G. Saron, "The Jews in Kruger's Republic," *Jewish Affairs* 26.5 (May 1971). For demographic information regarding South African Jewry in general, see A. A. Dubb, *The Jewish Population of South Africa: The 1991 Sociodemographic Survey* (Cape Town: Jewish Publications South Africa, 1994).

40. See, for example, and particularly for the early years of the Johannesburg Jewish community, M. Kaplan and M. Robertson, eds. *Founders and Followers: Johannesburg Jewry, 1887–1915* (Cape Town: Vlaeberg Publications, 1991).

41. See John Simon, "Pulpit and Platform: Hertz and Landau," in *Founders and Followers,* ed. Kaplan and Robertson.

42. Mendelsohn, *Sammy Marks.*

43. For the story of Free State Jewry, see M. Pencharz and D. L. Sowden, "In the Orange Free State," in *The Jews in South Africa,* ed. Saron and Hotz; and S. M. Aronstam, "A Historical and Socio-Cultural Survey of the Bloemfontein Jewish Community with

Special Reference to the Conception of Jewish Welfare Work" (Ph.D. diss., University of the Orange Free State, 1974).

44. He wrote again on Feb. 22, 1892, expressing his regrets that the campaign for Russian Jewry had not gone well in the Free State. These letters and much other valuable material concerning Reverend Joel Rabinowitz, who lived a full and fascinating "frontier" life, are in an album of letters and press cuttings kept in the Manuscripts and Archives Department at the University of Cape Town, ref. BCS 428.

45. In 1965 the Country Communities Department of the Board of Deputies reported that there were 8,500 Jews living in 220 rural localities.

46. M. Shain, *The Roots of Antisemitism in South Africa* (Charlottesville: University Press of Virginia, 1994), 116.

47. Ibid., 118ff.

48. For some account of the Greyshirt movement and anti-Semitism in South Africa generally, see ibid.

49. For a recently published account of the participation of Jews in the Freedom Struggle, see I. Suttner, ed., *Cutting through the Mountain* (New York: Viking Press, 1997).

50. "Prog" is a reference to the Progressive party, later called the Progressive Federal party, now the Democratic party. "UP" is the United party, the party of J. C. Smuts, long the official opposition until many of its members, dissatisfied with its insufficiently vigorous opposition to the government, broke away to form the Progressive party.

51. The South African Jewish Board of Deputies, modeled on the British Board of Deputies, was formed in 1912 as a result of the amalgamation of the Transvaal Board (founded in 1903) and the Cape Board (founded in 1904).

52. All the board's reports and statements quoted or referred to in this chapter can be found in the archives of the board in Johannesburg and Cape Town or in the Jacob Gitlin Library, Cape Town.

53. This entitled the government, through the security forces, to hold a suspect for questioning for 90 days without charging him and without his being allowed legal representation. It was later extended to 180 days.

54. In the early 1970s a Jewish sociologist, Melville L. Edelstein, conducted a survey which demonstrated that the "social distance" exhibited by black students toward Jews was exceeded only by that exhibited toward Afrikaners. See M. L. Edelstein, *What Do Young Africans Think?* (Johannesburg: Institute of Race Relations, 1972); M. L. Edelstein, "The Urban African Image of the Jew," *Jewish Affairs* 27.2 (Feb. 1972).

55. G. Saron, *The South African Jewish Board of Deputies: Its Role and Development* (Johannesburg: The Board, 1973), 22.

56. This was the term applied by antigovernment elements to the so-called self-governing black homelands, the creation of which was a cornerstone of the policy of Dr. H. F. Verwoerd, first as minister of native affairs and later as prime minister, who has been termed "the architect of 'grand' apartheid." Ethnic grouping was said to be the first step to constitutional development for blacks, who were—so the policy was explained—to have political rights in their own homelands. The policy was entirely discredited and abandoned even before the 1994 elections.

57. An unofficial body of representatives of the black community of Soweto, a huge black town adjoining Johannesburg.

58. For some examples of the attitudes expressed by the rabbis, see S. Kessler, "The South African Rabbinate in the Apartheid Era," *Jewish Affairs* 50.1 (Autumn 1995).

59. The percentages are approximate and apply to 1936. According to the inflated 1991 census, Jews constituted 0.3 percent of all South Africans and 1.8 percent of whites; if the multisource estimate is used, the proportions are 0.3 percent and 2.1 percent. In 1980, the proportions were 0.5 percent and 2.6 percent, respectively. The downward trend continues. The statistics are taken from Dubb, *Jewish Population of South Africa*.

3 Living within the Frontier: Early Colonial Australia, Jews, and Aborigines

PAUL R. BARTROP

The first permanent European settlement on the continent of Australia was established when the eleven ships of what became known as the First Fleet set down their cargo of English and Irish convicts at Sydney Cove, New South Wales, on 26 January 1788. Among these convicts were at least eight (and possibly up to fourteen) Jews, whose presence at the very foundation of European colonization signaled what was later described as the "normalcy" of the Australian Jewish situation. Because Jews were in Australia from the beginning of the British presence, it has been argued that they have "never been considered to be aliens to quite the same extent as elsewhere."[1] The position of Jews in Australia throughout the nineteenth century was on the whole different from that of foreigners in that Jews, though not Christian, were nonetheless British by nationality and thus as much subjects of the Crown as any other British citizen. They shared all the same civil and legal rights as other Britons, and justice was truly blind in dispensing impartial judgments regardless of religion.

Judaism did not, however, enjoy equal religious rights with Christianity, and this was to form the main focus of Jewish grievance in the Australian colonies throughout the first half of the nineteenth century. For the overwhelming majority of Jews during this time, the quest for recognition of equality of religion was the key feature of what might be termed "frontier life"; though rarely roughing it "on the frontier," nonetheless colonial Jewry found itself in a struggle on the frontiers of legal emancipation. They already enjoyed social equality, but the question of religious equality was a major drawback—if not *the* major drawback—to full political equality, and until this was achieved Jews in colonial Australia could never feel totally and unconditionally accepted as full citizens.

The Jewish position in Australian society was inextricably bound up with the common settlement experience shared by all. Convict settlement in New South Wales, Van Diemen's Land, Queensland, and Western Australia was directly responsible for a Jewish presence in those colonies, as there were Jews among the convict populations in each outpost. The planned free colony of South Australia had a Jew, Jacob Montefiore, as one of its original commissioners. Port Phillip—the future colony of Victoria—saw an early ingress of young middle-class Jews into what was essentially a free colony in the process of being settled by emancipated ex-convicts and would-be landowners keen to settle the rich lands of what an early explorer, Major Sir Thomas Mitchell, dubbed "Australia Felix." Everywhere Jews went, the nature of their settlement characterized the prevailing ethos of the specific colony in question; the "normalcy" of their position was reinforced by the manner of their arrival and subsequent settlement.

If there was little unusual in Jewish settlement relative to the British experience in the early Australian colonies, it must be stressed that all such settlement took place at the expense of the continent's indigenous population. The Aborigines had no say in who came into Australia, where they came from, or in what numbers they arrived. In a different application of the term "frontier," it was the Aboriginal presence which from the outset formed the boundary line between those parts of the continent which were colonized by the British, and those which were yet to be—even though, according to the doctrine of *terra nullius,* British claims embraced the whole continent and it was expected that one day the entire land would be colonized. The indigenous population, in this process, would gradually be pushed to one side, such that the outer limits of British settlement would always mark the boundary between colonial and Aboriginal habitation. The history of the nineteenth century was to show that for the Aborigines this line would continually shrink, as British settlement expanded and Aborigines were forced further and further back into the interior of the continent.

This is the frontier notion most clearly described by James O. Gump, in his paraphrase of previous work by Howard Lamar and Leonard Thompson.[2] According to this, the frontier is "a zone of interaction between two or more previously distinct peoples, and the process by which relations among peoples begin, develop and crystallize. The frontier 'opens' when these peoples initially make contact, and 'closes' when one of the peoples gains ascendancy over the other."[3]

Such "ascendancy," in the Australian colonies, was represented by the unleashing of forces against the Aborigines which were, if not genocidal in intent, at the very least genocidal in effect, and differed enormously from the frontier experience of Jews at the same time in the same colonies.

In contemporary Australian historiography there is now a need to reconsider the frameworks within which the dispossession and destruction of the Aboriginal peoples took place throughout the nineteenth century, though space unfortunately does not allow for an elaboration of this in the current essay. We need to know *why* Aborigines were dehumanized and degraded, as well as *how* this took place during the period of Australia's early European settlement; just as important, we need to know the psychological basis which allowed the settlers to perpetrate and/or endorse mass murder as a means to "solve" the Aboriginal "problem." Generally speaking, the colonial experience was characterized not only by mass destruction on a genocidal scale, but also by land dispossession, population dislocation and transfer, forced assimilation, and language displacement. Later, those who survived this physical destruction were confronted by the specter of cultural and social destruction, which for most proved to be, at least in part, irresistible.

The notion of the frontier in colonial Australia is thus not as straightforward as it might initially appear, for when applied to the cases of Jews and Aborigines we are in fact looking at two quite different applications of the term. Moreover, when looking at the frontier experience in other geographical locations we are more likely to be exposed to the "invader-indigenous" relationship than the kind faced by Jews as "outsider-insiders" in colonial Australia. We therefore need to consider carefully the nature of the frontier in its Australian context, as this can help us to better appreciate why it was that Jews and Aborigines evoked different responses from broader British colonial society, and how each responded accordingly.

It has been calculated that most of Australia's Jews up to the 1890s were either English-speaking migrants from Britain or their Australian-born descendants.[4] This must certainly have added to the normalcy of their situation, for, apart from religion, they passed in colonial society indistinguishable from the general population. Throughout much of the later nineteenth century, such happy integration worked remarkably well. Jews were able to play a full and important role in Australian development in the areas of economics, politics, and the arts, quite unimpeded by discriminatory legislation or social restrictions. The battles for political emancipation—battles which, as we shall see, characterized the Jewish "frontier" experience—had been fought earlier in the century. Israel Getzler, the historian who has considered this issue, has prefaced his account in the following way: "Jews were not persecuted in the early Australian colonies. They had civil and political rights and religious freedom, but they did not have full religious equality and they worked continuously until they got it."[5] The issue of religious equality was, in Getzler's words, the "sole grievance" of Jews in colonial Australia; it was to be achieved throughout the southeast of the continent by the end of the 1850s.

In this environment, Jews confidently set up their own charity organizations, while at the same time providing gratuitously for public welfare groups such as existed in the wider community. They found no conflict in patriotically supporting the Empire of which Australia formed a part, and later many would loyally do their duty in undergoing military training for the Empire's defense. In every major sphere of enterprise and activity, Australian Jews played their part with the same vigor as Australian non-Jews, such that up to the end of the nineteenth century Jews were (and were seen as) a thoroughly integrated and committed element within Australian society.

This analysis is somewhat at variance with the position of Jon Stratton, elaborated elsewhere in this volume.[6] His argument that Jews were racialized and cast into the role of "other," moreover, makes sense only if we note that such feeling came to light in colonial Australia from the 1880s onward, *after* the specter of large numbers of foreign (that is, non-British) Jews appeared destined to be heading for Australia's shores in the aftermath of the Russian pogroms. It might even be suggested that it was in the first instance their "foreignness" that rendered them undesirable, with their Jewishness a hastily-added secondary justification for keeping them out (and for racializing them). This is an area that has not yet received the fullest attention of Australian scholars,[7] which is a pity in view of the fact that it might well give a better understanding of why Australians—both governments and the public—adopted precisely this stance fifty years later during the Nazi era.[8] Exploring the racialization of Jews during the late nineteenth century, furthermore, might well provide us with important appreciations of just how far Jews had come since the 1850s, at a time when the position outlined by Stratton certainly did not prevail.

Indeed, the situation prior to the 1880s had not been quite so clear-cut as Stratton might contend. True, the Jewish convicts were no better treated than any other convicted felon, and in the class-dominated society of late eighteenth- and early nineteenth-century Britain had few civil rights other than those reserved for criminals and pariahs. But even they were not discriminated against on the basis of their religion. W. D. Rubinstein, in a neat summary of the Jewish experience during the convict period, has noted that the Jewish convicts were transported for having committed crimes which, "though common enough in the London slums of the day would probably strike nearly everyone today as incredibly trivial. Daniel Daniels, for example, was sentenced to seven years' transportation for stealing a copper pot, a pewter porringer, and a pair of shoes. Joseph Levy was transported for life for stealing a watch."[9] They would have been set to work on tasks common to all convicts, such as laboring, timber-felling, building, and agricultural and domestic work. Most would have been "assigned out" to free settlers, as a cheap labor force.

The convict era lasted from 1788 until its cessation in 1852, its overall contribution to the colonial population numbering an estimated 145,000. Of these, at least one thousand were Jews, a percentage of about 0.66 of the total number of transported convicts.[10] (The proportion of Jewish population relative to non-Jews in Australia has more or less remained constant ever since, at around one half of 1 percent.) The average age of the Jewish convicts, male and female, was in the mid-twenties, with over 90 percent being men.[11] Until the arrival of Jewish free settlers in sufficient numbers to form congregations and the other trappings of communal life, there was little opportunity for the early Jewish presence to develop beyond a collection of individuals who knew they were Jewish and were acknowledged as such by their peers.[12]

Following the commencement of Jewish free settlement in the mid-1820s, Jews did not have an acknowledged religious equality, even though life was in all other respects conducive to a relative contentment. Although at first small, the various Jewish communities found life in the Australian colonies congenial enough to establish solid congregations, the first established in Sydney in 1832. This was followed by Melbourne in 1841, and the other major cities over the next sixty years: Hobart, 1845; Launceston, 1846; Adelaide, 1848; Brisbane, 1865; Fremantle, 1887; Perth, 1892; and Newcastle, 1901. Other synagogues were also established in the city suburbs and regional centers (for example, Geelong, Ballarat, Bendigo, Broken Hill, Bathurst and Kalgoorlie).

Daily life for the Jewish colonists was on the whole different from that seen in many other lands of recent settlement at this time. There was not much in the way of itinerant peddling or hawking—of which more below—and the often crushing inner-urban poverty so characteristic of Jewish immigrants in North America, particularly later in the century, at no time prevailed in the Australian colonies. The social and cultural milieu from which the Jewish immigrants came in no way proved to be so alien to the wider Australian population as to foster animosity. Hilary L. Rubinstein has noted that acceptance by the general community "came easily . . . [for] the basically middle class Jews of colonial Australia," as their British character rendered them little different "from the majority of their fellow-colonists":

> They were clearly distinguishable only by religion, and it is significant that from an early period they described Judaism as a "denomination" which emphasised their resemblance to other citizens and demonstrated their assumption that Judaism was equal with Christianity and would be treated as such. . . . [Jews] were determined to play a full part in the life of the general community while retaining their identities as Jews. Indeed, they believed that they could best ensure the respect of non-Jews by being seen to respect their religion and themselves. . . . In short, they would integrate but they would not assimilate.[13]

By retaining their sense of identity as Jews, and campaigning for equality in all fields, they were thus able to ensure that their presence was more than merely accepted under sufferance; by the end of the 1850s, and for much of the rest of the century, Jews were an established part of colonial society, neither subjected to discrimination nor targeted as other than legitimate Britons with a right to live in the country.

As stated earlier, this was to change later in the face of racializing processes which were applied to *foreign* Jews. Interestingly—and this was the case throughout the twentieth century, as well—those identified as *British* Jews were not racialized for the purpose of vilification or exclusion (which would have been illegal in any case, in view of their British nationality). Jews in the early colonial period up to the middle of the nineteenth century, on the other hand, were not isolated as an "other" group standing outside the mainstream of society; their "normalcy," previously discussed in this essay, overrode any notions people may have had about their legitimacy as a constituent part of colonial society.

A sense of otherness was, it would seem, almost exclusively reserved for people of a different skin color to that of the colonists. Chinese were definitely "other"; so too were Afghans, Indians and Pacific Islanders. But without doubt the most vilified, isolated, and debased "others" were the Aborigines, who presented particular problems for the settlers in view of the fact that they had not arrived as immigrants and could therefore not be kept out or repatriated back to their country of origin. In a very real sense it is possible to argue that the dispossession of Australia's Aborigines was accompanied by processes which were, if not genocidal in intent, at the very least genocidal in scope and effect.

As one example of the kind of issue being discussed here, we can consider the opinion of Bishop Broughton, appearing before the House of Commons Select Committee on Aborigines in 1835. Under examination, Broughton was asked whether it could be said that the Aborigines "have gradually retired before the progress of our [i.e., British] civilization."[14] His response was instructive: "They do not so much retire as decay; wherever Europeans meet with them they appear to wear out, and gradually to decay: they diminish in numbers; they appear actually to vanish from the face of the earth. I am led to apprehend that within a very limited period, a few years, . . . those who are most in contact with Europeans will be utterly extinct—I will not say exterminated—but they will be extinct."[15]

Asked to elaborate on whether this situation came about as a result of Europeans "interfering with their usual habits, and depriving them of their means of hunting," or whether on account of "direct ill treatment," Broughton replied that it was

> Less by ill treatment than by depriving them of the means of subsistence; because, wherever the country is cultivated, the kangaroo disappears; and another very serious cause is the introduction of intoxicating liquors, which destroy very great numbers of them. . . . Without any absolute ill usage of them, [European contact] certainly does appear to affect them injuriously; without outrage practised against them. I do not attribute it to actual destruction of them by force, but there is something in our manner and state of society which they appear to decay before.[16]

What the Bishop did not say was that in "depriving the Aborigines of the means of their subsistence" the settlers frequently employed violent—and often murderous—means, to the extent that, as calculated by Henry Reynolds, "it is reasonable to suppose that at least 20,000 Aborigines were killed as a direct result of conflict with settlers,"[17] though this figure is, as Reynolds's subsequent research shows, "little better than an informed guess" which probably only serves to preface a death toll which "may have been much higher."[18]

Death owing to frontier violence has a certain air of deliberation and intent accompanying it, but was it genocide? This is a key issue, probably one of the most important historical difficulties yet to be resolved in Australian scholarship. The dean of Australian historians on nineteenth-century Aboriginal-European relations, Henry Reynolds, is unequivocal in stating his position: "Was it a case of genocide? In a literal sense clearly no. The Aborigines survived the invasion."[19] This conclusion is, it must be stated, based on a false definition of genocide, for if an event becomes a genocide only if all the people do not survive, then by virtue of the fact that there are always some who survive any genocide, there have never been any acts which thus qualify. It is not, moreover, just a false definition: it is also flawed logic to assume that an act such as genocide cannot have gradations. Genocide is not clear-cut; for an act to be genocidal does not rest upon the assumption of total annihilation. A closer reading of both the theory and practice of genocidal experiences would have shown Reynolds this.

At least, however, Reynolds has tried. Few other Australian scholars have attempted to apply genocide theory to a discussion of frontier life in the nineteenth century. As one example, the final chapter of Michael Cannon's *Who Killed the Koories?*—a chapter entitled "Genocide, with the Best of Intentions"—sees the term employed as a throwaway line, without any pursuit of the deeper theoretical dimensions implicit in the concept.[20] Explanations of Australian Aboriginal destruction have traditionally not allowed for genocide, and this position, in spite of recent scholarship to the contrary, is still accepted as authoritative. The preference by Australian scholars for such words as "massacre," "murder," and "dispossession" has in the past demonstrated a reluctance (and for some, an outright refusal) to address the Aboriginal-European relationship using conceptual tools designed expressly for the purpose of giving meaning to that experience. To date the best discussion is by Melbourne scholar Tony Barta, in an essay from 1985.[21] "Why," asks Barta,

> has the term been skirted so warily by historians of Australia? There is no dispute that the basic fact of Australian history is the appropriation of the continent by an invading people and the dispossession, with ruthless destructiveness, of another. There can be no doubt about the disintegration of Aboriginal society, traditional culture and religion, the destruction of the Aborigines' economic existence, their languages, their personal security, liberty, health, and dignity. About the loss of lives we have the most appalling evidence. . . . Throughout southern and eastern Australia the processes of colonization and economic expansion involved the virtual wiping out of the Aboriginal population. If ever a people has had to sustain an assault on its existence of . . . [a genocidal] kind . . . it would seem to have been over the last two hundred years in Australia.[22]

Barta's position is clear: "Most Australians have never seriously been confronted by the idea that the society in which they live is founded on genocide."[23] To illustrate his point, Barta needs to provide just a few examples:

> Thousands of Aborigines died violently at the hands of white settlers, whole peoples were wiped out by disease, degradation, alcohol and despair. But who planned it? Who carried it through? It seemed simply to happen. By 1850 the original inhabitants of Sydney and Newcastle were all gone. By 1886, after only fifty years of settlement in Victoria, a population of more than 10,000 Aborigi-

> nes was reduced to 806. Round Adelaide, the decline was from 650 to 180 in fifteen years.
>
> Perhaps a fifth of those killed died "by the rifle" as the settlers advanced; however, the greatest killer was undoubtedly small-pox.[24]

A figure of one-fifth killed by gunfire would probably by itself be sufficient evidence that some serious murdering had taken place, but what do we make of mass death brought about through other causes?

The position of Henry Reynolds, building on his estimate of 20,000 violent frontier deaths, is that what he refers to as "secondary effects" of the British invasion, such as "disease, deprivation [and] disruption," were responsible "for the premature deaths of many more," although "it is almost impossible to arrive at a realistic figure."[25] A scholar who has made a major investigation of this issue, Noel Butlin, has concluded that not only was the introduction of smallpox the single most effective killer of them all, but that such introduction was deliberate, and planned for the purpose of extermination.[26] This is a clear, and very controversial, position. Many disagree with Butlin's argument concerning the intent of the settlers to deliberately introduce diseases such as smallpox, but such criticisms, if accepted, would work to exonerate those who distributed diseased blankets and clothing, who failed to offer medical assistance, who circulated among Aboriginal communities while already diseased, and who brought these same communities into a condition of debility though venereal disease and the onset of malnutrition.

Admittedly, there are certainly occasions on which I sometimes have difficulty describing *all* cases of Aboriginal population destruction in the nineteenth century as genocide (as some contemporary Aboriginal activists and political spokespersons are wont to do). The onset of disease does not always imply a deliberate policy of killing instituted by the colonial authorities. It is important that all instances of population destruction be considered on a case-by-case basis, and that generalizations to the entire continent not be made in order to "prove" the existence of a "policy" of European genocide against Aborigines. This is why I am so much more comfortable with the notion of "genocidal destruction," or "destruction on a genocidal scale." The ultimate effect remains the same, and this should not be lost sight of; the people die, or are killed, and at the end of the process their numbers are substantially (sometimes staggeringly) reduced. But to label an act as being an "act of genocide" says a great deal about ascribing responsibility for the deaths of those in question. Sometimes, such responsibility is misplaced, unfairly cast, or simply nonexistent. Hence we need to be extremely careful when applying this term to Aboriginal population losses in the nineteenth century; there will be occasions when "genocide" is an inappropriate descriptor, and "genocidal destruction" fits better. Either way, it must be reiterated that such decisions can only be made by looking at every situation individually—unless evidence of a full-scale Colonial Office preference for wholesale and total destruction can be found, which would change the focus of our investigations radically. (I would suggest, however, that the finding of such a directive will never occur, as the mindset needed to develop it had not yet been formulated).

Developments of a thoroughly destructive kind, however, did characterize life on the frontier throughout the nineteenth century. While different expressions of racial violence took place in different colonies at different times, nonetheless the Aborigines' status of "other" relative to the British always worked to their ultimate disadvantage. One scholar, John H. Bodley, has attempted to understand why indigenous peoples around the world proved unable to withstand European invasion during the nineteenth century, and his work explains clearly the process whereby Europeans were able to overcome local inhabitants. In a study from 1982 Bodley examined the nature of life and death on the frontier; the punitive raid; full-scale wars of extermination; the unequal contest between guns and spears; the impact of the extension of government control over native peoples; the issue of land dispossession; the quest for "progress"; and the imperative of Western-style economic development.[27] These features, it could be argued, are applicable to all genocides of indigenous peoples, of which the case of Australia's Aborigines is a leading example.

The idea of genocide as the major expression of life on colonial Australia's Aboriginal frontier is, as previously suggested, far from universally accepted among Australian scholars. The views of Henry Reynolds have already been outlined, and although he has problems with the notion of genocide he nonetheless does recognize that massive depopulation took place as a direct result of both frontier violence and the dispossession process. Lest it appear as though the story is one of uninterrupted sorrow, however, it must be pointed out that mutually beneficial relationships were also established and did take place. In *With the White People,*[28] Reynolds's attempt to complement his earlier work on frontier violence by showing the ways in which Europeans and Aborigines could actually get along and work together, we are taken on an altogether different journey. Here, we see the innumerable ways in which Aborigines were welcomed into colonial society—as guides, interpreters, laborers, trackers, troopers, stockworkers, mineworkers, servants, domestic helpers, and pearl-divers. Reynolds is keen to point out that, just as scores of thousands of Aborigines died throughout the nineteenth century as a result of European efforts, so also were Aborigines paradoxically deeply involved in the pioneering activities of those same frontier settlers: "From the earliest years of settlement blacks were on both sides of the frontier, the same skills, the same bushcraft, being used alike to enhance and resist the progress of the pioneer. And while we have to accept the brutality of the white frontiersman we cannot avoid making the same judgement about Aboriginal stockmen, troopers and trackers who were so often by their side. They too were engaged in the destruction of tribes which impeded the pioneer's path. They too had blood on their hands."[29]

Such collaboration was not an occasional feature of frontier life; it was everywhere. Reynolds has calculated that "as many as one in four of all Aborigines killed in frontier skirmishing fell victim to the guns shouldered by other Aborigines"[30]—guns shouldered, it should be added, on behalf of either European bosses or colonial police forces. In southeastern Australia and the area of Western Australia south of Perth, "Aborigines assisted the pioneers," while in the north and the center "they were the pioneers."[31] The majority of Aborigines left alive after the killing had stopped "sought security in a difficult and threatening world and in doing so made many adaptations to, and compromises with, European society."[32] Building on themes such as these, it is important to realize that nineteenth-century Australia was not a discrete society with a single Aboriginal policy based on a single non-Aboriginal set of values or assumptions, from which could come a single Aboriginal response. Reynolds does highlight one issue, however, which was just as important (in theory if not in scope) for the general Aboriginal situation as it was for the Jewish one. Referring to those Aborigines who interrelated "with the white people," he has noted that "these were the people who wanted to be accepted as equals by Europeans but who were perpetually beaten back by the racism of colonial society and the impenetrable caste barrier erected in its name. For the most part they didn't want to deny their kin and the Aboriginal heritage or to forget where they had come from. They wanted to be accepted as they were and in so doing they looked forward to, and indeed were the frustrated pioneers of, what in recent times has become known as the multicultural society."[33]

Jews in colonial Australia could be described in similar terms, an observation which raises fascinating questions concerning perceptions of inequality, acceptance, identity, and hegemony among (and between) oppressed peoples and those responsible for their distress.

For Jews, of course, the distress experienced in colonial society could in no way compare to the situation of the Aborigines. There was nothing even remotely approaching the persecution or vilification suffered by the indigenous population; the nearest Jews came to this was the occasional anti-Semitic article or cartoon in the press, and even this was in the main later in the century, after Jewish immigrants, albeit in very small numbers, began arriving from eastern Europe.[34]

In view of this, therefore, what was the "frontier" through which Jews were attempting to break in the middle period of the nineteenth century? It must be remembered that the range of occupations in which the majority of Jews were engaged up to the 1850s—"clothiers, drapers, general storekeepers and tavern keepers"[35]—did not allow for much in the way of political influence on the one hand, nor for the stimulation of anti-Semitic hostility from the non-Jewish population on the other. To put it bluntly, most Jews simply got on with the business of living—and that they were left free of the added burdens of racial harassment stands in marked contrast to what their fellow-Jews were experiencing in many other countries at this time (as several of the essays in the current collection testify). This is not to say that they were at all times free from molestation; from time to time there were unenlightened expressions of anti-Jewish sentiment based on traditional images of the Jew as moneylender, capitalist, non-Christian (or anti-Christian) alien, and the like. But these expressions were for the most part exceptional up to 1850, and cannot be regarded as typical attitudes coming from non-Jewish society.

It must not be felt that Jews were exclusively urban-dwellers facing the same problems common to all Jews in similar environments. Rural districts and small towns—areas which could certainly be described as belonging to the colonial frontier—saw comings and goings of Jews during the nineteenth century. Indeed, the early issues of the *Australian Jewish Historical Society Journal,* a publication which this author has in the past criticized for its overemphasis on colonial and anecdotal matters,[36] provide a wealth of material concerning not only Jews during the colonial period generally, but Jews "on the frontier" more specifically.[37] The stories recounted invariably follow a similar path: the arrival of enterprising Jews in a growth area requiring services which they could provide; the establishment over time of a small congregation, and perhaps acquisition of a building to serve as the focus of communal activity; and the gradual decline of the same community as the reason for the original growth disappeared and larger congregations in the major cities were able to offer greater chances of religious and social continuity.

Hilary L. Rubinstein has shown that most Jews in nineteenth-century Australia "were involved in some kind of merchandising,"[38] and it is interesting to note that most of this activity began in the larger cities, which acted as a base from which enterprise could move into the country areas. So far as colonial development was concerned, such endeavor was both necessary and appreciated (to say nothing of lucrative), as Rubinstein demonstrates:

> The 1830s witnessed a push into the bush by Jewish traders, who sensed the opportunities which existed there for storekeepers, hotel (or tavern) keepers and hawkers (or pedlars) supplying their respective wares to remote settlements. Old rural commercial directories show that Jewish storekeepers and hotel keepers were to be found in many of the little outback towns and wayside stations and, during the 1850s, on the goldfields of New South Wales and Victoria. They were filling the traditional Jewish role as middlemen which their people had practised for centuries in Europe and which they maintained in other frontier societies besides Australia—the United States and South Africa are two obvious examples. . . . Little wonder, then, that many of the Jews who occupied this indispensable position became well-respected figures in their localities and that so many of them became mayors and other civic leaders in colonial Australia. Here, as in other frontier societies during the nineteenth century, Jews were accepted on equal terms with others seeking to tame the environment.[39]

This final point is a telling one, and gets us back to the central issue dominating Jewish-Gentile relations in the first half of the nineteenth century, that of religious equality and acceptance.

Hilary Rubinstein has accurately written that "no legal enactment safeguarded the equality of Australian Jews," who "owed their favourable position to the tolerance and fair-mindedness of their fellow citizens and the liberalism of the civil authorities."[40] Despite the preferences of some in the colonies—and it is worth bearing in mind that prior to Federation in 1901 there was no singular Australian polity, but rather six distinct colonies each with their own legislature—there was neither an official state religion nor a requirement that only Christians could be elected to public office. This did not mean that Jews could afford to be complacent; on the contrary, the Jewish conception was that this did not go far enough. When the issue of state aid to organized religion surfaced in the various colonies in the 1840s and 1850s, Jewish communities fought to have such aid extended to include them. In New South Wales, Van Diemen's Land and Port Phillip it was quite a battle, but as Rubinstein has written, "in the absence of legislation ensuring their rights, the Jews came to regard state aid as approximating official ratification of their equality in Australia."[41]

The argument was a simple one: state aid—that is, financial assistance for religious denominations provided by the government from funds raised through the taxation of all—should not be denied to Jews where Jews had contributed to those taxes. It reached into the very core of Jewish ideas of acceptance, and calls for tolerance toward the Jews on the part of some well-meaning philosemites did little to placate Jewish sensitivities on this issue. They did not want to be "tolerated," for to do so would be to acknowledge a certain form of "otherness" which was unacceptable to people who saw themselves as being as British as anyone else, and whose only difference was that they were "Englishmen of the Mosaic persuasion."[42] The issue was stated no more clearly than in a petition presented to the Legislative Council of Victoria on 17 March 1854. Signed by 504 members of the Victorian Jewish community, it stated, inter alia, "While Your Petitioners ask neither for toleration in a Colony where all Her Majesty's subjects are based upon an equality, nor favour from those who are bound to mete out justice to all, they claim as a right, being good citizens and loyal subjects, that they not be excluded from participation in [the grant of state aid for religion] or that they not be compelled to bear an equal burden in the State with the recipients of such Grant."[43] It had to be all of one or all of the other, and was, in many respects, a clear cry of "no taxation without representation." The struggle, to use Suzanne D. Rutland's phrase, "was a matter of principle rather than finance."[44]

The question of state aid was resolved in the Jews' favor at different times during the 1840s and 1850s. In New South Wales, after a decade of rejections, victory was achieved in 1855; in Van Diemen's Land, where the greatest anti-Jewish opposition was forthcoming from Lieutenant-Governor Sir John Franklin, it came in the same year, after it had been granted in New South Wales; in Victoria, building on the experience of the other two colonies, in 1859; and in South Australia, which because of the nature of the colony's founding was different from the others and where state aid did not have to be fought for to the same degree as elsewhere, a measure of equality had actually been established as early as 1846—at which time there were but fifty-eight Jews in the whole colony.[45] Israel Getzler has concluded that South Australia was thus "the pioneer among Australian colonies not only in the abolition of state aid and the separation of church from state, but also in religious equality for Jews,"[46] a strange irony when we consider the fact that a century and a half later South Australia has become the focus of anti-Semitic agitation and racist political movements for the rest of the country.

The colonial "frontier" with which Jews had to deal—and through which they had to break—was thus vastly different from that experienced at exactly the same time by the continent's Aborigines. The major field of activity for Jews in colonial Australia was the city, even though there were a few Jewish bush pioneers who shared the life of all other frontiersmen. When placed alongside what was happening to the Aborigines, the state aid grievance might seem insignificant, even trivial. Yet as Israel Getzler has concluded, the grievance over state aid appears trifling

> only when looked at as a mere Australian phenomenon. It gains in significance and weight when viewed against the wider background of mid-nineteenth-century Jewish history: the vicissitudes of Jewish emancipation in Europe, especially in the post-1848 years of counter-revolution, the protracted fight of Jews in England for equal political rights and the coming to self-consciousness of the Jewish people in the aftermath of the "Damascus blood libel" of 1840. Seen in this perspective, the struggle of Jews in the Australian colonies for religious equality may be regarded as the Antipodean extension of a world-wide movement toward Jewish emancipation and as an integral part of nineteenth-century liberalism.[47]

Given the backgrounds and occupations of the majority of colonial Jews, it is perhaps not surprising that they should be in the vanguard of a movement of this nature. Australia was a "new, expanding, dynamic, money-making society, with a distrust of unearned privileges."[48] The majority of Australian Jews came from the United Kingdom; those who did not mainly hailed from one or other of the German States. As Hilary L. Rubinstein has written,

> They might have had memories of predominantly Jewish neighbourhoods in London and elsewhere, but very few of them had first-hand experience of life in a traditional European ghetto, cramped and confined, with its isolation from non-Jewish culture, the civil disabilities of its inhabitants, its legal restrictions and curfews, its narrow streets and crowded tenements. The English and emancipated German Jews who together constituted the majority of the Australian Jewish community came from societies in which Jews regarded themselves as equal citizens. And in Australia, too, Jews regarded themselves as not merely *in* the land, but *of* it.[49]

In these circumstances, the newness of Australian colonial society had a large role to play; many of the prejudices, biases and social consciousnesses of Europe were not appropriate to life in the new country, and were thus rejected. There was, furthermore, nothing in colonial Australian society even approximating the status of South Africa's *kaffireatniks,* nor the teeming tenements of the United States later in the century. The post-1880 Jewish immigrants to Australia, most of whom came from similar backgrounds to those who went to Johannesburg and New York City, were, on the contrary, assimilated fairly rapidly into Sydney or Melbourne's mainstream Anglo-Jewish middle class, living according to social patterns which had been laid down forty years before. Their newness and foreignness, it could be argued, did not—even in the 1890s—serve as a prohibition to them gaining acceptance as future Australians. The emergence of racial anti-Semitism in some sectors in the final decade of the nineteenth century did not overturn that fundamental development, and much of this can be put down to the earlier social and religious acceptance of the previous generation.

There was never a possibility, therefore, that Jews would accept the status of "Other" in Australian colonial society. Aborigines, who were unable to resist being given such a status and occupied land wanted by that same society, suffered massive depopulation owing to settler depredations, in spite of their attempts to either physically resist or reach accommodation through cooperating with those invading their land. Although some colonists in the 1850s would have preferred the conversion of Jews to Christianity for their own souls' sake, at no time was there a perceived need to destroy their culture, social networks, or ways of living in order to have them replaced by a "British" model. Jews in colonial Australia were British already. In this, we see a total contrast with the Aborigines, who were the archetypal "Other" so far as a majority in colonial society were concerned.

How, then, can a comparison of Jews and Aborigines in colonial southeastern Australia be measured? Indeed, in light of the above, is such a comparison even legitimate? The argument of this essay is that it is, and in three important ways. In the first place, each sought *equality* within colonial society, on their own terms and without being compelled to surrender their ways of life by external (that is, hegemonic) forces. Secondly, each found themselves forced to *struggle* in order to achieve this, the Jews by means of petitions and public agitation, the Aborigines through warfare[50] or accommodation. Finally, and perhaps most decisively for both communities, the *outcomes* of this struggle were to condition the long-term future role of both Aborigines and Jews in Australia, a legacy which still prevails down to the present time—Jews as heirs of what has become a culture which eschews anti-Semitism as anathema, Aborigines as the enduring target of a European-derived racism which continues to capitalize on a process of dispossession and genocidal destruction which took place during the nineteenth century.

A final issue which needs to be addressed concerns the possibility of Jewish-Aboriginal contacts on the physical frontier. Aborigines could in no way play a role in Jewish emancipation, but did Jews play a role in the persecution and dispossession of Aborigines? In light of the evidence which has come down to us today, the prospects seem slight. It will be recalled that Jews accounted for only about one half of 1 percent of the total European population, and the vast majority of these lived in the cities in any case. (From the middle of the 1860s, incidentally, so did a majority of all colonists). Opportunities for Jews to engage in frontier warfare were thus few at the best of times, but there is more. Settler actions against Aborigines "on the frontier" took place for the most part in areas where there was no Jewish presence at all—in the Western District and Gippsland in Victoria, in western and northern New South Wales, and, later in the century, in North Queensland. With *very* few exceptions, moreover, Jews did not form part of the squatting class—those who took up large landholdings which sometimes incorporated lands occupied by Aborigines—nor were they so-called selectors farming smaller parcels of land. On the whole, it may be concluded that Jews were not involved in settler violence against Aborigines. The degree to which this can be put down to the influence of Jewish religious ethics or the lack of opportunities to so involve themselves, however, must remain a matter for conjecture, as the numbers in question were so slight and our capacity to look into the minds of those so charged is circumscribed by a lack of data. We may in fact never know for certain how frontier Jews in colonial Australia felt about Aborigines.

To say that the two peoples, Aborigines and Jews, underwent different frontier experiences would be superfluous. The notion of the physical frontier, a construction of the invading society rather than of those being invaded, is a thoroughly appropriate way of describing *where* European-Aboriginal contact took place, and the images accompanying the term came to characterize (and continue to characterize) how the colonists saw their settlement and their actions. For Jews, however, life on the frontier had an altogether different meaning. True, very few shared the pioneering lifestyle of the bush, the homestead, and the small town, but for the majority the idea of the frontier represented limited religious rights, a barrier which had to be penetrated and left behind for the betterment of all. In this sense it might be said that Jews in Australia ceased being a frontier people by the middle of the nineteenth century, outliving that other frontier by several decades. From this point onward, Jews progressed into the world of the majority society, and began to capitalize on their triumph. The Aborigines, denied similar success as a result of their inability to beat back those who had created the frontier in the first place, were in no position to enjoy such a luxury—their fate presumably sealed until the frontiers of other minds, at a later time, had been traversed. It must be said, with honesty, that one and a half centuries later, despite the enlightenment that has come to inform so much of our thinking in so many areas, we still await such a crossing.

Notes

1. W. D. Rubinstein, *The Left, the Right, and the Jews* (London: Croom Helm, 1982), 163.

2. Howard Lamar and Leonard Thompson, eds., *The Frontier in History: North America and South Africa Compared* (New Haven, Conn.: Yale University Press, 1981).

3. James O. Gump, *The Dust Rose like Smoke: The Subjugation of the Zulu and the Sioux* (Lincoln: University of Nebraska Press, 1994), 1.

4. Rubinstein, *The Left, the Right, and the Jews*, 163.

5. Israel Getzler, *Neither Toleration Nor Favour: The Australian Chapter of Jewish Emancipation* (Melbourne: Melbourne University Press, 1970), 1.

6. See Jon Stratton, "The Color of Jews: Jews, Race, and the White Australia Policy," in this volume.

7. Hilary L. Rubinstein has, however, made a start by looking at the response of the existing Australian Jewish community in this regard. See Hilary L. Rubinstein, "Australian Jewish Reactions to Russian Jewish Distress," *Australian Jewish Historical Society Journal* (hereafter *AJHSJ*) 8.5 (1978): 444–56.

8. This notion of Jews being rejected as foreigners *as well as* Jews is precisely the position that served as the backdrop to my previous work on this subject. See Paul R. Bartrop, *Australia and the Holocaust, 1933–45* (Melbourne: Australian Scholarly Publishing, 1994).

9. W. D. Rubinstein, *The Jews in Australia* (Melbourne: AE Press, 1986), 23.

10. Ibid.

11. Ibid., 24.

12. Those with an interest in exploring further the story of the Jewish convicts should consult J. S. Levi and G. F. J. Bergman, *Australian Genesis: Jewish Convicts and Settlers, 1788–1850* (Adelaide: Rigby, 1974); and J. S. Levi, *The Forefathers: A Dictionary of Biography of the Jews of Australia, 1788–1830* (Sydney: Australian Jewish Historical Society, 1976).

13. Hilary L. Rubinstein, "Australian Jewry: A Brief Historical Overview," in *When Jews and Christians Meet: Australian Essays Commemorating Twenty Years of Nostra Aetate*, ed. John W. Roffey (Melbourne: Victorian Council of Churches, 1985), 4.

14. Jean Woolmington, ed., *Aborigines in Colonial Society, 1788–1850: From "Noble Savage" to "Rural Pest"* (Melbourne: Cassell, 1973), 60.

15. Bishop Broughton, cited as evidence in the *Report from the Select Committee on Aborigines (British Settlements)*, House of Commons, June 26, 1837. See *Historical Records of Victoria*, vol. 2A: *The Aborigines of Port Phillip, 1835–1839* (Melbourne: Victorian Government Printing Office, 1982), 62.

16. Woolmington, *Aborigines in Colonial Society*, 60–61.

17. Henry Reynolds, *The Other Side of the Frontier: Aboriginal Resistance to the European Invasion of Australia* (Ringwood, Victoria: Penguin Books, 1982), 122.

18. Henry Reynolds, *Frontier: Aborigines, Settlers, and Land* (Sydney: Allen and Unwin, 1987), 53.

19. Ibid.

20. Michael Cannon, *Who Killed the Koories?* (Melbourne: William Heinemann Australia, 1990), 263–65.

21. Tony Barta, "After the Holocaust: Consciousness of Genocide in Australia,"

Australian Journal of Politics and History 31.1 (1985): 154–61. A second essay from Barta, more refined than the first, draws similar conclusions. See Tony Barta, "Relations of Genocide: Land and Lives in the Colonization of Australia," in *Genocide and the Modern Age: Etiology and Case Studies of Mass Death,* ed. Isidor Walliman and Michael N. Dobkowski (Westport, Conn.: Greenwood Press, 1987), 237–51.

22. Barta, "After the Holocaust," 154.

23. Ibid.

24. Ibid., 156.

25. Reynolds, *Other Side of the Frontier,* 122.

26. N. G. Butlin, *Our Original Aggression: Aboriginal Populations of Southeastern Australia, 1788–1850* (Sydney: Allen and Unwin, 1983), chaps. 2, 5.

27. John H. Bodley, *Victims of Progress,* 2d ed. (Menlo Park, Calif.: Benjamin/Cummings, 1982).

28. Henry Reynolds, *With the White People* (Ringwood, Victoria: Penguin Books, 1990).

29. Ibid., 232.

30. Ibid.

31. Ibid., 231.

32. Ibid., 233.

33. Ibid.

34. In this regard, see especially Hilary L. Rubinstein, "Manifestations of Literary and Cultural Anti-Semitism in Australia, 1856–1946," *Melbourne Chronicle,* Oct.–Nov. 1983, 2–4; *Melbourne Chronicle,* Feb.–Mar. 1984, 2–4.

35. Rubinstein, "Australian Jewry," 5.

36. Paul R. Bartrop, "The Role and Record of the Australian Jewish Historical Society: How Have Australian Jews Remembered their Past?" *AJHSJ* 9.3 (Nov. 1991): 570–80.

37. As just a few examples, see the following: Nathan F. Spielvogel, "The Beginning of the Ballarat Hebrew Congregation," *AJHSJ* 1.4 (1940): 110–14; Sydney B. Glass, "Jews of Goulburn," *AJHSJ* 1.7 (1942): 239–48; Rabbi Dr. A. Fabian, "Early Days of South Australian Jewry," *AJHSJ* 2.3 (June 1945): 127–43; Rabbi Dr. Israel Porush, "The Jews of Tamworth," *AJHSJ* 3.4 (Dec. 1950): 193–202; L. E. Fredman, "Bendigo Jewry," *AJHSJ* 4.4 (Aug. 1956): 175–83; George F. J. Bergman, "Edward Davis: Life and Death of an Australian Bushranger," *AJHSJ* 4.5 (Dec. 1956): 205–40; Rabbi Lazarus Morris Goldman, "The Early Jewish Settlers of Victoria and Their Problems, Part 1: Before Separation," *AJHSJ* 4.7 (May 1958): 335–412; Rabbi Lazarus Morris Goldman, "The Early Jewish Settlers of Victoria and Their Problems, Part 2: After Separation, 1851–1865," *AJHSJ* 4.8 (Dec. 1958): 415–97. This is but a sampling of an extraordinarily rich source of material on early Australian Jewry, and the appearance of such scholarship persists in the present day, in spite of the enormous growth of works concerning the later nineteenth and twentieth centuries. For our purposes, see especially G. F. J. Bergman, "George Mocatta (1815–1893): A Notable Pioneer Squatter," *AJHSJ* 8.1 (June 1975): 62–71; and M. Z. Forbes, "The Jews of NSW and the Gold Rushes," *AJHSJ* 12.2 (June 1994): 282–326.

38. Hilary L. Rubinstein, *Chosen: The Jews in Australia* (Sydney: Allen and Unwin, 1987): 10.

39. Ibid., 11–12.

40. Ibid., 40.

41. Ibid.

42. Ibid., 37.

43. Getzler, *Neither Toleration Nor Favour,* 96.

44. Suzanne D. Rutland, *Edge of the Diaspora: Two Centuries of Jewish Settlement in Australia* (Sydney: Collins Australia, 1988), 42.

45. Ibid., 43.

46. Getzler, *Neither Toleration Nor Favour,* 118.

47. Ibid., 1.

48. Rubinstein, *Chosen,* 36.

49. Ibid., 36–37.

50. In a telling statement, Henry Reynolds has addressed the following to all who perceive the Aboriginal-European relationship simply from the perspective of one long series of relentless persecutions:

> An overemphasis on the significance of massacres tends to throw support behind the idea that blacks were helpless victims of white attack; passive recipients of promiscuous brutality. Such an argument runs easily along well worn channels of historical interpretation. Paternalism and sympathy have often merged in support of the view that the Aboriginal experience was a story "infinitely pathetic—children as they were, stretching out frail hands to stay the flood tide."
>
> Such an assessment parodies the Aboriginal role in frontier conflict. Blacks did not sit around their camp fires waiting to be massacred. They usually knew the dangers accompanying white settlement even before the Europeans arrived and took action to minimize those perils. (*Other Side of the Frontier,* 124)

Such "action" certainly included warfare, a point made time and again in the works of Reynolds and others. See R. H. W. Reece, *Aborigines and Colonists: Aborigines and Colonial Society in New South Wales in the 1830s and 1840s* (Sydney: Sydney University Press, 1974), app. 1, for a listing of all recorded conflicts between Aborigines and Europeans between 1832 and 1845 and a list of deaths on the frontier of Aborigines and Europeans between 1836 and 1844.

4 Alaskan Jews Discover the Last Frontier

BERNARD REISMAN

The motto of the State of Alaska is "The Last Frontier." Alaskans proudly affirm their frontier status—it explains what attracted most of them to choose to live in Alaska. Living in a frontier community is a source of pride for the residents, and is a primary determinant of what is distinctive about their lifestyle. It is therefore important, at the outset, to set forth the distinguishing characteristics of a frontier. There are four criteria which define frontier settlements. The first criterion is that the area is distant from more settled sections and undeveloped—it exists mainly in its natural state. Second, there are few people living in the area; it has a low population density. Third, there are limited services—organizations or programs to respond to the needs of the frontier settlers. Finally, the far-away location of the frontier community limits access to parents and extended family networks.

Alaska meets all these criteria and is a classic frontier society. It is the largest of the fifty states—occupying over 16 percent of the total land mass of the "Lower 48" (the term Alaskans use to remind visitors that their state is one of the fifty U.S. states).[1] The area is predominately undeveloped, with extensive forests, mountains, rivers and lakes. Further, Alaska has the lowest population density in the United States: 1.08 persons per square mile compared to 74.31 persons per square mile for the Lower 48.[2] Anchorage, Alaska, where more than half of Alaska's Jews live, is over 2,000 miles from Seattle, Washington, the nearest big city in the Lower 48. To travel by plane from New York City to Anchorage is at least a thirteen-hour trip.

My interest in Alaska was initially generated when I discovered, on a 1993 vacation trip there, organized Jewish communities in each of the Alaskan cities I visited. This was surprising, given the historic propensity of Jews to settle in or near urban centers. Not only is Alaska predominantly rural, but it is quite distant from the major urban centers where the vast majority of American Jews live. The data from the 1990 National Jewish Population Survey indicated that only 5 percent of all Jews were living in non-metropolitan areas.[3] As I began to get involved in studying about the Jews of Alaska, I became aware that this residential settlement was part of a new demographic trend: that Jews living in the Lower 48 have been increasingly choosing to live in small, rural communities.

In general, American Jews are a highly mobile population. The demographers, Sidney Goldstein and Alice Goldstein of Brown University, have documented this phenomenon in their recent book, aptly titled *Jews on the Move.* The Goldsteins point out that, at the time of their study, 57% of all American Jews were living outside their country or state of birth.[4] This is more than double the figure for the general American population, "among whom only 29% had changed their state of residence during their lifetime."[5] The Goldsteins identify two other recent demographic changes among American Jews which further explain the emergence of a Jewish community in Alaska. The first is a general shift in the geographic distribution of American Jews. The most significant changes in residential concentration of American Jews over the past sixty years (from 1930–90) is the decline in the proportion of Jews living in the northeast region of the United States (from 68.3 percent to 50.6 percent) and a similar level of change, in this case an increase, in the proportion of Jews living in the western region (from 4.6 percent to 18.8 percent; see table 4.1).[6] The growth of the western region is particularly

Table 4.1. Distribution of U.S and Jewish Populations by Regions, 1930 and 1990

	Jewish Population[a]		U.S. Population[b]	
	1930	1990	1930	1990
Northeast	68.3%	50.6%	27.9%	20.4%
Midwest	19.6	11.2	31.4	24.0
South	7.6	19.3	30.7	34.4
West	4.6	18.8	10.0	21.2

Source: Data for the Jewish population in 1930 is from *American Jewish Year Book,* 1931; for 1990 from *American Jewish Year Book,* 1991. Data for the U.S. population is from U.S. Bureau of the Census, Washington, D.C. This table is adapted from Sidney Goldstein and Alice Goldstein, *Jews on the Move: Implications for Jewish Identity* (Albany: SUNY Press, 1996), 38, 39. The author is grateful to Sidney Goldstein and Alice Goldstein and the SUNY Press for permission to use this material.

important since 50 percent of the Jews who moved to Alaska lived in the western region prior to the move.[7]

This changing pattern in the residential distribution of American Jews has important implications for Jewish identity. The Northeast has been the dominant center of Jewish settlement since the eighteenth century. It is an area of high Jewish density with well-organized Jewish communities, offering a full range of Jewish programs and services. The Jewish communities in the West are of more recent vintage, they are more dispersed, and they are attracting a younger population of Jews. Most important, with respect to the issue of Jewish identity, a recent Council of Jewish Federation demographic survey of Jews living in the West indicates a much higher rate of assimilation among the Jews living in the western region, as compared to the other regions.[8]

The second important demographic finding, highlighted in the Goldstein analysis and relevant to the emergence of the Alaskan Jewish community, is the association between high levels of education and residential mobility of American Jews. Studying the mobility rates of American males from the 1970–71 National Jewish Population Survey, Goldstein concludes: "More of those with higher education were involved in all kinds of movement—local, intrastate and interstate—than were those with less education, and the differentials were greatest for destinations involving longer distances."[9]

Clearly, a move to Alaska involves a long distance. With regard to level of education, one of the most distinctive characteristics of Alaskan Jews is their unusually high level of education. As noted in table 4.2, 54 percent of the Alaskan Jews received some graduate education beyond a bachelor's degree. This compares to 8 percent of all Alaskans, 9 percent of the total U.S. white population and 25 percent of Jews in the Lower 48.[10]

The high level of education of Alaskan Jews is clearly associated with

Table 4.2. Levels of Education

	Alaskan Jews	Alaskans	U.S. White Population	Jews in the Lower 48
High school graduate or less	4%	42%	62%	30%
Some college	22	28	17	21
Four years of college	20	22	12	23
Some graduate or professional school	54	8	9	25

Sources: Alaskan Jewish data from Bernard Reisman and Joel Reisman, 1995; Alaskan data from Alaskan Department of Community and Regional Affairs, 1990; U.S. data from U.S. Bureau of the Census, 1988; Lower 48 data from National Jewish Population Survey (NJPS), 1990.

their vocations. Almost four out of five (78 percent) of Alaskan Jews work as professionals or managers. That is more than twice the proportion of professionals and managers among the general U.S. white population (31 percent) and 29 percent more than Jews of the Lower 48 (49 percent) who are professionals and managers.[11] These data, along with the information I obtained from many personal interviews and group workshops, confirm that Alaskan Jews are a highly acculturated population. In their typical urban residences in the Lower 48 many of these acculturated Jews have effectively achieved a synthesis of living in two cultures. They are immersed in the general secular society. At the same time they maintain a connection with the Jewish community. My sense is that, because they feel sufficiently secure in both of these cultures, these Alaskan settlers are able to risk a move to a very different frontier environment, without the assured support of family and Jewish community.

Typically, frontier areas have attracted few Jews, and those who are attracted usually are minimalist or assimilated Jews. That has not been the case with a significant proportion of the Alaskan Jewish settlers of the past two decades. The results of our 1995 demographic survey of Alaskan Jews indicate that their level of observance of Jewish customs and rituals and their positive feelings about their Jewishness are significantly higher than the Lower 48 respondents to the 1990 NJPS. This unexpected finding suggests that it is not a flight from their Jewishness that explains the move to Alaska. Indeed, the higher level of Jewish interest and behavior of these recent Alaskan Jewish settlers, coupled with their initiatives to organize or align with Jewish communities in Alaska, suggests that they view their Jewishness as a resource to be cultivated as a means of adjusting to the frontier and shaping a secure and fulfilling lifestyle.

That, today, positively identified Jews are choosing to settle in Alaska is further confirmation of the Goldstein thesis of the changing residential pattern of American Jews. I view Alaska as a prototypical frontier—the edge of an unexplored region, and a "social laboratory." Studying the Jews of Alaska I hope to understand better the phenomenon of Jews moving to small towns and rural areas with limited Jewish populations, and of the implications for Jewish continuity. My research focused on three questions:

1. Who are the Jews who move to Alaska, in terms of their demographic and Jewish interests?
2. What are their motives for moving to a frontier society such as Alaska?
3. What happens to their Jewish identity living in a frontier area?

THE FRONTIER OF THE FRONTIER

Eighty-one percent of the approximately 3,000 Jews who live in Alaska live in the three largest cities: Anchorage, Fairbanks and Juneau (see table 4.3); 19 percent of Alaskan Jews, some 530 individuals, live in 40 smaller cities, all of which are rural, and whose general populations are under 10,000 and whose Jewish populations range from 1 to 71.[12] In order to understand more fully the frontier aspects of Alaska, I will focus on the Jews who live in the small, rural communities, which I have designated as "the frontier of the frontier." To provide a sense of the Alaskan Jews who live in these frontier communities, I have created a composite frontier community, Cascade, which is meant to be representative of the many small, rural communities in which Alaskan Jews live.

Cascade is over 900 miles from Fairbanks, the nearest of the three big cities. It has a total population of 2,500 individuals. There are eight Jewish households in Cascade with fourteen adults and fifteen children. (In this project, the definition of a Jewish household is one in which at least one adult identifies as a Jew). Each of the nine Cascade Jewish residents I will introduce are people I met during my visits to the small Alaskan communities. I do not identify the actual name or city in which they live so as to assure confidentiality. However, the information about them and their stories are very real, modified only if some detail might compromise confidentiality.

Table 4.3. Population of Ten Cities and Towns in Alaska with Largest Numbers of Jews

		Jewish Population	
City or Town	Total Population	Number	Percentage
Anchorage (borough)	257,780	1,605	0.6
Fairbanks (borough)	84,380	578	1.0
Juneau (borough)	29,228	306	1.0
Sitka	9,194	71	0.8
Kenai	7,006	63	0.4
Homer	3,836	56	1.4
Ketchikan	8,557	55	0.6
Soldotna	3,990	49	1.3
Haines	1,363	31	1.2
Bethel	5,195	30	0.6
Other towns	205,371	172	0.5
	615,900	3,016	0.5

Sources: General population data from Alaskan Department of Community and Regional, Affairs, Juneau, 1995; Jewish population date from 1995, Reisman Survey.

Before describing the Jews of Cascade it would be helpful to discuss the phenomenon of the Jewish community group. In at least nine of the cities in Alaska in which Jews live (which includes over 95 percent of all Alaskan Jews) there has emerged some type of formal Jewish communal organization. In Anchorage, there are two synagogues, one Reform and one Lubavitch, and each has a rabbi. In Fairbanks there is a synagogue (a recently purchased building converted to serve as a synagogue) and the community is now trying to raise enough money to hire a full-time rabbi. Currently they have student rabbis from the Hebrew Union College spend the summer with them. In Juneau, Bethel, Haines, Kenai, Ketchikan, Kotzebue, and Sitka there are Jewish community groups that meet to observe Jewish holidays, Jewish life-cycle events, and some meet more regularly to have Friday night services and/or programs of Jewish study. The religious services are held in rented facilities of churches or community organizations, and other programs take place in people's homes. All of the community groups have a modest program of Jewish education for children, organized and taught by parents. The consistency of the meetings of the Jewish community groups and the extent of their Jewish activities is primarily a function of the quality of the "convener" (I use this term to refer to the person in the community who assumes the key leadership role). At the outset this role involves identifying the Jews who live in the area and then bringing them together in some type of organization.

The convener serves to remind people of community meetings and assure that decisions reached by the Jewish community are carried out. Another important leadership function, especially in Alaska, is to help defuse or resolve tensions or conflicts among members of the community, which tend to occur with some frequency.

THE JEWS OF CASCADE

Three general pieces of information about the Jews of Cascade: (1) Of the eight Jewish households, seven involve a mixed marriage, and all identify their household as Jewish; (2) The age of the fourteen adults ranges from thirty-five to sixty-one, and the average age is forty-one; (3) None of the adults was born in Alaska—they arrived in Alaska between 1970 and 1986.

These are the stories of at least one adult from each of the Jewish households in Cascade.

Rachel Lupo

I'm a social worker. I grew up in Brooklyn in an Orthodox household. I went to the Yeshiva of Flatbush. My husband is Tom, who also grew up in New York.

He does construction work, which means he is away a lot because these days there isn't much building going on, so he has to travel to where there is work in the state.

Tom and I moved to Cascade right after our marriage. My family in Brooklyn are Orthodox and were very much opposed to my marrying Tom, who was reared as a Catholic. Tom and I realized that we couldn't stay in New York. When we thought about where we would like to live, Tom came up with the idea of Alaska. At first we laughed and thought it was crazy. But both of us love the outdoors and hiking, and we're both kind of adventuresome, so we just did it. We figured if we were to go to Alaska we should go all the way and not live in any of the big cities. We came across an advertisement for two and one-half acres of undeveloped land in a town called Cascade. It was cheap, so we used our wedding-gift money and bought it. We packed our belongings into Tom's old car and headed off to Alaska. Our families weren't too happy.

When we finally got to Cascade, after a ride that seemed to take forever, we were excited to see our two and one-half acres of wooded land. It was beautiful! We couldn't see any other houses in the area because the woods were so dense. We decided we would build our own home out of logs we cut down on *our* land. We did get some help from a guy we met who had power tools, but we did most of the building ourselves.

Once that was finished my next project was to try to meet other people in the Cascade area. It was early spring and I was aware that in a few weeks it would be Passover and I couldn't imagine not having a Passover Seder. But, I also couldn't imagine having a Seder with just Tom and me. On a lark I sent an item into the local newspaper, the *Cascade Clarion,* saying we would be having a Seder and if there were any Jews in the area who were interested they should call me. Well, would you believe I received ten phone calls, and that Passover eight of them joined us at our Seder. It was a great evening. That night we agreed to form "The Jewish Community Group of Cascade."

Tom and I have two children: Samuel, who is fifteen, and Sarah, who is twelve. Tom likes the idea that I keep a Jewish household, because he believes it is good for children to have a religious identity.

I put in a lot of time with our Jewish community group because I feel it is very important for helping provide a sense of Jewishness for our two adolescent kids. Together with several of the other women about five years ago we organized a Sunday School which gives the kids some type of Jewish education and also Jewish friends. Both of our kids are the only Jews in their classes in the Cascade Junior High and High School.

Bob

I do mostly carpentry work and I also work with a guy who has a linoleum and carpet store and I help him put down floor coverings. I was born in New York City and, would you believe, I am a graduate of City College of New York.

After finishing college the only job I could get was selling insurance. It took me only a few months to realize that was not a job for me. Besides I just felt life in New York was too much of "rush-rush" and "dog eat dog." I felt too hemmed in. Also, my girlfriend, now wife, June, who came from a small town in upstate New York, couldn't stand living in New York City. So on a lark we decided to see what it would be like to live in Alaska. Well, would you believe we like it.

I consider myself a "cultural Jew." I would never go to synagogue and I can't stand organized religion, but I do read a lot about Jewish affairs and I'm proud of my Jewish background. June is Catholic and she takes that seriously. She goes to church most Sundays, and usually takes our three kids. I can't say I'm happy about that, but I don't make a big deal about it.

Nancy

I'm a widow; my husband, Oscar died twelve years ago. I'm sixty-one years old and I'm the oldest person in the Cascade Jewish community group. Also I've lived here the longest. Oscar and I came here in 1970. That's when Oscar opened his hardware store. Now I work in the store. I go in most mornings, but our son Fred really runs the store.

Oscar was Jewish. In fact, when we first got to Cascade he was the only Jew in town. The people in town all loved Oscar and made a big deal about the fact they got along so well with him. That was mostly true, but behind Oscar's back a few people said mean things about Jews. Even these days there are some anti-Semites in Cascade (mainly the Christian fundamentalists), but most of the people are fine and the Jews are comfortable here. I was reared as a Protestant, but after I married Oscar I thought of myself as being Jewish, and our three kids were brought up as Jews. But, guess what, the two who are married both married non-Jews. Although Fred's wife said if they have kids she would go along with raising the kids as Jews. As far as our youngest son is concerned, he says he would like to marry a Jew, but he just never meets any.

Andrea

I'm the dean of the branch of the University of Alaska which is located in Cascade. I've been here for fifteen years. Before coming here I was on the faculty of Temple University in Philadelphia. I'm not too active in the Jewish community group in town. Mostly I come for religious services on the special Jewish holidays, like Passover and the High Holidays. On those days I'm more aware of my Jewishness and I think about my parents, so it feels good to have an opportunity to reconnect to my Jewishness on those occasions.

This past year I celebrated my fiftieth birthday. My partner Gail and I bought a very nice house just outside of town a couple of years ago. It is close to where both of us work. She is a physical therapist and has a busy practice. We've been together going back to Philadelphia, which is where we first met. We got hassled a lot by both of our families and decided they would never accept the fact that we're lesbians. So when I came across a notice about the Dean's job here in Alaska, we both were ready for the move. And it's worked out great for both of us. Here in Cascade we're fully accepted, both by the Jewish community and generally in town. Gail considers herself a "non-practicing Methodist." She often comes with me when I come to the Jewish community group to observe the Jewish holidays.

Margie

My husband Paul and I have been in Cascade for four years now. Paul is a physician and he came here to work in the veteran's hospital. He owes the government some years of service because they financed his tuition expenses for medical school. He likes what he is doing because he is working with so many different kinds of health problems—almost all of his patients are natives. But I think in another year or two we'll both be ready to return to the Lower 48. I guess we miss family and neither of us likes living in a small city. We don't have too many friends outside of the people Paul works with at the hospital. I've become somewhat friendly with a few of the people in the Jewish group in town. Paul isn't Jewish. He speaks of himself as a "C/E Christian"—a Christmas/Easter Christian—meaning those are the only days he goes to church. I'm a little better when it comes to observing the Jewish holidays. I enjoy taking part in the gatherings of the Cascade Jewish group. Paul is usually too busy to attend any of the programs of the Jewish community group. But, I guess the truth is that religion really is not particularly important to either of us.

Paul is a good bit older than me—I'm forty-one. He has two grown children from his first marriage. We don't have any children and we won't have any.

I have a good job with the local public radio, television station. I had been working in public radio in Detroit, where we lived before we moved to Alaska.

Charles

I grew up in a comfortable Jewish household in Los Angeles. I was turned off by the materialism and phoniness of that upper-middle class Jewish society. Frankly, my folks were not much better than their friends in that regard. You could only drive certain cars and buy clothes from certain stores. To me it was just so much bullshit. I attended UCLA as a pre-law major for a couple of years, but I wasn't too interested in writing papers and doing the boring reading assignments. So, I dropped out at the end of my second year.

I decided I would take a trip to Washington and Oregon. I got involved in some type of commune in Seattle. I was starting to run out of money, and my folks weren't too happy with my lifestyle. I got a job working in a restaurant, where I met Fran, a waitress in the same restaurant. Fran was born in a town near Cascade in Alaska. She married a native man when she was only seventeen, and they had two kids. But the marriage didn't work out and that was when she moved to Seattle. Her husband used to beat her up regularly.

We lived together for two years and then Fran's mother got very sick and Fran decided she had to go back to Cascade to care for her mom. I figured I would go with her. Soon after moving to Cascade I got a great job as an assistant chef on one of the tourist boats that stops in Cascade. It has worked out very well for all of us. The kids like me—I'm their father, and I enjoy that role.

One night, a few months after we were living in Cascade, I got a phone call from Rachel Lupo, inviting me to come to the next meeting of the Cascade Jewish community group. I really appreciated that call and I've become very active in the Jewish group. Fran isn't Jewish but she enjoys the group and she and the kids like the idea of observing Jewish holidays and customs. Being Jewish makes us more of a real family.

Judy and Peter

Peter: We're both artists and we love living in Cascade. Have you ever seen such a beautiful studio? We bought this house because of its lovely view of the mountains and then we added on this studio with these large windows. The light in here is great for painting.

I was pleased to hear that you were coming here to learn about the Jews of Cascade. I was reared in a traditional Jewish home in Los Angeles and I miss the old Jewish neighborhood in Los Angeles where just about everyone was Jewish. There are only a small group of Jewish families in Cascade and we get together pretty regularly. I usually lead the davening when we have religious services since I had a strong Jewish upbringing. There are only one or two other people in town who could lead religious services. It's important for me and also our two kids—Jerry who is nine and Miriam who is six.

Judy: I even got into the Jewish act, although I'm a *shiksa* (gentile). I love the Jewish holidays and customs and it's nice for the kids. I grew up as a Catholic, and I went to parochial school but I hated it and the nuns were always calling my mother to complain about me. But, if you want to know about complaining, you should have heard the fit my mother had when I told her I planned to marry Peter. She actually liked Peter, but she sure had a hard time explaining to her Irish-Catholic family in Trenton, New Jersey that her daughter was going to be married to a Jew and *by a rabbi!* Well, that was almost ten years ago and now they realize what a great son-in-law they got with Peter. Both of my brothers married Catholic girls and both of their marriages broke up.

Last week when I spoke to my parents on the phone and I told them that our kids—whom my parents are crazy about, started going to the Jewish Sunday School in Cascade, they didn't say anything bad about it. Peter asked me if I thought my parents would come to our son Jerry's bar mitzvah. I told him I'd rather wait a while before I ask, since that's almost four years away. But, you know something, I'll bet they'll be very proud of Jerry—he's so smart, and I even think they'll be proud of me.

Robert

I'm an attorney who did my law school training at Harvard. I was recruited right out of law school by a hot-shot new law firm here in Cascade. They promised me I would be a partner within three years and, if I remained three years, I would get a six-month sabbatical. They also offered me a hell of a lot more money than the firms in Boston and New York and they helped to get a job for my wife Mary Jo, who is also an attorney. Mary Jo has been very pleased with the law firm she's with. The real good news is that Mary Jo is now five months pregnant with our first child. Mary Jo is asking for a long-term leave, to raise the new baby. We want to have at least one other child and since we're both in our mid-thirties we don't have too much time.

I grew up in Chicago in a classical Reform Jewish household. We belonged to the prestigious Reform Temple on Lake Shore Drive and I went to Sunday School for about five years. Actually I liked Sunday School and going to the Temple. One of the things I miss living here in Cascade is going to Temple. The nearest synagogue is in Anchorage and it is about an eight hour drive. I did it the first year I was here, but I fell asleep on the drive home and almost had a bad accident. I've tried to get Mary Jo to come with me but she said: "Hey, my parents never went to church and I never did, so don't expect me to start going to synagogue at this point in my life." I didn't argue with her.

It will be interesting to see what we do about religion when we have our first child. I know, if it's a boy, I definitely want him to have a *bris* [ritual circumcision]. I remember Mary Jo and I once had a conversation about circumcision when we got an invitation from my sister and her husband to come to the *bris* of their son—my first nephew. We couldn't go because of some work obligations I had, but I remember Mary Jo saying she would never attend such a "barbarous" ceremony. Well, maybe we'll have a girl.

THE CHALLENGES FACING THE JEWISH COMMUNITY GROUPS

I have addressed the first two of the three questions posed in this analysis of Jewish life in Alaska frontier communities: "Who are the Jews who move to these communities?" and "Why do they come?" There remains the final question: "What happens to their Jewish identity?"

For Alaskan Jews living in small cities, the primary resource for nurturing Jewish identity, beyond the family, is the Jewish community group. I have identified the vital role played by the convener in contributing to the effectiveness of the community group. In this concluding section I will define the several challenges which face the convener in seeking to give leadership to the community group.

Almost by definition providing leadership to the indigenous Alaskan Jewish community groups is problematic. A significant majority of the people who choose to live in the frontier communities are individualists. They have an inherent antipathy to organizations or to being part of "organized religion"—Jewish or otherwise. They also are suspicious of authority. Conveners, or any leader, are viewed as either—or both—on an ego trip, or seeking to constrict the autonomy of the folk.

How might this analysis of the characteristics of the small Alaskan cities be defined so as to give direction to leaders of these communities? My reflections led to the formulation of two "syndromes." The first I define as "The No-Exit Syndrome," and is attributable to the small number of Jews living in these frontier cities. The second I define as "The End-of-the-Roaders Syndrome," and emerges from the highly individualistic nature of the frontier Jewish settlers.

The No-Exit Syndrome

While the members of the frontier Jewish Community Groups may share similar reasons for choosing to live in the frontier cities, they generally have many different views about the Jewish agenda and practices of the Jewish community group. They also have different ideas about the priority people should be expected to give to the Jewish group. But the most vexing problems arise from tensions in relationships among individuals or subgroups among the members. This is a problem in all groups of people, although it is reasonable to expect that the individualistic nature of Alaskan frontier settlers brings more than the usual distribution of "turbulent" people. These conditions are exacerbated in the frontier cities by virtue of the small numbers of Jews and by the "No-Exit Syndrome." In most Lower 48 synagogues, in the face of serious interpersonal tensions among congregants, or problems with the rabbi, or with ideological differences, the members have two options: leave the synagogue and join another one, or find other disaffected members and form a new synagogue. In the Alaskan frontier communities, given the small numbers, these are not feasible options. There is "no-exit," other than to drop out of the Jewish community.

The End-of-the-Roaders Syndrome

In virtually every one of the community groups I visited I encountered one person, and sometimes more, who carry their individualism to an extreme, and this creates problems for the group. A recent article in the *Wall Street Journal* identified these individuals as "end-of-the-roaders." The author offered this description of the "end-of-the-roaders": "Some of these almost pathologically disruptive individuals are merely oddballs, who adapt or drift away. Others, however, are sociopaths who can't seem to get along anywhere. Drawn by escapist fantasies and frustrated when they find no more road to move down, they are bringing problems, and violence, to Alaska's frontier communities."[13]

Because the "end-of-the-roaders" are usually attracted to the smaller communities their presence in these towns is more pronounced and their impact is more pervasive—in a negative sense. One such person, for whom the designation "end-of-the-roader" applies, is Fred Adler. In the eight years Fred has been in Alaska he has lived in three different small cities. Fred is in his late forties. He grew up in Los Angeles in a household which he described as "intellectually stimulating, Jewishly skeptical, and emotionally not too stable." His father left the family soon after Fred was born and Fred has never met him. Fred attended the University of Oregon during the early 1970s and became active in radical leftist political organizations. He moved to Alaska in 1979 in quest of "a different lifestyle." He has earned a living doing house painting and working as a crew member on fishing boats. Since 1989 Fred has been living with a woman and her young child in one of the small Alaskan towns on the West Coast.

I first met Fred at a meeting of his Jewish community group. An item on the agenda, which was meant to be a brief announcement, proved to be the main piece of business that evening. It was a suggestion by two women in the group for setting up an adult Jewish study program. Everyone reacted favorably to the idea and thanked the women for taking this initiative. Someone suggested putting a story in the local newspaper to bring the program to the attention of other Jewish people in town. People agreed that would be desirable to do. Then Fred stood up and indicated he had something to say. He began by saying he didn't want to comment about the Jewish study program itself, but was strongly opposed to putting a notice in the newspaper. He explained: "There's already too many different groups going their separate ways in this city: Natives, Greeks, Russians, Armenians, Chinese and others, and we Jews shouldn't add to that pattern of divisiveness." He continued to argue against publicizing the program, becoming increasingly agitated as he spoke.

The other people couldn't seem to understand Fred's position, noting that the proposed program was a voluntary one, and if any other ethnic or religious group wanted to develop a similar program to learn more about their background, that would be fine. Fred's opposition and rhetoric escalated but he received no support from anyone else. Finally someone said, "It seems like everyone else thinks the adult Judaica discussion group is a good idea, so why don't we just put it to a vote, since I know we still have three or four important items on our agenda to discuss." Everyone nodded in agreement. Fred then rose. His face was flushed, and as he spoke his voice trembled with anger: "Okay, if you folks want to railroad this idea, which *I strongly* oppose, I want you to know that I and my wife and kids will immediately withdraw from the Jewish community group."

With that announcement, Fred gathered his two daughters, who at the time, were playing with other children in the back of the room, and they walked out of the meeting. There was an extended silence. Finally, someone said: "Hey, if the guy feels that strongly about this matter I'm ready to give up on the Judaica program. We can't let any of our people feel that we would ever make a decision which would go against a person's deep-felt convictions."

No one was prepared to counter that argument. Someone volunteered to call Fred and tell him that the decision was reversed because they wanted to keep him and his family in the Jewish community group. As people began to leave, several of the veterans made a point of telling me privately that this was not the first time that Fred had such a tantrum and, as a result, manipulated the group to come to his preferred decision. They made clear that their patience with Fred and his controlling tactics was running out.

But the reality was that no action was taken to implement the proposed Judaica discussion group. Moreover, several of the veteran settlers left the meeting quite annoyed with the community group. This reaction was typified by the angry comments made to me by the host of the meeting, Harry Fried, after the others left: "I've had it with this group. We never can come to any decision without a big hassle or someone like Fred having a fit. My time is too valuable to come to these community meetings and always have bickering. We never manage to accomplish anything. Next time I'll sit home and watch television."

CONCLUSION

In his keynote address at the July 1996 conference on "Jewries at the Frontier," which was the basis for his introduction to this volume, Sander L. Gilman highlighted the pervasiveness of issues of frontier, boundaries, margins, and of center and periphery, across centuries of history. These issues arise for two reasons: first as a consequence of the constant persecution of Jews throughout their history, and their being forced or choosing to live in different countries. Second, in an ideological sense, originating in the Bible, two places are defined in which Jews might live: the first is in their own land,

Eretz Israel, the Land of Israel, the preferred location and the center. The alternative location is the *Golah* (exile), also referred to as the Diaspora (dispersed). To live outside of Israel connotes both a peripheral geographic status as well as the idea of banishment, by God, for not adhering to the moral standards God defined for His people.

Gilman's core thesis suggests that rather than view the persistent *Golah* Jewish settlements as "marginal" or of lesser importance, that they be recognized as authentic, and indeed as having shaped the essence of the evolving sense of Jewish identity.

Gilman is aware that "terrible things can happen at the frontier—massacres, banishments, rapes, and murders. . . . But it is in this liminal space that all parties are forced to understand and define themselves in the light of their experience of the Other."[14] Here Gilman refers both to Jews' self-perceptions as well as to the perceptions of Jews by non-Jews. It is at the margins of countless countries that Jews have interacted and benefited from the exchange with many different cultures. In these recurring encounters and conflicts, Jews have sharpened their capacity to accommodate and to clarify the ways in which they are different (distinctive) from non-Jews.[15] And, in a larger sense, the culture of the Jewish people has been shaped.

Viewed from this historic perspective, the small frontier Jewish community of Alaska might be more Jewishly prototypical than marginal or exotic. Also, this perspective helps explain the unanticipated high levels of Jewish behaviors and positive Jewish attitudes which characterized the research findings of Alaskan Jews. Just as countless generations of their ancestors adapted to ever-changing Jewish frontiers, these modern nomadic Jews, who voluntarily chose to settle in "the last frontier," also seem to have adapted very well. Their Jewishness has taken on a higher salience for them than it had in their more mainstream mode of life in the Lower 48.

Perhaps, over the course of their history, Jews have evolved both an attraction and a special aptitude to function in challenging environments, such as the frontier. This finding is of particular relevance to the earlier discussion of the new demographic trend of American Jews to leave traditional urban centers and to settle in small, rural areas. The typical response of leaders of the American Jewish community to this development has been to assume that such a move is both an expression of assimilation and a portent of further assimilation.

An alternative interpretation is to view the new settlements in the small rural communities and places like Alaska, as the latest frontier in the historic saga of "Jews on the move." From that perspective the expectation is that these settlements will enrich and energize Jews about to enter the twenty-first century in the same spirit as the *goldene medinah* (golden country)—America—accomplished this objective for their great grandparents a century ago.

Notes

1. J.Gregory Williams, *Alaska Population Overview, 1995 Estimates,* ed. Diana Kelm (Juneau: Alaska Department of Labor, July 1996), 64.

2. Ibid.

3. Sidney Goldstein and Alice Goldstein, *Jews on the Move: Implications for Jewish Identity* (Albany: SUNY Press, 1996), 49.

4. Ibid., 57.

5. Ibid.

6. Ibid., 38, 39.

7. Bernard Reisman and Joel I. Reisman, *Life on the Frontier: The Jews of Alaska* (Waltham, Mass.: Brandeis University, Cohen Center for Modern Jewish Studies, 1995), 49.

8. *Reinventing Our Jewish Community: Can the West Be Won?—A Report to the Jewish Communities of the Western United States and the Council of Jewish Federations* (New York: Council of Jewish Federations, 1994), 19.

9. Goldstein and Goldstein, *Jews on the Move,* 139.

10. Reisman and Reisman, *Life on the Frontier,* 40.

11. Ibid., 43.

12. Ibid., 28–30.

13. Bill Richards, "Where Roads End: Dreams of the Frontier Lure Misfits to Alaska, Then Reality Breaks In," *Wall Street Journal,* Aug. 31, 1994.

14. Sander L. Gilman, introduction to this volume.

15. Ibid.

PART 2 Identity

5 From One Frontier to Another: Jewish Identity and Political Orientation in Lithuania and South Africa, 1890–1939

GIDEON SHIMONI

The foundations of South African Jewry's communal institutions were laid by Jews who had come with the emigrant waves from England in the first quarter of the nineteenth century and established the first congregation in Cape Town in 1841. Most of these Jewish joiners into the advancing "frontier" society of southern Africa were either born in Britain, or they were born in Central Europe or Czarist Russia but had lived in Britain for some period before coming to South Africa. By 1880 they numbered an estimated 4,000, and may have reached as many as 10,000 out of the estimated 24,000 Jews in South Africa on the eve of the Anglo-Boer War of 1899–1901.[1] However, by that time there already were a large number of immigrants from Czarist Russia—an estimated 14,000 by 1899. When the first census of the Union of South Africa was held in 1911 it showed 46,926 Jews in South Africa, representing 3.7 percent of the white population. In 1936 (the census data closest to our present survey's closing date of 1939) there were 90,645 Jews representing 4.5 percent of the total white population. It may be roughly estimated that in the period 1912 to 1936 some 23,685 East European immigrants came to South Africa, primarily from the Lithuanian region (and after 1918 the Lithuanian state).[2]

The remarkable salience of "Litvaken" (Yiddish for Lithuanians) among these immigrants led the Zionist leader Nahum Sokolow (who visited South Africa in 1934, during his tenure as president) to call the Jewish community in South Africa "a colony of Lithuanian Jewry." The description "Litvak" is to be understood in a far broader sense than coextensiveness with the East European state known as Lithuania. Its connotation in Yiddish speech, folklore and literature, was of any Jew who stemmed from somewhere within the pre–World War I boundaries of the northwestern Czarist Russian provinces of Kovno, Vilna, Grodno, and northern Suwalki, whose ethnic composition was mainly Lithuanian and Polish, and of Vitebsk, Minsk and Mogilev, which were mainly Byelorussian and Russian in character. This was what might be called "historic Lithuania."

Elsewhere I have marshaled the available evidence for the view that the overwhelming majority of the immigrants from Eastern Europe to South Africa were indeed Litvaks in the aforementioned sense, but not without adding the caveat that the nature of this evidence is not definitive.[3] It is further noteworthy—and for the purposes of the present essay, even more significant—that a high proportion of the immigrants came from the Kovno province, towns such as Kovno, Ponevez, Riteva, Plungian, Yanoshek and Shavli featuring prominently. It is estimated from Czarist Russian statistics that some 33,800 emigrated from the Kovno province from 1896 to 1914. A considerable proportion of this number came to South Africa.[4] The independent state of Lithuania, which came into existence in 1919 and endured until 1939 when it was reincorporated into the Russian imperial ambit in the form of the Soviet Union, was but a truncated version of the territory avidly claimed by Lithuanian nationalists, especially since Vilna and its environs were lost to the Poles in 1920. Vilna was regarded by the Lithuanians as their national capital. By default Kovno became the Lithuanian capital. However, from the vantage point of the present inquiry, Kovno province being the predominant source of the migration flow to South Africa, there was considerable continuity between the Czarist Russian period and the period of Lithuanian independence. Indeed even the disparity in numbers between, as it were, the mother and daughter communities was not enormous. At most, the mother community was not much more than twice the size of the daughter. The 1923 Lithuanian census recorded 157,527 Jews (by religion) constituting 7.26 percent of the total population. By comparison, South African Jewry in 1926 numbered 71,816, constituting 4.3 percent of the white population.

JEWISH IDENTITY

Prior to 1919, these Jewish immigrants to South Africa from the "Lithuanian" provinces of the Russian Pale of Settlement were not coming from an established society in the national sense, since the Lithuanian national group did not enjoy independence. Nor were they coming from a well-developed and modernized economy; the Lithuanian provinces were among the least developed in the Russian Empire. Most of the Jews of the Lithuanian region of the Pale lived in the towns and *shtetlakh* (villages) and more than 80 percent were small merchants, artisans and salaried workers; only about 6 percent owned businesses of considerable size or were professionals.[5]

Hence, for these immigrants the contrast with South Africa as a "frontier" society was not as significant as it might have been for immigrants from more industrially and commercially developed countries, such as Britain or Germany. It could be argued that once Lithuania gained its independence, it assumed the character of a new society; in a sense it was also a frontier society from the national and economic points of view. That is to say, in new old-world Lithuania not much less than in new-world South Africa, the Jews were in some respects cofounders. Indeed, at the inception of the independent Lithuanian state the Jews were co-opted as political allies by the Lithuanian nationalists. Particularly important for the Lithuanian nationalists' struggle to retain Vilna was the fact that no more than 3 percent of Vilna's population was ethnically Lithuanian. Most were Poles and Jews, the latter numbering 60,000.[6] These considerations mitigate the significance of the frontier as *the* differentiating factor in comprehending South African Jewry's development. It is arguable that for the Jewish emigrant from Lithuania, by contrast with his emigrant counterpart from the already highly developed economy of Britain, the frontier situation of South Africa was not crucial as a formative factor. By and large, upon arrival he sought his livelihood in occupations similar to those he had known in Lithuania. He found work as an artisan—many claimed to be tailors or carpenters—became a peddler in Cape town or a "smous" peddling into the far-flung countryside, or a shop-keeper-merchant, or an employee in or owner of a "kafereeta" eating house for African mine workers on the gold reef of Johannesburg.[7] The main difference was that in the developing South African economy the immigrant Jew's upward economic mobility and passage to prosperity proved to be incomparably speedier and more complete than in Lithuania.

Far more significant than the frontier as a formative factor was the plural societal environment in which the Jewish immigrants found themselves in South Africa. But this environment too had something significant in common with that of the Lithuanian region of the Czarist Empire—both were ethnically heterogeneous. In the region whose Jews were called Litvaks, that is the whole northwestern area of the Pale, there were about 15 million inhabitants, of which 30 percent (4,500,000) were ethnically Lithuanian, and another 30 percent (4,500,000) were Byelorussians. The Jews were the third largest ethnic group, constituting 15 percent and numbering 2,500,000. Poles were 10 percent (1,500,000) and various others such as Germans and

Latvians made up the remaining 15 percent (2,250,000).[8] Furthermore, even though the truncated area of independent Lithuania had a clearer Lithuanian ethnic majority—83.9 percent according to the Lithuanian census of 1923[9]—also there the societal reality remained fundamentally pluralist, much like South African society.

The foregoing comparative observation is predicated on a serviceable distinction that may be made between two models of societal pluralism forming opposite theoretical poles of a continuum in which one may locate a variety of heterogeneous societies. One model is laissez faire in the sense that the state adopts a neutral attitude to ethnic supplementation, given an overarching linguistic and cultural uniformity. It therefore allows for a degree of ethnic cultural supplementation on a voluntary basis, that is to say, not supported by the state. Within this conceptual continuum, pluralism as understood in the United States approximates to the ideal laissez faire model. The opposite pole of the continuum might be labeled "mandatory pluralism," sometimes termed in the sociological literature "institutional pluralism."[10] It is characterized by parallel institutionalization of ethnic groups within the same political and economic system. This segmentation may be sustained by inveterate social norms but is at its most rigid if enforced by legal sanctions, as was the case in South Africa under apartheid. Both the Lithuanian region of Czarist Russia and the independent State of Lithuania were characterized by a societal structure that falls close to the "mandatory" pole of the continuum. To be more specific, in Lithuania the average Jew could and did live his entire life from birth to burial within the linguistic, social and educational environment of the Jewish ethnic group, not to speak of the distinctive religion to which he belonged. Indeed, in independent Lithuania this linguistic and institutional segmentation was perpetuated by dint of firmly established norms.

By comparison, South African society as a whole was, of course, far more rigidly segmented than Lithuanian society, the boundaries being defined in terms of race and color. It was, however, a compound segmented pluralism: its primary segmentation was into racially defined castes, one of which—the whites—was in all respects dominant, but all of which possessed parallel, if unequal, sets of social and cultural institutions. Its secondary segmentation divided even the dominant caste into Afrikaners and English-speakers by compelling further institutional duplication in certain cultural spheres, particularly language and education. Since the Jewish immigrant had entrée into the dominant white segment, by virtue of his skin color, it was the looser cultural dualism of the whites rather than the overall rigid, caste-like pluralism of the entire society, that determined the situation of the Jews.

Before World War I, in the Lithuanian region of the Pale of Settlement, the indigenous Lithuanian population, although demographically a majority, was predominantly of the peasant class. Not only was it subject to absolutist Czarist rule from St. Petersburg, but locally it was subordinate as well to a mainly Polish landowning gentry. Indeed, even the Catholic Church, to which most Lithuanians adhered, had a largely Polish clergy. Although even this economically backward region of Russia underwent some modernization in the course of the nineteenth century, the attendant acculturation of the Jewish population was relatively tardy and tended, if anything, toward the Russian language and cultural institutions (or, toward German in the area of Memel on the Baltic coast). Hence the Jews constituted a very distinct ethnic segment of society. Indeed, given the circumstances of Lithuania's newly-gained independence in 1919 and, in particular, its official commitment to sanction cultural-linguistic rights for its minorities, the Jews may be said to have constituted a national entity in interwar Lithuania.[11] According to the 1923 census, out of a total population of 2,028,971, the Lithuanians, numbering 1,701,863, constituted 83.9 percent. But the Jews were the next largest national group, numbering 153,743 or 7.6 percent. They were followed by the Poles, 3.2 percent; the Russians, 2.5 percent; Germans, 1.4 percent; and Latvians, Byelorussians and others each less than 1 percent.[12] More significant, within the Kovno province in 1909, the urban Jewish population constituted 49.9 percent of the total compared to Lithuanians with 20.6 percent, Russians with 17.7 percent, Poles with 8.3 percent, and Germans, Latvians and others with 3.5 percent. But in the villages the percentages were Jews, 2.5, to Lithuanians, 74.9. In 1933 the Kovno province had 20.4 percent of all Lithuania's Jews and the Jews numbered 31,428 out of 191,864 (16.4 percent of the total population).[13]

The essentially national identity of Lithuanian Jewry is best exemplified by a description of Jewish schooling. Although the foundations were laid in the first five years of Lithuania's independence, when the prospect of Jewish autonomy was most promising, the reality of educational autonomy survived the disappointment that ensued as the Lithuanian authorities first prevaricated and then reneged on the promise after the collapse of parliamentary democracy in 1926. By 1925, the Jewish elementary schools encompassed some 93 percent of Jewish children and the Jewish secondary schools 80 percent.[14] Although in the mid-1930s the percentage of Jewish children attending Lithuanian schools was on the rise, the Jewish schools still encompassed by far the majority: in 1935–36 they still accounted for 80.6 percent at elementary schools.[15] In the twenty-year interwar period as a whole it is estimated that no less than 60,000 received their education in the Jewish schools, some 6,000 of them graduating from the Jewish secondary schools (gymnasiums). Until the end, the Lithuanian government, although increasing its control, reducing its support, and demanding more use of the Lithuanian language, did not entirely withdraw state funding of the elementary schools, and also the secondary schools received partial support.

The Jewish schools were of three main types: secular-Hebrew, orthodox-religious, and secular-Yiddish. The first type was the creation of the Zionists and constituted the Tarbut network. Modern Hebrew with the Sefardi accent current in Palestine was the language of tuition. Already in 1920–21 it accounted for 32.3 percent of all pupils and for as much as 70 percent by the mid-1930s.[16] It spanned kindergarten to gymnasium, encompassing, in 1930–31, 15,446 pupils (10,941 of which were in elementary schools) and 543 teachers in 122 institutions of schooling. It also maintained a teacher-training seminary of its own. The orthodox-religious schools were called "Yavneh" and came to be sponsored by the Ahdes (Agudat Israel) as well as partly by the Mizrahi (orthodox Zionists). They too taught Hebrew, although in the old Ashkenazi accent. In 1920–21 they had 2,362 pupils in thirty schools. By 1928, one-third of all schools were affiliated with Yavneh.

The secular-Yiddish network underwent several transformations in consequence of the authorities' repression of Communist influences, which were indeed prevalent in these schools. Yiddish was the language of tuition and the Yiddishist orientation included that of the socialist workers Bund, the Left-Poalei Zion wing of socialist Zionists, as well as the liberal democratic Folksparty. The latter became the dominant influence in the network especially in its two gymnasium schools, one in Wilkomir (founded in 1920) and the other in Kovno (founded in 1926). The Yiddish schools never exceeded 15–20 percent. In 1920–21 there were 1,754 pupils in sixteen schools. In addition to these three main types there were "Pshore Shulen" (Compromise Schools) which had 2,850 pupils in sixty-eight schools in 1920–21. They taught in Hebrew but combined a degree of orthodox traditionalism with a generally Zionist orientation. In sum the Jewish schooling system was the most profound and enduring expression of Jewish identity as a national-cultural minority of predominantly Zionist orientation.

Passing to a comparison with South African Jewry, the field of education provides a major contrast between the development of the two communities. In South Africa, as in Britain and the United States, the thrust of Jewish immigrant aspirations for their children was toward linguistic acculturation. In the period prior to the Anglo-Boer War of 1899–1901, because the Boer Republic did not provide schooling for non-Protestants, the Jews there had no choice but to provide their own elementary schooling or send their children to private Catholic schools. But from the outset of British control over all of South Africa the Litvak immigrants sought fully to integrate their children into the English-medium state schools and settled for merely supplemental tuition in *heder* and Talmud Torah afternoon schools.[17] Neither the orthodox rabbis and synagogue organizations nor the powerful Zionist Federation created Jewish day schools, although, to be sure, the idea was repeatedly debated at conferences of the South African Zionist Federation in 1916 and 1919, and again in 1928, when at last a Jewish Board of Education was formed. Yet it was only after World War II that the Jewish Boards of Education in the Transvaal and Natal and in the Cape Province began to create the network of elementary and secondary Jewish day schools that eventually came to encompass some 70 percent of the age groups from nursery to secondary school by the 1990s. Their funding had to be from voluntary communal sources and parents' fees, although some state support was eventually obtained. However, unlike the Hebrew or Yiddish language schools of Lithuanian Jewry, even these schools were, and remain to this day, essentially English-language frameworks that provide only supplementary teaching of the Hebrew language and rudimentary aspects of Judaistic learning.

The ideological formula underlying this voluntary network of Jewish education was "broadly national-traditional." This formula was a compromise between the secular Zionists and the Mizrahi rabbis, the "national" aspect implying an essentially Zionist orientation, while the "traditional" implied no more than that the prevailing atmosphere and conduct of the school's activities must be consonant with orthodox religious norms. Notwithstanding the vast difference between the development of Jewish education in South Africa as compared with Lithuania, in the comparative perspective of Jewish educational models in other countries of the New World, especially Britain and the United States, it is clear that the South African model had a relatively more national orientation. In this sense, the Litvak influence, however vitiated, is still identifiable.

Another sphere of identifiable but much attenuated Litvak legacy is that of South African Jewry's religious life.[18] The historical record shows a tremendous lapse from religious observance by the immigrants. Although orthodoxy in the *misnagdi,* or non-hasidic, mode was the sole form of Judaism until as late as 1933 when the first Reform congregation was formed by Rabbi Cyrus Weiler, and remained preeminent even thereafter, the mode of observance that characterized its adherents has aptly been described as "non-observant orthodox." The determinate factors in this development were, on the one hand, the exigencies of making a living in a socioeconomic environment that made sabbath observance difficult, and on the other hand, the preexisting foundations of a Jewish clergy trained in the mold of Anglo-Jewry's British-acculturated United Synagogue. To be sure, some of the Litvak immigrants found this mode of synagogue decorum objectionable and balked at the style of English-medium "Reverends," the likes of Alfred Bender, in Cape Town. There were intracongregational tensions on this score resulting in splits and the formation of independent congregations more compatible with Litvak modes of religious conduct. Yet, by the 1920s these differences had subsided and, particularly under the tenure of Juda Leo Landau as Chief Rabbi of the United Hebrew Congregations and, after 1933, of the Federation of Synagogues, a uniform mode of moderate, acculturated orthodoxy became normative throughout the Jewish community.[19] It was, however, an orthodoxy closely aligned with Zionism. From the outset, the various reverends of Anglo-Jewish training identified with Zionism, the only important exception being Alfred Bender in Cape Town, who evinced a negative attitude paralleling that of Chief Rabbi Adler of the United Synagogue in London. However, even he came around to support Zionism after the issue of the Balfour Declaration in 1917. A considerable number of rabbis became associated with the religious Zionist party Mizrahi founded in 1919, and it was they who exerted a considerable influence on the "national-religious" formula for Jewish education.

Overall, the determinate factor in reinforcing the ethnic-national character of the Litvak majority of South African Jewry, as well as inclining the Anglo-Jewish element toward Zionism, was the dual segmentation of the white societal environment. The Afrikaner segment harbored an organic nationalist sentiment, closely linked to their Calvinist, Dutch Reformed churches. While Afrikaners appreciated it, if and when Jews adopted the Afrikaans language (as only a minority in fact did), no Jew could become an Afrikaner in the full national sense, any more than a Hebrew-speaking Christian could be recognized as a Jew. The predominantly urban, English-speaking segment, on the other hand, was far less cohesive and its identity was relatively amorphous. It soon became the predominant reference group for acculturation of the Litvak Jews, who gradually moved out of occupations involving close contact with rural Afrikaners. Already by 1911 the Union of South Africa's census showed an urban Jewish population of 42,487 as compared with only 4,280 in the rural areas.[20] Yet, although the English-speaking segment certainly exerted an assimilatory attraction for Jews, it had nothing like the valence of the uniform English culture of Britain. South African society left considerable leeway for preservation of a distinctive Jewish ethnic identity. Moreover, there is abundant evidence that right across the spectrum of Afrikaner political leadership—from Smuts, who followed a policy of conciliation between Afrikaners and British, to Afrikaner nationalists such as J. B. M. Hertzog and Daniel Malan—there was recognition of the legitimacy of Zionism as a natural expression of that distinctive Jewish identity. Indeed, in Smuts's case—and he was a preeminent political figure in the period under discussion—there was positive encouragement of and support for Zionism.[21]

POLITICAL ORIENTATIONS

The Lithuanian region of the Russian Empire, and particularly the important city of Vilna with its large Jewish population—about 60,000 on the eve of World War II—produced major pioneers of the various modern political movements that burgeoned in late nineteenth-century Russian Jewry. The founder of the first sectional Jewish socialist group, Aharon Lieberman, was a product of Vilna, although his group was formed in London. Vilna was the birthplace and cradle of both the socialist workers' organization, the Bund (Algemeyner Arbeter Bund in Polen, Rusland un Lita), founded in 1897, and of the Eretz-Israel (Palestine)-oriented Hibbat Zion movement that anteceded Theodor Herzl's Zionist Organization, also founded in 1897. Well before World War I the Bund had undergone a change in its position on the national question. Although it started out with an "internationalist" outlook modified only by the tactical and practical need to function sectionally among Jewish workers, many of whom knew only the Yiddish language, the Bund had incrementally adopted the demand for Jewish cultural autonomy along the lines first formulated by Austro-Marxists such as Karl Renner and Otto Bauer on the one hand, and the liberal historian of the Jews, Simon Dubnow, on the other hand.

However, as I have noted, the Jews who migrated to South Africa were mostly from the small towns of the Kovno heartland of Lithuania, rather than from Vilna. On the whole, their upbringing had been traditionalist-religious. However, In contrast to the hasidism prevalent in the Polish provinces further to the south of the Pale, which vigilantly resisted all *haskalah* (Enlightenment) influences, Lithuanian Jews were predominantly of the relatively more broad-minded *misnagdi* type. Whatever exposure to modernity they experienced was mediated by the Hebrew *haskalah* influences that had penetrated even the student body of great Lithuanian yeshivas, such as that of Volozhin and Ponevez. Thus, in the midst of the mass of still traditionally raised Litvak immigrants to South Africa in the period 1880–1910 one finds a number of typical *maskil* types to whose reports and articles in the maskilic Hebrew press, notably *Ha-tzefira* (published in St. Petersburg) and *Ha-melitz* (published in Warsaw), we owe much of our historiographical knowledge about the early years of the Jewish community in South Africa. The foremost of these writers was N. D. Hoffman (1860–1928), who stemmed from Neustadt-Sugind in the eastern Kovno province and wrote a series of articles, commencing in 1890, that appeared in *Ha-tzefira*. Another was M. D. Hersch (1858–1933), who wrote eight articles in 1892–93 that were published in *Ha-tzefira* in 1895, and another eleven articles published in 1895–96. As I shall show, it is also evident from the historical record that the stream of Litvak emigrants to South Africa from 1880 to 1910, although mostly of traditionalist background and with limited secular education and political awareness, was not devoid of individuals who had already been exposed to the various political ideologies that had gained followings in late nineteenth-century Russia. The range included the Eretz-Israel-oriented Jewish nationalism of Hibbat Zion, Dubnowian diasporic nationalism, sectionalist Jewish socialism of the Bund, and internationalist social-democracy.

By 1919, when independent Lithuania was established, political awareness had grown considerably, especially in the wake of the world-shaking Russian Revolution, on the one hand, and the spurt of Zionism stimulated by the Balfour Declaration, on the other. The state of Lithuania was a much truncated version of the traditional Lithuanian territorial homeland. Within its precarious first two years of independence, the city of Vilna and its environs changed hands, from the Poles to the Soviet Russians and to the Lithuanians and again to the Poles who annexed it, to the smoldering chagrin of the Lithuanian nationalists.[22] Concomitantly, the Jews living in independent Lithuania were but a small part of Litvak Jewry as a whole. Vilna had been the cultural and intellectual heart of Litvak Jewry. Its detachment also had important consequences for the political orientations of Litvak Jewry, most notably the weakening of the socialist Bund. Never a major force in the Kovno province, the Bund was reduced to relative insignificance in interwar Lithuania, which was undeveloped industrially, and whose governments tried to suppress its activities together with those of the Communists. This contrasted greatly with the Bund's prominence in the political life of neighboring Poland's Jewry, which included significant numbers of proletarians in industrial centers such as Bialystock, Lodz and Warsaw. But in Lithuania as in Poland, the Communists and their various front organizations continued to attract a small but extraordinarily disproportionate number of Jews.[23] As we shall see, there was some apparent "transfer" of this involvement to South Africa, since the Bund had no more than an ephemeral existence there, whereas Communism did attract a disproportionate number of Jewish adherents from the Litvak immigrant generation and its South African-born offspring.

With a broad sweep of the brush, one may depict the political spectrum of interwar Lithuanian Jewry thus: the major political orientation was toward Jewish nationalism aspiring to autonomy. This meant that Jews, by and large, were not participants in the political parties of the Lithuanian ethnic majority. They functioned politically as an ethnic-national segment of the Lithuanian state. As such they were at first wooed as allies for Lithuanian nationalist aspirations, particularly in regard to the demand that Vilna be incorporated into the independent Lithuanian state as its capital city. But within less than a decade, the attitude of the Lithuanian nationalists changed; they reneged on their promise of autonomy and followed a "Lithuania for the Lithuanians" policy. Only the Jewish Communists—a tiny minority among the Jews—were averse to the demand for national autonomy. As advocated mainly by the Folksparty, such national autonomy was to be actualized within the Lithuanian state and expressed through the Yiddish language. As envisioned by the mainstream Zionists, particularly the General Zionists and the Tzeirei Zion-Zionist Socialists, the ultimate goal was a Jewish state in Palestine as the national home for all Jews, but this did not preclude the enjoyment of cultural autonomy, emphasizing the Hebrew language, also in the Lithuanian state. Indeed, the demand for local autonomy was part and parcel of their Zionist program. Only the He-halutz Organization and the youth movements, such as Ha-shomer ha-tzair and Gordonia, whose aspirations focused on settling in Palestine, tended to turn their backs on the *Gegenwartsarbeit* (the term used to describe local Zionist work) implicit in the demand for autonomy.

For the Bundists, who were not a major force in independent Lithuania, national revival in Palestine was extremely objectionable and advocacy of Yiddish-language autonomy took second place to the revolutionary struggle of the working class. This revolutionary socialist outlook, and preference for Yiddish, was shared by the Left-Poalei Zion, but the socialist development of a Jewish working class in Palestine remained a positive part of their ultimate goal. Also a formidable force were the non-Zionist liberal nationalists who advocated an ideology of Diaspora cultural autonomy, already formulated in the period of Czarist rule by the Jewish historian Simon Dubnow. They were known as the Folksparty.

For the majority of orthodox Jews of the Agudat Israel party, which went under the name "Ahdes" in Lithuania and was headed by rabbinical luminaries, the Zionist project in Palestine was a gravely objectionable travesty of the messianic role of the Holy Land, but this did not preclude settlement of religious Jews there. Ahdes came a strong second in the political race throughout much of the interwar years. However, a significant minority of orthodox Jews, the members of Mizrahi, rejected this outlook and adopted the Zionist position, while striving to influence the Zionist project in Palestine in accord with orthodox religious principles.

Focusing more specifically on the Zionists, we should note that in the first decade or so of the interwar period the General Zionists were preeminent and provided most of Lithuanian Jewry's political leadership in the institutions of autonomy. But in the 1930s the Labor Zionists became the major force, while Revisionist Zionism led by Vladimir Jabotinsky also was on the ascendant, its youth movement, Betar, becoming second in size to the leading movement Hashomer ha-tzair. Mainstream Labor Zionism developed out of the Tzeirei Zion that was associated with the world movement known as the Hitahdut, which was Labor Zionist, but not explicitly socialist. In the post-Russian Revolution period of ideological effervescence that characterized all labor movements, divisiveness developed within the party—known since 1921 as Tzeirei Zion-Socialist Zionists—between those who identified with the explicitly socialist World Confederation of Poalei Zion, and others who clung to the Hitahdut affiliation. By the time the Sixteenth Zionist Congress met in 1929, two separate Labor parties from Lithuania gained representation. But in the 1930s, after the fusion of the two world unions, Hitahdut and Brit Poalei Zion, first in Palestine and then worldwide, Lithuanian reunification adopted the name The United Zionist Socialist Party (Mifleget ZS hameuhedet). It became paramount in Lithuanian Zionism. Thus in the elections to the 1933 Congress this party gained seven mandates out of the total of eleven sent from Lithuania.[24]

At the Paris Peace Conference of 1919, Lithuania, along with Poland and other new states in Eastern Europe, undertook to grant extensive minority rights. For the Jews, in addition to full civic rights this included the right to Jewish national representation in the legislature, a special minister for Jewish affairs in the government, the use of Jewish languages in governmental and judicial institutions, organs of Jewish autonomy based on the local communities (*kehiles*) as units, binding on all Jews and with power to levy taxes, and state support for Jewish schools on equal terms with other schools.[25]

Within the incipient framework of cultural autonomy, the political life of Lithuanian Jewry was conducted on two interrelated levels—the internal communal level and the Lithuanian state level. On the first level, in January 1920 an all-Lithuanian Jewish conference was convened in Kovno. Eighty-two different *kehiles* were represented by 141 delegates. The Zionist parties—

General Zionists, Tzeirei Zion, and Mizrahi—were the dominant group with sixty-one delegates. (The extreme left, whether Communists or Left-Poalei Zion, boycotted the conference). The second strongest group was the anti-Zionist Ahdes with fifty-four delegates, and the clash between orthodoxy and secular nationalism was the dominant issue under debate owing to the Ahdes demand that the *kehile* be defined as a religious institution and that Jewish schools under the auspices of the Jewish autonomous framework be religious in character.[26] Notwithstanding this dissension, the Lithuanian Jews, in contrast to Polish Jewry, which was also engaged in a struggle to attain autonomy, succeeded in establishing a united National Council, the Natzional Rath. The president was a Zionist and the vice president a member of Ahdes.

In January 1920 the Lithuanian government enacted a provisional law that empowered the *kehiles* to function and tax their members, and in April 1921 it established the promised Ministry for Jewish Affairs. However, all of this was still far from formal and final institutionalization of Jewish autonomy. The struggle to attain institutionalized autonomy continued to dominate Jewish public concerns. It was hampered by internal conflict between the non-Zionist orthodox camp and the secular camp (both nationalist and non-nationalist) and frustrated by the successive Lithuanian governments' prevarications and vacillations with respect to the final legalization of genuine autonomy. The internal schism between the orthodox and the secularists centered on the question whether the *kehile* units were to be essentially religious in nature or secular-national. The external frustration of Jewish aspirations for autonomy was spearheaded by the clerical-nationalists of the Lithuanian Christian Democratic Party. An important aspect of this frustration was the Ministry of Education's retention of ultimate control over Jewish schools rather than their being wholly within the jurisdiction of the organs of Jewish autonomy, as wished by the Jews. The forces resistant to the implementation of real autonomy won out by September 1924 when the minister of the interior dissolved the Jewish Natzional Rath.

The Lithuanian Jewish parties were able to establish a single Jewish list in the elections to the first Lithuanian parliament. It consisted of two representatives each of the Zionists, the Folksparty and the Ahdes.[27] However, the intensified internal dissonance frustrated attempts to form a second unified Jewish list for the elections to parliament in 1922 and in 1923. Three separate lists—Zionist, Folksparty and Ahdes—competed for the Jewish vote. In late 1923 a United Jewish list was formed for national elections and joined forces in an electoral bloc with the German, Polish and Russian minorities. Fourteen delegates were elected, half of whom represented the Jewish minority. The last properly democratic elections to be held in Lithuania were those of

1926. They were marked by acrimonious conflict between the Ahdes party (which appeared as the "Jewish Economic-Religious List") and the nationalist Zionists and Folksparty, who received three mandates to the Ahdes' one. But Lithuanian democracy had reached its end; shortly after the elections a right-wing coup took place and established an authoritarian regime.[28]

Turning now to a comparison with the pattern of political orientation in South African Jewry, it must be noted that in the period before the First World War, immigrant Jews from Russia were on the whole far too alien and preoccupied with their own "greener" troubles to become involved in the political and social issues of their new environment. It is evident that as they acculturated to the white society, Jews internalized the racial prejudices current among the privileged whites. It is likely that the feeling of superiority, at times even of contempt, which characterized the Litvak Jews' view of the Lithuanian peasants facilitated the adoption of similar attitudes toward the equivalent farm laborers and urban workers of black and colored pigmentation whom the immigrant now encountered in South Africa.[29] There is no indication that the average Yiddish-speaking immigrant drew a parallel between the treatment of Africans or Indians on the one hand, and the discriminations from which Jews suffered in the Russian Pale of Settlement on the other, although some cases were in fact quite similar. Like other whites, Jews quickly got used to regarding Africans as inferiors, fit only to be workers and servants. In the words of Leibl Feldman, who was speaking from his observations as a part of this generation of Litvak immigrants: "Immediately upon their arrival . . . they were, thanks to their white skins, taken into the ruling section of the population. . . . In their behavior towards the Africans they conducted themselves in accordance with their surroundings. . . . One accepted the privileges 'with both hands' and one allowed oneself to be served by the Africans just as all other whites did."[30]

Yet, even before the First World War it is evident that some individual immigrants began to apply radical leftist outlooks brought with them from the Russian Empire. The outstanding example was a man named Yeshaya Israelstam. Born in Waksne, Lithuania in 1870, he had first wandered to the United States at the age of sixteen. In 1900, he came to South Africa. The interim of fourteen years outside of Eastern Europe makes it difficult to determine whether the radical socialist ideas that he evinced were imbibed directly from the Eastern European background or indirectly through his exposure to radical elements in the well-formed Jewish labor movement in the United States. Be that as it may, one finds Israelstam involved in a group styling itself "The Friends of Russian Freedom" which came into existence to support the Bund's self-defense activities in the wake of the 1905 pogroms in Russia. He also attempted to form a Social Democratic Workers' Party along the lines of De Leon's party of the same name in the United States.[31]

Another example of exceptional Jewish involvement in opposition to the norms and laws of racial discrimination that underpinned absolute white supremacy was the close association of a number of Jews with Mohandas Gandhi's Satyagraha struggle on behalf of the Indians in South Africa between 1903 and 1914. The closest of Gandhi's white friends and associates were in fact Jews, notably Henry Polak, from England, and Hermann Kallenbach, who was a Litvak by birth but had studied in Germany.[32]

Throughout the period surveyed in this essay there was a continuous ideological presence, through various organizational transformations, of Yiddish-speaking leftist groups. The first of these was the already mentioned Society of Friends of Russian Liberty. Set up to aid the self-defense organization of the Bund in Russia, it took on the character of a fraternal organization oriented politically toward the Bund. It clashed with a rival self-defense club formed by a group of Zionists in support of Zionist self-defense activities in Russia. In 1907 there was a resurgence of support for the Bund when it invited Sergius Riger, a prominent leader of the Bund, to speak in South Africa.[33] However, after World War I there is no record of any significant presence of a Bund group in South Africa.

More significant was the Yiddish-Speaking Group which affiliated to the International Socialist League, forerunner of the South African Communist Party. Founded in Johannesburg in February 1917, it appears to have commanded a following of a few hundred.[34] Its militant challenge to Zionism met a response within the same universe of discourse put up by another group formed in about 1919—Poalei Zion. This group adopted the ideological orientation of Left Poalei-Zion rather than that of Tzeirei Zion, which, as I noted earlier, was the mainstream party of Labor Zionism in Lithuania. Thus the members of Poalei Zion favored Yiddish over Hebrew. According to Leibl Feldman, who was a member of this Poalei Zion group, it succeeded in gaining the defection of a number of the Yiddish-Speaking Group's members, while others had to be expelled for evincing sympathy with Zionist "chauvinism."[35] Be that as it may, the Yiddish-Speaking Group disintegrated in 1921, its members being absorbed into the Communist Party of South Africa. As for the Poalei Zion group, seeking a Zionist-leftist synthesis, it occupied a position on the Jewish political spectrum somewhere between the small minority of Yiddish-speaking, leftist radicals and the majority of bourgeois-aspiring Zionist immigrants. Yet even Poalei Zion remained well off the mainstream of Zionist sentiment. Consequently, it too faded out of existence within a few years.

More durable was the Yiddisher Arbeter Club (Jewish Workers' Club) founded in 1929.[36] Its members condemned the "pernicious" grip in which they said Zionism held South African Jews and described Zionism as a shameful form of bourgeois chauvinism and danger to the working-class Jew. Its organ, *Die Proletarishe Shtimme,* accused the Zionists of unrealistic utopianism, sought to expose "the great Zionist bluff" and considered the Arabs innocent victims of Zionism.[37] Small but persevering, the Arbeter Club remained an uncompromising opponent of Zionism until as late as 1948, when it quite suddenly collapsed. Its demise is explicable in terms of the accelerated upward occupational mobility of the Jewish population, particularly during World War II, which ran counter to its working-class sentiments and ideology. By 1948, many of its own members were already well-to-do employers of labor. Moreover, it lacked a following in the next generation, even some of the most ardent members of the Club finding that their children were caught up in the great upsurge of Zionist youth movements which took place after 1945, especially in Ha-shomer ha-tzair and Habonim.

Of a broader nature but also catering to the anti-Zionism of Yiddish-speaking leftists, were the cultural literary organizations that emerged in South Africa. The first was the Yiddisher Literarisher Farein founded in October 1912 in Johannesburg. Its aim was to foster Yiddish cultural life through discussions, plays, a Yiddish library, and so on. During 1916 it produced a printed literary journal, *Dos Neie Wort.* The Farein's subscribing membership reached about 250, but the circle of Jews who participated in it was much wider, reaching a peak in 1922 when packed halls throughout the country welcomed Peretz Hirschbein, the first famous Yiddish writer to visit South Africa. The Farein, although an arena for ideological controversy, was not politically committed either way. At its founding, its Zionist members were able even to introduce a point in its constitution to the effect that "Hebrew should have a place where possible." However, in due course the left-wing Yiddishists began to dominate its activities. Its tone became distinctly anti-Zionist and its orientation shifted toward the Soviet Union and sympathy with the Communist cause in South Africa. When the Farein established the first Yiddish afternoon folkshul in 1929, it met with hostility from many Zionists who, although themselves Yiddish-speaking, regarded it as a threat to the Hebrew Talmud Torah school system.[38] As a result, the folkshul never incorporated more than sixty children and two teachers and after only two years it had to close down for lack of support. Not long after, in June 1932, after twenty years of activity, the Farein itself ceased to exist.

A parallel development of the leftist minority in the late 1920s and the 1930s was related to support for Jewish colonization on the land in the Soviet Union.[39] The Zionist Federation, prodded by the World Zionist Organization, strongly opposed these efforts. In 1932 an organization called Afrikaner Geserd (Society for Settling Jewish Workers on the Land in the USSR) issued from the activities of the Russian Colonization Fund. The Geserd declared its aim to be "to render effective material and moral support toward Jewish socialist reconstruction in the Soviet Union and particularly in Birobidzhan." It issued a printed monthly organ in Yiddish and English called *Geserdword* which also sought "strenuously to combat Zionism in all its manifestations," and "to shake off the harmful and illusory dream of establishing a 'National Home' in Palestine through an alliance with British imperialism."[40] The Geserd represented the peak of leftist Jewish opposition to Zionism in the history of South African Jewry. It even managed to create a small youth section called Yugend Geserd, the only anti-Zionist Jewish youth movement ever to have emerged in South Africa. Associates of the Geserd began publishing a monthly journal called *Farois* (Forward) and reestablished a *Kulturfarein* (cultural federation) in 1937 and an afternoon Yiddish folkshul under the guidance of I. Charlash who had come out from Lithuania as a Yiddish cultural emissary.

In sum, the evidence suggests that the left-wing segment of Litvak Jewry's "genetic" legacy was not absent from the history of South African Jewry. It undoubtedly served as the nursery out of which there developed a disproportionately salient number of Jewish organizers of various Labor Unions, especially those that balked at the color line,[41] and of Jewish participants in the radical leftist movements that challenged, however unsuccessfully, the entire societal system of capitalist white supremacy.

Nevertheless, it is equally evident that these leftist groups remained a peripheral factor in the political orientations of South African Jews, relative to the strength of the Zionist movement. Even the Geserd and the Kulturfarein remained fringe groups. *Geserdword* lasted only until September 1935 and *Farois* until February 1940 and only 200 children passed through the Folkshul in the first five years of its existence. The Geserd itself disintegrated with the outbreak of World War II. The Zionists had a far greater command of the Jewish press. In English there was the veteran weekly *Zionist Record* and the weeklies *SA Jewish Chronicle* and *SA Jewish Times*. Moreover, in Yiddish there was the Zionist weekly *Der Afrikaner Yiddisher Tzeitung*, founded in 1933 in succession to *Der Afrikaner*. In addition there were at this time a number of short-lived weeklies of Zionist character, such as the *Yiddisher Express* (1933–37) and the Zionist socialist *Yiddishe Shtimme* (1938).[42]

Even in the Yiddish-speaking generation the Zionist organizations were predominant; how much more so in the next generation of South African–

born Jews. Already by 1936 it was estimated that over 78 percent of all Jews under thirty years of age were South African–born.[43] Even if it still heard Yiddish at home, the first generation of locally-born South African Jews was more likely to be attracted to the Zionist youth societies and movements. Nor could the leftist elements look to immigration for replenishment. The last waves of immigrants prior to the Quota Act of 1930, which drastically reduced Jewish immigration, were more Zionist than ever. They included many graduates of the new Lithuanian Tarbut schools, as well as many who had first gone to Palestine.[44]

There can be no doubt that, judged by almost any criterion—membership, press resources, fundraising capacity, youth affiliates—the Zionist Organization was the preeminent institution in the life of the community.[45] Founded as early as 1898, the Zionist Federation was in fact the first Jewish institution to achieve a national organizational framework. Indeed, in the circumstances that developed immediately after the Anglo-Boer War, that Federation became de facto the first representative institution of the community in relation to the governmental authorities. Its leader, Samuel Goldreich, averred "that nothing which concerns the Jew is foreign to us. The South African Zionist Federation is charged with the proper care of the local aspects of the Jewish question."[46] By 1910 it embraced well over sixty Zionist societies spread throughout southern Africa.[47] Indeed, it was only after a struggle and with grave reservations that the early Zionist leaders permitted the establishment in 1912 of an overall representative organ in the form of the South African Jewish Board of Deputies, modeled on the body of that name in London. Thenceforward the institutional structure of South African Jewry developed on the lines of Anglo-Jewry, in contrast with the *kehile* model of Lithuanian Jewry. However, in a sense the existence of some twenty Litvak *Landsmanschaften* (mutual benefit societies) up until the 1950s perpetuated something of the Lithuanian *kehiles* from which their members originated.

The fact that the Litvak immigration did not encounter an established communal structure and a veteran leadership committed to the ideal of integrating as "Jews of the Mosaic faith," as was the case in Britain and the United States, is of crucial importance in explaining the hegemony that Zionism gained over South African Jewry. By the same token, the fact that middle-class Jews from England and Germany took to Herzlian Zionism with enthusiasm and assumed leadership roles in the Zionist Federation is indicative of their sense that such overt ethnic identification was compatible with the pluralistic and inchoate character of South African society at the "frontier." It is in this respect that they most differed in their identity and political orientation as Jews from those of their highly acculturated and integrated contemporaries in England and the United States.

The extent of identification with the Zionist Organization was extraordinary, especially when viewed in the comparative perspective of other Jewries in the Anglo-American world. The percentage of the Jewish population that purchased the *shekel,* signifying membership and voting rights in the World Zionist Organization, exceeded that of almost every other Jewish community in the world. Indeed, although the *shekel* is indicative merely of formal identification, rather than of the inherent strength of Zionism, it is of interest that throughout the 1920s and 1930s no fewer *shekels,* and sometimes more, were purchased by South African Jews than by the Jews of Lithuania itself. For instance, from 1937 to 1939, 41,735 *shekels* were purchased in South Africa, compared to only 25,500 in Lithuania.[48]

Given the difference in the financial positions of Jews in Lithuania compared to South Africa, another sphere in which the Zionism of South African Jews was far more developed than Lithuanian Jewry's Zionism was, as might be expected, fundraising for the Keren ha-yesod (the Zionist Organization's Foundation Fund), founded in 1922. Indeed, in the Fund's first two decades South African Jewry's per capita contribution, in absolute figures, was second only to the United States: $3,898,985 to the U.S.'s $16,113,852![49]

Whereas Lithuanian Jewry's Zionism was the continuation of the already highly politicized and variegated Zionist ideologies and organizations of the Jews in the Russian Empire, the internal political variegation of South African Zionism only began to develop after World War I. Before that time all South African Zionists were General Zionists. Two exceptions were the formation of the aforementioned Poalei Zion group at the end of 1918 and a small Mizrahi Party formed in 1919. By the end of 1921 Poalei Zion had dissolved. In the 1920s the immigration of Litvak Jews, some of them after spending a period in Palestine, created both a group of Tzeirei Zion and a Revisionist Zionist group. But full politicization of the Zionist Federation was only effected as late as 1943 when, at the combined insistence of the Revisionists and Tzeirei Zion, the former individual "best man" system of election to World Zionist congresses was replaced by elections on the basis of party lists.

South African Jews evinced a special receptivity to Jabotinsky's militant views, although the strength of Revisionism in South Africa was more than counterbalanced by the Tzeirei Zion, which attracted a considerable following in the South African-born generation during the late 1930s and became known as the Zionist Socialist Party. By 1939 its Yiddish-speaking Litvak founders relinquished the leadership roles to South African–born personalities such as Felix Landau (son of Chief Rabbi Landau) and Louis Pincus. Both settled in Israel, the former becoming a judge and the latter rising to the chairmanship of the World Zionist Organization-Jewish Agency in the 1960s. The hypothesis that Revisionism had special appeal in South Africa because of the white regime's right-wing political climate is not borne out by the evidence. As has been mentioned earlier, the exposure of Jews to leftist ideas was far from negligible in South Africa, and Jews were seminally involved in labor organization and the ideological left throughout the 1920s and 1930s. The most important factor of which account must be taken in attempting to explain the appeal of Revisionism would appear to be the purely personal impact of Jabotinsky himself when he visited the country in 1931, 1937 and 1938. The Revisionists' New Zionist Organization of South Africa was the only political group to have its world leader—and a very charismatic leader at that—serve as a local leader while he was in the country. This proved to be greatly to its advantage.

Of crucial importance in promoting the Zionist mode of identity were the youth movements. Whereas in other western countries, particularly in the United States and Britain, some major youth organizations were fostered by non-Zionist community agencies, in South Africa the Zionist Organization virtually had a monopoly over all youth activity. By 1920 there were already thirty-three Young Israel Societies, as the first youth groups were called, affiliated to the Zionist Federation.[50] In 1931 the first uniformed junior youth movement, Habonim, was founded to cater to the ten- to fifteen-year age group. In the late 1930s a group of young Yiddish-speaking Litvak immigrants formed the Ha-shomer ha-tzair youth movement with a leftist ideology and the promotion of pioneering (*halutz*) settlement in the kibbutzim of Ha-shomer ha-tzair in Palestine. By the 1940s the youth movements had multiplied on the basis of political alignments and included the Revisionist youth movement Betar, and the Ha-shomer ha-dati (later Bnei Akiva) affiliated with Mizrahi, the Zionist Socialist Youth and the General Zionist Youth. The ubiquitous influence of these movements had the effect of exposing successive generations of South African–born Jewish youth to a mode of Jewish identification determined exclusively by Zionism.

According to the 1936 census, Yiddish was still the home language of 19.37 percent of the Jews (17,561 out of 90,645). There can be no doubt that most of these were supporters of Zionism. Even the offspring of Yiddish-speaking leftists were more likely to be attracted to these Zionist youth movements than to continuation of their parents' political orientation, especially since the political orientation of the Ha-shomer ha-tzair movement, the Zionist

Socialist Party and its youth section, as well as Habonim by the 1940s, was something of a synthesis of Jewish ethnicism and leftist-liberalism. It is a noteworthy fact that they not only tended to align themselves with political forces opposed to the entire South African system of absolute white supremacy, but became a nursery for the arousal of awareness of South Africa's societal evils. A number of individuals who later threw themselves wholly into the resistance movements that fought the apartheid regime after 1948, either as Liberals or as Communists or Trotskyists, were first nurtured in this Zionist seedbed.[51] The recently published autobiography of Baruch Hirson provides a prototypical example of this phenomenon. Hirson relates how, having grown up devoid of any social awareness relating to the system of white supremacy, such awareness was first aroused when he became involved in Ha-shomer ha-tzair. Its brand of socialist Zionism was the ideological nursery and passageway for his eventual adoption of Trotskyism and for the involvement in the African Resistance Movement that resulted in his arrest and imprisonment for nine years.[52] It must therefore be noted that, notwithstanding the essentially ethnicist thrust of all Zionist activity in South Africa, it also consciously served as a stimulant of general social and political awareness, and, however unintentionally, as a conduit for involvement in the local South African resistance movements, both of the Liberal and Leftist strains.

CONCLUSION

What can one learn from this comparative examination of two Jewries at the "frontier," the "mother" community in Lithuania and its "daughter" community in South Africa? It falls short of enabling a definitive evaluation of the relative significance of the Litvak "genetic" heritage on the one hand, and the South African environment on the other hand, in shaping the character of South African Jewry. However, it is does show clearly that the essentially national identity of the Litvak immigrants who constituted the majority of South African Jewry was preserved in South Africa to a degree that is remarkable when compared to other new communities formed or reinforced by the post-1880 waves of emigration from Czarist Russia and its successor states. It is my contention that the explanation for this lies in the commonalities revealed by a comparison between the "frontier" societal environments of Lithuania and South Africa; commonalities that provided "mandatory" forms of ethnic pluralism in both places. In plain terms, what this means is that the same type of Litvak emigrant who settled in Britain or in the United States of America did not experience so great a degree of reinforcement of his "genetic" Jewish national identity.

This distinctiveness of South African Jewry's identity profile was reflected in the pattern of political orientations that characterized Jewish life in South Africa. Neither in British Jewry nor in American Jewry was Zionism, in all its internal ideological variety, as normative and institutionally dominant as it was in South Africa. Having established that, however, a caveat is necessary: in South Africa no less than in Britain and the United States of America a non-normative minority of Jews played a remarkably disproportionate role in the radical left of the country's political spectrum. In South Africa this involvement also meant opposition to the racist assumptions that underlay the maintenance of white supremacy.

Yet the comparison with the continuation of the Litvak "genetic" heritage in independent Lithuania from 1919 to 1939 and the development of South African Jewry in the same period makes it equally evident that, much as happened in Britain and America, the acculturation of the Litvak immigrants did, in the final analysis, vitiate their national identity. In stark contrast with developments in Lithuania itself, South African Jews did not entertain even the very notion of gaining recognition as a national minority, let alone of enjoying national minority rights in South Africa. They rapidly adapted themselves to those purely voluntary principles and institutional structures of communal life that were already in the process of formation by the Anglo-Jews who had settled in South Africa prior to the Litvak migration from the 1880s onward.

South African Jewry's predominantly Zionist political orientation, although marking it off so distinctively from other New World communities and British Jewry, was not of the same quality as that of Lithuanian Jewry itself. For a significant segment of the Zionists in Lithuania (although by no means for the majority) personal settlement in Palestine was an ideological imperative. Moreover, they aspired not only to national statehood in Palestine but also to parallel attainment of national-cultural autonomy in Lithuania. In short, they regarded themselves as part of the Jewish nation, not merely as an ethnic or religious minority. In contrast, the Zionism of South African Jews meant no more than the upholding of the attributes of Jewish ethnicity—its religion, its languages (primarily Hebrew but also Yiddish), its sense of common origin, solidarity and destiny, and its connection to the now renascent territorial homeland, Zion. In practice this translated mainly into a form of vicarious support for Jewish statehood in Palestine as a solution for persecuted Jews everywhere and as the pivot of all Jewish identification and creative ethnic-cultural continuity. Only a marginal, although influential, segment of the Zionists in South Africa regarded personal settlement in Palestine as an ideological imperative. In the light of these differences, I would suggest that whereas the normative mode of identity and political orientation of Litvak Jewry in Lithuania itself was *nationalist,* the normative mode of the Litvak Jews who acculturated to South Africa is better described as *ethnicist.*

Notes

1. Gustav Saron and Louis Hotz, *The Jews in South Africa* (Cape Town: Oxford University Press, 1955), 89; Gideon Shimoni, *Jews and Zionism: The South African Experience, 1910–1967* (Cape Town: Oxford University Press, 1980), 12.

2. Saron and Hotz, *Jews in South Africa,* 100, 377–81. According to Gustav Saron's estimates, in the thirty-year period from 1880 to 1910 some 40,000 Jewish immigrants had entered South Africa, 21,980 of whom came from 1900 to 1912. He further estimated that another 30,000 came from 1912 to 1952. Subtracting the known figures for the period 1940 to 1952, viz., 2,676, this leaves an estimated 27,300 for the period 1912 to 1939. If we subtract another 3,615 known to have come from Germany in the period 1933 to 1936, this leaves an estimated 23,685 immigrants probably from Eastern Europe in the period 1912 to 1939.

3. Shimoni, *Jews and Zionism,* 5–7.

4. Dov Levin, ed., *Pinkas ha-kehilot: Lita* (Jerusalem: Yad Vashem, 1996), 26.

5. Masha Greenbaum, *The Jews of Lithuania* (Jerusalem: Gefen, 1995), 208.

6. Leib Garfunkel, "Ma'avakam shel yehudei lita al zekhuyot leumiyot," *Yahadut Lita,* 4 vols. (Tel Aviv: Am Hasefer and Igud Yotzei Lita, 1972), 2:35.

7. On the economic and occupational development of South African Jewry, see Marcus Arkin, ed., *South African Jewry: A Contemporary Survey* (Cape Town: Oxford University Press, 1984), 57–78; Saron and Hotz, *Jews in South Africa,* 348–69; Mendel Kaplan, *Jewish Roots in the South African Economy* (Cape Town: Struik, 1986).

8. See Greenbaum, *Jews of Lithuania,* 208.

9. Levin, *Pinkas ha-kehilot,* 46.

10. Cf. M. G. Smith, "Institutional and Political Conditions of Pluralism," in *Pluralism in Africa,* ed. L. Kuper and M. G. Smith (Berkeley: University of California Press, 1969), 29–67.

11. This analysis of Lithuanian society and the place of the Jews within it is especially indebted to Ezra Mendelsohn, *The Jews of East Central Europe between the World Wars* (Bloomington: Indiana University Press, 1983).

12. Levin, *Pinkas ha-kehilot,* 46.

13. Ibid., 26, 47.

14. See Greenbaum, *Jews of Lithuania,* 262–70; Levin, *Pinkas ha-kehilot,* 55–57.

15. Dov Lipets, "Ha-khinukh ha-ivri ve-ha-tnua ha-ivrit be-lita ha-atzmait," *Yahadut Lita,* 2:117.

16. This summary of the educational institutions draws on Levin, *Pinkas ha-kehilot,* 56–58, and Greenbaum, *Jews of Lithuania,* 265–69. In 1920–21, Yavneh schools had 23 percent, the Yiddish schools 17 percent, and the Pshore schools 27.5 percent.

17. On Jewish education in South Africa, see Meyer E. Katz, "The History of Jewish Education in South Africa 1841–1980" (Ph.D. diss., University of Cape Town, 1980).

18. On the development of religious life and institutions in South Africa, see John I. Simon, "A Study of the Nature and Development of Orthodox Judaism in South Africa up to c. 1935" (M.A. thesis, University of Cape Town, 1996). See also Jocelyn Hellig, "Religious Expression," in *South African Jewry,* ed. Arkin, 95–116.

19. Only much later, in the 1970s, did a tendency toward strict observance along ultraorthodox lines, particularly of the Hassidic Habad variety, begin to emerge in South Africa.

20. "Statistics of the Jewish Community in South Africa 1911–1960" (compiled from the Official Census reports of the Union of South Africa), 1972, file 132A, Archives of SA Jewish Board of Deputies, Johannesburg.

21. For a detailed discussion, see Shimoni, *Jews and Zionism,* 40–50.

22. The Germans evacuated Vilna in November 1918. Poland occupied it in April 1919. In June 1920 the Russians overran it, and in October 1920 the Suwalk Treaty between the Poles and the Lithuanians ceded Vilna to Lithuania. However, this did not hold. The Polish army again occupied Vilna and notwithstanding all of Lithuania's protestations, including those to the International Court of Justice at the Hague, the Poles incorporated Vilna into Poland in April 1922. Kovno became the provisional capital of Lithuania; Vilna remained its capital in name only.

23. See Mendelsohn, *Jews of East Central Europe,* 232. The Lithuanian Communist Party was small. By 1939–40, when Soviet Russia occupied and incorporated Lithuania, it had no more than 2,000 members (of all ethnic extraction). See Dov Levin, "The Jews in the Soviet Lithuanian Establishment, 1940–1941," *Soviet Jewish Affairs* 10.2 (May 1980): 24.

24. At the 1933 Zionist Congress the other four mandates were Revisionist Zionists (one), General Zionists (A Group, one) and Mizrahi (one). In 1931 the Ha-shomer hatzair youth movement was the largest with 4,150 members, followed by Betar with 1,500. Shmuel Elyashiv-Friedman, "Tnuat eretz Israel ha-ovedet," *Yahadut Lita,* 2:199–202; Levin, *Pinkas Hakehilot,* 63–70.

25. See the text of "The Declaration of the Lithuanian Delegation to the Jewish Delegations at the Paris Peace Conference, 5 August 1919," translated from the French, in *Yahadut Lita,* 2:41. See also the reiteration of minority rights commitments, although in attenuated form, in the Lithuanian government's declaration of May 12, 1922, to the League of Nations, in ibid., 2:58–61.

26. Garfunkel, "Ma'avakam shel," 2:43–45.

27. See Garfunkel, "Ha-yehudim ba-seimim ha-litai'im," *Yahadut Lita,* 2:73–83.

28. See Mendelsohn, *Jews of East Central Europe,* 230–31.

29. As it happens the Yiddish term *poyer,* applied to the peasants in Lithuania, is etymologically related to the Afrikaner word *boer.* But in South Africa, not the Boer but the African was the equivalent of the Lithuanian peasant.

30. Leibl Feldman, *Yidden in Johannesburg* (Johannesburg: South African Yiddish Cultural Festival, 1956), 241–46. Thus every African, no matter of what age, was addressed as "boy;" even white children called an adult African "boy." An African woman was referred to as a *shikse.* The word *kaffir* was adopted into Yiddish. As it happens the etymological origin of the word lies in the Semitic languages where it originally meant "infidel."

31. There are references to these activities in the *Rand Daily Mail,* Jan. 29 and June 2, 1904. See Feldman, *Yidden in Johannesburg,* 137–41.

32. See Shimoni, *Jews and Zionism,* 80–81.

33. I had been under the impression that the Bund group faded out of existence soon after, but research by E. A. Mantzaris has shown that this is not so. See Evangelis Mantzaris, "Bund in dorem afrika," *Unser Zeit* 6 (1981): 44–46, and Evangelis Mantzaris, "Sergei Riger (Baron) in dorem afrika," *Unser Zeit* 9 (Sept. 1983): 42–43.

34. See, in brief, Shimoni, *Jews and Zionism,* 53–54, 173–74. Also E. I. Mantzaris, "Radical Community: The Yiddish-Speaking Branch of the International Socialist League," in *Class, Community, and Conflict: South African Perspectives,* ed. Belinda Bozzoli (Johannesburg: Ravan Press, 1987), 160–76. This thoroughly researched unearthing of the Yiddish-Speaking Group's activities is marred only by a tendency to treat Yiddish as the preserve of the leftist working-class Jews in assumed contrast with Hebrew as the language of the "middle-class" Zionists. In fact very few Litvak Zionists spoke Hebrew. Yiddish was no less theirs in practice and they by far outnumbered the anti-Zionist leftists even among working class Jews.

35. Leibl Feldman, *Yidden in dorem afrika* (Johannesburg: G. Gleckina, 1937), 102–16.

36. See the illuminating unearthing of the Yiddisher Arbeter Club's history in Taffy Adler, "Lithuania's Diaspora: The Jewish Workers Club, 1928–1948," *Journal of Southern African Studies* 6.1 (Oct. 1979): 71–92. However, Adler tends to attribute use of Yiddish too exclusively to anti-Zionist working class Jews.

37. See, e.g., "The Shameful Role of Zionism in South Africa," *Proletarishe Shtimme,* Sept. 1932.

38. See *Zionist Record,* Jan. 20, 1929.

39. See Shimoni, *Jews and Zionism,* 56–60.

40. The quotations are from *Geserdword,* Feb. 1932, May 1935. See Shimoni, *Jews and Zionism,* 56–58.

41. On the role of Trade Union leaders such as Gabriel Weinstock and Solly Sachs, see Shimoni, *Jews and Zionism,* 87–89. See also the groundbreaking study by Evangelos A. Mantzaris, "Jewish Trade Unions in Cape Town, South Africa, 1903–1907: A Socio-Historical Study," *Jewish Social Studies* 49 (Summer–Fall 1987): 251–64.

42. See A. P. Poliva, *A Short History of the Jewish Press and Literature of South Africa from Its Earliest Days until the Present Time* (Johannesburg: Prompt Printing, 1961); Michael P. Grosman, "A Study of the Trends and Tendencies of Hebrew and Yiddish Writings in South Africa since Their Beginnings in the Early Nineties of the Last Century to 1930" (Ph.D. diss., University of the Witwatersrand, 1973).

43. H. Sonnabend, "Survey of Johannesburg Jewry," ts., SA Jewish Board of Deputies, Bureau of Jewish Statistics and Research, 1936, Archives of SA Jewish Board of Deputies, Johannesburg.

44. See Shimoni, *Jews and Zionism,* 59.

45. I have traced at length the development of Zionism in South Africa in *Jews and Zionism.* See also G. Shimoni, "Zionism in South Africa: An Historical Perspective," *Forum* 37 (Spring 1980): 71–91.

46. *Report of the Executive to the First Conference of the South African Zionist Federation, 1905,* Archive of the South African Jewish Federation, Johannesburg. The quotation is from Goldreich's presidential speech.

47. *Report of the Executive to the Fourth Conference of the SA Zionist Federation, 1911,* Archive of the South African Jewish Federation, Johannesburg.

48. *Report of the Executive of the Zionist Organization and Jewish Agency for Palestine Submitted to the 21st Zionist Congress at Geneva, August 1939,* 40, Archive of the South African Jewish Federation, Johannesburg. Of course, purchase of the *shekel* was far more difficult financially for the average Lithuanian Jew than for the Jews of South Africa, and in addition the report of the executive noted that the *shekel* campaign in Lithuania had suffered from "strained relations" between the rival Zionist political groupings. Account must also be taken of the fact that in the late 1930s the Lithuanian authorities disallowed the conduct of elections to the Zionist Congress.

49. See Shimoni, *Jews and Zionism,* 36. It should be noted that in 1939 South African Jewry numbered only 90,700 to U.S. Jewry's 4,975,000.

50. See L. Pinshaw, "The South African Young Israel Federation," in *The South African Jewish Yearbook,* ed. M. de Saxe (Johannesburg: South African Jewish Historical Society, 1929), 257–62.

51. See Shimoni, *Jews and Zionism,* 188–92.

52. See Baruch Hirson, *Revolutions in My Life* (Johannesburg: University of Witwatersrand Press, 1995), esp. 94–139.

6 A Frontier Experience: Israeli Jews Encounter Diaspora in Cape Town, South Africa

SALLY FRANKENTAL

Demographically, Israeli Jews in South Africa constitute a tiny minority, barely visible within the Jewish minority, which in turn constitutes about 2 percent of the minority white population.[1] Although total Jewish immigration to South Africa since 1970 is small in absolute numbers, Israeli-born Jews made up 21.2 percent of that total between 1970 and 1979, and 61.4 percent between 1980 and 1991.[2] Given that at least some accompanying adults were Israeli citizens not born in Israel, this immigration constitutes a not insignificant influx into a community diminishing in size and proportion since the 1970s.

Yet, with the minor exception of pupils in Jewish Day Schools, Israelis are significantly absent from communal Jewish life. Furthermore, Israelis in South Africa have not created "ethnic enclaves," nor established specifically Israeli institutions. Nor do they exhibit any particular enthusiasm for rapid integration into the local community. These "absences" distinguish them from most populations reported in the extensive literature on migrants, including Israeli migrant populations in Los Angeles and Chicago.[3] It is also unlike the behavior of most Jewish migrant populations of the past, and even of the present.

This chapter explores some of the reasons for the "absences" through a consideration of mutual perceptions of difference among Israelis and local Jews, including different conceptions of Jewishness.

ISRAELI MIGRANTS IN SOUTH AFRICA

Several difficulties arise in attempting to calculate the number of Israelis in South Africa.[4] Nevertheless, DellaPergola and Dubb estimated the number at over 6,000 in 1987,[5] and Dubb estimated a maximum of 9,634 legally resident in South Africa in 1991.[6] This is probably an underestimate as fieldwork evidence indicates considerable flux in the number and official status of Israeli residents in Cape Town at any given time. However, there is no more reliable means of assessment.

While South Africa attracts only a very small proportion of all Israeli emigrants (the majority choose North America), table 6.1 shows the increase in the proportion of Israelis in the total number of immigrants to South Africa in recent years. These figures are based on the category "by country of previous permanent residence" and thus probably include some returning South Africans.

Table 6.2 summarizes the available published data on the Israel–South Africa migration flows and shows a net positive balance for South Africa. Close examination of yearly figures shows several ups and downs in the size of Israeli migration, through a long-term upward trend. Immigration peaked in 1990, with 945 immigrants with Israel as "country of previous residence," of whom 772 were Israeli-born, and 914 had Israeli citizenship. Yearly figures show a marked decrease since then. Such fluctuations always reflect, among other things, specific events in the country of departure. The increase in the mid-1960s coincides with a period of severe economic recession in Israel. Forty-two percent of the 1970s migrants arrived during 1975 and 1976, a pe-

Table 6.1. Immigrants and Israeli Immigrants to South Africa, 1950–93

		Israeli Immigrants	
Year	Immigrants	Number	Percentage
1950–59	156,366	457	0.08
1960–69	333,378	1,007	0.29
1970–79	328,944	1,765	0.30
1980–89	229,868	4,030	1.75
1990–93	45,388	2,120	4.67

Sources: South Africa, Central Statistical Services, Report No. 19-01-11 (1983-85); ibid., Report No. 03-51-01 (1986-93).

Note: According to the Department of Statistics, "immigrants are persons who, according to statements compiled at the time of entry into South Africa, intend to reside in South Africa permanently" (CSS Report No. 19-01-10, 1982).

Table 6.2. Israeli Migrants to and from South Africa, 1950–93

	1950–59	1960–69	1970–79	1980–89	1990–93
Immigrants to South Africa					
Previously resided in Israel	457	1,007	1,765	4,030	2,120
Born in Israel	278	574	1,178	2,628	1,562
Israeli citizenship	402	388	1,640	2,053	2,076
Emigrants from South Africa					
Moving to Israel	269	2,818	2,025	249	
Born in Israel	59	324	362	78	
Israeli citizenship	48	396	436	57	

Source: South Africa, Central Statistical Services, Report No. 19-01-11 (1983-85); ibid., Report No. 03-51-01 (1986-93).

riod of low morale in Israel in the wake of the 1973 Yom Kippur War. It is noteworthy that the increase continued despite the 1976 Soweto uprising in South Africa. This trend reflects relative lack of concern with political events in the receiving country, an observation further supported by the significant increases of the 1980s, a period of considerable civil unrest in South Africa.

In the 1990s, the Gulf War and the uncertainties initiated by the beginnings of the Middle East peace process may have operated as "push" factors. However, fieldwork evidence suggests that since the late 1980s, the "pull" factors of perceived economic opportunities in South Africa, particularly during the political transition, have been more significant motivators.

Instrumental personal considerations and the absence of emotional commitment to the host country are characteristics shared by the vast majority of the research population, irrespective of period of arrival. The most common response to apartheid, in the earlier period, and to the current rapid transformations in South Africa was, "It's their problem, it's not my state." As all Israelis know that they can return to Israel whenever they so wish, it is not surprising that they are less anxious about the uncertainties of South Africa's future than many South Africans. However, while no official migration figures are available beyond 1993, many Israelis are known to have returned to Israel just before the first South African democratic elections in 1994.

THE RECEIVING ENVIRONMENT

The Wider Society

The rate of population flows between sending and receiving countries is always dependent on the social, economic and political conditions prevailing in each, as well as on the nature of the relationship between them. During the 1970s and 1980s in particular, when both Israel and South Africa were viewed by many as "pariah states," the relationship between the two governments was closer than at any previous time.[7] According to Arkin, the rationale for the relationship was part of a "mutually beneficial long-term policy of effective collaboration" and not based on the need to meet "some sudden and temporary emergency."[8]

While the "mutually beneficial" claim was hotly contested by significant segments in both societies, growing interaction led to increased mutual public awareness and interest in both countries. Since South Africa's successful transition to democracy, the new government has maintained full diplomatic relations with Israel. It has also maintained earlier immigration policies. Israelis are thus neither favored nor discouraged and are subject to the same facilities and constraints as any other immigrants.

The Local Jewish Community

The South African Jewish community is comprised of all Jews who acknowledge their Jewishness in some way. The main concerns of organized Jewry in South Africa are similar to those of all diaspora Jewish communities: protecting the rights and interests of all Jews vis-à-vis the wider society, preserving the Jewish heritage through a range of religious and educational institutions, safeguarding the welfare of Jews through charitable and other organizations, and promoting Zionism and maintaining strong links with Israel. The South African community differs from other diaspora communities in the greater degree of cohesiveness in its internal organization, and in the degree of consensus and intensity regarding Zionist commitment.[9] These differences stem partly from the community's relatively homogeneous origins and partly from its position as a community of whites within the formerly dominant white minority in a highly ethnically conscious wider society.

Since the beginnings of the political transition to majority rule in South Africa, Jews, like everyone else in the country but most particularly whites, have grown increasingly anxious about prospects for the future. In one sense little has changed: Jews continue to live in (formerly) "white" suburbs, to be overrepresented in the professions, and to maintain above-average education and income levels. All Jewish communal institutions continue to function—some are even expanding—and their traditionally strong support for Israel has not been threatened despite increased, sometimes militant, criticism of Israel's policies and despite the (new) presence in South Africa of Palestinian representatives. Yet Jews share with all South Africans the sense of profound change. While they certainly welcome the relatively peaceful transition to constitutional democracy, they are fully aware that the decades of protected privilege by virtue of a white skin belong to the past.

While many Jews, like many others, are optimistic about the future and foresee expanded prospects in an open society, others are less certain and more fearful. Their anxieties operate on two levels: at the personal level they worry about the growing crime rate, about the impact of affirmative action on job prospects for their children, about standards of education, and more generally and diffusely, about the impact of the recent changes on their middle-class and relatively affluent lifestyles. At the Jewish communal level, many are apprehensive about the continued adequacy of the material base and future leadership capacity of their institutions. They recognize that the community is diminishing in its human and material resources, both because it is aging[10] and because of emigration.[11]

Against this background of simultaneous continuity and profound change, one might expect that an influx of Israeli Jews would be actively welcomed as a source of enrichment, particularly as there is some evidence that the community is turning inward, focusing increasingly on specifically Jewish matters.[12] But this is not the case.

Alternatively, one might expect the presence of increasing numbers of Israelis in South Africa to create a dilemma for the local community. Given near universal Jewish support for Israel, and approval of Zionist efforts at recruitment for *aliya*,[13] together with a clear commitment to Jewish continuity, should Israelis be shunned as deserters, or welcomed in an effort to keep them within the Jewish fold? Unlike in the United States,[14] there has been no formal debate on this topic within local Zionist circles, nor any attempt to devise communal policy.

INTERACTION WITH THE "PROXIMAL HOST" COMMUNITY

Mittelberg and Waters present what they call the "proximal host model" to describe a process of possible identity-formation following migration.[15] The model suggests that the identity of recent immigrants in the host country is influenced by the existence of a proximal host group, that is, the ethnic group to which newcomers are assigned by natives of the host country. Recent immigrant groups might reject their identification with the "proximal" hosts or might integrate into the wider society through assimilation into the "proximal host group." Waters's findings from her work among West Indian immigrants to the United States suggest that the socioeconomic background of the newcomers and the social status of the "proximal host group" are the relevant factors.[16] Two issues pertinent to the current study arise from the foregoing: (1) the way in which South Africans in general and Jewish South Africans in particular categorize "Israelis"; (2) the extent to which socioeconomic criteria differentiate the migrant population.

There is no evidence to indicate that South Africans in general identify Israelis as a distinct ethnic category. As shown, they comprise a tiny proportion of all whites and a small proportion of all immigrants. Despite some residential and occupational clustering in both Cape Town and Johannesburg (where most are resident), their numbers are insufficient to create Israeli ghettos or distinctive occupational niches. They come to South Africa as individuals, utilizing the conventional channels open to all immigrants, and there is no evidence to suggest that they constitute a particular category in the eyes of the state although they are, like all immigrants, distinguished for statistical purposes. Occasional press reports of criminal activities have identified Israelis but these have not evoked xenophobic or other negative reactions from the general populace. Nor have there been television or radio programs about Israelis as a local "ethnic community," as there have been about Greeks, Indians, Jews, and Portuguese in South Africa.

South African Jews, on the other hand, clearly perceive Israelis as a subcategory of Jews "other" than themselves. Many Jews, but particularly people actively engaged in communal affairs, often refer to "the Israelis" as if they constitute a well-defined entity.[17] Most local Jews become aware of an Israeli presence in Cape Town through chance encounters. Some have more experience of Israelis—because they visit Israel, have relatives there, are involved with voluntary organizations whose work is centered on Israel, or are graduates of the local Jewish school which has an active interest in Israel and in Zionist education. Such Jews often express differences between themselves and all Israelis, local migrants or Israelis in Israel, irrespective of whether they know any or not. And such expression is usually couched in well-established popular stereotypes.

Within the Jewish community there is no specific organized communal body whose exclusive brief it is to deal with Israeli migrants, although of course all communal institutions are as available to Israelis as they are to any Jew. Local Jewish communal organizations and their officials, lay and professional, often comment on the noninvolvement of "the Israelis" in communal affairs. However, none have made this a central concern.

In terms of socioeconomic status, the local Israeli population in Cape Town can be differentiated both internally and in relation to local Jews. The Israeli population contains fewer professionals, and a larger proportion of Sephardim.[18] Israeli Sephardim in Israel, unlike South African Sephardim (usually from Rhodes via Zaire and Zimbabwe), tend to be overrepresented in lower socioeconomic categories.[19] Fieldwork evidence indicates that apart from the smaller proportion of professionals, Israelis are as likely as South African Jews to be self-employed, are distributed similarly across occupational categories, and income levels are related more to the length of time in South Africa than to standard of education or specific occupations. Moreover, unlike Israeli migrants in Chicago[20] and Los Angeles,[21] distinctions between Sephardi and Ashkenazi migrants in Cape Town are not based on socioeconomic criteria. More important, both from observing the identity of members of social networks and from comments Israelis make about themselves and local Jews, differentiation rests more on the criteria of age, common interest, nationality of spouse, and cultural "style" *within a perceived shared "Israeliness,"* than on socioeconomic distinctions.

Yet the local Jewish community can be regarded as the "proximal host" for Jewish Israelis. All Israelis in Cape Town acknowledge their Jewishness in some way—some with considerable ambivalence (see below)—although the meaning of the label and its salience for individuals varies greatly. Furthermore, all are as interested and informed about Jews elsewhere in the diaspora as most South African Jews—in other words, they see themselves as part of "the Jewish People," even if this is not at the center of their consciousness. And certainly the history of Jewish migration in all periods and places—except perhaps for contemporary Israeli migration—records the eventual assimilation of newcomers into local communities where they existed.

One might therefore expect that if Israelis remained in South Africa long enough, they too would "disappear" as an identifiable population. But there are four major differences between diaspora Jewish migrants and Israelis in Cape Town. First, and most important, these migrants emigrated from a Jewish state, unlike most Jewish migrants of the past two millennia. The implications of having been socialized within a dominant Jewish majority in a sovereign Jewish state are elaborated below.

Second, most Jewish migrants of the past, as well as many diaspora migrants of today, left their places of origin with no intention of ever returning, and few did. Almost all Israelis in Cape Town express the intention of returning "sometime." Whether they eventually operationalize that intention or not—and some have been in South Africa for more than thirty years—a sense of "sojourn" surely colors the way they live their lives in the meantime.

Third, as a consequence of their intention to settle, most other Jewish migrants engaged with the local communities they found on arrival, even when that interaction was acrimonious. By contrast, Israelis in Cape Town do not and have never influenced or tried to influence Jewish public life, and are conspicuously absent from almost all organized communal activities. For most, their social interactions *of choice* are almost exclusively with other Israelis, or, in the case of South African–Israeli couples, with other "mixed" couples.

Most of the wide range of Jewish communal events, though organized independently by various organizations, are open to the public and extensively advertised in the Jewish and general press. The only regular event at which there is always a notable Israeli presence is the Israel Independence Day celebration, and Israelis were also visible at communal meetings held during the last two Israeli elections. They were conspicuously absent from the communal memorial service for the late President Yitzchak Rabin. Occasionally, when a guest speaker is a well-known Israeli public figure, a few Israelis may attend, larger numbers attending if it is made known that the address will be in Hebrew. Only two of the many communal organizations has an Israeli as a committee member, and the Sephardi synagogue is the only institution that has Israelis (including Ashkenazim) as active members.

Fourth, most other migrants, before and/or until they merge with their "proximal hosts," build their own community—whether in pockets, as with the *landsmannschaften,* or in order to protect or further their interests, or simply to provide a sense of *Gemeinschaft.* Local Israelis express no need for formally structured frameworks. Despite seeking and preferring the company of Israelis for social interactions of choice, their networks are not comprised exclusively of Israelis. Although there is some residential concentration, they can be found in many parts of the peninsula—there is no area of Cape Town that resembles a "Chinatown" for Israelis. These findings for the most part confirm those of Shokeid for New York,[22] Mittelberg and Waters for kibbutz-born,[23] and Uriely for Chicago.[24] Gold, however, provides evidence of a far wider and deeper sense of community among Israelis in Los Angeles, as well as numerous examples of organizations and institutions catering to specifically Israeli needs.[25] I return to the differences between Los Angeles and Cape Town in the section below on "the lack of community building." Most important, in Cape Town, the reference by Israelis to a local Israeli collectivity, an "imagined community,"[26] is unusual, infrequent, weak and sporadic (that is, not consistent or sustained)—except in contradistinction to South African Jews.

Reference to local Jews usually occurs during discussions about various others and is also couched in stereotypical terms. In such conversations Israelis may refer to "Israelis" when differentiating them from local South African Jews around specific issues, often, but not only, to do with religion. For example: "They must belong to a *shul* [synagogue]—what else makes them

Jewish?—they need religion, we don't"; or, "Israelis don't need to contribute money to the IUA [Israel United Appeal, a fundraising organization]—we have already given blood." Quite often reference is to particular groups of Israelis that the speaker is differentiating from him- or herself: "I'm not interested in those Israelis [who meet regularly at a well-known café]. I don't think most of them would be my friends in Israel, so why should I be friendly with them here—just because they are Israelis?" or, "They [young, single newcomers] get into trouble and give Israelis a bad name. I'm not interested in them." In other words, distinctions are drawn along classical "us-them" lines according to the situation, the topic, and the perceived attributes and values of whoever "the other" is assumed to be. Much is made of difference in these comments and attitudes; little is made of internal solidarity.

There are several possible explanations for the marked nonparticipation of Israelis in local Jewish communal life. One possible explanation relates to their situation as newcomers, people who have to work harder than settled citizens and are thus too "tired" to do what essentially amounts to charity and/or fundraising work. Other reasons relate to the migrants' perceptions and beliefs about the local community and its concerns, and thus implicitly to their own self-definition(s) and concerns. And some explanations relate to the past, to having been socialized as members of a dominant majority rather than as members of a self-conscious minority.

These three sets of "explanation," taken together, also relate to the voluntarism so characteristic of all organized Jewish communities in the diaspora.[27] Whereas Israelis in Israel join voluntary associations because of some personal interest shared with others, the basis of the association is rarely, if ever, ethnic Jewishness. In Israel, Jewish ethnicity is expressed at the national level, even while "country of origin" ethnicity and/or a specific religious identity (one among many Jewish possibilities) may be expressed through affiliation to voluntary associations. Diaspora Jews also form voluntary organizations based on country of origin or specific religious identification. However, by definition, self-conscious Jewish ethnicity is the basis of all Jewish communal voluntary associations and whatever their specific instrumental goals, the preservation and promotion of positive Jewish identification is always part of their *raison d'être*. Such an orientation is simply foreign to most Israelis.

Another explanation defines Israeli migrants, despite their formal status of "immigrants," as "[transmigrants] whose daily lives depend on multiple and constant interconnections across international borders and whose public identities are configured in relationship to more than one nation-state. They . . . settle and become incorporated in the economy and political institutions, localities, and patterns of daily life of the country in which they reside."[28] This research population, while it indeed "becomes incorporated" in the local daily reality, remains uncommitted to "the local" and retains an orientation of "permanent sojourner."[29] The balance of this chapter describes some of the differences Israelis perceive between themselves and local Jewry and attempts to account for these perceptions in terms of both past socialization and current transmigrant position.

ENCOUNTER WITH LOCAL JEWRY

Following Gilman (in his introduction to this volume), the encounter with diaspora constitutes a frontier "where the complex interaction of the definitions of self and Other are able to be constructed." This is a frontier of material and conceptual space, a space in which boundaries are both perceived and constructed. The encounter-as-frontier contains "contestation and accommodation," doubts and dangers as well as challenges and new possibilities. The encounter gives rise to both closure (around constructed entities/selves) and, simultaneously, a constant traversing of the constructed boundaries. For a small minority, the simultaneity creates discomfort: a sense of liminality, betweenness, or a sense of being in limbo, belonging nowhere. For the majority of Jewish Israelis in Cape Town, however, *comfortable* contradiction is achieved. The majority are not situated *between* worlds—rather they locate themselves *in relation to* the various worlds that together constitute their reality.

Interaction and Its Limitations

Four overlapping categories of Israeli migrants in Cape Town engage with the Jewish community in particular contexts. The first, *shlichim* (emissaries from Israel), have formal positions in Zionist organizations or as teachers in the Jewish day schools. The nature of their work requires them to engage with the community. They come to South Africa on two- to three-year nonrenewable contracts which oblige them to return to Israel at the end of the specified period. Outside of the workplace and formal occasions associated with work, the adults' social networks are comprised almost exclusively of other *shlichim*. Although their school-age children interact freely with local Jewish children, this seldom results in parental friendships. Because *shlichim* are selected on the basis of their intense ideological commitment to the Zionist enterprise, it is not surprising that they relate and refer to other Israeli migrants as *yordim* and are judgmental of their presence in South Africa. Some of the other migrants resent this attitude, but all purport to understand it and personal relationships do develop across the *shlichim/yordim* boundary, though most *shlichim* socialize more among themselves.

The second category comprises those Israelis, with or without children, who have married Jewish South Africans and thus interact with the extended kin networks of their spouses. In most cases the wives are the South Africans and interaction of the Israeli spouse with his or her affines occurs mainly in the context of family "occasions," including the celebration of Jewish festivals. The non-kin social networks of these couples tend to comprise other "mixed" couples like themselves. Compared with the available U.S. data from the detailed studies of Gold, Shokeid and Uriely, there appear to be proportionately more such "mixed" marriages in Cape Town, possibly reflecting the comparatively greater Zionist commitment and Israel-connectedness of South African Jewry. In such families, the South African and Israeli spouses each tend to have circles of same-sex friends who are exclusively South African or Israeli. The amount of time spent in South Africa does not affect this pattern. While other factors, such as class, or stage in the life-cycle, obviously influence choice of friends, the cohesiveness and longevity of several networks of "mixed" couples is nevertheless striking.

The third category comprises those Israelis, whether married to South Africans or not, who have children who attend Jewish day schools and/or youth movements. Through their children these adults interact more frequently with local Jews than do other Israelis. However, their own friendships tend to be with other Israelis or with "mixed" couples.

The fourth category, also the smallest, comprises the religiously observant. Most work as teachers or religious officers, are usually not emissaries, and were recruited by employers to fill positions for which there were no suitably qualified South Africans. Their social relationships beyond work tend to be formed with other observant Jews but the closest (most frequent and intense) amongst these are with observant Israelis.

It is thus immediately apparent that all categories of Israelis prefer other Israelis for their interactions of choice, and limit interaction with non-Israelis. For some, their work relationships too are with Israelis. Several singles interact more with non-Jews but they too prefer relationships with Israelis like themselves.

Notions of "The Other"

Despite publications with titles such as *Judaism beyond God*[30] and movements such as Secular Humanistic Judaism, there is no doubt that the Judaic component of Jewishness is considered essential by most, insiders and outsiders alike, in any definition of Jewishness. In South Africa the designation "Jewish" distinguishes Jews from all Gentiles in the minds of both sets, with little attention paid to distinctions between ethnic and religious affiliation. In official parlance too the reference is usually religious, in phrases such as "Christians, Muslims and Jews." Most Jews use the label "non-Jew" for "the other" and, whether or not they are personally observant, implicitly accept religion as a crucial component of both referents.

In Israel, however, although the designation "Jewish" also distinguishes Jews from all Gentiles, the significant societal-level cleavage is between Jews and Arabs, whether the latter are Christians, Muslims or secular. The terms used by most Jewish Israelis are "Israelis" (for Jews) and "Arabs"; Arabs use "Jews" and "Arabs." In the context of the history and current reality of the region, the differentiating designations used by Jewish Israelis thus emphasize sociopolitical distinctions, implicitly national rather than religious.

Yet in at least one official aspect Israeli Jewishness is presented (imposed?) rather differently: One of the ten questions on the Israeli census form asks "Are you (1) Jewish (2) Moslem (3) Greek Orthodox (4) Greek Catholic (5) Latin (Catholic) (6) Christian—other (specify) (7) Druze (8) other (specify),"[31] and, according to Dominguez, there is no parallel question such as "Are you (1) Jewish (2) Arab, etc." In other words, the most official Israeli definition of "Jewish" is religious.

Within Jewish Israeli society, there has always been significant differentiation in religious terms but it has grown steadily, and in recent years, exponentially. There is no doubt that the religious-secular cleavage is a pervasive and powerful element in identity-formation in Israeli society, increasingly becoming a basic criterion of "othering" within Israeli Jewry.

The conceptual categories internalized before migration, in both ethnic and religious terms, constitute a major part of the "cultural baggage" the migrants bring with them to diaspora.

Israelis as "Other" for South African Jews

As indicated, local Jews are generally pro-Israel in attitude and many are ideological Zionists. A larger proportion relative to other diaspora communities has visited Israel, and many participate in organizations through which they learn a great deal about the country and its people. Despite the relative familiarity and positive sentiment, most local Jews conceptualize Israelis, both those in South Africa and those in Israel, in stereotypical terms relating to perceived Israeli behavior (cultural style), values, and beliefs. As with all stereotypes, the depictions imply "difference" from the commentator and are often negative: Israelis are thus "loud and pushy," South Africans reserved and restrained; Israelis are dishonest in business, South Africans are "above-board"; Israelis are "only out to make a fast buck," South Africans are communally-minded; Israelis don't care about tradition—they go on vacation on Jewish festivals whereas South Africans accept responsibility for perpetuating Jewish tradition and mark the festivals appropriately.

Local Jews as "Other" for Israeli Migrants

In his study of Israeli emigrants, Sobel asserts that "there existed a certain confusion with regard to distinctions between Jewishness and Israeliness,"[32] while Shokeid insists that "The Israeli experience . . . sharply separate[d] Israelis and other Jews."[33] From the fieldwork, it would seem that both authors are right. On the one hand Israelis discuss Jewish topics, issues, and concerns *as* Israeli topics, issues, and concerns—suggesting "confusion." On the other hand, they explicitly distinguish themselves from Jews, and most particularly from diaspora Jews, as in the following quotations:

> I'm an Israeli, I cannot become a Jew. I don't know [how] to think like a Jew.
>
> When I meet new people, all sorts of people, they know I'm an Israeli—not a Jew, an Israeli.
>
> I'm an Israeli—I could never be a diaspora Jew.
>
> Israelis and local Jews are *completely* different.—There's a basic difference in mentality between Israelis and South African Jews, maybe all diaspora Jews.

The apparent contradiction between Sobel's and Shokeid's conceptions lies in the terms of reference and/or the nature of the discourse. Another way to interpret the seeming confusion between Jewish and Israeli matters would be to understand it as the conflation of Jewishness with Israeliness and vice-versa,[34] *and to appreciate the "taken-for-granted-ness" of that conflation.* The first and most common evidence for this is the almost universal use of the label "Israeli" to mean Jewish Israeli. A qualification is added only when non-Jewish Israeli citizens are referred to, as in, for example, "Arab Israeli." Even Sobel and Shokeid do not bother to inform readers that the term "Israeli" designates only a part of that population, albeit the dominant part.

Evidence abounds to support the observation that Israeli Jews take for granted the intertwinedness of Jewishness and Israeliness. For example, the causes of the high rate of Jewish-Gentile intermarriage in the United States (based on the 1990 National Jewish Population Survey) were widely debated in the Israeli press. There was never any question that this American sociological and demographic statistic was of direct relevance and interest to an Israeli readership. Or, despite vastly differing opinions about individual rights or levels of national responsibility regarding Russian Jewish immigrants (including the irony of casting doubt on the very identity for which they were victimized in Russia), all Jewish Israelis take for granted both the legal and moral right of Russian Jews to settle in Israel, and the moral obligation of the state to both rescue and "absorb" the immigrants. (The same is true for the smaller Ethiopian immigration.) Or, while there has been a great deal of (often acrimonious) debate about the relationship between religion and state, no Israeli doubts the validity or legitimacy of expending so much political energy on Jewish religious issues. Finally, no contradiction is seen between laying historical claim to the territories designated Yehuda and Shomron in terms of Jewish history, while making the emphatic distinctions quoted above between being an Israeli and being a Jew.

What then is the discourse within which the distinction is made? What is the referent for "Jew"? The most striking fact that emerged when the term "Jewish" was introduced into any discussion with respondents was the immediate association with religion. Given the popular characterization of Israel as a secular democracy, and of most Israelis as non- (and many as anti-) religious, this almost automatic association seemed surprising.[35] No matter how the topic arose, no matter whether the response related to belief or observance, or whether it was proud and affirming, apologetic, or stridently antagonistic, it was always in terms of religion, as in the following examples:

> My life here is good at the moment, but I belong there not here. I'm an Israeli—I can't be a diaspora Jew. That is, they're good Jews, better than I am. They go to *shul* [synagogue] . . . and all those things. But I'm an Israeli—it won't help [*lo ya'azor,* "nothing can change that"]. (Full text of the third quote above)

> Israelis and local Jews are *completely* different. Sure there are religious Israelis, but most are secular. For Israelis being Jewish is a cultural matter, national, not religious. (Full text of the fourth quote above)

> You see, in Israel it's clear—you are either religious [*dati*] or you're not religious. When I first came to South Africa, I was told that a certain person keeps kosher. Then I saw him driving on *shabbat* [the sabbath] and it made no sense. So I asked him, "What happened to your kosher?" and he didn't even understand [the connection]. (In discussion with the author and a South African Jew about how to raise children.)

While the association of "Jew/Jewishness" with religion is striking, it was not the only assumption made. Unless the conversation was specifically and explicitly about religious Jews in Israel (and the terms used then were *datiim* [the religious] or *haredim* [the ultra-orthodox] i.e., not the terms "Jew" or "Jewish"), it was always assumed that "Jew" meant "diaspora Jew." For example,

> There's a basic difference in mentality between Israelis and local Jews, maybe all Jews in the diaspora. The Israelis are secular and the Jews are involved with *shul* and *kashrut* [dietary laws] and the IUA and if their children will marry *goyim* [Gentiles]. We have to worry about wars and taxes and mortgages and new immigrants, from Russia or Ethiopia, even South Africa. (Full text of last quote above)

> The South African Jews, when they hear I'm an Israeli, they're immediately friendly. They're sure we're on the same wavelength just because we're both Jews. But we're not. We're not even similar—[we] simply don't relate to the world in the same way. . . . I don't exactly know [how] to explain . . . maybe, something like this: The Jews here are always worrying about something—will the daughter marry a *goy*? is the neighbour an anti-Semite? All the time they think "Jew." We don't think like that. We, the Israelis, we don't worry so much—we're Israelis, and Jewish, and proud of it, and that's that.

Perceptions of Difference beyond Religion

All the respondents without exception talk first, and at length, about missing relatives and friends: "Real friends, that you grew up with, from your neighborhood, from school, from the army. You can't compare even the best new friend with that kind of intimacy. In Israel [*ba'aretz*, 'in the Land'[36]], friends are like family." The emphasis on absent relatives is striking, even for those respondents who indicate quarrelsome relationships with some family members, and particularly when all the respondents, in one formulation or another, mention their own sense of independence. For example, "I've been here only a year, but my little sister has decided to get married in July, so I have to go. I didn't plan to travel so soon and the money [is] a bit of a problem, but we'll do something . . . she's my little sister, I have to be there." Or, "I left home, actually, when I enlisted and I even lived in America for a year and a half, so that's nearly ten years, and they don't run my life or anything, don't misunderstand, but I miss them [*hem chaserim li*], specially if there's something special, like the *chagim* [festivals]. You know how it is—family is family, there's no substitute."

It is not very surprising that recent migrants, particularly those who arrived alone, feel the absence of close family. It becomes more interesting when expressed as a particularly Israeli trait:[37]

> It's strange, I've been here for three years and I have lots of good friends . . . but I still miss the family [*hamishpacha adayin chasera li*]. So I have to go home once a year to see them. Sometimes they drive me crazy but that's the way it is. Maybe it's Israelis. Lisa [a South African friend] and I talk alot about our mothers, and we laugh . . . because they both nag, you know, like all Yiddishe mamas. But it's still different—my parents and my brother and sister, they know me, they know where I go, and who with. Lisa's mother doesn't know her friends, they don't just pop in, like *ba'aretz*.

The last quotation captures several of the conceptual dichotomies and ambiguities identified here. The phrase "Yiddishe mama" demonstrates the conflation between Jewishness and Israeliness in that this very Jewish concept is being applied to an Israeli mother. The same phrase also denotes the presumed affinity between Jewish Israelis and diaspora Jews by implying that all Jews have "Yiddishe mamas." Yet simultaneously the speaker also insists on differentiating Israelis from South African Jews—in this instance by reference to cultural style.

Respondents with South African relatives often praised them and expressed appreciation for assistance, but many agreed with Rachel that "it's not the same. They're South Africans, our whole way of relating is entirely different." In other words, while loyalty to family is always expressed, perceived differences, sometimes explicitly construed as Israeliness, sometimes with the "Israeliness" of self implicit in the characterization of "the other," are also clear.

All the respondents, irrespective of age, marital status or period in South Africa, identified similar "trait lists" of South African ways of acting and interacting, contrasted unfavorably with imputed Israeli characteristics of informality/spontaneity, "openness," and honesty or straightforwardness (*dugriut*). Some associated negative attributes specifically with Jews, others generalized; but all, implicitly or explicitly, were engaged in self-definition of Israeliness, of difference, of boundary-formation, when making such judgments.

Raffi, twenty-six and single, echoed many with his complaints about formality: "You always have to make arrangements. Even the young people, even though you can call them at the last minute, you still have to call, you can't just appear. *Ba'aretz* if you're a friend and you feel like visiting, you appear—it doesn't matter if it's after nine!"

Nurit, a thirty-three-year-old married woman with young children and in Cape Town six years, focused on the children: "You always have to fix everything before. I'm surprised each child doesn't have a diary. . . . But that's the way it is here—there's no neighborhood life [*chayei shchuna*]. Obviously you get used to it—you have to, otherwise your children lose. . . . Life is wonderful for children *ba'aretz*—they're so free, and they become independent much sooner. They're not pampered [*mefunakim*], like here."

Sharon, thirty-one years old, married to a South African and mother of a two-year-old, has been in South Africa four years. She also echoed many with her comments on frankness and hypocrisy: "They're so false here, two-faced. They say one thing but they mean something else. Not everyone, of course, there's good and bad in every nation [*am*]. For instance, you meet someone and they say, they all say, 'you must come over'—but they never say when, or where. And they repeat it every time, but nothing comes out of it. I think they're more honest in business here but I think we're much more honest in our personal relationships. I prefer to know where I stand."

Dalia and Yossi's older son returned to Israel and married an Israeli. Another son lives in Cape Town and is married to a South African Jew. After a recent visit to Israel, Dalia commented on the quality of relationships: "Even after twenty-five years there is still a difference. Friendship between Israelis is more intimate, warmer—there and here. With the locals, there's something superficial, artificial—even after so many years, and even with good friends. [I] don't know why, but that's the way it is. Even with my daughters-in-law . . . [they are] both a hundred percent. But with Sharon [the South African], there's a kind of distance that there isn't with Orna."

Shachar, thirty-three and single, was particularly scathing about South African Jews:

> I talk straight [*dugri*]—if they don't like it, too bad. If they think I'm rude, well, that's their problem. . . . I can't stand this *golah* [diaspora] mentality: everything must always be *nice* [said and repeated in English]—"he's nice," and "she's not nice," and "it's not nice" to do this or that, and "you must be nice to people." . . . Why? why *must* I be nice to people? I do my job, I talk straight, and I have friends and there are other people I do business with, and these are all normal relationships. But they're not all the same. With them [South African Jews], you never know what's going on, because they're always so *nice*. Clearly that's nonsense—they're not always nice, no one is nice always. They have to pretend, they have to show a nice face to the *goyim*. We don't have time for such nonsense *ba'aretz*.

Several points of note emerge from these self-and-other assessments of difference. First and most striking is the degree of similarity among the views expressed, the degree to which images of self and other are shared. Also noteworthy is the degree to which the self-image approximates the Zionist ideal of "the new Jew": free, independent, open and honest, assertive and down-to-earth. The Zionist ideal was, of course, formulated within an ideology of negating diaspora, and by extension, of negating the traits assumed to characterize diaspora Jews. Here, without for the most part mentioning Jews, Zionism or diaspora, these Israelis provide a self-description (indeed, almost a caricature) which would gladden the hearts of the ideologues of yesteryear.

While virtually identical characteristics were identified by most respondents, not everyone assessed them in the same way. Some expressed admiration, though mostly for public rather than interpersonal behavior: "They are so polite—it's a pleasure. Everyone waits in queues without pushing or shouting. I don't think the bureaucracy is different from Israel—one clerk passes you to another, exactly like there. But here everyone accepts it quietly."

Second, while informants experienced dissonance in terms of opposing interaction styles—frankness/pretense, formality/spontaneity, independence of spirit/concern with the opinions of others—and considered the positive attributes markers of Israeliness, the dissonance itself was not viewed as problematic, but simply as a fact of life-away-from-home. Though all were judgmental in their comments, they did not suggest that the identified differences would impede interaction with non-Israelis. When questioned explicitly, however, most expressed preference for Israeli company. Observation of the composition of social networks on occasions of "socializing by choice" confirmed that this preference is indeed practiced.

Third, in most aspects these immigrants conform to what we have learned about all migrants especially in the early period after arrival: they miss their families, enjoy speaking their own language,[38] are quickly comfortable with complete strangers who are also Hebrew-speakers, and they readily formulate a set of stereotypes about "others" which is highly suggestive about their self-definition.

Two aspects, however, stand out as specifically "Israeli." The first relates to the emphasis and positive attitudes respondents expressed toward family and friends in Israel. Why should this merit comment? After all, many people have strong positive feelings about their kin, and, by definition, about friends. But the intensity of feeling expressed is reminiscent of small face-to-face communities[39] and not usual for members of highly technological, highly urbanized and increasingly consumerist societies. I believe these attitudes are closely related to what respondents call *chayei shchuna* (neighborhood life)—in other words, to Israel's urban geography and population density. Most of the Israeli urban population lives in apartment blocks in neighborhoods dotted with small grocery (and other) shops, whose proprietors also live in the area. Because most people own their apartments, which are very expensive relative to earning power, residential mobility is not high. Most children attend state schools, zoned in neighborhoods, and most extracurricular activities for school-age youth also take place within neighborhoods. Immediately after high school the overwhelming majority of the population enters the army for three years compulsory national service. The result is that strong, intense, long-term bonds are formed both in the neighborhood and in the army.

This residential norm has been changing rapidly over the past few years as rising affluence has led to the spread of single family suburban housing, formerly the preserve of only the wealthiest. However, the norm outlined is valid for most of the migrants described here, and accounts at least in part for their emphasis on the intimacy of social relationships as a mark of Israeliness that distinguishes them from locals.

The second aspect has to do with their concern with news about Israel. All migrants show particular interest in news from "home," but the frequency and intensity of concern of Israelis is probably unique, though understandable in the light of Israel's ongoing security problems. All the migrants expressed dissatisfaction at the paucity of Israeli news easily obtainable in Cape Town, all watch CNN for news of Israel, all communicate directly with Israel—greatly facilitated by electronic technology—whenever and as soon as they hear of any "incident."

This intense concern stems partly from habit—in Israel everyone is accustomed to hearing news regularly, and, in many cases, hourly. Buses, supermarkets, and many offices tune into the headline news for reassurance that nothing disastrous has happened anywhere in the country in the past hour. It also stems partly from the small size of the country, coupled with the fact that virtually all Israeli Jews are army reservists for a considerable period of their adult lives. There is thus a good chance they might know someone involved in whatever incident might occur and/or might themselves be called up (via the radio) if some serious action were to take place. For people inexperienced in war, this sounds melodramatic; for ordinary Israelis, it is all too real.

The Lack of Community-Building

At one level, in Jewish terms, there is no need for the migrants to build "community." There exists a "ready-made" community for them to engage with and integrate into if they so wish. To the extent that Israelis wish to participate in ritual activity—primarily prayer and rites of passage—they have the same access to existing Jewish institutions as any local Jew. Kosher food, if desired, is readily available, and the free Jewish communal library contains newspapers, books and periodicals in Hebrew. Organizations to safeguard Jewish interests and welfare also serve all Jews. Israelis utilize these facilities as and when the need arises, but with the exception of members of the Sephardi synagogue, do not participate in ongoing programs or fund-raising activities.

However, given the distinct cognitive, affective and behavioral boundaries Israelis perceive between themselves and local Jews, such *Jewish* ethnic structures cannot provide *Israeli* ethnic solidarity. By contrast with the variety of formal frameworks described by Gold for Los Angeles,[40] the migrants in Cape Town have not created frameworks for the collective expression of Israeliness. Their experience and expression of Israeliness is limited to individual and/or informal means (also described by Gold): intense, ongoing connectedness with family and friends in Israel; Israeli newspapers, books and videos; and Hebrew-speaking frameworks, both the relatively restricted compass of family, and the more extended, more or less loosely structured, personal networks they create.

The differences between Los Angeles and Cape Town can, I believe, be explained by four interrelated factors: (1) the greater (critical) mass of Israelis in Los Angeles allows for greater viability of formal organizations such as Hebrew schools and social clubs; (2) the sharper sense of impermanence in South Africa, due to generalized uncertainties about South Africa's future, underlined by the pervasiveness of "emigration discourse" among whites in particular, and in the popular media. This sense of contingency leads to a larger proportion than in Los Angeles manifesting what Uriely distinguishes as a "sojourner" or "permanent sojourner" (rather than "settler") orientation;[41] (3) the larger proportion of "mixed" marriages in Cape Town, which reduces demand for specifically Israeli (and Hebrew-based) programs and gatherings; (4) the "comprehensive" (i.e., nondenominational) nature of the Cape Town Jewish day school, with its emphasis on Hebrew and its active Zionist and pro-Israel activities, a supportive environment for Israeli identification.

At another level, however, the lack of internal Israeli community-building relates to issues of rootedness. I have referred to the Israelis throughout this chapter as "migrants" rather than "immigrants" and have shown how they are located not within their current or former local worlds but rather in relation to the various worlds they inhabit simultaneously, as individuals and families. The overwhelming majority say they intend to return to

Israel "sometime"; most either own or plan to acquire property in Israel; and all maintain intense and extensive ties with "home," greatly facilitated by electronic technology. While many are informed about South African affairs, their behavior and expressed sentiments suggest that this knowledge is casual, for purposes of short-term self-interest, rather than an indication of involvement in or commitment to South Africa, including South African Jewry. Through the links maintained with Israel, including visits, and through their display and use of Israeli objects and foods, and their interactions within largely Israeli social networks, these migrants "construct and reconstitute their simultaneous embeddedness in more than one society."[42] But while the embeddedness is simultaneous, it is not equally "deep" in all its aspects in each setting.

The contingency implicit in such behavior and sentiments raises the issue of moral allegiance. Israelis exhibit no confusion about this. They do have what might be termed "dual loyalty" but each aspect of the "duo" is of a different order. Their emotional loyalties and sense of belonging relate to the "nation" at two levels: to the Israeli (Jewish) nation, the closest thing to a territorialized nation-state, at least in its self-perception; and to "the Jewish people," a deterritorialized nation. Their civic loyalties, rights and duties are firmly embedded within the local, with some extension to Israel in terms of legal and property rights. In behavior and attitudes they thus distinguish, albeit not formulated this way, between membership of a state (i.e., citizenship) and membership of a nation.

While they experience a sense of loss—of family, friends, neighborhood life, of language, of ways of doing and ways of being—they in fact remain mutually implicated in the lives of those who are absent, and by so doing connect the past to the future through the present.

Their earlier socialization in Israel facilitates their ability to relate simultaneously to several worlds. It includes wide experience of cultural, including linguistic, diversity, as well as experience, vicarious or personal, of family separation and reunification. Many have not grown up in three-generational families, having lost many, if not all, relatives in the Holocaust. While the fact that their children are separated from grandparents because of their own migration often induces a sense of guilt and sadness, not having grandparents on hand is something they are familiar with. The Israeli migrants are cosmopolitans in Hannerz's use of the concept: as an orientation, a perspective, a state of mind. It entails "a relationship to a plurality of cultures," "a stance, an attitude to diversity itself."[43] These migrants are versed in cosmopolitanism in this sense. They are experienced in its practice even though hegemonic Zionist state policy has had, until recently, a consciously homogenizing ideology.

Their cosmopolitanism is both constituted by and constitutive of their experienced realities—constituted by Israeli society's social and cultural diversity and multilingualism, and constitutive of the ways that that past interacts with the here and now. Most of the Israelis in this study could well echo Marianne Hirsch: "For me displacement and bilingualism preceded emigration, they are the conditions into which I was born."[44]

Rather than expressing apathy or negative disengagement, the respondents' lack of community-building can thus be seen as a rational response to their situation: their instrumental use of local Jewish facilities satisfies certain needs, and their simultaneous embeddedness in both Israel and South Africa, expressed through personal networks, provides sufficient *Gemeinschaft.* They display a broad spectrum of attitudes to the negative connotations of betrayal implied in the notion of *yerida:* some deny the accusation of desertion because they intend to return; some dismiss the concept as outdated, no longer applicable to "normal" citizens (which resonates with current debates about post-Zionism); and others emphasize the legitimacy of individualistic values and aspirations. I would argue that this situation reflects the migrants' confidence about their relationship to the Israeli state, contrary to the "neurosis" proposed by Yehoshua.[45] It also reflects a shift in values away from the collective to an emphasis on self-realization.[46] That is, verbally and behaviorally the Israelis express confidence in the viability and endurance of the Israeli state, value that state positively, and feel free to exercise their personal current residential preference, albeit expressed as temporary.

TOWARD EXPLANATION

Perceptions of a Shared Past

The conflation of Jewishness with Israeliness is most taken for granted most often with respect to the past. Despite considerable variation among dispersed Jewish communities during two thousand years of "exile," and despite continued manifestation of that heterogeneity in both Israel and the diaspora, the sense of a common origin, of a shared historical experience of exile and persecution, and creativity, and of a shared religious tradition, is still profound. Furthermore, there is consensus that the existence of the State of Israel is largely due to the efforts of the Zionist movement, a Jewish movement of national liberation, albeit one that arose at a particular historical moment in European history. There also exists virtual consensus that Israel is and must remain a Jewish state although there is no agreement on the meaning of the adjective nor how it relates or should relate to the secular and democratic principles espoused in the Declaration of Independence. In addition, in both rhetoric and deed, identifying Jews everywhere have retained a strong sense of mutual responsibility. Liebman and Cohen, in their comparison of Israeli and American Jews, add to the above a shared set of symbols and what they call "familism," viewing "the Jewish people" as an extension of "my family."[47]

The broad consensus sketched here, which offers a large range of particular items and can accommodate many interpretations precisely because it is so broad, goes some way toward explaining the taken-for-granted identification by Israelis of Jewishness with Israeliness. It is in the selection from that broad canvas, of specific symbols, of particular values and perspectives, all of which emerge in the particular sociohistorical context of Israeli and diaspora societies respectively, that creates differentiation both within Israeli society and between Israel and the diaspora. And it is that differentiation that accounts, at least in part, for some of the seeming contradictions delineated above.

Such conflation clearly does not exist for South African (or any diaspora) Jews. While personal identities certainly include both Jewish and South African components, the criteria for each are distinct: (religious) ethnicity for the Jewish element, and citizenship ("nationality," in formal terms) for the South African component.

The Association of Jew/Jewish with Religion

An additional factor to those itemized above in relation to Israeli perceptions of "the other," and supported by fieldwork data, concerns the prominence of religious issues in Israeli public life over the past ten or fifteen years.[48] The so-called status quo agreement between the religious and secular,[49] so carefully crafted and upheld during the Ben Gurion era and beyond, has been progressively eroded. While at one level there has always been significant cleavage between the two categories, the status quo agreement at the level of public life and party politics, combined with the closed (ghettolike) character of ultraorthodox lifestyles, had, in the past, succeeded in minimizing, or masking, the extent of the cleavage. Since the "Begin era" (1977) at least, that cleavage has been increasingly exposed.

This is clearly reflected in informants' responses. The younger generation (under thirty-five) is much more likely to be more emphatic in their self-definition as secular, as "Israeli, not Jewish," more consistent in describing various processes in Israel as religious "coercion," and more disparaging of religious public figures and political positions. They are also more likely to associate Jewishness with religion. Furthermore, this generation displays very little concern with the notion of *yerida* with its implications of betrayal and/or desertion.

The older generation is more likely to introduce the concept *yerida* into conversation—while taking care to distinguish themselves from *yordim*—and to discuss Jewishness as emerging from historical consciousness and "tradition."

For most South African (and other diaspora) Jews, the labels "Jew/Jewish" are assumed to include reference to religion when applied in general. When applied to themselves, the label usually connotes ethnicity.

Conditions of Collective Existence

Elsewhere I have discussed the major divides within contemporary Jewry, between the Orthodox and all others, and between Israel and the diaspora.[50] With regard to the first divide, I argue that while *in certain major respects* the divergence between the observant Orthodox and all other Jews has already taken place, there are simultaneous indications of rapprochement, including increased cooperation between the Israeli and diaspora components of each of these "sides," *around other issues.* I claim that the second divide is essentially between non-Orthodox Israelis and non-Orthodox diaspora Jews,[51] including the non-observant Orthodox-affiliated. In Gilman's terms, the first divide transcends the center-periphery model and creates a new, albeit internal, frontier. The second divide, though shaped by material and existential space, does not contain the implied value hierarchy of the center-periphery model.

The Orthodox/non-Orthodox distinction relates to a specific aspect of "the tradition," *halakha* (Jewish Law), and assumes that its content, meaning, purpose and value are salient and valid for its adherents and comprise the most important ingredient of their Jewishness. This does not imply that "the Orthodox" constitute an undifferentiated category—analytically and empirically they can be, and are, differentiated according to various criteria ranging from ideological to behavioral. But in this sense the distinction treats the non-Orthodox as a residual, albeit majority, category, classified as such only by what they are not. The focus here, however, is not on the coherence or looseness of the non-Orthodox category—which indeed manifests much greater diversity than the Orthodox—but rather on the perceived divide, within the category, between Israelis and diaspora Jews, in this case South African Jewry.

The most critical divide, and also the most obvious, relates to the collective level: Jews in Israel are a national majority within a sovereign democratic state, defined as "Jewish." The implications of a Jewish majority, to date, are that national symbols, holidays, and language are Jewish and public, and that the majority of the individual Jew's relationships—work, neighborhood and leisure—are with other Jews. The implication of an independent state with a Jewish majority is that the destiny of its citizens is decided by them, albeit not in isolation from the rest of the world, Jewish and Gentile. The implication of democracy is that diverse Jewish voices, of which there are many, have representation in decison-making. The consequence for all Jewish Israelis is that they neither have to be reminded nor do they need to remind themselves self-consciously that they are Jewish. They are immersed, willy-nilly, in matters Jewish. Jewish issues, dilemmas, celebrations and commemorations are present all around them, daily and always.

Diaspora Jewry, including South African Jewry, is everywhere a minority for whom collective expressions of Jewishness are dependent on the tolerance of the host society; where national symbols, holidays and language are other than Jewish; where minority Jewish voices merely add points of fission because there is no overarching framework which is in any way binding; and where the majority of the individual Jew's relationships are with other Jews only if he or she makes a conscious effort to create and maintain such relationships. The consequence for all diaspora Jews, in the absence of daily public immersion, is that they must self-consciously choose whether and how to be Jews. For South African Jews, minority self-consciousness runs particularly deep: they are a minority both because of the color of their skin and, within the white minority, because of the pervasiveness of religion in South African life. In addition, because of their strong Zionist commitment, they have always been keenly aware of the possibility of being accused of dual loyalties.

Mutual perceptions of difference thus largely account for the nonintegration of the local Israeli migrants into the "proximal host" community. And these perceptions can be seen to be firmly located, in each case, in the social context within which members of each collectivity were socialized.

Self-Confidence and "Comfortable Contradiction"

A minority of the transmigrants in this study are troubled by their liminal situation—in, but not of, *golah*. These migrants—mostly older, and not all born in Israel—are acutely aware that even after the so-called normalizing Zionist revolution, and despite aspirations to become a secular democratic state "like all others," the animating issues, the deepest fissures in Israel, in public and private domains, are not only about the obvious—taxes, schooling, and so on—but include conflicts about the nature, the very character, of their nation-state. Their ongoing engagement with life in Israel keeps these issues "alive" for them; but their present lives in diaspora underline the degree to which neither the Jewish state, nor the condition of "the Jewish people," has been normalized. To this extent they resemble diaspora Jews. However, having been successfully socialized to negate diaspora, yet now finding themselves in it, they are ambivalent about many aspects of their own lives. They are unable and unwilling to become "compartmentalized" Jews, but recognize the difficulties of imparting their version of Jewishness to their children in the conditions of *golah.* For these migrants, the contradictions in their lives create discomfort and they are pleased and relieved when their children choose *aliya.*

For the majority of Israeli migrants in Cape Town, however, this is not the case. While they may resemble their forebears in their unrooted cosmopolitanism, their style of adaptation is quite different. As Jewish-Israelis/Israeli-Jews, socialized as a dominant majority, they are neither troubled nor ambivalent about their own identities or positions but display self-confidence in their ethnic-national identity, and contrast it proudly with the self-consciousness of diaspora Jewry. In this sense they have been "normalized"—they carry none of the social or psychological baggage of a "minority." In every sense they closely resemble other middle-class transmigrants, who live simultaneously in more than one world, and link the past to the future through their own present. Their adaptation to diaspora thus constitutes a definitive break with Jewish adaptive patterns of the past. And in this sense they are at the frontier of the twenty-first century—exemplars of the possibilities of living *comfortably,* albeit with contradictions, in a globalized world.

However, from a Jewish perspective, *outside of Israel* this very "normalization" contains an inherent threat to Jewish continuity. Self-confidence and positive sentiment per se say little about distinctive content or the extent to which Jewishness is valued relative to the many other available options for identification. The very taken-for-grantedness of the equation between Jewishness and Israeliness can lead to the (false) assumption that this relationship is inevitable, "natural," automatic, somehow self-perpetuating. It can undermine the basic requirements for the continuity of cultural particularity: the conscious will to acquire distinctive cultural knowledge, and the ability, desire and means to transmit it to the next generation.

Notes

1. A. A. Dubb, *The Jewish Population of South Africa: The 1991 Sociodemographic Survey* (Cape Town: Jewish Publications—South Africa, 1994), 7.

2. Ibid., 25.

3. S. Gold, "Patterns of Economic Cooperation among Israeli Immigrants in Los Angeles," *International Migration Review* 28.1 (1994); N. Uriely, "Patterns of Identification and Integration among Israeli Immigrants in Chicago: Variations across Status and Generation," *Contemporary Jewry* 16 (1995).

4. For a full description of these difficulties, and attempts at resolution, see S. DellaPergola and A. A. Dubb, "South African Jewry: A Sociodemographic Profile," *American Jewish Year Book* 88 (1988); S. Frankental, "Israelis in South Africa: Profile of a Migrant Population," in *Papers in Jewish Demography, 1985,* ed. U. O. Schmelz and S. DellaPergola (Jerusalem: Hebrew University, 1989); and Dubb, *Jewish Population of South Africa.*

5. DellaPergola and Dubb, "South African Jewry," 75.

6. Dubb, *Jewish Population of South Africa,* 17.

7. B. Beit Hallahmi, "Israel and South Africa, 1977–1982: Business as Usual—and More," *New Outlook* 26.2 (Mar.–Apr. 1983); N. Chazan, "The Fallacies of Pragmatism: Israel's Foreign Policy towards South Africa," *African Affairs* 82.327 (Apr. 1983); K. Osia, *Israel, South Africa, and Black Africa: A Study of the Primacy of the Politics of Expediency* (Washington, D.C.: University Press of America, 1981); G. Shimoni, "South African Jews and the Apartheid Crisis," *American Jewish Year Book* 88 (1988).

8. M. Arkin, ed., *South African Jewry: A Contemporary Survey* (Cape Town: Oxford University Press, 1984), 89.

9. See G. Shimoni, *Jews and Zionism: The South African Experience, 1910–1967* (Cape Town: Oxford University Press, 1980).

10. According to Dubb, *Jewish Population of South Africa,* 117 and 122, between 1970 and 1980 the 65+ age cohort had increased from 11.7 percent to 17.2 percent of the total Jewish population (118,200 in 1970; 117,963 in 1980) and the number of those aged 75+ had virtually doubled. By 1991 the total population had declined by about 10 percent and those aged 65+ by about 17 percent. However, the proportion of those aged 75+ had grown from 5.8 percent to 7.3 percent. As Dubb notes (118), this is the group most likely to require public assistance. In addition, large-scale emigration of younger people over the same period has left many elderly without the support of their children.

11. The most recent migration estimates, compiled from a variety of sources in 1991 (see Dubb, *Jewish Population of South Africa,* chaps. 1–2), show 21,000 Jewish emigrants for the period 1970–1980 (17.8 percent of the Jewish population in the 1970 census) and 18,000 emigrants for the period 1980–90/91 (15.2 percent of the Jewish population in the 1980 census). 22,500 immigrants and return migrants entered the country between 1970 and 1990/91. Dubb (3) also shows that in 1991 Jews constituted 0.3 percent of all South Africans and about 2 percent of whites, a decline from the 0.5 percent and 2.6 percent, respectively, in 1980. Furthermore, by 1991 there had been significant net losses in the 0–9 and 25–34 age groups.

12. S. Frankental and M. Shain, "Accommodation, Apathy, and Activism: Jewish Polical Behaviour in South Africa," *Jewish Quarterly* 40.1 (1993): 11.

13. The Hebrew terms for migration to and from Israel, *aliya* and *yerida,* are biblical in origin and differ from the term for migration in general (*hagira*). The term *oleh,* Jewish immigrant to Israel, means "one who goes up" (to the Holy Land) thereby fulfilling the Zionist injunction; *yored* (pl: *yordim*), "one who goes down," designates the (Jewish) Israeli who leaves Israel, and implies desertion. The terms thus have both emotional and ideological connotations. See A. Friedberg, "Yerida: The Pull and the Push," *Forum* 61 (1988); D. Kass and S. Lipset, "Israelis in Exile," *Commentary* 68.5 (1979); and M. Shokeid, *Children of Circumstances: Israeli Emigrants in New York* (Ithaca, N.Y.: Cornell University Press, 1988), for discussion of *yerida* as a "problem," and Z. Sobel, *Migrants from the Promised Land* (New Brunswick, N.J.: Transaction Books, 1986), for its treatment in the Israeli media.

14. S. M. Cohen, "Israeli Emigres and the New York Federation: A Case Study in Ambivalent Policymaking for 'Jewish Communal Deviants,'" *Contemporary Jewry* 7 (1986); Shokeid, *Children of Circumstances,* 52.

15. D. Mittelberg and M. Waters, "The Process of Ethnogenesis among Haitian and Israeli Immigrants in the United States," *Ethnic and Racial Studies* 15 (1992).

16. M. Waters, *Ethnic Options: Choosing Identities in America* (Berkeley: University of California Press, 1990).

17. For example, the author of an article in the June 1996 issue of the *Cape Jewish Chronicle,* about a function held during the last Israeli elections, refers to the presence of "an unusually large number from the Israeli community."

18. "Sephardim" (also known in Israel as "orientals") is the traditional classificatory term for Jews descended from the Jews who lived in Spain and Portugal prior to their expulsion in 1492. Today the term is used for Jews who themselves or whose antecedents came from Muslim countries and who reside predominantly in Israel and France. The term "Ashkenazim" is used for Jews originally from eastern and central Europe who today reside predominantly in Israel, Latin America, and English-speaking countries.

19. E. Ben Rafael and S. Sharot, *Ethnicity, Religion, and Class in Israeli Society* (Cambridge: Cambridge University Press, 1991); S. Smooha, *Israel: Pluralism and Conflict* (London: Routledge and Kegan Paul, 1978).

20. Uriely, "Patterns of Identification."

21. Gold, "Patterns of Economic Cooperation."

22. Shokeid, *Children of Circumstances.*

23. Mittelberg and Waters, "Process of Ethnogenesis."

24. N. Uriely, "The Rhetorical Ethnicity of Permanent Sojourners: The Case of Israeli Immigrants in the Chicago Area," *International Sociology* 9 (1994); Uriely, "Patterns of Identification."

25. S. Gold, "Israeli Immigrants in the United States: The Question of Community," *Qualitative Sociology* 17.4 (1994).

26. B. Anderson, *Imagined Communities: Reflections on the Origin and Spread of Nationalism* (London: Verso, 1983).

27. D. Elazar, *People and Polity: The Organizational Dynamics of World Jewry* (Detroit: Wayne State University Press, 1989); C. Liebman and S. Cohen, *Two Worlds of Judaism: The Israeli and American Experiences* (New Haven, Conn.: Yale University Press, 1990).

28. N. Schiller, L. Basch and C. Blanc, "From Immigrant to Transmigrant: Theorizing Transnational Migration," *Anthropological Quarterly* 68.1 (1995): 48. For a critique

of the authors' use of the terms "immigrant," "international," and "nation-state," see S. Frankental, "Transmigrants, Cosmopolitans, and the Meaning of Home" (ms., Department of Social Anthropology, University of Cape Town, 1995).

29. See Uriely, "Rhetorical Ethnicity of Permanent Sojourners."

30. S. Wine, *Judaism beyond God: A Radical New Way to Be Jewish* (Michigan: Society for Humanistic Judaism, 1985).

31. Quoted in V. Dominguez, *People as Subject, People as Object: Selfhood and Peoplehood in Contemporary Israel* (Madison: University of Wisconsin Press, 1989), 154.

32. Sobel, *Migrants from the Promised Land,* 50.

33. Shokeid, *Children of Circumstances,* 210.

34. S. Herman, *Jewish Identity: A Social Psychological Perspective* (London: Sage, 1977), was the first to provide evidence of this for Israelis in Israel. The present study shows that the taken-for-grantedness of the conflation is part of the internalized "cultural baggage" Israeli migrants take abroad.

35. Although most respondents defined themselves as secular, or "non-practicing traditional," this discourse too needs to be examined, particularly in the light of the Guttman Report (1994), which challenges the conventional wisdom that Israel is a secular society and concludes instead that "Israeli society has a strong traditional bent." See C. Liebman and E. Katz, eds., *The Jewishness of Israelis: Responses to the Guttman Report* (Albany: SUNY Press, 1997). More important for this discussion, whereas the response of "secular" in Israel assumes "secular Jewish," in the diaspora this is articulated as "Israeli, not Jewish."

36. All the respondents use *ba'aretz,* "in the Land," to refer to Israel. This usage is common to all Israelis. Correspondingly, "abroad" is phrased as *chutz la'aretz,* "outside of 'the Land.'" While the usage is unselfconscious and does not signal a particular ideological or political position (unlike the varity of terms used for the West Bank and Gaza), it does nevertheless point to the Zionist success in creating a linguistic/cognitive map that distinguishes clearly between "the Land," meaning "our" land, and everywhere else. This kind of language usage thus, in most cases, also demarcates Israeliness.

37. See Liebman and Cohen, *Two Worlds of Judaism,* chap. 2.

38. Language doesn't only mean semantics, accent, or vocabulary. It is interconnected with meanings of home, family, and displacement. As Gilman emphasizes, language is a crucial and constant marker of frontier. In John Hollander's words, "When you have to go there [home], the way they talk is yours." ("It All Depends," *Social Research* 58.1 [1991]: 47).

39. A similar point is noted in Liebman and Cohen, *Two Worlds of Judaism,* 22, referring to the work of Kevin Avruch (*American Immigrants in Israel: Social Identities and Change* [Chicago: University of Chicago Press, 1981]), although the characterization there uses the term "traditional" rather than "face-to-face."

40. Gold, "Israeli Immigrants in the United States," 332–34.

41. Uriely, "Rhetorical Ethnicity of Permanent Sojourners."

42. Schiller et al., "From Immigrant to Transmigrant," 48.

43. U. Hannerz, "Cosmopolitans and Locals in World Culture," *Theory, Culture, and Society* 7 (1990): 238–39.

44. M. Hirsch, "Pictures of a Displaced Girlhood," in *Displacements: Cultural Identities in Question,* ed. A. Bammer (Bloomington: Indiana University Press, 1994), 77.

45. A. B. Yehoshua, *Between Right and Right* (Garden City, N.Y.: Doubleday, 1981).

46. E. Schweid, "Is There Really No Alienation and Polarization?" in *The Jewishness of Israelis,* ed. Liebman and Katz, 156; R. Wistrich and D. Ohana, *The Shaping of Israeli Identity* (London: Frank Cass, 1995), viii.

47. Liebman and Cohen, *Two Worlds of Judaism,* chap. 2.

48. M. Aronoff, *Israeli Visions and Divisions: Cultural Change and Political Conflict* (New Brunswick, N.J.: Transaction, 1989); C. Liebman, ed., *Religious and Secular: Conflict and Accommodation between Jews in Israel* (Jerusalem: Keter, 1990); Liebman and Katz, *Jewishness of Israelis;* Z. Sobel and B. Beit Hallahmi, eds., *Tradition, Innovation, Conflict: Jewishness and Judaism in Contemporary Israel* (Albany: SUNY Press, 1991).

49. The term "secular" tends to be used very arbitrarily. Only a very small minority of identifying Jews, in Israel or the diaspora, holds a conscious intellectual position on this issue and purposefully rejects notions of the divine or the sacred, and its extensions to law (*halakha*) and religious ritual practice. Such Jews are, for the most part, knowledgeable in these matters and concerned with "the state of the nation." They tend to emphasize the universalistic and social justice content of "the tradition," and those among them who recognize the Jewish calendar and the value of ritual tend to interpret or practice these as historical commemorations and/or occasions for strengthening family or national solidarity. The vast majority of the so-called secular are considered such in terms of practice, and are secular by default rather than by intent: they do not ask themselves what they believe, and practice whatever takes their fancy from whatever they happen to know or remember. Theirs is not an intellectual position, but rather an empirically observable phenomenon. It should be clear from this chapter that the implications of "secularity" are different for Israelis and diaspora Jews.

50. S. Frankental, "Klal Yisrael and Jewish Continuity: The Future," ms., Department of Social Anthropology, University of Cape Town, 1996.

51. The reference here is to identifying Jews only, whatever their means or criteria of identification. Those who have opted out, whether consciously and deliberately, or by default, are excluded. With possible individual exceptions, they can be considered already lost to the Jewish people and to Judaism.

7 Bifocality in Jewish Identity in the Texas-Jewish Experience

SETH L. WOLITZ

A FIRST ENCOUNTER WITH TEXAS JEWRY

Having moved to Texas some twenty-three years ago, I needed the services of a *mohel* (ritual circumciser) for our newborn native Texas son. The local *mohel* had a shaky hand and so I looked elsewhere and found a fifth-generation Texas Jew from Houston reputed to have the speed and accuracy of a Texas gunslinger! His plane arrived on time at our city airport, but, expecting a bearded *mohel* dressed in traditional garb, I could not find him. Disconcerted, I paged the *mohel* and a man appeared in full Texas dress—the ten-gallon hat, the silver belt buckle, blue jeans and boots—saying he was Doctor Geller. I panicked. "Are you the *mohel*?" I asked. "I am," he said in drawl and lifted his ten-gallon hat and showed his yarmulke to me and then pulled out a string of *tsitsit* (ritual fringes on special undergarments of Orthodox Jews)! Well, the rest of the story is familiar, a normal *bris* (circumcision ritual). But let me add, at its conclusion, the leading university anthropologist fainted! Howdy Pardner, Welcome to Texas Jewry![1]

THE HISTORICAL UNIQUENESS OF TEXAS JEWRY

The Texas Jewish experience is distinct from other parts of the United States because the history of the State of Texas itself is unique. From 1836 to 1845, Texas was a sovereign nation and this experience has marked the people and the memory of the state. Jews, while few in number, were part of the fight for independence from Mexico and Jews entered and participated in Texas life from the beginning of the Anglo-Texan hegemony. The Jews were in the Alamo and even served in the Texas Navy. They helped colonize the state and founded the cities and towns of Waco and Castroville.[2] In the nineteenth century, the majority of the Jews came from Germany and entered into banking, cattle ranching and especially the mercantile sector, establishing the great department stores, the most famous of which, to this day, is the Dallas Neiman-Marcus store. The Jews did not come in groups but as individuals and spread throughout the state. In the main cities, Galveston, Houston and San Antonio, the Jews organized burial societies by 1855, and in Houston, chartered the first synagogue, Beth Israel, in 1859, which started orthodox and ended up reform by 1879.[3] The Jews participated fully in civic affairs and one was even elected to the U.S. Congress. Many served in the Confederate Army during the War of the States. This dramatic event gave further shape and integration of the Jews into their Texas milieu. By 1900, according to the statistics of the American Jewish Yearbook (1900), there were approximately 15,000 Jews in the state.

The character of the Jewish community of Texas would hardly alter with the arrival of the Eastern European Jews who entered Texas from its main seaport under a program called the Galveston Movement. Jacob Schiff in New York, the leading German-Jewish-American philanthropist, was aware of the growing tensions brought about by the mass immigrations to the United States along the Eastern Seaboard, and sought to reroute the new Jewish immigrants to the West.[4] This project functioned from 1907 to 1914. Although it brought in ten thousand skilled and unskilled Jews, it nowhere approached the original plans which foresaw at least tenfold the entrants. Galveston was chosen because of direct shipping lines to Germany and its cooperative local community under the leadership of Rabbi Henry Cohen, a legend in Texas-Jewish life.[5] It was the first time that Texas Jews functioned as a concerted community on behalf of World Jewry.[6] By coming straight to Texas, these immigrants of the Galveston Movement entered into the dominant culture, as had the earlier Jewish immigrants, and needed to accommodate immediately to the new physical and cultural realities. Being Eastern European Jews, their sense of definition and identity based on distinct cultural/religious and social practices placed upon them greater burdens of adjustment than their earlier German counterparts who had already gained some social and cultural advantages from the German *Aufklaerung*. Forced to encounter the Other—the dominant Anglo-Texan, the subaltern African-American and Mexican-American—the new immigrant was hastened on the path of Americanization or, better, Texanization. The Eastern European Jewish immigrant also faced the class barriers of the German-Jewish elite, the memories of which are not yet all erased.

The Texas experience provided no mediating space. The New York world, by contrast, by the sheer number of immigrants, permitted the creation of a transitional culture. It became a centrum of a distinct Jewish-American experience, the importance of which is now recognized worldwide.[7] Even though New York functioned and functions today as the center of Jewish-American life, the Texas Jew, while accepting his peripheral condition from the New Yorker's perspective, does not feel decentered. The Texas Jew sees New York as the alternative vision and considers the Texas-Jewish experience no less valid and perhaps more desirable. Most Jewish-Americans have folk memories of the squalid East Side tenements of Manhattan, but the Texas-Jewish community has an almost pastoral memory of growing up in peaceful Texas towns and small cities from Amarillo to Laredo, from Beaumont to El Paso. The Texas Jews have, in imitation of the dominant Texas culture, created a mythic sense of homeland: a landedness, a centeredness, in short, a sense of Texas as home with all its incongruities. The Galveston Movement, with its descendants ultimately fusing with the German-Jewish earlier stock, set the character of Texas Jewry. By 1930 there were approximately 50,000 Jews in Texas and the population remained steady until the 1970s when the influx of Northern Jews began and increased significantly in the last fifteen years. The Jewish population of Texas today is approximately 110,000 and is growing rapidly.[8] Although there is some dilation of the Texas-Jewish habitus by the rapid growth, not unlike Israel's absorption of the Russian Jews, the powerful myth of Texas—even if tongue-in-cheek, and it is more than that—envelops the newcomer willingly and unconsciously, and his native-born descendant becomes the absolute imprimatur of authenticity by birthright. By being present at the origin of the republic and of the state, the Texas Jew lays claim to originary rights which, if at times are contested by anti-Semites, nevertheless carry psychological meaning and weight to both Texas Jews and Gentiles. The New York Jewish experience, beginning in 1654, starts off with a clash of wills between Pieter Stuyvesant and the newcomers. They came as a group and have maintained and functioned over the centuries with highly organized group-consciousness and solidarity. Texas Jewry has a different history and therefore a different mentality.

CONFIGURATIONS OF THE TEXAS-JEWISH PERSONALITY

In studying the problem of Jewish identity in its acculturation into Texas, I shall interpret three self-consciously Texas-Jewish writers/performers whose texts reflect the inheritance of the Galveston Movement of the first and third generations. This study will show how the first generation observes the

Other, the hegemonic Other, from the perspective of the minority culture and attempts to justify and recognize its own accommodations and future perspectives, and, secondly, how the third generation interprets the Other as a co-equal, revealing the problematics of contemporary Jewish identity in the delightful aporia called the "Texas Jew." This essay argues that by the third generation the Jews have acculturated to Texas to such a degree that they have reshaped the label and traditional meaning of the noun and concept. They have created a Texas Jew who fits the dominant normative practice of Texas. In their texts, they have reinscribed this Texas Jewishness back into the original Jewish culture of the first generation so that the ancestors are proto-Americans or proto-Texans. The gaps and tears of the Atlantic crossing are thereby sutured into a smooth Foucauldian genealogy which answers to contemporary Texas-Jewish wants and needs. In this condition, there is no consciousness that there is any significant difference between the present Jewish identity and that of the past, except in language and greater religious laxity in traditional observance, but not in ethical fervor or identity. What I shall reveal is a paradigmatic shift, a reorientation of ethnicity in which, using the terms of Simon During, the "dominant social values [were] internalized."[9] This essay forces the question of what is and who determines Jewish identity while offering a Texas-Jewish variant.

TWO GENERATIONS ENCOUNTER THE TEXAS EXPERIENCE

Since I am working in the dangerous area of Weberian ideal types, I have chosen to make use of the most creative texts of each generation to underline the paradigmatic shift I have theorized as producing the Texas Jew. This is immediately evident in the generic choices and possibilities. The first generation of the Galveston Movement mainly wrote memoirs, which were as much attempts at reflexivity and locating the self after the rupture of the old life as they were capturing the wonderment and bewilderment of the new. The memoir was an *apologia pro vita sua* which both recorded the instabilities in life, the breaks with the past, the justifications of accommodations, if not attainment of success. One unique figure, Rabbi Alexander Ziskind Gurwitz (1859–1937), supplies the only detailed picture of the Galveston Movement as a participant, capturing the trek from Kharkov to San Antonio at the age of fifty-one. His work, *Memories of Two Generations,* was written in Hebrew and Yiddish and published at his own expense in New York in 1935.[10] He may have had a limited aesthetic sensibility to Western forms, but the subtext of his entire work reflects the biblical master-narrative of the Joseph story to which he makes constant allusion: "It was the will of God that we should come [first] to America from where we would be able to save our children from the hell of Russia" (247). The third generation reflects its vision of the Jewish condition through the performative arts. The shift in generic production itself underscores the move from the first-generation personal and closed world of narrative reflexivity to a public-oriented dissemination of a Jewish vision which seeks its representation as opposed to invisibility. Most of the memoirs were never published. The use of performative arts demands a public hearing. Its efforts are persuasive and establish rights of presence of unquestionable legitimacy. Mark Harelik's 1985 play, *The Immigrant,* about his immigrant grandfather settling in the rural town of Hamilton, Texas, continues to be performed in every major repertory theater in the United States, and his 1996 play, *The Legacy* (first produced at San Diego Playhouse, Summer 1997), about the second generation in Texas and its accommodations, continues the family story and Texas-Jewish saga of the Galveston Migration.[11] Harelik's plays reenact the complex shift of perspective in the two generations. *The Immigrant,* in two acts, follows the continuous Texanization of grandpa, Haskell Harelik, in his quest for security and respect. Kinky Friedman encapsulates in his sharply satiric country-western songs circa 1972 the intersection of race, culture and language which locates the sites of resistance between the would-be hegemonic culture of Anglo-Texas and the assertive egalitarianism of the Texas third-generation Jew, who functions within the dominant culture's parameters which have been appropriated into a Jewish-Texas one.[12] By offering a third-generation high-culture text and a popular culture textual exemplum, I seek to point out the presence and integration of the Texas Jew into the broadest cultural life of the state and nation. This does not preclude discontinuities and resistances but also locates a new cultural authority in which the Texas Jew has attained to a large extent what the French call *le haut du pavé.*[13]

We may gain more from approaching the paradigmatic shift and creation of the modern Texas-Jewish vision from an inductive view. Let us look at the song of Kinky Friedman composed in 1972 in Austin and performed with his combo, with its aggressively appropriated anti-Semitic slur, The Texas Jewboys, which asserts Jewish presence and claim to legitimacy. This song was recently performed at the annual Fourth of July Luckenbach Folk Festival in 1996, where it still brought cheers and at points boos from the Texas audience.

> A redneck nerd in a bowling shirt
> Was guzzling Lone Star Beer
> Talking religion and politics for all the

world to hear
They ought to send you back to Russia boy
or New York City one
You just want to diddle a Christian girl
And you killed God's only son

I said has it occurred to you, you nerd
That that's not very nice
We Jews believe it was Santa Claus
that killed Jesus Christ.
You know, you don't look Jewish he said
Near as I can figure
I had you lamped for a slightly anemic
well-dressed country nigger

Oh they ain't making Jews like Jesus anymore
They don't turn the other cheek the way they
done before
He started in on shouting and spitting
on the floor, Lord
they ain't making Jews like Jesus anymore.

He says, I ain't a racist but
Aristitle [*sic*] Onassis is one Greek we don't need
And them niggers, Jews, and Sigma Nus
All they ever do is breed
And wops and micks and slopes and spics and spooks
are on my list
And there's one little heb from the heart of Texas
Is there anyone I missed?

Well, I hits him with everything I had
Right square between the eyes.
I said, I'm gonna get ya, you son of a bitch, ya,
For spouting that pack of lies.
If there's one thing I can't abide
It's an ethnocentric racist.
Now you take back that thing you said
about Aristitle Onassis.

They ain't making Jews like Jesus anymore
We don't turn the other cheek the way
We done before
You could hear that honky holler
As he hit the hardwood floor
They ain't making Jews like Jesus anymore.

They ain't making Jews like Jesus anymore
They ain't making carpenters who knows what nails are for
The whole damn place was cheering as I
Stole right out the door, Lord
they sure ain't making Jews Like Jesus anymore.

This song's title, "They Ain't Making Jews Like Jesus Anymore," ironically and stunningly appropriates the Christ figure very much as Chagall and the Jewish painters and Yiddish poets did in the teens and twenties of this century, claiming Jesus not only as a Jewish soul-brother, thus reducing blasphemously a God-figure to a Jewish subaltern mortal, but appropriating and inscribing the essence of Christian virtue to the normative habits of the Jews: a passive, good-natured people "turning the other cheek." The rhetorical strategy of the song sets stereotype against its mirror image: the populist Texas Bubba anti-ethnic against the meanest, toughest Texas Jew in the Texas public space of a beer hall. The song celebrates Jewish muscle and Jewish rights to win the day in a mythic Texas fashion: a brawl. The song confirms that the Texas Jew is as Texan as the Redneck. The title begs the question: What type of Jew then is being made? The new Jew, the Texas Jew; tough, unbending, no "turning the other cheek, the way they done before." Here is the Texas mythic tradition where individual muscular performance carries truth and right.[14] The knockout rebuts every anti-Semitic accusation a Texas Redneck might harbor:

—the Jews are foreigners who should go back to where they came from;
—they are communists or damn Yankees;
—they are sexually threatening, they breed too much;
—they are a criminal peoplehood having committed deicide;
—their bodies are diseased and weak;
—they are vulgarly flamboyant in a material way, overdressed;
—their race is not white but something inferior;
—they belong to negative ethnicities.

The satirical song puts down the Texas Bubba braggart getting his comeuppance from an unexpected co-equal. The knockout not only reduces the Redneck to his mortal banality, but by being called a "Honky," he is debased and reintegrated into the Texas economy of ethnic slurs.

What is invisible in the song is the new cultural space in which the scene is performed, for the narrative's transparency shields the total Jewish appropriation of the Texas Redneck's cultural assumptions that a show of might makes right. Jewish traditional subalternity reappropriated ironically and scandalously as Christian piety is found wanting in opposition to the Other's violence. The assumption of the Other's violence is now inscribed back into the Jewish worldview and ethos. The "remasculinization" of the Jew through aggressivity absorbed from the dominant culture shapes the new Texas-Jewish ethos.[15] One barely recognizes the subtextual suggestion that this is the David and Goliath story replayed in a Texas saloon.

The song posits the image of the new Texas Jew as the obverse of the Redneck's slurs:

—the Texas Jew is as native a Texan as anyone else;
—his Judaism or Jewishness as creed is as good as any Christian one;
—he refutes the claim that Jews killed Jesus Christ as just another child's tale like Santa Claus (that Christians are to blame for the threat to Christianity is from commercialization represented by the Santa Claus myth);
—the Jewish body is tough, strong, aggressive and sexually potent;
—the Jew is intellectually, morally and physically the equal of anyone else and prepared to show it;
—the Jew will no longer put up with racism or ethnocentrist slurs by direct action.

The song completes the mythic ideal of Texas by the fact that "The whole damn place was cheering as I stole right out the door!" confirming that a Texas Jew who stands up and physically defends and wins his fight deserves respect. That respect won by violence inverts the older Jewish values but the new Texas-Jewish values places external respect higher than the older virtue of passivity, which gains no outside respect. The new Texas Jew therefore is no longer inner-directed but outer-directed in the old Riesman terminology. This song therefore posits unconsciously the assumption of the Other's value system now inscribed as Jewish. The very use of the country music idiom and the twangy Texas accent underscores transparently the new Texas Jewish configuration and integration instanced in the song. It could well be the Texas Anthem of contemporary Texas Jewry!

Language marks a major symbolic and metonymic role of identity across the generations.[16] The transfer of linguistic medium marks the paradigmatic shift most sharply.

Gurwitz's *Memories of Two Generations* was written in Hebrew and Yiddish and divided into two books. The first book reflects the traditional life of a Lithuanian Jewish rabbinical student and his adulthood in Russia. The second book records the years in Texas with an ironic eye, which twenty years of hindsight in San Antonio has given him. It also gave him time to construct his literary persona as the quintessential inept Talmud *khokhem* (wise man) gazing humorously both at himself, his peer group, and at the accommodation to the Gentile world of Texans.

As a Hebrew teacher and *shokhet* (ritual slaughterer) for eighteen years in the Talmud Torah in San Antonio, the switch to English was traumatic.[17] The new president of the Talmud Torah fired him because he "was not adept in English" (266) enough to teach in a modern Talmud Torah. He accepts this reality willy-nilly, being already seventy, but it marks a divide, for English was the language of the land but not of Yiddishkayt. The powerful traditional perspective from which Gurwitz functioned understood the fracture and the cost. He was aware that his Talmudic inheritance was not valued in the new conditions, but he was determined to save what was possible. Language is reflected in Harelik's *The Immigrant* as well, where Haskell starts the play speaking Yiddish, then pidgin English, then accentless English, and in senility returns to Yiddish. The second generation in *The Legacy* can understand a Yiddish joke, but all is lost by the third. For Gurwitz, Yiddish is the natural medium of his existence and serves as the division between himself and the new beyond which he could not reach. He functioned in an irresolvable bifocality: Yiddish was for Gurwitz the private code of the Jews and English is the speech of accommodation. Harelik and Friedman function with a cultural linguistic bifocality too: for the contemporary performers, English is their normative language and Yiddish is the symbol of the old barely-known monolithic culture lurking with nostalgia (a fact an Austin klezmer band takes advantage of by performing Yiddish songs with jazz motifs and Tex-Mex beats for mixed audiences with no Yiddish speakers). A further proof of Texas-Jewish hybridization and believed Jewish continuity!

Yiddish had less staying power in Texas than, say, German, or Czech, or certainly Spanish. These populations which spoke a particular language tended to settle as a community in a small town or in a rural area and maintained their language by their isolation. The Jews were too few in number in Texas and never settled as a community. They came as individuals and they spread throughout the state. Only in Dallas, Houston and San Antonio did the Jews have literary and culture clubs in which Yiddish literature was discussed or performed. The immigrant generation obviously spoke Yiddish to each other in the synagogue, kosher butcher shop, and other Jewish social settings, but their children entered the English mainstream through the public schools rapidly. Yiddish died out by lack of usage in the rural areas and towns where there were only one or two Jewish families. In the cities, it held on longer. But the language was reduced for the second generation to a house tongue. Those Yiddish newspapers or books which entered Texas remained in the hands of the first generation. The second generation did not use Yiddish except with their parents, and most spoke English with them as well. Jewish identity was not tied so sharply as with the Germans and Czechs to linguistic markers. English was the language of Texas politically, economically and socially, and the Yiddish speaking Jews, following the German Jews before them, sought to use English as the mainstream tongue. And it was a necessity for business. The Texas Jew did not come to Texas to live an isolated existence but to partake of the Texas commonwealth. (Neither German Jews nor Eastern European Jews ever settled in German-speaking communities like Fredericksburg or Boerne. They avoided single ethnic settings of immigrants and always chose Anglo-Texan towns where English was the linguistic medium.)

Bifocality courses through the Jewish generations in Texas, for each looks out from his perspective and constructs a culture of reference. For the first generation of Gurwitz/Haskell, the old country is referred to as a place of instability with cultural practices which, if authentic, needed adjustments for the reality of contemporary life. There is never a mention of any return. The new life meant an arrest of nomadism and oppression and the satisfaction of law and order as well as hope. Gurwitz states: "This country is the finest 'city of refuge'" (250). His cultural authorities are always drawn from traditional Jewish practice. He can problematize what his gaze apprehends. For example: "In such a beautiful free land where the cultures of all lands flowed so smoothly, it seemed inconsistent and wrong to distinguish between one race and another. How had these blacks sinned? Was it just because they were born with black skins? We asked our nephew about this and he explained that this was no governmental decree" (210). He is not impressed. Memories of the bad times in Russia serve as a subtext to his observations. The social reality of Texas continued to disturb him. The poverty of the little Mexican huts "constructed like a sukkah, covered with rusted tin" (212) reveals his Jewish moral fervor at the class differences in San Antonio which, he notes, remains continuously divided into "white, black and yellow races, Anglos, Mexicans and Negroes" (213). His gaze reflects the resident alien. Gurwitz maintains an Eastern European Jewish mental site which accepts dislocation, unlike Haskell Harelik who seeks the fusion of mental, physical and social enfranchisement into one site: Texas as home.[18]

Gurwitz thinks in terms of the Jewish people and its survival in mainly religious/ethnic terms to the end of his life. He shrewdly notes, "the newcomers did not come here seeking Judaism [*yiddishkayt*]. That they had in the old home. They came seeking a livelihood" (250). Gurwitz stands between two worlds and is able to accept many of the changes. His main orientation was protecting and developing Jewish institutions and his pride that San Antonio has them in place reinforced his sense of accommodation and comfort (285). His real center was the future Israel. "We do not have a country of our own, with our own government as other nations do" (249). The Balfour Agreement, he argued, "impelled every Jew to get involved in the upbuilding of Eretz Yisrael" (253). America was a wonderful place but it is a city of refuge. "American Jews should consider themselves among the most fortunate Jews in the world" (249). His vision of the possible may be summed up in this statement: "The wedding [of his youngest son] was outstanding, in that it combined the best features of American custom and religiously correct ritual" (248). That was his accommodation. His grandchildren are still in San Antonio. The Gurwitz memoirs are so important because they reveal an older man's adjustment to Texas. He remained an accommodating essentialist.[19]

In the play *The Immigrant,* a young Haskell Harelik wanted to accommodate rapidly to the Texas reality. The Old World was a place to escape from and Texas a place to start a new life. Living in Hamilton, Texas, alone with his Jewish family, Haskell was prepared to strip away most of his old country external dress, habits and food customs, for these seemed less meaningful as related to his Jewishness. He even changes his name from Chatzkell Garelik to Haskell Harelik (act 1, sc. 3, 25–28). The new life becomes possible due to the support of the Gentile Perry family, which is based on fact. The play privileges ideologically the theme of Texans sharing a world of cultural practices which make room for difference. Haskell's vision of America remains open-ended, a vision of order, security and accomplishment, and his ultimate success, from peddler of fruit to dry-goods salesman underwritten by the loans of the Perry Bank, comes to fruition. Haskell's vision from within the play celebrates Texas and America for its security and stability. "How many years have the Jews been wandering? Who says we can't wander to Texas and rest for a while" (act 1, sc. 9, 78). The presupposition is that the past is untenable; thus the new homeland is a refuge which must be accommodated.[20]

Haskell too has feelings for fellow Jews and, given events in Europe, he wishes like Gurwitz to help save his people. He encounters from his Gentile protector the isolationist position:

> [Milton Perry:] Haskell, what the hell are you on about? You're an American now. . . . You've been here thirty years.
>
> [Haskell:] They're my people. . . . Share my freedom with my own people. As an American. (act 2, sc. 5, 135–37)

The text captures the seeming dissonance of Haskell's identity caught in the classic dual loyalty trap. American citizenship does not preclude him from fighting against the quota which Perry places as a test of Americanness. Haskell's refusal to accept the Perry position brings on hegemonic rejection as Perry storms out. Haskell is fighting here both for co-equality and respect as American citizen, and marks his right as citizen to have an original peoplehood to whom fellow loyalty in their danger is legitimate.[21] Perry places Americanness as both a civic action of citizenship and as a peoplehood, which assumes his ancestry as the ur-American authenticity. He demands and claims of Haskell the choice of Ruth: your people are my people now. This scene characterizes an immigrant dilemma, but it is the third-generation Texas Jew placing in the mouth of the first generation its demand for recognition that citizenship in America is not a peoplehood in the *Blut und Boden* sense of nineteenth-century nationalism, but a societal contract, a *Gesellschaft* in Tonnies's terminology, in which people can claim different, legitimate and co-equal origins. Haskell is pleading for a level field of play. He refuses to be bullied into the Americanness argument of Perry who had been his benefactor.

> [Haskell:] You've helped me. I'm grateful. . . .
> [Milton, furious, leaves]: I've paid my debt to you! I don't owe you a god-damn thing! [In a fury he blows out the (Shabbes) candles.] (act 2, sc. 5, 142)

Putting aside the obvious theatrical closure of the scene, the blowing out of the candles, a blasphemous act, underscores the semiotic act of a dual rejection. Haskell is not going to be bullied by a fellow Texas-American nor by Jewish tradition! He wants respect: "I'm a person" (139). Haskell inscribes bifocality by underlining that the Jewish past is untenable and the present and future of Texas Jewry represents order, stability and respect. Is this only Haskell of the first generation speaking, or the third-generation descendant reinscribing his Texas-Jewish perspective? Assertiveness is within Haskell's character and possibility but its performative representation is a third-generation reinscription of co-equality in a "high culture" medium parallel to Kinky Friedman's tough Texan knocking down the honky in the popular culture medium.

Significantly this scene takes place on Friday night at home in Hamilton, while Haskell's sons, the second generation, are out hunting with their Texas peers—clearly alluding to the massive accommodation by the breaking of Shabbat and the non-Jewish act of hunting. The first generation still honors the Shabbat with prayers, but sits down to a *milkhiks* (based on milk products) meal: blintzes! The normative Eastern European Shabbat meal (*fleyshiks*, a meat-based meal) is inverted, for meat is so abundant in Texas that to honor the Shabbat they have reversed the tradition and made it their own "authentic" Jewish *milkhiks* Shabbos meal. I spoke to the actual Harelik family and discovered that to this day it is still traditional in their family to have Shabbes milkhikes even though the house was never kosher. This reinterpretation of tradition into a unique Texas-Jewish family follows a certain logic: through the physical dislocation and change of environment, the use of inversion of tradition admits a reinscription of the distinctiveness, in this case, of the Shabbat tradition.[22] Nothing is seemingly lost in the Texas-Jewish mentality.

Let us study the final scene of act 1 in which Haskell Harelik and his wife, Leah, battle over the problem of what is Jewish identity in Texas. This scene represents Haskell as the emergent Texas Jew, whereas his wife has not yet crossed the divide.

> Leah: Haskell! Look at this town! There must be thousands of places where we live. . . . Where there are Jews. . . . Haskell. Let's find our own people.
> Haskell: But, Leah, the store, the business . . .
> Leah: Look at you! Is your head covered? When did this stop? We don't eat kosher . . . you don't pray at sundown.
> Haskell: What difference does that make, Leah?
> Leah: What difference? You're a Jew. I married a Jew.
> Haskell: I'm still a Jew. . . . So we don't keep kosher. Where would we buy? My head is uncovered? I don't want to be strange either. These people are our customers. They buy, we eat. Do you think God will hate me for that? Why does He need me to wear a little piece of cloth on my head? (act 1, sc. 9, 72–74)

This scene might well have been played out in any provincial American or South African town where only single Jewish families lived, but the Texas setting exacerbates the isolation and forces a hastening of the paradigm shift to abandoning external Jewish customs and absorbing transparently the local culture. When Leah suggests moving to New York to preserve traditional Jewish identity, the role of the metropolis as centrum once again assumes its meaning vis-à-vis the Texas Jewish worldview: Leah admits to being decentered and wanting the *Gemeinschaft* of other Jews. The encounter with other Jews who actually live in a community of significant numbers, especially New York, actually astonishes the Texas Jew. After the discovery of shared commonality, however, comes the shock of difference; the Texan-ness of the Texas Jew emerges, which reflects both the dominant Anglo-Texan social values internalized and the laxity of Jewish ethnic identity superseded by the stronger religious sense of identity.

Haskell's negative response to going to New York reflects the immigrant's new centering in Texas and his sense of accomplishment and definition, and, indeed, of his psychological sense of self and siting. Haskell has made something of himself in Hamilton, Texas. His rooting is through an already Americanized sense of centering, the self-realization of his personal accomplishment, his business. Here is the paradigmatic shift in all its clarity: "But Leah, the store, our business . . . Here is our place! I'm not going to run again. No more running! No More!! Our place is here! That's the end! Yes?" (*Immigrant,* act 1, sc. 9, 75). Haskell's identity is Texanized to the place and site of his accomplishment. Gurwitz, in his memoirs, notes just this phenomenon when he argues that Yiddishkayt was the old country, Texas meant a livelihood. But it meant more: a new identity was in formation.

> Leah: For my baby, there is no life here. Yes, of course. I can learn to live in a different house. I can learn a different language. I can say howdy, grow a cactus by the door. But my baby, Haskell, can't make these shortcuts. He can't grow up without God. To cover his head, do I buy a cowboy hat? Pointy boots, big belt buckle? He'd fit right in huh?

Leah wants the Jewish religious structures which are totally absent in Hamilton, Texas. That she concedes she can adapt to local cultural practices articulates the comparative ease of collapsing the traditional Eastern European Jewish lifestyle. The inner structure of the Jewish culture reveals itself based on religious structures of identity associated with the ritual year and life cycle. Texas Jewry privileges its religious identity, for it conforms to both the lifestyle of the dominant culture which encourages religious affiliation and it secures the basic structures of Jewish identity.

> Haskell: Our baby won't be without God, Leah! This child will be a Jew. I don't know how, but when this person, this Jewish person is born, we will have brought something new, something old into a different corner of the world. . . .
>
> Leah: I'm still looking for land. (act 1, sc. 9, 77–78)

Haskell concedes that he has abandoned much of the old Eastern European external cultural practices but refuses to admit to an internal break. His voice reveals the desperation of embracing the new while seeking some accommodation with the old, yet not interrupting his passage. The play concludes with Milton Harelik, the youngest son, returning safely from World War II, taking over the business and continuing the Jewish presence in Hamilton, Texas. The play seamlessly passes the paradigmatic shift from immigrant to authentic Texas Jew who inhabits his chronotope as American as apple pie, and yet is aware of his Jewish inheritance. Jewish continuity is espoused: at one with its ancestors and yet renewed in Texas.

What Is the Texas-Jewish Inheritance Today?

In the third generation of Kinky Friedman and Mark Harelik, we see the bifocality significantly different from the first generation. The present is seen as a stable condition rooted in Texas with an identity called the "Texas Jew" which provides form and, I shall argue, an uncertain content, but which is conceived by the Texas Jew fully as an unchanged continuity from the past of the best values of Judaism. The past, represented by the immigrant, appears mistakenly more rooted. The third generation, Texanized, seeks its Jewish authenticity in a mirror response to the first generation seeking to Americanize.

The third-generation Texas Jew, however, is not sufficiently aware of the occlusions in which he works, for he has transparently absorbed the dominant cultural practices. He lacks the Jewish knowledge which Gurwitz noted was becoming the norm. For example, let us observe in *The Immigrant* errors of traditional Jewish cultural/religious practice. When Haskell enters Hamilton, the dramatist has Haskell remove his wedding ring and hide it. In the traditional Jewish world, the Jewish male never wore a wedding band. The ring placed on the woman's finger is the act of the completion of the contract and public ceremony of taking possession of the woman, not as coequal which a modern Protestant double-ringed marriage ceremony implies. When Haskell's children are born, he plants trees in their honor, which has a tradition back to the Talmud, but Mark Harelik adds, Haskell "places the baby in the middle of the yard" (104). This is no Jewish custom, but Harelik invented it to show how Haskell was rooting his child to the new land. In fact, only the dead in the Jewish tradition are spread on the ground. The third child is named Milton in honor of Milton Perry, the benefactor. This contradicts Ashkenazic tradition of naming a child only after the dead and never the living.

Traditional Jewish ethnic practices dissolve into a generalized Jewish continuity. In *The Immigrant,* we see that the pride in holding onto the old candlesticks and having a Shabbos dinner does not preclude the fact that the sons are off hunting. Obviously it is harder for isolated country Jews than for the Texas city Jews to maintain the yearly and life-cycle customs. (As late as 1980, Jews isolated in south Texas would move into rented rooms or apartments near the Orthodox synagogue in San Antonio for High Holidays, a tradition going back to the nineteenth century.) But we must not interpret the difficulties as a loss of Jewish identity. The text becomes the site for recovery.[23] By recognizing the dangers, the author seeks to reinforce his belief that his generation has not abandoned the inheritance. Its essence continues even if there is laxity in observance. His image of Haskell's Jewishness and its continuity to Milton Harelik is what the dramatist seeks to impress upon us. The Jewish values of Haskell are no less those of Milton and of the dramatist, three generations of Texas Jews. Fair play, social conscience, ethical performance—all Texan-American normative values are conflated and found inscribed within the Jewish inheritance. The differences of language and other Ashkenazic cultural activities are of little significance: in the Texas-Jewish mindset, the essential Jewish identity is maintained and preserved.

Differences between the actual practice and the idealized inheritance, however, does find expression. Kinky Friedman frames the passage from cultural meaning to mere formula in satiric verses, such as "We Reserve the Right to Refuse Service to You," which underscore how Texanized and conformist the contemporary Jewish religious structures have become:

> Well, I walked on in to my House of God
> Congregation on the nod
> Just the Chosen folks, doing their weekly thing
> Hear O Israel yes indeed
> The book was backwards, I couldn't read
> It but I got a good rise when I heard
> That Rabbi say: Baruch Atoy Adonoy
> What the hell you doing back there boy
> We reserve the right to refuse services to you
> Your friends are all on welfare
> You call yourself a Jew
> You need your tie and ticket to zip
> Your prayers on through
> We reserve the right to refuse services to you.

The song defends a lifestyle that seeks and protects social and ethical ideals which conform to the authentic Judaism the singer feels he represents. This is a voice of the third generation which will not accept interference into its lifestyle, and which the song implies is not banishing a Jewish consciousness for it is defending the real Jewish values, not bourgeois ones. Traditional Ashkenazic ethnicity here is surely gone, or at least distinctly transmogrified into a new Texas-Jewish expression. The contemporary Texas-Jewish religious institution is seriously challenged. The song mocks the appeal to a Jewish confessional conformism to Texas middle-class mores. The Rabbi has become its defender while eschewing issues of social justice, that unique meeting place in the America of the seventies, where Jewish religious and secular socialist ideals joined American civil rights concerns. The song becomes a textual site for questioning the failure of contemporary Judaism to respond to the pressing moral questions of the time. Notice, however, that it is the contemporary Texas-Jewish structure that is problematized, not the Jewish inheritance itself.[24]

The fact that an aesthetic structure is used for critical debate reveals how American and Texan the voice really is, for it underscores, like the plays of Harelik, the aestheticization of the Texas Jews who are using their art to interpret their Jewishness and what they problematize as their Jewish inheritance. The song claims the individual is the owner of the true inheritance and not the institution. The Texas Jew certainly sees himself as the possessor of the continuity of the true Jewish values. This is a transparent reading of American ideals which places emphasis on the personal over the communal structures and which is inscribed into Texas Judaism without any consciousness of this transference.

The Holocaust memory forces a powerful Texas-Jewish tie to his historical identity which transcends religion or customs or any other cultural practice. The Holocaust throws on the Texas Jew the only shadow of instability or doubting of rootedness. Its commemoration is an approach/avoidance encounter, but it may run deep. It transcends identity with the Lone Star State and joins a universal Jewish inheritance which provides the only real difference with his fellow Texan. Kinky Friedman gave song to this repressed fear and admission of association and inescapable identity which I find certainly reflected in my Jewish students at the University of Texas. The very Texan country-western style makes "Ride 'em Jewboy" a remarkable expression of Texas-Jewish folk culture, as in this excerpt:

> How long will you be driven
> Relentless around the world
> The blood in the rhythm of the soul
> Wild ponies all, your dreams were broken
> Rounded up and made to move along
> The loneliness which can't be spoken
> Just swings a rope
> And rides inside a song
>
> Dead limbs play with ringless fingers
> A melody which burns you deep inside
> Oh how the song becomes the singer
> May peace be ever with you when you ride

So ride, ride, ride, ride 'em Jewboy
Ride 'em all around the ol' corral
I'm, I'm with you boy
If I got to ride six million miles

Today Holocaust observances in Texas are ecumenical affairs.[25] The Holocaust no longer serves as a point of difference. Like intermarriage in Texas, the parties celebrate together and hold back their uneasiness. Texas Jews are aestheticized, and good manners is one southernism they espouse and fully share with their fellow Texans and Confederates, as opposed to those "rude" Yankees and New York Jews!

CONCLUSION

The contemporary Texas Jew delights in asserting and playacting, like any other Texan, the image of the idealized tough Texas macho. This is part of Texas folklore and it carries an added piquant for himself when that Texan is a Jew as well. He feels and acts the co-equal of his Gentile Texan counterpart and he feels himself the continuation of a Jewish inheritance that he believes is noble, ethical and valuable. What he is unaware of in his admiration of his inheritance is that he places his normative American-Texan values upon his Jewish past. He has inscribed unconsciously American values of personal reliance, co-equality of men and women, and all the democratic values of the Western Enlightenment tradition into his Judaism, which he believes were always there and to which his ancestors gave equal accord and appreciation. This forms the moral core and worldview of the Texas Jew and its aporia. What adds to his distinctiveness is his sense of rootedness, albeit the Holocaust gives him an added self-definition which he keeps deep inside. Identifying with the land of Texas, its folklore and its history, the Texas Jew enjoys fulfilling the role of Texan both as shared humor, but also seriously as a legitimizing fact that he belongs, rooted.[26] He functions as an individual and, while he freely associates with Jewish communal institutions, he holds his own counsel as to what is the true Jewish inheritance. As we have seen, ethnic identity is really reduced to a Texanized religious one. It is linguistically confirmed by the avoidance of the pejorative ethnic noun, "Jew," by using "Jewish," the adjectival noun which may connote a hint of ethnicity but defines safely religious affiliation. Belief is not as important as affiliation. Texas culture requires a religious affiliation, and a Judaic one is thus respectable. The system of Jewish identification is unquestioned and a bit Pirandelloesque: it's Jewish, if you believe it is so! Belief and identity are a private matter, affiliation is public. In such a cultural configuration, the Texas Jew has found his niche. His bifocality expresses itself in his civic and historical sense of union with his fellow Gentile Texans, and in his religious and historical sense of oneness with his fellow Jews and ancestral inheritance. He may even partake in private delight that Israel and Texas are both Lone Star States!

I would like to conclude on a personal note, with news of my native Texas son. He graduated from Stanford University, in California (a traitorous desertion), where he was president of the Texas Club which he formed with two Chinese Texans and eight Texas Jews! As you can see, that Houston, Texas *mohel* left an imprint.

Notes

This essay is dedicated to the memory of my father, Morris Wolitz, Antipol–New York–Del Ray Beach, and to his native Texas grandson, David Israel Berman Wolitz. The songs "They Ain't Makin' the Jews Like Jesus Anymore" (© 1974 by Kinky Friedman) and "We Reserve the Right to Refuse Service to You" (Kinky Friedman, Rick Goldberg, and J. Maizel; © by Kinky Friedman) and the excerpts from "Ride 'em Jewboy" (© 1973 by Kinky Friedman) are used here by permission of Kinky Friedman.

1. Tomas Rivera, the leading Chicano novelist, also attended my son's *bris* and, at the end of the ceremony, grabbed my arm and said, "Man, after that, I need a drink!" Most of the guests had never attended this ceremony before and it created quite an impression. Dr. Geller is the descendant of the Geller Family of Houston who, for generations, have been *mohels* to the Texas Jewish community. This tradition is noted in Shmuel Geller, *Mazkeres Ahavah, Remembrance of Love: A Biographical Account of Rabbi Yaakov and Sara Geller and Family—The Transplanting of Jewish Life from Galicia to Texas, 1863 to the Present* (Zichron Yaakov, Israel: Institute for Publication of Books, 1988). In Texas it is considered correct and natural to invite your non-Jewish friends and professional workplace colleagues (and vice versa) to major religious rites of passage.

2. Natalie Ornish, *Pioneer Jewish Texans* (Dallas: Texas Heritage Press, 1989), 51–66.

3. Ruth Winegarten and Cathy Schechter, *Deep in the Heart: The Lives and Legends of Texas Jews* (Austin: Eakin Press, 1990), 8.

4. Bernard Marinbach, *Galveston: Ellis Island of the West* (Albany: SUNY Press, 1983), xiv.

5. Winegarten and Schechter, *Deep in the Heart,* 84–85. See also Henry Cohen, "The Galveston Movement: Its First Year," *Western States Jewish History* 18.2 (Jan. 1986): 114–19 (rpt. from *B'nai B'rith Messenger,* Apr. 16, 1909).

6. Marinbach, *Galveston,* 193–94.

7. Ibid., 183–84.

8. Population statistics from the *American Jewish Year Book* (Philadelphia: Jewish Publication Society) of the cited year. The last year cited was 1996, vol. 96.

9. Simon During, "Introduction," in *Cultural Studies Reader,* ed. Simon During (New York: Routledge, 1993), 7.

10. Rev. Alexander Ziskind Gurwitz, *Sefer fun tsvey doyres* (New York: Eygns, 1935); translated into English ("Memories of Two Generations") by Rabbi Amram Prero, ms., Barker Library, University of Texas at Austin. All references and citations are from book 2 in the English version and were checked against the Hebrew and Yiddish of the original publication.

11. Mark Harelik, *The Immigrant: A Hamilton County Album* (New York: Ballantine Books, 1988). The manuscript for *The Legacy* (1996) was loaned to me by the dramatist, Mark Harelik. *The Immigrant* had its world premiere in the Denver Center Theater Company's Source Theater in February 1985 with Mark Harelik playing the role of Hashell Harelik. It has been performed at all the major repertory theaters in the United States, including the Mark Taper in Los Angeles, the Arena Theater in Washington, D.C., and the Alley Theater in Houston. It was performed twice at the Live Oak Theater in Austin, Texas, in January 1990 and again in 1994. (A special performance with Mark Harelik in attendence was performed for the Texas Jewish Historical Society at its annual meeting in Corpus Christi, April 1997, where the author announced the work has been commissioned for a musical.)

The Immigrant is a four-character play. It is set in Hamilton, Texas. Act 1 takes place in 1909 and follows Haskell Harelik's encounter with the Perry family, Milton (the local banker) and Ima, who take him under their wing as he moves from banana peddler to owner of a dry-goods store. He brings over from Russia his wife, Leah, who finds adjustment to Texas living in act 1 quite difficult. Act 2 presents the birth of the Hareliks's three sons and their continued successful integration into Texas. Leah finds contentment in Hamilton. Scene 5, the Shabbes dinner, contains the climax of the play, in which Haskell declares his independence from Milton Perry and his defense of his own authenticity. The year is 1939. The play brings about a bittersweet reconciliation with the dying Mr. Perry and the play ends with their youngest son's return from World War II to continue the Texas Jewish experience.

12. The texts of the songs were supplied by Kinky Friedman and Fruit of the Tune Music, Inc. Special thanks to Mango for handcopying the songs.

13. Michael Fischer, "Ethnicity and the Arts of Memory," *Writing Culture,* ed. James Clifford and George E. Marcus (Berkeley: University of California Press, 1986), notes the importance of ethnic autobiographical writing to which I subscribe: "Ethnic autobiographical writing parallels, mirrors and exemplifies contemporary theories of textualities, of knowledge, and of culture . . . powerful modes of cultural criticism . . . deploy[ing] a series of techniques: bifocality or reciprocity of perspectives, juxtapositioning of multiple realities, intertextualities and inter-referentiality, and comparison through families of ressemblances" (230).

14. Diane Ravitch, "The Educational Critic in New York," in *Creators and Distributors: Reminiscences by Jewish Intellectuals of New York,* ed. Bernard Rosenberg and Ernest Goldstein (New York: Columbia University Press, 1982), 386–94. Her memories capture the patriotic intensity in Texas and a Jewish reaction: "It meant a lot in Texas to be patriotic and there always seemed to be some doubt about whether Jews were fully committed as Americans. The Houston Jews I knew tried extra hard to show that they were as patriotic as non-Jews" (390–91). She continues: "The main emphasis among Jews seemed to be on succeeding, assimilating, being very low-key on Jewish issues in order not to antagonize non-Jews, and becoming just as Texan as other Texans" (391–92).

15. I have found Sander Gilman's thoughts in *The Jew's Body* (New York: Routledge,

1991) very suggestive and useful: "It is Christianity which provides all the vocabularies of difference in Western Europe and North America. . . . Anti-Semitism is central to Western culture because the rhetoric of European culture is Christianized, even in its most secular form" (18); and, "The same sense of difference impacts on the Jew who is caught in the web of power which controls and shapes his or her psyche and body. The assignment of difference to aspects of the body shapes how individuals understand their own essence" (235). Kinky Friedman's use of country-western music permits a very direct and strong expression of Jewish reappropriation of its body, essence, and selfhood. The allusion to the "anemic" body by the Texas anti-Semitic Bubba exemplifies what Gilman states: "The construction of the Jewish body in the West is absolutely linked to the underlying ideology of anti-Semitism, to the view that the Jew is inherently different" (Sander Gilman, "The Jewish Body: A Footnote," in *People of the Body: Jews and Judaism from an Embodied Perspective,* ed. Howard Eilberg-Schwartz [Albany: SUNY Press, 1992], 22). The physical violence of the Jewish response shifts the stereotype and revitalizes the Texas Jew out of the anti-Semitic stereotype.

16. I found most useful James Collins's clarifications and amplifications of Pierre Bourdieu's terminology in "Determination and Contradiction: An Appreciation and Critique of the Work of Pierre Bourdieu on Language and Education," *Bourdieu: Critical Perspectives,* ed. C. Williams, E. Li Puma, and M. Postone, (Chicago: University of Chicago, 1993), 116–38.

17. David Forgacs, "National-Popular: Genealogy of a Concept," *Cultural Studies Reader,* ed. During, 178–90, interprets Gramsci's thinking on language and culture change and underscores the theoretic significance of language change and its manipulation in creating new cultural practices and the power of political hegemony in bringing this about. Gurwitz, without the sophistication of modern theoretics, was making the same points with practical examples from his Talmud Torah experience.

18. Gurwitz is a classic example of the colonized intellectual who fifty years before Frantz Fanon (*The Wretched of the Earth* [Harmondsworth, U.K.: Penguin, 1969], 29, 41) fully recognized the the "Manichean" moment that divides the colonial space: the split between carceral space and dreams of possession. Gurwitz looks upon Russia as an imperialist entity dominating and colonizing the Jews. He understood this in Texas as well by the colonial treatment of Afro-Americans and Mexican-Americans. He had the sensitized frame of his colonized perspective as a Russian Jew to appreciate the suffering of his fellow man. Gurwitz's "performance of cross-referencing" with remarkable empathy—using the terminology of Homi Bhabha in "Archeology of the Archaic," *Literary Theory Today,* ed. Peter Collier and Helga Geyer-Ryan (Ithaca, N.Y.: Cornell University Press, 1990), 203–18—opens further studies to early inter- and crosscultural perspectives in American cultural practices. Texas is a transition, a respite for Gurwitz; a good one, but not the teleological ideal which his own tradition proposes: the Return to Zion. It is a *detour* for the *retour* that Edouard Glissant develops in *Le Discours Antillais* (Paris: Seuil, 1981), a variant on the Jewish experience par excellence. Writing a memoir becomes a protest to express that although power is lacking but desired, the colonized Jew is neither blinded or inarticulate. His voice, however, is entrapped in languages without echo—the tragedy of the immigrant. He decolonizes his mind by writing but ultimately he succombs to the local hegemony by his acquiescence to the security it does offer. His memoirs are fit study for Subaltern Studies.

19. Gurwitz's refusal of the idea that "the necessary price of emancipation was the destruction of difference" (using the language of Tamar Garb, "Modernity, Identity, Textuality," in *The Jew in the Text: Modernity and the Construction of Identity,* ed. Linda Nochlin and Tamar Garb [London: Thames and Hudson, 1995], 24) makes him either postmodern or a clear conservative—which he was (an interesting confluence of perspectives).

20. The entire history of Texas Jews fits the experience of a diasporic culture. There is a desire for fixity after nomadism, continuity after displacement. What astonishes me is that James Clifford could write a seminal article on "Traveling Cultures" (in *Cultural Studies,* ed. L. Grossberg, C. Nelson, and P. Treichler [New York: Routledge, 1992], 96–111) and the significance of "Diasporic cultures," offering theoretic/methodological possibilities that could easily apply to the Texas Jewish experience, and yet his study never mentions the originating people of the term "diaspora," or the remarkable example of its functioning among Jews for the past two thousand years!

21. Haskell's defense of an ethnic origin and pride in American citizenship and identity finds its theoretical elaboration in Werner Sollors, *Beyond Ethnicity: Consent and Descent in American Culture* (New York: Oxford University Press, 1986), and further elaborations in Werner Sollors, *The Invention of Ethnicity* (New York: Oxford University Press, 1989). Sollors tends to eschew the hegemonic play of tensions that certainly threatened the immigrants at the beginning of the century. Such a theatrical scene (act 2, sc. 5) would not have been written by either a first- or second-generation American Jew, for the confrontational encounter here is distinctly performative. The earlier generations more likely would have confined the raspy encounter to a memoir and the oral tradition of the family. The fact that it is written for performance by a third-generation Texas Jew reveals the attained levels of security and co-equality. Arthur Hertzberg shrewdly noted that the second-generation American Jew "believed neither in the melting pot nor in cultural pluralism. . . . Jews [second-generation] in the arts and letters almost always wrote or composed as 'general Americans' [i.e., Anglo-Americans]." Hertzberg noted that Gershwin and "Jewish artists and performers had a particular affinity in those days for expressing their Jewish angst through Negro characters. . . . Negroes in *Porgy and Bess* seemed to be Jews in blackface" (*The Jews in America: Four Centuries of an Uneasy Encounter: A History* [New York: Simon and Schuster, 1989], 273–74). Mark Harelik releases Haskell (and all American Jews) from psychological bondage by permitting Haskell a vigorous presentation of his position and a transgressive mien that rebuts the previous unequal social/psychological encounter by insisting on an even playing field. What distinguishes the Texas Jew here from the general East Coast Jew is the very performative rendering of this scene. Its remarkable quality of self-assertiveness is not found in Yankee Jewish playwriting. It is the new assertion of the Texas Jew saying he is the continuity of the inheritance when it is in fact a re*new*ed identity: old plus new.

22. This ability of adaptation explains how, in country Texas synagogues, such conditions existed for many years, according to Gurwitz and my informants: "In each of these country towns, the Jews are divided as they are in San Antonio: Traditional Jews and German Jews. Since they cannot afford to have two synagogues, and two rabbis, most of them have one synagogue, in partnership, with one Rabbi serving both ideological groups. In order not to discriminate, the Rabbi stands at the Ark, but the

worshippers are seated at each side of the synagogue. The Rabbi addresses each side, in turn, and delivers his sermons accordingly." On Rosh Hashanah and Yom Kippur, however, the rabbi has his work cut out for him. For the German Jews he conducts the service without a hat, and he faces them during the entire service. Then he puts on his yarmulke, turns to the other side, faces the Ark, and conducts the orthodox service. After this, he turns to the center, so that he is addressing both sides, and he delivers his sermon to both sides simultaneously (Gurwitz, *Sefer fun tsvey doyres,* 279–80).

23. My perspective on ethnicity in this text parallels the definition provided by Stuart Hall: "The term ethnicity acknowledges the place of history, language, and culture in the construction of subjectivity and identity, as well as the fact that all knowledge is contractual. Representation is possible only because enunciation is always produced within codes which have a history, a position within the discursive formations of a particular space and time" ("New Ethnicities," in *Critical Dialogues in Cultural Studies,* ed. David Morley and Kuan-Hsing Chen [London: Routledge, 1996], 446).

24. In an unpublished paper, "'The Jewish Civil War': *The Jewish Herald* and the Crisis of National Leadership," Bryan Edward Stone, who is completing his doctorate in Texas Jewish history at the University of Texas at Austin, notes that in the history of Texas Jews, the Jews follow fellow Texans in their propensity to "secede from things": "In 1878 Dallas Jews wrote their own prayerbook and discarded the Minhag America promoted by Isaac Wise. . . . During the Galveston Movement, Jacob Schiff was frequently at odds with Rabbi Henry Cohen. . . . in 1942 Congregation Beth Israel (Houston) [Reform] took on every national Jewish organization over the issue of Zionism. [They were opposed to it.] In the 1950s and 1960s, Texas rabbis urged the leaders of the Anti-Defamation League to cease sending Northern civil rights organizers into Texas for fear these 'outside agitators' would stir trouble for the local Jews." He continues: "All these episodes may indicate that the local identity of Texas Jews, that is the *Texas* half of the equation, was perhaps more important to them than their collective identity as Jews. Texas Jews never stopped thinking of themselves as Jews . . . but it was more important to be Texans and to put forth a vision of Texas Jewishness than to affiliate with a vague national Jewish culture whose leadership [in New York] they mistrusted." Regionalism is meaningful and centering to Texas Jewish identity and interests. I wish to thank Bryan Edward Stone for his kindnesses as an intellectual sparring partner, adviser on his vision of "le Texas profond," "deep Texas," and a superb critical native son who holds perspectives "mighty peculiar" still to a Yankee who is a "new-born" Texan.

25. In the 1998 CD release *Pearls in the Snow: The Songs of Kinky Friedman* (Kinkajou Records), all the leading Texas country singers, including Willie Nelson, Tom Waits, Dwight Yoakum, and Lyle Lovett, sing his songs, and Nelson sings "Ride 'em Jewboy" in what Friedman considers the finest rendition ever (personal communication, December 22, 1998). That the leading Texas country singer, a Gentile, chose to interpret this Holocaust song underscores how Texas-Jewish and general Texas cultural realities can and do mesh.

26. The University of Texas at Austin plays a unique role in helping maintain Texas Jewish continuity. It is a tradition of at least three generations to send the Texas Jewish offspring to the University of Texas to get an education, find and meet his or her

spouse either through the Jewish fraternity/sorority system, the Hillel House, or any other university activities. The marriages that took place over these generations have added to the bonding of a Texas Jewish community de facto across the state. The various cities and towns are joined together by kinship ties due to this continuous encounter at the University of Texas at Austin. Thus a state institution plays unconsciously a most sacral Jewish role as matchmaker by offering its facilities and mediation.

8 (Re)Creating Jewish Ethnicities on the Brazilian Frontier

JEFFREY LESSER

Academics often make the unfortunate assumption that those nations defined as "developing" (Third World, peripheral, underdeveloped, less developed, etc.) represent a frontier, be it economic or social. Yet this a priori notion ignores the fact that elites in these countries see the cities where they live as a "core" and their border regions as both physical and conceptual frontiers. This is certainly true in Latin America, where the language of the frontier mixes easily with that of the pioneer, yet only in reference to what is commonly denominated as "the interior." This makes "frontiers," in spite of a lack of industrial development, into critical components of national consciousness. Cartography has thus become a "nationalist" science (no single map is accepted by all countries) and Brazilians and Venezuelans frequently skirmish over "their" national spaces, while in 1995 Ecuador and Peru went to war over the placement of a border.

The frontier, however, is more than a physical space. Because of its importance to national identity, the frontier has become a place inhabited by heroes (of sorts) who gain both land and unusual freedom of action by their spatial choices of settlement. Nowhere is this more evident than in Brazil, where immigrants appear to have settled on the frontier as much for economic reasons as for the opportunity to create communities which would not be forced to follow strictly national acculturation and assimilation policies. For Jews on the northern and southern frontiers this freedom was critical in their decision to make Brazil a new home.

INTRODUCTION

On the surface, Brazil is a country of race. It is a place where blacks and whites and people of various shades seem to coexist in a superficial harmony that is tenuous at best. Thus when I saw a Brazilian *telenovela* that conflated nationality and ethnicity with its advertisement for "Portuguese, Japanese, Spanish, Italians, Arabs—Don't Miss The Most Brazilian Soap Opera on Television," I was somewhat surprised.[1] I should not have been since it only brought to the most extreme reaches of popular culture Brazil's world of immigrant ethnicity. In São Paulo you may find yourself in the "Japanese" neighborhood of Liberdade or the formerly "Jewish" and now "Korean" *barrio* of Bom Retiro. In Curitiba you will find a government that promotes a flawed multiculturalism and in Rio Grande do Sul you can visit the "German" town of Gramado or the "Italian" one of Caxias do Sul. In each of these cases the message is the same: this is not "Brazil" but alien territory.

The language of nationality used to describe these "alien" spaces masks a world where hyphenated identities are very real, even though elite Brazilian culture aggressively rejects the possibility of such social constructions. Indeed, Brazilian society does not even have linguistic categories that acknowledge hyphenated ethnicity and a third generation Brazilian of Japanese descent is called "Japanese" while a fourth generation Brazilian Jew of North African descent may become a *turco,* an *árabe,* a *sírio,* a *sírio/libanês* or a *judeu.* Since Brazil's social chemists have traditionally seen the country as a "racial laboratory" with "a singular ethnic composition" in which immigration was a social reagent that had to be handled with the greatest of care, there was, and is, little room for anything but Brazilians or foreigners.[2]

For many nineteenth-century intellectuals and politicians, immigration was the key to transforming Brazil's social identity and as ideology metamorphosed into policy, the question of who was denied entry became as important as who entered.[3] Immigrants simultaneously challenged simplistic notions of race by adding a new element—ethnicity—to the mix. Jews were particularly difficult for Brazilian elites to conceptualize because they were deemed both non-white and non-black, thus challenging the notions of Brazilian national identity that elites were trying to construct. Cultural difference was not the only factor that made Jews particularly visible: work in commerce and eventual residential concentrations in Brazil's urban centers challenged elite notions that all immigrants should be agricultural workers. The result was that Jews were presented with a series of different options about how they might fit, or not fit, into Brazilian society.

In order to examine the question of transnational ethnicity and how it is constructed among Jewish immigrants to Brazil this article explores how two different Jewish immigrant groups, in two different historical moments and on two different frontiers, (re)constructed their ethnic identities. The two groups mark the beginnings of both large scale Sephardic and Ashkenazic immigration to Brazil, and include the thousands of Moroccan Jews who began to settle in the mid-nineteenth century on Brazil's northern frontier, in the Amazonian state of Pará, and an equal number of Eastern European Jews who settled in farming colonies in southern Brazil. For both these groups, (re)constructing their ethnicities as "Brazilian" allowed them to more fully participate in their own premigratory cultures. Thus, North African Jews naturalized themselves as "Brazilian" in order to return physically to Morocco while the Eastern European group became "Brazilian" by accepting a place in a positivist social structure that allowed the maintenance of ethnicity as long as it did not interfere with political loyalty. What both groups shared was a realization that their success in Brazil was related to the negotiation of multiple identities, as farmers, as business people, as Jews, as foreigners, and as Brazilians.

THE AMAZONIAN FRONTIER

As early as 1823 a small North African Jewish community could be found in Belém do Pará, a city at the mouth of the Amazon. Little is know about this group, although a story was once told to me by an old man who wished to explain the integration of North Africans into Paraense society:

> *Becoming Brazilian*
>
> When the Jews arrived they came without women or rabbis. Many began relationships with indigenous women and wanted to marry, yet there was no rabbi among the immigrants to conduct conversion ceremonies. The leader of the immigrants thus appointed the most learned member of the group to teach all the fiancées about Judaism prior to marriage, emphasizing one principle—that the Jewish G-d was the one and only G-d. The day of the marriage the bride-to-be was brought into a room blindfolded and told that a spoonful of molten gold would be put in her mouth. If she really believed that the Jewish G-d was the one and only G-d, the gold would taste as sweet as honey. And every woman believed and the gold always tasted like honey.[4]

The presence of this small group led to a proliferation of images of Brazil in North Africa, and in the early 1860s a few hundred Moroccan (or Maghribi) Jewish families moved to Rio de Janeiro. The Spanish-Moroccan War (1859–60) may have been the catalyst for their flight but deeper issues propelled these migrants.[5] Historically Jews had worked as business agents for the Sultan, occasionally even receiving the title *tujjar al-sultan* (the Sultan's merchants). Yet living in a Muslim world gave Jews a profound sense of minority status and their multilingualism—Arabic and Spanish were used for business, French and Hebrew were studied at the Alliance Israélite Universelle (AIU) schools that had been set up in Tangier and other port towns, and Haquitia was spoken at home—gave them a transnational perspective.[6] As Moroccan economic opportunity diminished in relation to other areas of the Arab world, Muslim merchants became increasingly xenophobic and resentful of the economic ties that many Jewish merchants had to the French. Jews thus began to consider emigration, some leaving for Egypt and Algeria, but many of those educated at the Alliance schools choosing to leave the region altogether. According to a report from one of the AIU's directors, by the 1880s 95 percent of the boys completing their education at a Alliance school went to South America.[7]

By 1890 more than one thousand Maghribi Jews had migrated to the state of Pará, in the Amazon Region. The rubber economy appeared booming and cities and towns alike were filled with peddlers and small merchants who would soon become well-off.[8] Jews settled in both the city of Belém and in small towns along the bank of the Amazon where they traded city products like clothes, medicine, tobacco and cachaça (a sugar cane–based liquor) for country products like fish, Brazil nuts, rubber and copaiba oil.[9] Potential prosperity, however, was only one of the attractions for Morocco's Jews, who soon discovered that Brazilian naturalization certificates were obtainable after only six months of residence. This technicality of Brazilian law (or lack of it) had important repercussions, since many Maghribi Jews, in spite of their economic success, feared that "yellow fever [and] insects" made Brazil "a country of sickness." A new Brazilian nationality, however, allowed them to return to Morocco after seven or eight years with both a sense of security and significant sums of money. They experienced a leap in status because of their wealth and worldliness and there are reports that those Jewish men who had not migrated experienced a decrease in their marriage prospects.[10]

Mimom Elbás was typical in many ways. He emigrated to Belém at the end of 1892 and after a year moved to Rio de Janeiro. Six months later he was naturalized, apparently by giving a cash gift to a corrupt official, and returned to Morocco under the protection of the Brazilian government.[11] This did not please the Consul in Tangier, José Daniel Colaco, who complained that Elbás, who had left his family in Brazil, "does not know how to speak any language but Arabic which is typical of the Hebrews from the Eastern ports."[12] The questionable legality of Elbás's rapidly gained naturalization certificate was only a surface issue; the consul's real concern was the introduction of a new, and potentially dangerous, ethnic stream into Brazil. The problem was that Brazil's leaders had divided the potential immigrant world into two simple groups: undesirable Africans and Asians who were banned by law, and desirable European and North Americans who would be attracted with subsidies. Moroccan Jews arriving on their own, while seen as members of the undesirable category, were never part of the formal equation and so there were no legal barriers to their entry. This concerned diplomats in Rio de Janeiro, who often suggested that the Ministry of Justice be more careful in granting naturalization certificates in the future.[13]

No one took such measures. By the first years of the twentieth century there were over six hundred naturalized Brazilians living in Morocco, all of whom looked to Brazil for protection, especially in times of crisis. Simao (or Simon) Nahmiash moved to Pará in 1879 when he was twenty-three years old. Three years later he requested a naturalization certificate, based on his "firm intention to continue residing in the Empire and to adopt it as my fatherland."[14] The entire process took about a month and some years later Nahmiash returned to Tangier, Brazilian citizenship in hand. He set up an importing business and in 1901 became engaged in a land-rights battle with a local Muslim merchant and found himself arguing his case before the Shraa Tribunal (Native High Court). Not only did he lose the case, he also found himself held in contempt of court, an offense punishable by prison. As police arrived at Nahmiash's house to make the arrest, he raised the Brazilian flag, but to no avail.[15]

From prison Nahmiash contacted the Brazilian Consul, A. Mauritz de Calinerio, for help. Calinerio was less than excited about helping the "Hebrew" but feared that if he did not do so the "semi-barbarous" Moroccan political system would be perceived as having defeated the Brazilian "spirit of Justice."[16] Strong measures were needed and the Consul's threat to break Brazilian/Moroccan relations if Nahmiash was not released made international headlines.[17] There is no evidence that the publicity had any effect; what is clear is that Calinerio's "private representations" (probably in the form of cash) did lead to the release of Nahmiash. Yet the Nahmiash situation was just one of many. Time after time naturalized Brazilians demanded, and received, the help of the Consulate in Tangier. This angered both the Brazilians, who by 1900 had decided that only those Moroccans naturalized before 1880 would be considered Brazilians, and the Moroccan government, which had cordial relations with Brazil "in everything and for everything as long as it is not related to the Hebrew Moroccans, naturalized Brazilians."[18] "In everything and for everything," however, meant almost nothing since an examination of diplomatic documents suggests that Brazilian relations with Morocco seem to have revolved almost exclusively around the question of how to treat Brazilian Jews of Moroccan birth. On March 4, 1903, a solution to the mutual problem was found: Brazil closed its diplomatic offices and turned them over to the Portuguese.[19]

THE SOUTHERN CIMA DA SERRA FRONTIER

In 1904 a number of farming colonies were founded in southern Brazil by the Jewish Colonization Association (known in Brazil as ICA, an acronym; *Yidishe kolonizatsye gezelschaft,* or IKA), a European-based philanthropic group. The Eastern European Jews who populated the colonies in the state of Rio Grande do Sul never numbered more than a few thousand people. Yet the mere existence of the colonies challenged traditional images of Jews as exclusively and insidiously oriented toward finance and capital in urban areas. Furthermore, the colonists, by acculturating but refusing to assimilate, formed an immigrant community committed to its own ethnic survival while defying notions that Jews were uninterested in becoming citizens of Brazil.

The farming colonies brought Jewish immigration to the official attention of Brazilian leaders for the first time since the Inquisition. This occurred in part because the ICA enjoyed the diplomatic support of a British government committed to ensuring that emigrating Russian Jewry would resettle outside of the United Kingdom. It was further reinforced because some members of the ICA leadership were heavy investors in the Brazilian economy. The ICA thus provided legitimate refugee relief even while representing foreign interests in Brazil and as a result, a particularly strong relationship developed between the ICA and the Rio Grande do Sul government. Indeed, when the Rio Grande do Sul government sought to promote itself to potential emigrants at the St. Louis (Missouri) International Exhibition of 1904, its official English-language Descriptive Memorial of the State of Rio Grande do Sul singled out the Jewish colonies, and no others, as positive examples of colonization.[20]

Ironically, Brazil's Jewish agricultural colonies were established as a result of a rumor that circulated among the European Jewish elite in the late 1880s. As the story was told, a group of Russian Jews attracted by notices of cheap land for colonization had migrated to Argentina earlier in the decade.[21] The plans fell through and they were reduced to huddling "near the railway station, sustaining themselves with handouts from passengers."[22] News of the situation reached Baron Maurice de Hirsch de Gereuth (Moritz Baron Hirsch), a Bavarian-born Jewish philanthropist who had founded the Jewish Colonization Association in 1891 with the specific purpose of aiding poverty-stricken East European and Balkan Jewry by establishing Jewish farming colonies in the Americas. In 1893 the ICA set up its first colony in Argentina and in 1901 the ICA began to investigate expansion into Rio Grande do Sul, because of low costs, proximity to the Argentine colonies, and its government's desire for new colonists. Brazil was also attractive because the Positivist-influenced Rio Grande do Sul Republican Party (PRR) was tolerant in matters of religion, an important factor to Jewish immigrants being persecuted in the Russian Empire.[23]

In 1902 the Jewish Colonization Association purchased a large estate in a sparsely populated section of central Rio Grande do Sul, directly on the rail line between Rio de Janeiro and Montevideo, Uruguay. The colony was named "Philippson," after the Belgian vice president of the ICA, Franz Philippson, who was also president and owner of the Compagnie Auxiliaire de Chemins de Fer au Brésil, the dominant rail company in the state.[24] The railroad, it was hoped, would help the new colony flourish by transporting its goods to urban centers and exporting surplus lumber from newly cleared forests, and it made Colony Philippson a priority for PRR politicians who wanted to encourage further migration to underpopulated frontier areas.[25] According to a dispatch from the secretary of public works published in the PRR newspaper *A Federação,* "the aims of the [ICA] are for the public good . . . to encourage immigration and material progress."[26] In other words, it was "not sufficient only to introduce mass immigration . . . it is necessary to facilitate the exchange of products with the construction of good roads [that] permit rapid and economical transportation."[27] To the PRR, populating the state with immigrants helped increase the economic power needed to break the domination of the states of Minas Gerais and São Paulo in Brazilian national politics. At the same time, profit from the expanded economic base would ultimately flow upward to the state elite and often from there to the exterior. To the PRR and the foreign interests with whom it was allied, Jewish immigrants were an important cog in the economic development and political growth of Rio Grande do Sul.

Jewish colonists were supposed to begin arriving in Rio Grande do Sul in early 1904, and the Saint Petersburg Emigration Office of the ICA promoted Colony Philippson by distributing notices of the availability of free passages, animals, tools and land. Even so, the Jewish Colonization Association's four hundred Russian offices were not able to find the twenty-five to thirty families needed, since few Jews were interested in migrating to Brazil, with its image as a disease infested jungle with little real economic opportunity. This was accentuated by racist fears, and the well known Yiddish saying that Brazil was the *land fun di mahlpes* (land of the monkeys) compressed all the images into one simple phrase. One colonist who did go remembered "the disquiet provoked . . . by the active rumors of distant Brazil. Some [potential colonists] . . . said they had information from newspapers. Others had received notices from those already there. [But] the most talked about rumors of endemic diseases, like yellow fever, typhoid, [and] cholera and animal attacks."[28] Indeed, Brazil's reputation was so bad that Jews even refused to move there after the Kishinev pogrom of April 1903.

Eventually a few hundred candidates ignored the rumors and applied to migrate. By August 1904, thirty-seven Jewish families, totaling 267 persons, had been "selected with great care."[29] They began to arrive in September, and the first impressions were not favorable. Immigrants were shocked to find that the "extreme primitiveness of our hovels contrasted with the relative comfort of our old homes in Russia." Others complained that they had to work from sunup to sundown just to make the colony habitable.[30] The situation was compounded when Philippson's directors discovered that the Saint Petersburg Office had sent a group of "farmers" who knew nothing about Brazil and were "ignorant in particular of the agricultural conditions that they are encountering."[31]

The problems did not stop unscrupulous agents in Russia from telling potential immigrants that, if they paid their own passage, the ICA colonies would provide them with all the necessities for starting a farm. Soon hundreds of families, none sponsored by the ICA, "were transported to Brazil and dumped down on the Jewish Colonization estate." Ironically, these newcomers were viewed by the Philippson administrators as saviors because many did have the agricultural experience that the ICA sponsorees did not.[32] A lack of adequate schools and poor sanitary conditions impelled the official colonists, who were all "ignorant of the country and the local customs," to leave Philippson as quickly as possible. Alfred L. Moreau Gottschalk, the United States Consul-General in Rio de Janeiro, informed one inquirer in 1917, just thirteen years after the establishment of Philippson, that "the colonies cannot be accentuated to have been successes as the younger generation seems almost invariably to leave the land and take up commercial pursuits."[33] For the most part this rejection of agriculture was one of simple economic expediency and those who left the colonies went on to found a more prosperous Jewish community based in Porto Alegre, the state's largest city.

Although the ICA sent between five and ten new families to Colony Philippson each year, the growth of the settlement was minimal. Furthermore, the Rio Grande do Sul government, in spite of its encouragement of colonization and its willingness to let the immigrants maintain an openly Jewish way of life, gave little actual support to the colonies. Yet in June 1909,

Quatro Irmãos, a 360 square mile (87,000 hectares), largely forested estate in northeastern-central Rio Grande do Sul was purchased as a second Jewish colony. The new colony, like the first, was in strategic proximity to the rail lines of Franz Philippson's Compagnie Auxiliaire, near the São Paulo–Porto Alegre railway line.[34] Preparations in Quatro Irmãos far exceeded what had been done in Philippson. In order to attract East European recruits for the new colony, the ICA Information Bureau in Saint Petersburg began promoting Quatro Irmãos in its bimonthly Yiddish-language magazine *Der Idischer Emigrant* (The Jewish Emigrant). These articles, it was hoped, would help dispel the negative images of Brazil that had made colonists for Philippson scarce. The ICA Information Bureau also printed two thousand brochures directed at Russian-speaking, urban Jews who might want to establish themselves in business in the state.

Promotional materials and physical preparations did little to improve Brazil's image among Russian Jews and the Saint Petersburg office had little success in garnering immigrants. Finally, in July 1912, fourteen families and nineteen single men arrived from the Argentine ICA colonies. In August sixty additional families came from Bessarabia and, in April 1913, another group of forty-three families left Bessarabia for Quatro Irmãos. The conditions, however, were so bad that between 1915 and 1923 the outmigration of sponsored Jews from Philippson and Quatro Irmãos was constant.

It is not surprising, given the appalling conditions, that by 1923 the centers of Jewish life in Rio Grande do Sul were oriented away from the colonies. In the nearby cities of Passo Fundo, Santa Maria and Cruz Alta, Jews created alternative social and communal institutions, and small independent Jewish institutions in Porto Alegre, exploding in size with new arrivals from Europe and the Middle East, were incorporated into rapidly growing umbrella organizations. Jewish settlers now had more compelling reasons to move to urban centers and soon only a handful remained in the colonies where a series of rebellions would convince the last to leave. Such political disruptions and armed uprisings were common in Rio Grande do Sul throughout the 1920s but the ICA colonists, not actively involved in Rio Grandense politics, were usually untouched by the upheavals.[35] In late 1922, however, Quatro Irmãos found itself in the center of rebellious activity when a revolt began after electoral fraud in the state's first contested election in fifteen years led opposition leaders to rise up militarily against Governor Antonio Augusto Borges de Medeiros. The colony's large wooded areas and location near the Rio de Janeiro–Montevideo railway line made the colony, according to Rio Grande do Sul's subinspector of police, eminently "suitable as a hiding place for ill-intentioned persons," and insurgents could be found wandering throughout the colony.[36] In late January 1923, animals began mysteriously disappearing, but Quatro Irmãos's codirector managed to persuade a local *coronel* (warlord) to promise that "the colonists would be respected and all animals returned."[37]

The PRR army finally arrived in Quatro Irmãos and the rebels left the estate. Yet permanent protection was left to a municipal police force which had in fact disbanded and fled when the rebellion began. ICA administrators thus proposed the English government protect Quatro Irmãos since the ICA was officially a British corporation. This hope never translated into reality and the situation worsened throughout 1923.[38] In April, Borges's soldiers again liberated Quatro Irmãos but demanded that the colonists "loan" them materials and animals that were never returned. When the state troops left the colony, the insurgents again returned and also "requisitioned" materials without paying for them. Between January and June of 1923, hundreds of horses, cows (over 20 percent of those on the colony), chickens, oxen, and sacks of corn, beans, and manioc were looted.[39] This led to a two-thirds drop in cattle prices, and with little food "the already poor colonists were at the very end of their resources." This forced numerous Jewish families, including a group "of the most energetic and well-to-do colonists," to flee Quatro Irmãos for the relative safety of nearby cities.[40]

In September 1923, Quatro Irmãos's colonists again became the "victims of revolutionary lawlessness" when rebels occupied the entire colony and demanded a "war contribution" of 25,000 milreis (U.S. $2,550) or its railway would be destroyed and the entire ICA staff imprisoned. Eventually the "tax" was halved and the colony was given eight days to get the funds from the ICA Headquarters in Paris.[41] Paris refused to pay the bribe payments and contacted British Ambassador Sir John Tilley asking that "Our society being British subject dare taking liberty soliciting your urgent intervention before Federal Government."[42] Pressure was added by Lucien Wolf, a well-connected and powerful member of the Joint Foreign Committee of the Jewish Board of Deputies and Anglo-Jewish Association, who pointed out to the British undersecretary of state that "The JCA [*sic*] is an important philanthropic organization . . . and it possesses in various parts of the world, large colonies on which thousands of Jewish refugees have been successfully settled and which helps very appreciably to deflect from European countries the pressure of emigration from East Europe."[43] The fear that Eastern European Jewish immigrants who would normally go to Brazil might now stay in Great Britain led to action and a meeting between Foreign Minister Felix Pacheco and Ambassador Tilley led to two detachments of federal infantry being stationed on the colony.

In November 1923 an armistice was finally signed and later that year Rabbi Isaiah Raffalovich arrived in Brazil as the new local director of the Jewish Colonization Association. His first task was to guarantee the safety of the settlers on Quatro Irmãos since revolutionary activity had resumed after a group of forty-five "bandits" attacked the colony. An ICA observer from Paris had been awakened with a gun to his head, dragged into the woods, and threatened with death while some colonists were forced to pay bribes in order to avoid assassination.[44] A colonist named Raskin suffered the indignity of having his beard cut off, a clearly irreligious taunt at the traditional Jews who lived on Quatro Irmãos. Another colonist was found in the woods "disfigured by swords thrusts to the head and a bullet lodged in his chest."[45] The murder shocked Brazilians and immigrants alike, and not surprisingly all of the colonists deserted Quatro Irmãos. Isaiah Raffalovich's sad note to the British government said it all: "The colony [has] now broken up completely."[46]

In spite of the problems in the colony, Jews who migrated from the colonies to Rio Grande do Sul's urban centers, notably the capital Porto Alegre, found that the promises of religious and cultural freedom given by the PRR were legitimate. Indeed, Rio Grande do Sul was and is notable for the high levels of pre-migratory culture that are maintained, especially when compared to places like Rio de Janeiro and São Paulo. Throughout the state, Germans, Italians, and Jews lived in separate towns, and in Porto Alegre itself neighborhoods were far more monolithic in ethnic makeup than those in other cities. Thus, Bom Fim, the neighborhood traditionally associated with Jews in Porto Alegre, was actually a "Jewish" neighborhood (something not the case in São Paulo's "Jewish" neighborhood of Bom Retiro or Rio de Janeiro's of Praça Onze) throughout the 1960s, and it is more than suggestive that even the German-Jewish Congregation in Porto Alegre, the Sociedade Israelita Brasileira de Cultura e Benificencia (SIBRA), was located within walking distances of all the different "traditional" shuls, a situation that did not exist in other areas. Of course the movement of Jews from the ICA colonies to Porto Alegre helped to establish a traditional Jewish base that was not to be found in any other expanding Jewish community in Brazil, and the smaller numbers meant that the community could afford only one Jewish school, and thus did not separate its youth along political-educational lines as occurred in cities with competing Jewish schools. On Brazil's southern frontier, where political loyalty superseded ethnic difference, Jewish communal life remained much stronger than it did in nonfrontier areas of Brazil.

CONCLUSION

By examining how two Jewish immigrant groups constructed their ethnicities, I have tried to show how the frontier became a particularly viable place for the worlds of Brazilianness and neo-Brazilianness to coexist. I have suggested that Brazilian ethnicity can only be understood when rejection and inclusion of and by immigrant groups ultimately tell the same story, the search for "the spiritual integralization of Brazil."[47] It is in many ways like Greil Marcus's study of punk rock, *Lipstick Traces,* where history becomes the result "of moments that seem to leave nothing behind, nothing but the spectral connections of people long separated by place and time, but somehow speaking the same language."[48] The connections here are indeed spectral. On the Amazonian frontier North African Jews became Brazilian so they could return to Morocco. On the southern frontier Eastern European Jews became Brazilian so they could be Jewish. On Brazil's frontiers the society of sameness and the society of difference fused as the reality of the hyphen remained strong but always hidden from public view.

NOTES

The author gratefully acknowledges the financial support of the Lucius N. Littauer Foundation, the Memorial Foundation for Jewish Culture, the North-South Center, the J. William Fulbright Commission, and the National Endowment for the Humanities.

1. *Jornal do Imigrante* 4.422 (Sept. 1981): 2.

2. Sílvio Romero, *História da literatura brasileira,* 2d ed., 2 vols. (1888; Rio de Janeiro: H. Garnier, 1902–3), 67.

3. Jeffrey Lesser, *Welcoming the Undesirables: Brazil and the Jewish Question* (Berkeley: University of California Press, 1994), 7–8.

4. Interview with Sr. J. in Belem's main synagogue, Apr. 1994.

5. Michael M. Laskier, *The Alliance Israélite Universelle and the Jewish Communities of Morocco, 1862–1962* (Albany: SUNY Press, 1983), 133–37; Robert Ricard, "Notes sur l'émigration des Israélites marocains en Amérique espagnole et au Brésil," *Revue Africaine* 88 (1944): 11–17.

6. Edmund Burke III, *Prelude to Protectorate in Morocco: Precolonial Protest and Resistance, 1860–1912* (Chicago: University of Chicago Press, 1976), 36–37; Salomão Serebrenick, and Elias Lipiner, *Breve História dos Judeus no Brasil* (Rio de Janeiro: Ediçoes Biblos, 1962), 95.

7. Maïr Lévy, "Rapport sur l'Emigration à Tétouan" (1891–92), Archives of the Alliance Israélite Universelle (Tétouan), VI B 25, rpt. in Sarah Leibovici, *Chronique des Juifs de Tétouan (1860–1896)* (Paris: Editions Maisonneuve and Larose, 1984), 287–96; Laskier, *Alliance Israélite Universelle,* 137; Norman A. Stillman, *The Jews of Arab Lands in Modern Times* (Philadelphia: Jewish Publication Society, 1991), 38.

8. Barbara Weinstein, *The Amazon Rubber Boom, 1850–1920* (Stanford, Calif.: Stanford University Press, 1983), 50–51, 259–60; Abraham Ramiro Bentes, *Primeira Comunidade Israelita Brasileira: Tradições, Genealogia, Pré-História* (Rio de Janeiro: Gráfica Borsoi, 1989).

9. *Yehudim al g'dot ha Amazonas/Jews on the Banks of the Amazon* (Tel Aviv: Beth Hatefutsoth, Nahum Goldmann Museum of the Jewish Diaspora, 1987).

10. Robert Ricard, "L'Emigration des Juifs marocains en Amérique du sud," *Revue de Géographie Marocaine* 7.8 (2d and 3d trimesters, 1928): 3; Isaac Benchimol, "La Langue espagnole au Maroc," *Revue des écoles de l'AIU* 2 (July–Sept. 1901): 128.

11. See naturalization case of Mimom Elbás in Egon Wolff and Frieda Wolff, *Dicionário Biográfico IV: Processos de Naturalizaçao de Israelitas, Século XIX* (Rio de Janeiro: n.p., 1987), 211.

12. José Daniel Colaco (Consul) to Carlos de Carvalho (Minister of Foreign Affairs), Sept. 18, 1895, 02-Repartiçõoes Consulares Brasileiras, Tangier—Ofícios—1891–1895—265/1/11, Arquivo Histórico Itamarati—Rio de Janeiro (hereafter AHI-R).

13. Ministry of Justice annex to José Daniel Colaco (Consul) to Carlos de Carvalho (Minister of Foreign Affairs), Sept. 18, 1895. 02-Repartições Consulares Brasileiras, Tangier—Ofícios—1891–1895—265/1/11, AHI-R.

14. Letter of Simao Nahmias in Wolff and Wolff, *Dicionário Biográfico IV*, 349.

15. *Al-shogreb-Al Aksa* [Tangier], Aug. 27, 1902, 02-Repartições Consulares Brasileiras, Tangier—Ofícios—1900–1925—265/1/13, AHI-R.

16. Confidential letter of A. Mauritz de Calinerio (Consul in Tangier) to Olyntho Maximo de Magalhaes (Minister of Foreign Affairs), Sept. 15, 1902, 02-Repartições Consulares Brasileiras, Tangier—Ofícios—1900–1925—265/1/13, AHI-R.

17. *El Imparcial* [Madrid], Aug. 20, 1902.

18. Confidential letter of A. Mauritz de Calinerio (Consul in Tangier) to Olyntho Maximo de Magalhaes (Minister of Foreign Relations), Oct. 6, 1902, 02-Repartições Consulares Brasileiras, Tangier—Ofícios—1900–1925—265/1/13, AHI-R.

19. Letter of William R. Gordon (Brazilian Vice Consul in Tangier) to Itamarati, Mar. 4, 1903, 02-Repartições Consulares Brasileiras, Tangier—Ofícios—1900–1925—265/1/13, AHI-R.

20. Eugenio Dahne, ed., *Descriptive Memorial of the State of Rio Grande do Sul, Brazil* (Porto Alegre: Commercial Library, 1904), 29.

21. Lazaro Schallman, *Los Pioneros de la Colonizacíon Judía en La Argentina* (Buenos Aires: Ejecutivo Sudamericano del Congreso Judío Mundial, 1969), 16–19.

22. Judith Laiken Elkin, *Jews of the Latin American Republics* (Chapel Hill: University of North Carolina Press, 1980), 127; S. Adler-Rudel, "Moritz Baron Hirsch," *Leo Baeck Institute Yearbook* 8 (1963): 45.

23. Brazilian Constitution of Feb. 24, 1891, article 72, no. 3; Luiza H. Schmitz Kliemann, "A ferrovia gaúcha e as diretrizes de 'ordem e progresso,' 1905–1920," *Estudos Ibero-Americanos* 3 (Dec. 1977): 189.

24. Rapport de L'administration centrale au Conseil d'Administration of the Jewish Colonization Association (hereafter RACCA), 1903, 48, Arquivo Histórico Judaico Brasileiro, São Paulo (hereafter AHJB-SP).

25. Joseph L. Love, *Rio Grande do Sul and Brazilian Regionalism, 1882–1930* (Stanford, Calif.: Stanford University Press, 1971), 7.

26. *A Federaçao* [Porto Alegre], June 20, 1903.

27. Secretaria de Estado dos Negócios das Obras Públicas. *Relatório do Secretário de 1906,* code 105, 10, Arquivo Histórico do Rio Grande do Sul–Porto Alegre.

28. Jacques Schweidson, *Judeus de Bombachas e Chimarrao* (Rio de Janeiro: José Olympio Editora, 1985), 7. See also Martha Pargendler Faermann, *A Promessa Cumprida* (Porto Alegre: Metrópole, 1990); Marlene Kulkes, org., *Histórias de Vida: Imigraçao Judaica no Rio Grande do Sul* (Porto Alegre: Instituto Cultural Judaico Marc Chagall, 1989); Moacyr Scliar, *Caminhos da Esperança: A Presença Judaica no Rio Grande do Sul* (Porto Alegre: Riocell, 1990).

29. RACCA 1907, 142, AHJB-SP; Report of Maurice Abravanel in *Annuario do Estado do Rio Grande do Sul para O Anno de 1906* (Porto Alegre: Kruse and Co., 1905), 299.

30. Schweidson, *Judeus de Bombachas,* 8; Frida Alexandr, *Filipson: Memórias da Primeira Colônia Judaica no Rio Grande do Sul* (São Paulo: Editora Fulgor, 1967), 17.

31. ICA Head Office (Paris) to Philippson Administration, Sept. 15, 1904, no. 37, organized ICA file, box 12, plastic bag 1, AHJB-SP.

32. Isaiah Raffalovich, "The Condition of Jewry and Judaism in South America," in *Central Conference of American Rabbis Yearbook,* vol. 11 (New York: Central Conference of American Rabbi's, 1930), 5; Raffalovich (New York) to ICA Head Office (Paris), July 8, 1930, and Séance du Conseil d'Administration (hereafter SCA), Sept. 27, 1930, 2:57, Archives of the Jewish Colonization Association, London (hereafter JCA-L); *The Jewish Chronicle* [London], July 6, 1906.

33. Memorandum of Alfred L. Moreau Gottschalk, Jan. 19, 1917, "Immigration and Colonization in Brazil"; Purport Lists for the Department of State, Class 8: "Internal Affairs of the States," 8.32.55, "Brazil-Economic Matters-Immigration," National Archives and Record Center, Washington, D.C. (hereafter NARC-W).

34. *Deutsche Zeitung* [São Paulo], Feb. 11, 1915.

35. Isabel Rosa Gritti, "A Imigração Judaica para o Rio grande do Sul: A Jewish Colonization Association e a Colonizaçao de Quatro Irmaos" (M.A. thesis, Pontifíca Universidade Católica do Rio Grande do Sul, 1992), 66–70. The revolts in Rio Grande do Sul were part of a national movement of revolutionary young military officers (*tenentes*) that began with the abortive army revolt in Rio de Janeiro in July 1922, continued with the Prestes revolt in the Missoes district, and culminated in July 1924 with barracks uprisings in São Paulo, Manaus, Belém, and Aracaju. See Edgard Carone, *O Tenentismo: Acontecimentos, personagens, programas* (São Paulo: Difel, 1975), and Neill Macaulay, *The Prestes Column: Revolution in Brazil* (New York: New Viewpoints, 1974).

36. Letter of Braz de Albuquerque Braga to Jewish Colonization Association (Erebango), undated, FO 371/10608 A2300/124/6, 105, Public Records Office, London (hereafter PRO-L).

37. ICA Administration (Passo Fundo) to ICA Directorate (Paris), Feb. 12, 1923, no. 755, 3, LP 1922–26, 748–850 uf. AHJB-SP; ICA Administration (Passo Fundo) to ICA Directorate (Paris), Feb. 12, 1923, no. 755, 3, LP 1922–26, 748–850 uf. AHJB-SP.

38. ICA Administration (Passo Fundo) to ICA Directorate (Paris), Feb. 12, 1923, no. 755, p.3. LP 1922–26, 748–850 uf. AHJB-SP; ICA Administration (Passo Fundo) to ICA Directorate (Paris), Mar. 20, 1923, no. 757, 4, LP 1922–26, 748–850 uf. AHJB-SP.

39. "Liste des Requisitions Faites Par Les Forces du Government le 26 et 27 Avril, 1923," attached to letter of ICA Administration (Passo Fundo) to ICA Directorate (Paris), Aug. 17, 1923, no. 769, LP 1922–26, 748–850 uf. AHJB-SP; David Proushan to T.

C. Dillon (British Consul in Porto Alegre), Oct. 29, 1923, no. 774, LP 1922–26, 748–850 uf. AHJB-SP.

40. ICA Administration (Passo Fundo) to ICA Directorate (Paris), Sept. 11, 1923, no. 770, 3, LP 1922–26, 748–850 uf. AHJB-SP; "Movement Colons Quatro Irmãos á 25/7/23," attached to letter of ICA Administration (Passo Fundo) to ICA Directorate (Paris), Aug. 17, 1923, no. 769, LP 1922–26, 748–850 uf. AHJB-SP.

41. John Tilley, British Embassy (Rio), to the Marques Curzon of Kedleston, British Foreign Office (London), Sept. 15, 1923, FO 371/8431 A550/5630/287/6, 221, PRO-L; ICA Administration (Passo Fundo) to ICA Directorate (Paris), Sept. 11, 1923, no. 770, 3, LP 1922–26, 748–850 uf. AHJB-SP.

42. Paris to Passo Fundo, Sept. 9, 1923, LP 1922–26, 748–850 uf.; ICA Administration (E:echim) to British Ambassador (Rio de Janeiro), Sept. 11, 1923, no. 774, LP 1922–26, 748–850 uf. AHJB-SP.

43. Lucien Wolf (Geneva) to British Foreign Office, Sept. 12, 1923, FO 371/8431 E5501/5060/6, PRO-L.

44. ICA (Brazil) to ICA (Paris), Dec. 20, 1924, no. 805, LP 1922–26, 748–850 uf. AHJB-SP.

45. Relatório Policial sobre Assassinato de David Faigenboim, Aug. 8, 1924, organized ICA file, box 20, 8, AHJB-SP; ICA (Brazil) to ICA (Paris), Dec. 20, 1924, no. 805, 3, LP 1922–26, 748–850 uf. AHJB-SP; Relatório Policial sobre Assassinato de David Faigenboim, Aug. 8, 1924, organized ICA file, box 20, 2, AHJB-SP. Many years later an ICA administrator claimed that Faigenboim had been murdered for revenge by an ex-employee. See Samuel Chwartzman, "Um pequeno histrico [*sic*] sobre algumas das pessoas enterradas no cemitério de Quatro Irmãos vítimas de morte violenta, umas por acidente outras por assasinato," Archive of Samuel Chwartzman, Porto Alegre.

46. John Tilley, British Embassy (Rio), to Austen Chamberlain, British Foreign Office (London), Jan. 8, 1925, FO 371/8431 A5501/5630/287/6, 74, PRO-L.

47. Antônio Baptista Pereira, *O Brasil e A Raça: Conferencia Feita na Faculdade de Direito de São Paulo a 19 de Junho de 1928* (São Paulo: Empresa Grafica Rossetti, 1928), 17.

48. Greil Marcus, *Lipstick Traces: A Secret History of the Twentieth Century* (Cambridge, Mass.: Harvard University Press, 1989), 4.

9 Jews in Chinese Culture: Representations and Realities

ZHOU XUN

In modern China, the definition of the "Jew" or "Jewishness" is both problematic and complex. It is a symbol for money, deviousness and meanness; it can also represent poverty, trustworthiness and warmheartedness. It has religious as well as secular meanings. While it represents individualism, it also stands for a collective spirit. On the one hand it symbolizes tradition, on the other hand it can equally invoke modernity. One day the "Jew" is a stateless slave, another day the "Jew" is the dominant power in the world. The "Jew" is nationalist and at the same time cosmopolitan. He can be a filthy capitalist or an ardent communist, a committed revolutionary or a spineless loser. In other words, anything which is not Chinese is Jewish, at the same time that anything which is Chinese is also Jewish; anything which the Chinese need is Jewish, at the same time that anything which the Chinese despise is Jewish. These representations have had very little to do with the small Jewish presence in China. They were invented to fulfill contradictory and ambiguous roles, as distant mirrors, in the construction of the self by various Chinese intellectual and social groups since the turn of the century.

Although these representations seem to correspond to images of the "Jew" in Europe, it would be superficial to reduce them to purely "Western influence." Representations of the "Jew" have been endowed with indigenous meaning by modernizing elites. The images of the "Jew," for instance, were and still are generated by the *difference* of the "Jewish" race, which is marked by its "non-Chineseness," more specifically because Jews are seen not to be direct descendants of the Yellow Emperor. As a matter of fact, the animal radical of *Youtai,* the received character for "Jew" or "Jewishness" in

Chinese, indicates the *imagined* physical difference between the "Chinese" and the "Jews," which is rooted in the tradition of "picturing the alien groups living outside the pale of Chinese society as distant savages hovering on the edge of bestiality."[1]

By creating the "Jew" as a homogenous group, which acts as a constitutive outsider and embodies all the negative as well as positive qualities which were feared or desired, various social groups in China could thus identify themselves as an integrated homogenous "in-group," or the "Chinese" in this case. They are able to project their own anxieties onto outsiders like the "Jews." In this respect, it corresponds to a widespread fear as well as need of an "other" which can be found in many cultures and societies.

In reality, "Jews" have not existed in China in any significant manner comparable to Europe or America, and there was very little social contact between the "Chinese" and the "Jews" in both the colonial and the postcolonial period.

THE JEWS IN CHINA: THE REALITIES

The Jews of Kaifeng and Xinjiang

Any attempt to set a date for the beginning of Chinese consciousness of Jews as a different "racial" group would be arbitrary. The first known Jewish community in China is the Kaifeng community. It was discovered by a Jesuit missionary, Matteo Ricci, in 1605. Ricci, however, never reached Kaifeng himself. He was met by a local doctor from Kaifeng named Ai in the imperial capital Peking. According to Ricci's correspondence to his order, it was through his conversation with Ai that he became convinced that Ai and his community were the Chinese Jewish descendants. Ai and his clan were however less clear about their "Jewish identity." As a matter of fact, they regarded their religion to be the same as Christianity and they even invited Ricci to become their religious leader—as none among them were familiar with their religious practice.

The earliest received document we have suggesting that Jews were considered to be different from the local Chinese is also the writings of Ricci in 1605.[2] According to Ricci, the Jewish community in Kaifeng was referred to as the "blue-hat Western people" by the locals. It is obvious that the term "blue hat" was an outward mark of the Jews of Kaifeng. In contrast, the term *Huihui* was much more complex and perhaps more significant. It first appeared in China as a reference to Muslims in the Yuan Dynasty (1279–1368) under the Mongol rule. However, it has also been used in a wider context, referring to people from the western region of or outside the Chinese empire. The nature of the term "blue-hat Western people" indicates that in the sixteenth and seventeenth centuries, or perhaps even earlier, the Kaifeng Jewish community was considered to be more closely related to the Muslims than to the local Chinese. However, as the result of intermarriage and cultural assimilation, by the middle of the nineteenth century, when the Protestant delegates visited the Kaifeng Jewish community, these differences had eventually become insignificant. What was left to separate the so-called Jewish descendants in Kaifeng from other local Chinese was nothing more than fragments of Torah scrolls, prayer books, stone tablets and the faded memories of some members of the community.

Apart from the Kaifeng community, it was also suggested that Jewish communities existed in other parts of China before the thirteenth century. Recently, some scholars have discovered some documents in Uyghur which suggest that there were Jews in the northwest of China, such as the Xinjiang area, since the ninth century. These Jews arrived in China through the silk road. However, there is no suggestion that any kind of Jewish community existed there, and it is most likely that these Jews lived side by side with Muslims and Buddhists and formed the now so-called Uyghur minority in China. At the turn of this century, when some Jews escaped to Xinjiang from the pogroms in Russia, most of them chose to hide their Jewish identity in public and became part of the local Uyghur community. It has however been suggested that in their homes, many of them still kept their "Jewish" tradition. But the majority of the locals and Chinese were and still are unaware of the existence of the "Jews" in Xinjiang and their story remains untold.

The Sephardic and Ashkenazi Jews in China

In the second half of the nineteenth century, a group of Sephardic Jewish merchants arrived in China in conjunction with the British exploitation of China. At one time, some of them became the richest families in the Far East. Most of them, however, kept apart from the local Chinese community. Some of them presented themselves as British rather than Jewish and they were in fact some of the most prominent figures of the foreign community in Shanghai before 1949.

Needless to say, the privileges of certain British Jews in Shanghai, such as Sir Victor Sassoon (1881–1961), on the one hand induced the construction of the image of the "Jews" as "imperialists" in China. Being associated with the East India Company in the early years, the Sassoons and many other Jewish merchants in Shanghai had at one time or another engaged in the opium trading business. As opium had been seen as a destructive power which the foreign imperialists had used to destroy the "yellow race" and China, these British Jews did not gain a very good reputation among Chinese nationalists. Even in the 1970s, some Chinese still referred to them as "evil opium traders." Apart from opium trading, they also engaged in other economic activities such as banking and property business. Among them, Victor Sassoon and Silas Hardoon (1851–1937) became two of the most dominant figures in Shanghai's financial as well as political world early in this century. Both of them lived a rather luxurious and corrupt life. While Sir Victor Sassoon was described as being famous for his land speculation, having a lavish building named after him, and his high living,[3] the Hardoon garden was known as one of the most spectacular and expensive places of its day in Shanghai. Silas Hardoon, even until recently, is still sometimes referred to as a "British imperialist."[4]

While Sephardic Jews controlled the financial world of Shanghai, Ashkenazi Jews from Russia also brought vitality to the economic and social life of the northeast of China, especially in places such as Harbin, at the beginning of this century. Unlike the Sephardic Jews in Shanghai, the Ashkenazi Jews of Harbin were much more concerned about their Jewishness and their sense of community as a whole. They built their own bank, schools, hospitals and synagogues. However, during the Japanese occupation of Manchuria, many of the members of the community had to move, first to Tianjing, then to Shanghai.

The Jewish Refugees in Shanghai

The last and the biggest migration of Jews to China was after 1939, when anti-Semitism in Germany reached its highest and worst form. Shanghai became the home for many thousands of Jewish refugees. In the early days, life for the refugees was relatively easy and lively here; they were able to engage in business and various social activities. However, after Japan had formally declared war on China on July 7, 1937, an anti-Jewish policy was also enforced by some of Japan's so-called Jewish experts and the pro-Japanese parties in China. In their recent book, *Jews in the Japanese Mind,* David Goodman and Masanori Miyazawa have demonstrated that the Jewish myth had already appeared in Japan as early as the end of the last century.[5] The more immediate cause for the Japanese enforcement of an anti-Jewish policy in China during wartime, however, was a pamphlet entitled *Der kampf zwischen Juda und Japan* by Alfred Stoss, a retired German naval commander and an anti-Semite. This pamphlet described the Jews as a dangerous threat to Japan, especially in China where the rich Jews in Shanghai were attempting to control Chiang Kaishek's nationalist party in order to fight the Japanese. This work had obviously deepened Japan's xenophobia about the "mysterious Jew." The influx of Jewish refugees from Nazi Germany into Shanghai since 1939 was also seen as a threat to Japanese control over the city.

In order to eliminate the purported "Jewish threat" to the building of a "Great East Asia Sphere," some of the Japanese "Jewish experts" cooperated with Wang Jingwei's pro-Japanese nationalist government and the Xinmin Hui (People's Renovation Society). The Xinmin Hui was a Japanese-controlled organization, with its headquarters in Beijing. It attempted to promote the "Great East Asia Sphere" ideology and to justify Japan's occupation in China. Together they engaged in publishing anti-Semitic literature in China. It may also have been their aim to draw Chinese attention away from the Japanese aggression. In much of this anti-Semitic literature, the "Jews" were often described as the ancestors of all anarchists and communists.

In early 1943, almost a year after Roosevelt—described as the "puppet of the Jews"—had declared war on Japan, *Nanjing Republican Daily,* the official paper of Wang's government, began to publish articles to testify to the "Jewish danger" in China. An article entitled "The Jewish Imperialism in Shanghai" claimed that:

> The modern history of the Jewish invasion of China began in 1832, when a group of Jews, headed by the Sassoon family and seconded by the East India Company, entered China to become involved in the opium trade. Soon, these Jews, especially in Shanghai, built up an unshakable foundation in Chinese commercial business. However, they only engaged in illegal business, and never brought any benefits to the [Chinese] society. Their names are only associated with the opium trade, smuggling, or the nefarious property business. They use their banks and similar organizations to purloin money, or they control the stock market and use their lying skills to make huge profits. . . . A good example is the Ravens of the American-Oriental Banking Corporation. Their actual leader is Starr, who has a Jewish father or mother and is a typical Jew. He first went to Japan in 1920 in the hope of making big money in the East, but because of the Japanese people's nationalistic spirit and the Japanese law, he was not able to use his innate skills and therefore came to Shanghai. After he arrived in Shanghai, Starr got together with Raven. . . . He [Starr] opposes peace and supports Chongqing's terrorist activities; he continuously tries to deepen the hatred between China and Japan; he attempts to interfere in the harmony between China and Japan, and the achievements of the New Great Asia Sphere.[6]

Under the intense pressure of their German allies, in March 1943 the Japanese government passed the order to force the Shanghai Jewish refugees to move into the so-called designated area, or concentration camp. In order to justify such action, on March 15, *Shanghai People's News,* a Japanese-controlled paper, published an article which portrayed the Jewish refugees in Shanghai as "parasites," and they were characterized as evil:

> Although the Jews do not look very extraordinary from outside, their ambitions are overwhelming. They are like parasites, once they settle in a place, then they grow massively underground and suck everybody's blood. The European Jews are like this! The American Jews are like this! Now, the Jewish immigrants in China are also like this! That is why the Japanese army has to designate a restricted area [concentration camp] for the Jews. . . . The future settlement of the Jews in Shanghai must be dealt with urgently![7]

Thus, not only was the anti-Jewish policy in Germany justified by the "evils" of the "Jews," but Japan's decision to follow that country's example was praised as a wise step forward.

Although it is quite obvious that Japan attempted to project its sense of insecurity in occupied China onto the "Jews" by constantly repeating the theme of "Jewish imperialism," this certainly did not save it from becoming the main target of a growing nationalist movement in China. In fact, the majority of Chinese at that time had never even heard the name "Jews" and had no idea who they were. For most people in China the most immediate enemy was Japan. The so-called Jewish imperialists did not mean much to the bulk of the Chinese population. It is perhaps also important to point out that before 1949, apart from a small number of intellectuals, nationalists and communists, hardly any Chinese were familiar with the term "imperialist." The term which it might be considered comparable to is *guizi,* which literally means "devil" or "devils." However, while *guizi* has been used to refer to Japanese, Americans, British and many others, it has never been used to refer to Jews. In reality, together with millions of Shanghainese, both Chinese and foreign, the Shanghai Jewish refugees suffered as the victims of the Sino-Japanese War. After the War, many of them migrated to Palestine and North America. A few of them remained until the 1950s, when the Chinese communist government became intensely hostile toward foreigners in China.

At this point, it is important to note that, for the majority of local Chinese, both the Sephardic and the Ashkenazi Jewish communities, also later the Jewish refugees, were simply seen as sections of the foreign population in China. The construction of images of the "Jews" in China was limited to the educated sectors of the reading public. For them, images of the "Jews" had very little to do with the Jewish population in China.

THE EMERGENCE AND CONSTRUCTION OF THE IMAGE OF THE "JEWS" AT THE TURN OF THE CENTURY

For the modernizing elites, or reformers, in China at the turn of the century the "Jews" were an integral part of the new racial taxonomies they invented in order to represent the world as a collection of unequally endowed biological groups.[8] Described as a "historical race," the "Jews" stood in symbolic contradistinction to the historical "yellow race," as the reformers now referred to the Chinese. As early as 1903, Jiang Guanyun, one of the earliest modernizing journalists, had already established the "Jewish race" as a "historical Caucasian race" which had descended from the Semites. The physical appearance of the "Jewish race" (as well as other Semitic "races") was imagined by Jiang to be characterized by an oval face, big eyes, thin lips and convex nose. In the following years, similar descriptions prevailed in representations of the "Jew" in China. In 1910, for instance, when Zhang Xiangwen, a historian and geographer, visited the assimilated Kaifeng "Jewish" community, he perpetuated these stereotypes by claiming that some of the "Jewish" descendants had big noses and deep eyes and it was claimed that one could still distinguish them from "genuine" Chinese by their "Caucasian" physical features.[9]

On the one hand, for example, the circumcised penis—one of the most crucial marks of the Western image of the male "Jew"—was hardly mentioned by Chinese intellectuals, while on the other hand, the eagle-nose became the quintessential symbol of the "money-loving Jew." Blood, hair, color, shape of face or nose and other phenotypical features were perceived by these intellectuals to indicate the racial distinctiveness of the "Chinese" from the "non-Chinese."

Though these representations of the "Jewish" race in China were actively constructed by Chinese intellectuals themselves, the language of anti-Semitism was appropriated from Western sources to reconfigure and legitimize indigenous racial discourse. The Christian missionaries, in fact, first introduced the image of the "Jew" as the "seed" of Abraham. According to many of their writings in Chinese—especially those of the Protestants since the middle of the nineteenth century—people of the "Jewish race," although dispersed all over the world, were still bound together by a particular set of physical features.[10]

From the middle of the nineteenth century onward, travel to the West also provided opportunities for Chinese intellectuals to encounter and appropriate the arguments of anti-Semitic discourse. However, in contrast to the attitudes of anti-Semites in Europe, Chinese intellectuals' envy of Jews was often mixed with curiosity and interest. Why should the Jewish, not the Chinese, be the dominant culture of the world? Why should Judaism, not Confucianism, have been widely accepted as the guiding moral principle of human society? Why should a "Jew," not a "Chinese," be the richest man? While questions like these were asked, many modernizing elites also attempted to prove that Chinese culture was still superior to the "Jewish" one. By translating the German Assyriologist Friedrich Delitzsch's anti-Semitic work *Babel oder Bible?* into Chinese, Jiang Guangyun was able to demonstrate that the Mosaic law was not the oldest law code in the world and that the Hebrew culture was not the superior one in the world.[11] Furthermore, Jiang remarked that the moral code of Confucius preceded Mosaic law. On the other hand, Wang Tao (1828–97), an outstanding cultural intermediary who stood between tradition and modernity, found it most thrilling that an Eastern culture—the Jewish culture or Judaism—should survive within Western culture. He used it as an example to prove to the conservatives that they need not fear Western culture, because the Judaism which had survived and had an important role to play in the West had not managed very well at all in China. The assimilation of the Jewish community in China was for him powerful proof that Chinese culture was far superior to Jewish culture; therefore, it was still superior to Western culture. Thus, according to Wang Tao, opening the door to the West would not destroy the superior Chinese culture.[12]

THE "JEWS" AND MONEY

In order to construct the "Jews" as a "race" with biologically specific features, Jiang Guanyun even traced the Western anti-Semitic image of the "Jew" as financier back to its Semitic ancestry.[13] However, representations of the "Jew" as a financier were not always perceived to be entirely negative. Xue Fucheng (1838–94), a famous diplomat who regarded the development of commercial industry to be essential for China, saw rich "Jewish" financiers as a good illustration for his theory:

> England is one of the richest countries in the world, but the richest people in London are the Jews. Even the royal family in England could not compete with the Jews. . . . Nowadays, no country dares to compete with the wealthy Jews; every country which wants to take loans of millions of pounds has to discuss it with the Jews, otherwise, it cannot be done. The Jews have eventually be-

> come the patrons for many nations' loans. No matter whether it is peace or war, prosperity or poverty, on this earth there is nothing, including all the secrets of governments, the Jews do not know. The Jews also have shares in every big bank in the world. Although one regards the English as good at commerce, they themselves admit that they cannot compete with the Jews. Thus, the Jews are truly the most powerful people in the world.[14]

In other words, if China were as rich as the "Jews," then China would be the most powerful nation in the world. Although China did not become rich, as Xue had wished, Chinese merchants overseas sometimes did. Ironically, early this century in Southeast Asia, the Chinese were sometimes disparaged as the "Jews of the Orient."[15]

The translation of Charles Lamb's *Tales of Shakespeare* in 1904 was used to further consolidate the image of the "Jew" as a money-grabber. Shylock, the money-lender, soon became a household caricature of the "Jew" among the reading public in China. Furthermore, a number of historians even identified some commercial groups who had been engaged in money lending in the past in the western regions of China as Jews.[16]

THE "JEWS" IN THE "RACIAL" STRUGGLE

The dichotomy of Europeans into Aryan and Semitic "races" inspired some Chinese abroad to manipulate the "Jews" as a useful weapon in their "racial war" against the "white race." When Hong Jun, Xue Fucheng's contemporary and also a diplomat to Europe, was insulted by "white" people of a Western church, he fought back by claiming that Jesus was a Jew with black hair and eyes like himself, therefore the "whites" had no right to insult an Asian fellow-man of Jesus.[17] Dan Shili, one of the earliest Chinese female intellectuals who went to Europe, in her travel diary of 1910 passionately compared the anguish of the "Jews" under the rule of the "whites" with their freedom under the rule of the "yellows" in Kaifeng. The division between "Aryan" and "Semitic" races was thus projected onto a more fundamental opposition between the "white" and "yellow" races. Dan even warned the Chinese that if they did not learn from the lesson of the "Jewish race" they would not be able to win against the "whites."[18]

THE "JEWS" AS "NEW PEOPLE"

The myth of "Jewish" power in the West was of great attraction for Liang Qichao, one of the first reformers in the 1890s to propose a racialized world view. During his tour of the New World, he pondered over the survival of the Chinese people. He saw the "Jews" as an anti-image of the backwardness of the "Chinese" and found them to be a perfect example for his call for a "new people," or a collective nationalistic spirit, which he believed to be essential to the progress and social well-being of China:

> Jews are the most powerful and influential group among the immigrants in America. I heard that four tenths of the American banks are Jewish, and more than half the bankers in America are Jewish. . . . Jews completely control the local government of New York. No other group in the city can compete with the power of the Jews. The situation is very similar in other big cities. . . . The reason that Jews can be so powerful is because they are very united. In this respect, no other races can compare with them. . . . And amongst all the famous people of the world as reported by New York's *Monthly Journal,* there were forty-eight Jews. . . . Alas! For thousands of years, Jews have been stateless. But they survived as a race in the world with an enormous power, and they have also kept their own racial identity. In comparison, many other ancient people such as Babylonians, Philistines, Greeks and Romans did not survive.[19]

Therefore, according to Liang, if the "Chinese" race was going to survive, the "Chinese" must learn from the "Jews," or even better, become like the "Jews" and control the world economy and global politics. Hence, the future of China was projected onto the myth of "Jewish" power.

THE "STATELESS JEW"

With the rise of nationalism in China in the early twentieth century, some of China's revolutionary thinkers represented the "stateless Jew" as the imaginary prospect awaiting China. Articles on the pogroms in Russian began to appear in Chinese newspapers and journals after the Russo-Japanese War extended to the northeast of China in 1903. The Jewish problem, which was once completely unknown and uninteresting, now became of great relevance to the Chinese nationalists. The lamentation of the "stateless Jew" became a warning to the Chinese. The "Jewish race" was portrayed as an "ugly race because they do not have a country."[20] They were thought to have deserved their inhuman treatment. While stirring up the fear of becoming like the "stateless Jew," many of them reasoned: "We are not like the Jews!" According to them, the superior Chinese still had a country of their own. The argument went even further, with a very strong anti-Jewish tone: the Jews deserved the awful situation they were in because they had no nationalistic spirit nor any collective responsibility. The "Jews" were portrayed as victims of materialism and individualism. According to them, it was their love for money and personal happiness which finally drove the Jews into this terrible state. Schiff's huge loan to the Japanese in 1904 was seen by some Chinese as a bribe the "Jews" used to save themselves from the yoke of the Russians. The author of an article entitled "The stateless Jews" thus commented in a negative statement: "Stateless, though [they] have money, money cannot save them [the Jews]."[21] His solution for the Chinese was to avoid emulating the "Jews": not to love money more than one's country, otherwise the Chinese would end up stateless like them.

These nationalists further proclaimed that "if [one] cannot protect one's country, then one cannot preserve one's race."[22] Thus, the "Jews" were categorized as an "inferior race."[23] In order to avoid being like the "Jews" and to preserve the "Chinese race," China had to promote nationalism first.

THE "JEW" AS A "NATION"

With the fall of the Qing dynasty and the establishment of the Republic of China in 1911, racial nationalism was further promoted by Sun Yatsen. Nationalism, in the eyes of Sun and his followers, was the sole generator of the rise and fall of any "race." Zionism was now perceived as the nationalistic movement of the Jewish people, and it was thought that the nationalistic spirit of Zionism held the "Jewish race" together. While the so-called Jewish nationalistic spirit became an inspiration for these Chinese nationalists,[24] the image of the "ugly" and "stateless Jews" shifted to that of the "wonderful and historical nation."[25] And in the same way in which they portrayed the so-called Han Chinese as a pure biological entity, Sun and many of his contemporaries perceived the Jewish nation/race as a homogenous racial group characterized by common blood, language and culture. Since the "Jews" were perceived as a nation, with a common ancestry and territory, Palestine was accepted by many Chinese nationalists as "the national home of the Jewish people."

THE "JEWS" AS IMPERIALISTS

Together with nationalism, the newly founded Republic of China also provided the ground for an increasingly growing anti-imperialism. The "Jews" were sometimes portrayed as "imperialists." As in Europe, Chinese nationalists needed a scapegoat. Many of the articles on "Jewish imperialism" were drawn from Japanese or Western sources. They followed the age-old anti-

Semitic pattern by listing Jewish dominance in the world of finance, politics and the media, or they conflated Freemasonry with Zionism, the Jewish plot to control the whole world. The "Jews" were often portrayed as the epitome of imperialism and the driving force of evil in the capitalist world. In one article entitled "The Jewish Empire," the author declared that "If one does not know the truth about the Jews [Jewish imperialism], how could one say that he understands the truth about the West [Western imperialism]?"[26]

By the end of the 1920s, the anti-imperialism campaign was further intensified by Nationalist party members such as Dai Jitao. Dai was then the policy advisor for Chiang Kaishek and the nationalist government. He strongly believed that the main task of the Nationalist party should be to interpret and enforce in China Sun Yatsen's "Three Principles of the People."[27] This meant securing China's international equality and national liberty, in order to fight against "imperialism." As a result, Dai and his followers found the ideologies of French nationalists, such as Edouard Drumont and Charles Maurras, which had very strong anti-Semitic overtones, appealing and interesting. Zionism, which was portrayed by Drumont, Maurras and their supporters as a destructive danger to France, thus became almost comparable to the foreign danger—"imperialism"—which was feared and fought against by these Chinese nationalists. It is perhaps worth noting that not only Zionism, but also fascism, in its early years, was often conflated or equated with "imperialism" by these people. As with their misconceptions about Zionism, they never really understood fascism. In fact, an article entitled "Jews and Jewish Ideology"—translated from a work by one of Maurras's supporters—appeared in 1929 side by side with another article which discussed the rise of fascism in Europe.[28]

THE "JEWS" AS A SUPERIOR RACE

As mentioned earlier, having already classified the "Jewish" race as a branch of the "white" race, some Chinese intellectuals therefore also regarded it as a biologically "superior" race, alongside the "yellow" race, in contrast with the inferior "red," "black" and "brown" races.[29] The image of the "Jews" as a "wonderful and historical nation" was further defined as a "superior race," and it was claimed that such superiority was manifested in their intellectual ability. Hu Shi, a celebrated scholar and philosopher of modern China, stereotyped the "Jews" as an "intellectual race" with impressive academic ability and adventurous spirit.[30] The need to create such a representation was obviously rooted in the anxiety over the backwardness of China and the belief, shared by many Chinese intellectuals of the New Cultural Movement, that the intellectual class was the only hope for the reconstruction of their chaotic country. The New Cultural Movement first emerged in 1915 as a result of the demand for a new urban culture by the increasingly growing urban population in China.

According to You Xiong, one of the leading intellectuals of the New Cultural Movement, the reason the "Jews" were able to control world politics, world finance and the world in general was that "the 'Jewish race' has intellectual gifts of quick understanding, rational thinking, good judgement, good organization and fast action," and that they produced more superior lawyers, philosophers, thinkers, politicians, doctors, scientists, musicians and even chess players than any other race in the world.[31] Hence, in the same way that Liang Qichao had used the "Jews" as an example in his call for a "new people," intellectuals such as Yu Songhua also found in the "Jews" a model for the restoration of the "Chinese race": "From antiquity to modern time, the Jewish race has produced many of the world's first class geniuses. But in China, although a few [famous people] in history have attracted the admiration of the world, in modern times, no matter whether it is in academics, in politics or in commerce, China has not produced any talent able to compete in the world. How shameful we are when compared with the Jewish people and how disgraceful we are to our ancestors."[32] The present backwardness of the "Chinese" race, or more correctly, the anxiety within these intellectuals themselves, was explained as the result of a lack of talent in China. This did not, however, indicate that the "Chinese" race was less superior than the "Jewish" race, since China had also produced world-class geniuses in the past. Furthermore, Qian Zhixiu was able to prove that although the "Jewish" race and the "Chinese" race had very different characteristics, the latter shared all the advantages of the former, including intellectual ability. In conclusion, Qian proclaimed: "The Chinese will be the Jews [world power] of the future" and "China is the giant yet to be awakened."[33]

THE "JEWS" AS A PRODUCT OF RACIAL DISCRIMINATION

It would be an oversimplification to presume that all intellectuals in modern China articulated racial discourse in the same way. While the notion of "one homogenous race" prevailed among many Chinese intellectuals with regard to the "Jews," a few divergent voices, such as He Ziheng and Wu Qinyou challenged such a view. In his article entitled "The So-called Jewish People," He Ziheng used scientific methods to undermine the idea of the "Jewish race."[34] By using various statistics, He showed that a large percentage of Jews in different countries did not have the so-called Semitic nose, shape of head, deep dark eyes or black hair, and "no one can tell a Jew from an American or a European unless the Jews write the word 'Jew' on their forehead." He also dismissed the idea that all Jews shared "common blood," pointing out instead that intermarriage between Jews and other "races" was commonly practiced throughout history. He concluded that the "Jews" were not a race but merely a product and victim of racial discrimination.[35]

But for many left-wing intellectuals of the 1930s, the representation of the "Jews" as an oppressed people had a much more profound and symbolic implication in their own struggle against the immediate enemy—the Japanese "imperialists"—and their own imagined enemy—the "white" imperialists of the West. As Wu Qinyou put it: "The significance of the Jewish people is not in whether they can be seen as a race or not, but in their common goal to unite together with all the oppressed people and to liberate the human race."[36] The old dichotomy between the "white" and "yellow" race was reconstructed by merging the social notion of "class" with the biological myth of "race." As the problem of "race" was reconfigured into a question of "class," the symbolic role of the "Jew" was remodeled: "The tears, blood and death of the Jewish people have awakened the oppressed Chinese."[37] The oppressed "Jews" had become the comrades of the oppressed "Chinese" in their struggle against all oppressors.

THE OLD MYTH AND NEW PHENOMENA, 1949–95

With the official banishment of racial discourse by the Communist government after 1949, the myth of the "Jew" seemed no longer to be current in communist China. The notion of "race," however, did not disappear completely. Mao Zedong, for instance, defined "nation" as a distinct racial and cultural group. In the same way, Israel was perceived in China as the "Jewish nation state": the old "Jewish" race with its *new* country and *new* language. Like the left-wing intellectuals of the 1930s and 1940s, Mao also conflated the notions of "class" and "race" into a vision of the struggle of the "colored people" against "white imperialism." China's political role in Afro-Asian solidarity since the 1960s meant that the Jews in Israel, as the enemy of the oppressed Palestinians, could no longer be defined as the oppressed people; instead, they had become "the poisoned knife which the American imperialists pushed into the heart of Palestine."[38]

After the death of Mao and the collapse of the Cultural Revolution at the end of the 1970s, the "class" hatred between the "Jewish" race in Israel and the "Chinese" people came to a close. However, the myth of the "Jew" in China did not stop there. On the contrary, interest in the present state of

Israel and the "Jew" has reached unprecedented levels since the 1980s. Professor Pan Guang, the director of the Centre of Israel and Judaic studies in Shanghai, comments that "China's Jewish-Israel studies have reached a new and exciting stage."[39] The old myth of the "Jew" continues to distort the perceptions of many people in China. With the appearance of a new market economy, particularly in cities such as Shanghai, the symbolic link between the "Jew" and money has again emerged. While Shanghai eagerly opened its arms to welcome "Jewish" investments from all over the world, Kaifeng, the city which once had a small Jewish presence, also declared itself to be a "Jewish economic zone" in order to attract "Jewish" money.[40]

China's recent interest in Jewish issues is not exclusively economic. In recent years, especially in the post-Tiananmen era, interest in Jewish studies as shown by some intellectuals, such as Zhang Sui, is a response to efforts to reconfigure indigenous identities of race and nation. As Zhang Sui puts it: "In order to have a real deep understanding of the vitality of Chinese culture, one must first study the interesting anthropological fact that the Hebrew race, well known for its immutability, was assimilated by the Han race and became Chinese-Jewish descendants after entering China."[41] The superiority of the Han race and Chinese culture, it is claimed, seems to be manifested by the assimilation of the "Jewish" race. Such dubious studies are also encouraged in order to cover up the discrimination against so-called minority groups. Thus, the assimilation of the "Jewish" community in China is portrayed by scholars like Wu Zelin, a respected anthropologist, as a demonstration of "the traditional magnanimity and the tolerant spirit of the Chinese race, not only toward the Jewish people, but also toward all other races. Therefore, she [the Chinese race] can always live in harmony with all other races." (It is interesting to observe that, in his youth, Wu himself described the "Jews" as "laughable, despicable, pitiable, admirable, enviable, and hateful.")[42] More recently, the so-called Jewish descendants in Kaifeng have been given a monthly allowance from Beijing and have been freed from China's birth control policy. In other words, an entirely new category of the "Jews" is about to be constructed in China.

The death of Deng, as well as the handing-over of Hong Kong, in 1997 brings China the opportunity of further changes. Great speculation from both inside and outside is currently haunting the country. However, no matter what the change/s may be, the myth of the "Jews" will carry on in China as it has in the West, as well as in other Eastern countries. Such myths are an intrinsic part of the politics of identity in which one group's power, privilege and status is based on the exclusion of other groups. Although the images and representations of the "Jews" might transmute from negative to positive, from "inferior" to "superior," from "ahistorical" to "historical," from "stateless" to "nationalistic," from "rich" to "smart," or to "eternal" in the course of history, the "Jews" as the "other," or as the mirror to the construction/reconstruction of the "self" will always remain. This "other" may be anybody, from the "Jew," the "black," to the "homosexual," but the attempt to draw racially defined boundaries between people has been and still is an important part of many contemporary cultures and societies.

Notes

This chapter is largely based on a doctoral dissertation written under the supervision of Timothy H. Barrett of the School of Oriental and African Studies, University of London. I would like to express my gratitude for his constant support over the years. I also wish to thank Frank Dikötter, of the same institution, for his enormous contribution to both the dissertation and the present chapter. Then, there is J. G. Feinberg of the United Medical and Dental Schools of Guy's and St. Thomas's, University of London, who read and commented on the first draft, particularly on English language usage.

1. Frank Dikötter, *The Discourse of Race in Modern China* (London: Hurst and Co., 1992), 4. For more discussion on the use of the word *Youtai,* see Zhou Xun, *A History of Chinese Perceptions of the "Jews" and Judaism* (Surrey: Curzon Press, forthcoming), chap. 2.

2. Matteo Ricci, *Opere storiche del P. Matteo Ricci S.I.,* ed. Pietro Tacchi-Venturi S.I., 2 vols. (Macerata, 1911–13), 2:290–93.

3. Jerome Ch'en, *China and the West: Society and Culture, 1815–1937* (London: Hutchinson, 1979), 213. See also Zhang Zhongli, *Shaxujituan zhai jiu-Zhongguo* (The Sassoon Corporation in China before 1949) (Beijing: Renminchubanshe, 1985).

4. Xu Zhucheng, *Hatong waizhuan* (Unauthorized biography of Hardoon) (Hong Kong: Wuxinji Chubanshe, 1982); Li Chandao, *Damoxianjia Hatong* (Hardoon, the adventurer) (Beijing: Qunzhongchubanshe, 1979). For more discussion see Chiara Betta, "Silas A. Hardoon, 1851–1931: Case of Cross-Cultural Adaptation amongst Sephardic Jews in Shanghai" (Ph.D. diss., University of London, 1997), chap. 7.

5. David Goodman and Masanori Miyazawa, *Jews in the Japanese Mind: The History and Uses of a Cultural Stereotype* (New York: Free Press, 1995).

6. Tang Liangli, "Shanghai de Youtai diguozhuyi" (Jewish imperialism in Shanghai), *Nanjing minguo ribao* (Nanjing Republican Daily), Feb. 25, 1943.

7. "'Wuguo zhi min' de lianpu" (The mask of the "stateless people"), *Shanghai guomin xinwen* (Shanghai people's news), Mar. 25, 1943.

8. Much of the following material has also been used in Zhou Xun, "*Youtai:* The Myth of the 'Jews' in Modern China," in *The Construction of Racial Identities in China and Japan,* ed. Frank Dikötter (London: Hurst and Co., 1997), 102–45.

9. Zhang Xiangwen, "Daliang fangbeiji" (A report on the visit to the stone tablets

in Kaifeng), in *Nanyuan conggao* (Contemporary Chinese Historical Documents Series, no. 30), vol. 1 (Shanghai: Wenhai Press, n.d.), 282.

10. For a detailed discussion see the chapter on Protestant expansion in China in Zhou Xun, *History of Chinese Perceptions.*

11. Jian Guanyun, "Shijie zuigu zhi fadian" (The oldest law code of the world), *Xinmin congbao* 34 (1903): 31–34; see also vol. 33 of *Xinmin congbao.*

12. Wang Tao, *Taoyuan chitu* (Essays of Wang Tao), n.p., n.d., 86. For further discussion, see the first chapter of Zhou Xun, *History of Chinese Perceptions.*

13. Jiang Guanyun, "Zhongguo renzhong kao" (Inquiries into the Chinese race), *Xinmin conbao* 40–41 (1903–4): 4–5.

14. Xue Fucheng, *Chushi Ying Fa Yi Bi siguo riji* (Diaries of England, France, Italy, and Belgium) (Hunan: Yuelu Shushe, 1985), 793.

15. Wachirawut (1910–25) is the son of Chulalongkorn of Siam. See Wachirawut, *The Jews of the Orient* (Siam, 1914), which is an anti-Chinese pamphlet. Cf. Benedict Anderson, *Imagined Communities,* rev. ed. (London: Verso, 1992), 100–101.

16. Zhang Xingliang, "Gudai Zhongguo yu Youtai zhi jiaotong" (Communications between China and Jews in antiquity), in *Zhongxi jiaotong shiliao huibian* (A collection of documents concerning communications between China and the West), 4 vols. (Beijing: Furen University, 1930), 4:4–20. See also Hong Jun, *Yuanshi yiwen zhengbu* (Supplement to the translation of the history of the Yuan dynasty) (1897; Shanghai: Shangwu yinshuguan, 1937), 2:454–55; Tao Xisheng, "Yuandai xiyu ji Youtairen de gaolidai yu toukou shoushuo" (The high-interest money lending and the poll tax of the west regions of China in the Yuan dynasty and of the Jews), *Shihuo* 1.7 (1935): 54–55.

17. Hong Jun, *Yuanshi yiwen zhengbu,* 455.

18. Dan Shili, *Guiqianji* (Travel diary of Europe) (Changsha: Hunan Renmin Chubanshe, 1981), 196–211.

19. Liang Qichao, "Xindalu youji" (Travel diary of America), *Xinmin congbao* (special supplement) sec. 12 (1903): 49–52.

20. "Eguo luesha Youtairen" (Slaughtering of the Jews in Russia), *Youxue yibian* 9 (1903): 93.

21. "Youtai yimin" (The stateless Jews), *Dongfang zazhi* 4 (1904): 10.

22. Ibid.

23. "Lun nuli" (On slaves), *Guomin riribao huibian* 4 (1904): 18; "Eren luesha Youtairen" (The slaughtering of the Jews by the Russians), *Jiangsu* 4 (1903): 133.

24. Yin Qing, "Minzu jingsheng" (National spirit), *Dongfang zazhi* 16.12 (1919): 11. See also Sun Yatsen, *Sanmin zhuyi* (Three people's principles) (Shanghai: Shangwu Shudian, 1927).

25. See Sun Yatsen's letter to N. E. B. Ezra in 1920, Archives of the Hebrew University, Jerusalem.

26. Qian Liu, trans., "Youtairen zhi diguo" (The Jewish empire), *Dongfang zazhi* 8.9 (1911): 17–19.

27. See Dai Jitao, *Guomin geming yu zhongguo Guomindang* (The national revolution and the Nationalist party of China) (Shanghai: Dai Jitao's Office, 1925).

28. Zhuochao, trans. "Youtairen yu Youtai zhuyi" (The Jews and Jewish ideology), *Xin shengming* 2.9 (1929). The original article was written in French by R. Lambelin, the author of *Le Règne d'Israel chez les Anglo-Saxons* and the translator of *The Protocols*

of the Elders of Zion. Also in the same issue is Xiong Kangshen, "Faxishidang de ducai zhengzh" (The totalitarian politics of fascists). *Xin Shengming* was one of the nationalist periodicals whose main purpose was to discuss and promote Sun Yatsen's "Principles."

29. For further readings, see Dikötter, *Discourse of Race,* chaps. 3–4.

30. Hu Shi, *Hu Shi koushu zizhuan* (An oral autobiography of Hu Shi), ed. Tang Degang (Beijing: Wenhua Press, 1989), 33.

31. You Xiong, "Youtai minzu zhi xianzhuang jiqi qianli" (The present situation of the Jewish race and its potential), *Dongfang zazhi* 18.12 (1921): 23.

32. Yu Songhua, "Youtairen yu Youtai fuxing yundong" (Jewish people and the Jewish renaissance movement), *Dongfang zazhi* 24.17 (1927): 27.

33. Qian Zhixiu, "Youtairen yu Zhongguoren" (The Jews and the Chinese), *Dongfang zazhi* 8.12 (1912): 40–46.

34. He Zhiheng, "Shijieshang you chuncui de minzu ma?" (Is there any pure race in the world?), *Xueshu jie* 1–2 (1943): 12–16.

35. Ibid., 16.

36. Wu Qinyou, "Youtai minzu wenti" (Problems regarding the Jewish race), *Xin Zhonghua zazhi* 4.4 (1936): 7.

37. Li Zheng, "Guanyu pai-You" (Regarding anti-Semitism), *Yibao zhoukan,* Dec. 7, 1938, 235.

38. "Mao Zedong sixiang shi Baleshitan renmin de zhinan" (Mao's ideology is the compass for the Palestinians), *Renmin ribao,* May 16, 1967, 5.

39. Pan Guang, "The Development of Jewish and Israel Studies in China," Occasional Papers of the Harry S. Truman Research Institute for the Advancement of Peace, No. 2 (Jerusalem: Hebrew University, 1992), 3.

40. Li Li, "The Jewish Economic Zone in Kaifeng," *Xianggang lianhebao,* Jan. 9, 1995.

41. Zhang Sui, *Youtaijiao yu Zhongguo Kaifeng Youtairen* (Judaism and the Chinese Jews of Kaifeng) (Shanghai: Sanlian Shudian, 1990), 1.

42. Wu Zelin, "Preface," in Pan Guangdan's *Zhongguo jinle Youtairen de ruogan lishi wenti* (The Jews in China: A historical survey) (Beijing: Beijing Daxue Chubanshe, 1983), 11.

10 The Enemy Within: Some South African Jewish Writers

MARCIA LEVESON

Of course, the Jew is rather ugly: Not uglier than the Southern European, but uglier, without question, than the typical Briton.
—Sarah Gertrude Millin, 1933

I saw that she was very ugly. Ugly with the blunt ugliness of a toad. . . . She had the short stunted heavy bones of generations of oppression in the Ghettos of Europe; breasts, stomach, hips crowded sadly, no height, wide strong shoulders and a round back.
—Nadine Gordimer, "The Defeated" (1953)

Muizenberg . . . was a horrible place, crowded with vulgar, loud, ugly people whose grammar was worse than her Aunt Lydia's. They came down every year from their tasteless houses in Johannesburg, fat women with red lips, moustaches and diamonds, and fat men with wet lips and flashy cars who stood about in indecent bathing-trunks talking at the tops of their voices about money and business. . . . They spread their gorged flesh everywhere. . . . Gross, gregarious, philistine Jews!
—Jillian Becker, *The Keep* (1967)

"Ugly," "vulgar," "gross." These expressions of anti-Semitic disgust, of physical recoil from Jews, were not written by Gentile anti-Semites but by South African Jewish authors. Why, one may ask, in a century which has witnessed the Holocaust, in a country which has experienced ongoing Jew-hatred both overt and covert, do these authors seem to be assuming self-imposed roles of the traditional anti-Semite? Why are these "enemies" to be found among the Jews?

This phenomenon may be studied within both global and particular parameters. As Sander Gilman has pointed out, "the overarching model for Jewish history has been that of the center or core and the periphery."[1] Thus the precarious situation of the Jew, perpetually "at the periphery" in Western society, requires consideration. But Gilman suggests that the notion of "periphery" has in more recent times become transvaluated. And, indeed, it is clear that the condition of colonialism involves yet another variation of the notion of center and periphery. The peculiar location of South African Jews, as immigrants in a colonial dispensation, not merely a symbolic but an actual frontier and therefore *doubly* at the periphery of society, may give rise to specific tensions. Some of these tensions are expressed within the framework of literature.

HISTORICAL BACKGROUND

Some professing Jews arrived with the British settlers at the beginning of the nineteenth century. In an attempt to penetrate the center of society, they set about integrating themselves into the English-speaking community. This group was expanded by other Jewish immigrants from Germany or from Germany via England. It is notable that during the nineteenth century in Germany there was an unprecedented degree of Jewish assimilation or conversion. Many of the immigrant Jews were therefore highly acculturated. Thus, from early times assimilation has been a feature of Jewish participation in Cape society. The Jewish community, proportionately small and slowly growing, which continued to shed large numbers through conversion and intermarriage, was comfortable and well tolerated. Several Jews were engaged in public affairs and became prominent citizens. By the time of the granting of Responsible Government to the Cape Colony in 1872, Jews were regarded by the broader society not so much as a specific outgroup on the periphery but rather as a subgroup of the dominant white caste.

The heavy immigrations of Jews from Eastern Europe between 1880 and into the 1920s radically altered the demographic picture and gave rise among the white population to a very different and far more hostile perception. These Eastern European immigrants were often poverty-stricken and struggled to survive in the new country. Those longer-settled Jews, who had earnestly sought to throw off the trappings of marginalization, were embarrassed by the interlopers, who had all the markers of Otherness. They feared that the newcomers would undermine their precarious social position and draw attention to their own Jewishness, propelling them once again to a social position on the periphery.

The general white community was not inclined to ignore the inferior categorization the Eastern European Jews had brought with them from Europe. The influx of poverty-stricken Jews was seen by the Gentile community not only as an unfavorable social occurrence but also, and more significantly, as an expansion of the powerful and threatening black outgroup.

"BLACK JEWS"

In South Africa, at the beginning of the twentieth century, whites often categorized Jews with blacks. Both perceptually and in terms of legislation, Jews were classified with the indentured Chinese and Indian laborers who had been imported into the country at the same time as the arrival of the Jewish immigrants, as well as with the indigenous "kafirs."

In newspaper articles Jews were branded as "unsuitable immigrants, the equivalent of Chinamen and Coolies."[2] "Clean and respectable people would like to see [them] fenced in like the Chinese ought to be, in a location."[3] On the Rand, most Eastern European immigrants settled in the slums of Ferreirasdorp. Many were awarded concessions to trade on the mines among the black workers, or to set up eating houses—*kaffireatas*. Joseph Sherman has shown how the racially prejudiced white society viewed those who provided services to blacks with contempt as "white kaffirs,"[4] and by all accounts, the *kaffireatas* were places of degradation and despair.[5] Those Jews who were involved in illegal liquor dealing among blacks[6] were lambasted as "the most blackguardly race of men in existence." It was said that "[they] . . . have not the slightest sense of decency or modesty in them, and a more depraved race never existed."[7]

In Cape Town many Jews settled in District Six, among the colored population. A contemporary newspaper report sneered: "Cape Town at the present time is full of those Polish Jew hawkers who live in a dirtier style than kafirs. . . . Respectable Europeans should order these people from their doors. . . . Let these people do manual work."[8]

Sander Gilman reminds us that "it is the function of language and/or discourse [to act] as a marker of Jewish identity [*sic*]."[9] In 1902 the Immigration Restriction Bill was passed which excluded anyone who could not sign his or her name in European characters. Ostensibly aimed at controlling the influx of Indians and Chinese, it again drew attention to the Otherness, indeed the blackness, of Jews, and posed a direct threat to Jewish immigration. Only in 1906, under pressure from the Cape Jewish Board of Deputies, was Yiddish accepted for the purposes of the act as a European language, but throughout the twentieth century in the perception of Gentiles, and more insidiously the Jews themselves, it remained a negative label of Jewish Otherness.

The tacit connection of Jews with blacks as racial Others is recorded in colonial fiction of the Cape, particularly that of the diamond rush of the last quarter of the nineteenth century. Abdul JanMahomed has highlighted as a characteristic of the colonial text a "manichean opposition between self and Other."[10] The most common model portrays an opposition between white colonizers and the physically threatening Other, the colonized black. Diamond field fiction, however, sometimes replaced the figure of the black Other with a Jewish Other, reflecting not a physical but an economic opposition, since the Jew is almost invariably linked with criminal activities, usually IDB (illicit diamond buying).

In fact, the substitution of Jew for black as representative of the Other has earlier precedents. Sander Gilman agrees that the concept of color is not intrinsic but is merely a function of Otherness. He argues that the association of Jews with blackness is well established in Christian tradition, where medieval iconography frequently juxtaposed the black image of the synagogue with the white image of the Church.[11]

Gilman has also suggested that during the nineteenth century the categories of "black" and "Jew" again became interchangeable. The colonized black embodied colonial anxieties but he was distant and therefore ignorable, while the Jew, increasingly demanding access to society, whether that be metropolitan or colonial society, was a more immediate threat.[12]

With Jewish immigration into colonial society a further variation of these models is reflected in the early acceptance by white colonists at the Cape and in Australia of "English" Jews. Here the difference lies in the fact of those Jews' prior acceptance into *British* society, where they brought with them cultural givens which at first resisted appropriation by the category of "the Other."

In *IDB; or, The Adventures of Solomon Davis,* a novel published in 1887 by an Englishman, W. T. Eady, there is scathing reference to the Jews' continued drive toward assimilation—toward a shedding of vestiges of the category of Other—signalled if no other way than by the label of the Jewish name. The central character, a Jew from Whitechapel, makes his fortune at the diggings, and takes the unlikely Gentile name of "Montague Vaughan." The novel suggests that through dishonesty and cunning, the Jew and his wife, inveterate social climbers, have clawed out a spurious social niche for themselves: "They are aspiring to further promotion; and the lady talks to her confidential friends of the possibility of her being presented at an early Drawing-room; while the husband, over his prime Cubans and midnight hock-and-seltzer, occasionally lets fall a whisper as to his being elected at one of the leading West End Clubs" (344). At this time a bill introduced to the Cape parliament contained a clause which regulated the right to assume a new surname or alter an existing one. Although the bill was not passed this represents an attempt at ensuring that the Jewish name as label of outsiderhood would remain indelible.[13]

Once again, during the 1930s and 1940s, with the growth of the "Shirt Organizations," Jewish immigration was seriously threatened. Gideon Shimoni has noted that: "The core of Greyshirt ideology was . . . racist anti-Semitism. Greyshirt theory held that the Jews were not a European but an Asiatic race." [14] The Aliens Act passed by Parliament in 1937 not only effectively ended Jewish immigration but seemed also to legislate Jews as "Asiatics" and to imply their racial impurity. This would be particularly threatening in the light of the terrifying developments taking place in Nazi Germany.

In opposition, the National party had been in sympathy with the Greyshirts, and itself harbored numerous Nazi supporters. When it came to power in 1948 and continued to govern seemingly indefinitely, the threat of racial discrimination remained.

During the course of time, the physical threat against Jews outwardly receded. The second and third generation were upwardly mobile, and the white population increasingly closed ranks against people of color, grudgingly accepting all Jews as part of the white "race," and in this way drawing them once again into the center of a racially divided society. Nevertheless, in the Jewish community a subliminal layer of fear remained. As Sander Gilman has pointed out, models of Jewish identity are constructed by a combination of "knowing who you are (identity) and knowing how you came to be who you are (history)."[15] For the South African Jews these categories were threatening. In the construction of their identity, fear of the threat contained in their past and more recent history, as well as consciousness of colonial discrimination, led to a sense of their being particularly vulnerable to losing their fragile purchase on the white hegemony. The specter of racial discrimination against them was to haunt their consciousness and that of their descendants. An attitude at once defensive and defiant might result in an internalization of racial prejudice, leading to a situation which some might regard as the psychopathology known as "Jewish self-hatred."[16]

"JEWISH SELF-HATRED"

The origins of this phenomenon are obviously not specifically South African. The ways in which Jews relate to the majority culture in which they live has always been problematic, but intensified throughout the process of acculturation and assimilation during the period of the Enlightenment. Finding that freedom from the constrictions of the ghetto did not lead automatically to social integration, and that they were never accepted as anything other than a minority group, consigned to an invisible ghetto, some Jews internalized the assumptions and prejudices of the majority culture. Often they became marginal people with a confused sense of identity, believing themselves inferior and stigmatized by their Jewishness. In their attempt to rid themselves of this barrier to the fullest participation at the center of society, many Jews adopted Christianity. Some attempted in various other ways to deny or escape from their Jewishness. Some might turn their aggression inward onto the self—hence the origin of the identity problem known as "Jewish self-hatred."

The early Jewish immigrants at the Cape, with their high incidence of assimilation, were, of course, heirs to this tradition. The Eastern European Jews, on the other hand, were newly arrived from the ghetto. Their descendants, however—the group to which the aforementioned writers belong—might find themselves in the position occupied by the Jews of the Enlightenment, moving away from their parents, distancing themselves from the Jewish label. Throughout the twentieth century the tension between the assimilated and the less-assimilated Jews persevered. In both groups, in different ways, the consciousness of stigma became an internal threat, an "enemy," hampering their aspirations to integrate fully into white South African society with its status and privilege.

THE LITERATURE

Sarah Gertrude Millin (1889–1968), the well-known Jewish author, had an intellectual and emotional grasp of many of these historical and social determinants, and documented them in her writing, both fictional and nonfictional. Born in Lithuania, she was brought as a small child to South Africa. Her parents settled on the Vaal River diamond diggings near Kimberley, in an isolated area where there were few whites. They felt threatened by the surrounding mainly "colored" population.

At the same time, the colored people were scorned, as evidence of miscegenation between the white and black groups. In fact they represented examples of the very loss of caste and privilege that the Jews feared for themselves. Millin grew up among the colored children and observed the way in which the stigma of race operated. She noted the parallel between their exclusion from white society and her own sense, as a Jew, of exclusion from Gentile society.

In 1924 she published a novel, *God's Stepchildren,* which has become notorious as an apparently racist denigration of the colored people.[17] Recently Lavinia Braun has attempted to demonstrate the fallacy of this reading by pointing out that Millin's treatment, far from being condemnatory, is based on a dramatization of both her own and the colored characters' consciousness of stigma.[18]

Further, Braun argues, Millin's unpublished writing proves that, as a Jew, she believed herself to be of the ranks of those "negrophiles" who are "seeking to escape from their ranks of the inequal . . . of the pitiable into the ranks of the pitying, escaping from their own plight as sort of untouchables." Millin had written: "I should imagine the high percentage of Jewish negrophiles of our day has to do with (1) their understanding of racial separateness (2) their desire to escape it themselves."[19]

A few years later, Millin again tackled the subject of minority groups, particularly the Jews, in her 1928 novel *The Coming of the Lord.* "Old Nathan," an elderly Eastern European immigrant, is an outsider in the country community in which he lives. He feels: "I am here popular like the idiot of the village" (4). His son, Saul, has studied overseas and aspires to be part of the Gentile community. His most earnest wish is to escape from "the undesirable society of his fellow-Jews" (99). In being rejected by the Gentiles, he is "filled with resentment that he belonged to a race that so hampered simplicity of progress" (101). For him "progress" means the ability to move into the Gentile world. In vain his father warns him:

> Every anti-Semite has his favourite Jew . . . of whom he says: "This one is different from the rest. I will take him to myself." Sometimes that gives the Jew pleasure. He is happy not to look or seem like his brothers, because it is not what a person can call a fashionable thing to look like a Jew. . . . It is besides, an achievement, a triumph, for a Jew to be accepted as an equal by those who have hitherto despised him, even when, in his secret heart he despises them. . . . Old Nathan . . . found a passage in Esther. "Think not," he read, "that thou shalt escape in the King's house, more than all the other Jews. . . ."
>
> "A Jew stays a Jew, Saul." (97–98)

Escape, as Millin suggests, is an illusion, but is earnestly sought by those Jews who fear being compromised by the stigma of Jewishness.

Although elsewhere in the novel Millin dramatizes the fellow-feeling that grows between Saul and a black man, and shows their parallel sense of outsiderhood, she also depicts Gentile animosity toward Jews, particularly those Jews bent on assimilation. A Gentile regards a successful Jewish attorney as "a small, ugly Jew called Bramson, with thick lips and bandy legs." He muses: "What I always came back to was why a Jew called Abrahamson should take the name of Bramson" (36). The narrator comments: "He meant (though he did not know what he meant) that a Jew should not attempt to take a protective colouring and so lose his natural handicap" (36). This replicates the situation depicted in much diamond-field fiction.

The desire to escape from the restrictions of being Jewish, is seen by Millin to result in social maneuvering. In a speech which she delivered during the First World War, Millin observed: "The Jew is by nature a climber . . . and very often the only way a Jew can mark [h]is ascent—can distinguish himself from the others—is to deny his Judaism. And this, I believe largely accounts for the fact that so many Jews who rise in the world try to cast from them their Jewishness & assimilate. It is simply one way of self-assertion."[20] Echoing the phraseology used during the Gentile outcry against the Jewish "scum" entering the country at the time she was writing, she herself goes on to deprecate the first-generation Eastern European Jewish immigrant to South Africa as "the down-trodden, under-sized, undeveloped fugitive from the ghetto." She seems not to notice, or perhaps she notices only too well, that her own parents could be categorized in this way. She would seem to ally herself with the upwardly mobile second generation who thrive and improve their appearance, become estranged from their "oriental" parents, and may exchange religion for socialism: "They look differently, they speak differently, most of all they think differently. . . . [T]hey are far far more like their gentile neighbours than they are like their own progenitor. . . . The result is, often . . . [an] estrangement not only from family life but from Jewish life."[21]

Here Millin has identified the crisis of identity of so many second-generation South African Jews. Nevertheless, perhaps signalled by her cool third-person analysis, she shows evidence of having internalized and projected Gentile assumptions and Gentile prejudice. In an article, "The Right to be Ugly," which she wrote in 1933 during a peak period of anti-Semitism, she pours scorn on Jewish appearance using the key epithet "ugly," favorite of anti-Semites:

> The Jewish face is not liked by the other nations.
>
> It isn't even much liked by the Jewish nation. One can't, after all, hear for thousands of years that one's appearance is not what is should be [*sic*] without developing a self-consciousness about it. . . .
>
> A Jew must often ask himself: to what extent does his foreign ugliness affront his host? . . . For that it does affront his host he cannot doubt. . . . And yet it is only lately he has begun to appreciate to the full how quite repulsive he must be to strangers. It needed the Germans to smash in his Semitic nose to make the Jew see himself adequately mirrored.[22]

Millin's analysis of Jewish attitudes was viewed with suspicion. The article, which she wrote for a Zionist paper on her return from a visit to Palestine, was angrily rejected by the editor.[23]

In the same way that Millin's treatment of the colored people is still today regarded as basically racist, so, equally, could her characterizations of Jews and her remarks about them be regarded as anti-Semitic. It would seem that she herself suffers from the condition of Jewish self-rejection which she had fictionalized in the character of Saul Nathan.

Even more famous than Millin was in her time is Nobel prize-winning novelist Nadine Gordimer. Despite her current worldwide reputation as a courageous opponent of the racist apartheid regime, close scrutiny of the most significant texts in which Jews are featured demonstrates that her writing displays a form of racism, specifically of an animus against Jews.

In her first novel, *The Lying Days,* published in 1953, a Jewish man is described as "grunting" (149). The narrator comments: "He reminded me of some heavy, thick-skinned animal, a rhinoceros or a boar" (151–52). In a passage from a short story, "The Defeated," written at the same time, a Jewish woman is shown as "very ugly. Ugly with the blunt ugliness of a toad" (198). The use of animal imagery to deride Jews, and the ubiquitousness of the epithet "ugly," is a marked feature of the anti-Semitic texts of the colonial period, and these features continued to be used by some Gentile writers throughout the present century as a mode of disparagement of Jews.

Both in the novel and the short story, reference is made to several Eastern European immigrant Jews and their customs. Apart from the character of Joel Aaron, the attractive and more assimilated son of concession-store owners, Jews are treated by the narrators—significantly Gentile women—with fastidious disdain. Both texts record a child's visit to a concession store and a *kaffireata,* described as threatening places inducing nausea and repulsion. In *The Lying Days,* the Jewish storekeeper is "a short ugly man with a rough grey chin. . . . His shirt was open at the neck and black hairs were scribbled on the little patch of dead white skin. . . . as I came to the door of the eating house, a crescendo of heavy, sweet, nauseating blood-smell . . . assailed me . . . and a big white man in a butcher's apron [was] cutting a chunk of bruised and yellow fat-streaked meat from a huge weight impaled on a hook" (19). At first the narrator makes a connection between the Otherness of both Jews and blacks: "There were people [Jews] there, shadowy, strange to me as the black man" (20). But she goes on, in both texts, to describe in some detail the vitality, energy and exuberance of the blacks.[24] This is opposed to the defeat, poverty, dirt and ugliness inscribed in the construction of Jews. Thus, while both Jews and blacks are constructed as Others, there is a significant difference in the authorial treatment of these Others.

The motivation for Gordimer's idealization of one outgroup—the blacks—and the disparagement of her own outgroup—the Jews—is complex.

Some of the paradoxes of Gordimer's work were identified by Stephen Clingman, referring to a number of what he calls "split positions." These, he maintains, Gordimer occupies by nature of her colonial background, and because, while she has attempted to overcome the class and race structures of apartheid, she is simultaneously contained in them.[25] Other "split positions" which Clingman does not identify may be regarded as functions of a problematic personal identity. One such position is her identity as a Jew in a Gentile society.

Gordimer's attempt to distance herself from her Jewish background can be traced in a number of interviews she has given during the course of her career, in which she has dismissed her Lithuanian immigrant father and claimed closer connection with a "Scots" mother.

At approximately the time that her early works of fiction were appearing, she wrote of her childhood influences in an article in the *New Yorker* in 1954. She tells of the way in which her father paid dues to the "ugly little synagogue." Here the word "ugly" has been extended from Jewish appearance to Jewish worship. She records how she was sent to a convent school and regarded herself as belonging not to the Jewish community but to "our little colonial tribe, with its ritual tea-parties and tennis parties." She relates how her mother distanced herself from her "particular section of the community": "She got on much better with the Scots ladies of the town." She adds: "Our life was very much our mother's life."[26] As late as 1991 she spoke of the way in which her mother despised her father's background: "We didn't ever go to synagogue. . . . We didn't keep kosher—we ate bacon," she said.[27]

Some critics have been deceived by this sleight of hand and believe that Gordimer's mother was not Jewish but Scots. It would seem that Gordimer has colluded with this assumption, and like those assimilationist Jews at the beginning of the century, has abetted those who construct for her a different, and less "Jewish" identity.

There is a further "split position" inscribed in her comments about her family background, and found in her fiction: that between the station held by her father, the lower-class, foreign, Yiddish-speaking immigrant Jew, and the "superior" white anglophone culture to which her mother aspired, and to which her own upbringing, education and sympathies predispose her.

This split is fictionally treated in a 1991 story, "My Father Leaves Home," from *Jump and Other Stories,* concerning the narrator's visit to an Eastern European country, and the memories evoked of an immigrant father. Given the circumstances of Gordimer's family background, this story appears to have an autobiographical content. In terms very similar to Gordimer's published interviews, the narrator describes the family in South Africa:

> If the phylacteries and skull-cap were kept somewhere the children never saw them. . . . He went fasting to the synagogue on the Day of Atonement and each year, on the anniversary of the deaths of the old people in that village . . . went again to light a candle. . . . In the quarrels between him and his wife, she saw them as ignorant and dirty; she must have read something somewhere that served as a taunt: You slept like animals round a stove, stinking of garlic, you bathed once a week. The children knew how low it was to be unwashed. And whipped into anger he knew the lowest category of all in her country, this country.
>
> You speak to me as if I was a kaffir. (64)

The more assimilated mother, who is not an Eastern European immigrant, stigmatizes the father as an "animal," which the father, significantly, understands as "the lowest category of all in her country"—the "kaffir." The children appear to share the mother's contempt.

Through an examination of South African Yiddish literature, Joseph Sherman has shown that immigrant Jews themselves recorded in their fiction their acute consciousness of occupying a shifting frontier "marginalised by the white ruling class, but socially and politically privileged over black workers." It became necessary, as Sherman writes, "for them to negotiate an identity for themselves."[28] This was particularly critical in cases where the Jews found employment in occupations where they were in close contact with blacks, as in the concession store and the *kaffireata*. In her earlier work, Gordimer has treated these very occupations. In "My Father Leaves Home," the narrator returns to the setting of the concession store, and notes the father's harsh treatment of his black worker: "When I began to know him in his shop . . . he shouted at the black man on the other side of the counter who swept the floor and ran errands and he threw the man's weekly pay grudgingly at him. . . . I saw there was someone my father had made afraid of him. A child understands fear and the hurt and hate it brings" (66). She shows how the Jew, despised by his wife for his Jewishness, revels in a relationship in which he has power over someone he considers to hold a status inferior even to himself. Thus the Jew, stigmatized on racial grounds, becomes himself a racist.

In this story, perhaps unconsciously, Gordimer crystallizes the "split position" she occupies as the assimilated daughter of an immigrant father. The father's anxiety—*"You speak to me as if I was a kaffir"*—expresses the Jew's fear of social slippage and his precarious negotiation of social caste.

It is obvious that Gordimer was acutely aware of her own situation in South Africa. Her early writing appeared in the 1950s, a period when Nazi-inspired anti-Semitism had so recently threatened the status of Jews. The fear of slippage from a position barely acceptable because it is acculturated might lead Gordimer herself to displace those prejudices and hostilities which are part of her colonial inheritance from the black—most obvious candidate for the role of the Other, but unacceptable to her in terms of her developing liberal sympathies—to that hidden Other in her own blood. This hidden and repressed Other, more shameful and more difficult to come to terms with—in fact the "enemy"—is not merely the Jew as such, but the foreign, Yiddish-speaking Jew, typified as ugly and reviled as "scum" in the South African mythos.

Having distanced herself from Judaism, in her writing she assumes for herself a Gentile point of view. This is evident, for example, in her choice of Gentile narrators, and her unashamed projection of Gentile assumptions concerning Jews. Like the immigrant Jews, Gordimer has herself attempted to negotiate a new identity. It should be noted that this is an identity which would situate her more centrally at the center of society, while simultaneously her increasing radical political beliefs tended, on a different level, to distance her from the center of South African white culture.

As her career developed, her work was to become more sharply focused on opposing the evils of apartheid and on charting South Africa's social and political "history from the inside."[29] This very political activism may also contribute to what Letty Pogrebin has identified as the "Rosa Luxemburg syndrome."

Pogrebin suggests that some Jewish women activists tend to ignore what Luxemburg termed "special Jewish sorrows," because they consider them too self-serving. She ponders the way in which those women who are full of compassion for oppressed groups have nothing but contempt for their own group. "Rather than identify as Jews," she argues, "they had preferred to count themselves as feminists, anarchists, leftists, Marxists, civil rights workers, defenders of minorities and oppressed peoples. They did not recognize in their own denial of Jewish oppression proof of the impact of anti-Semitism."[30]

Gordimer's literary treatment of Jews remained compromised by a failure to move beyond those stereotypes set up since the fiction of the diamond rush and developed during the twentieth century. *A Sport of Nature,* published in 1987, for example, presents a gallery of Jewish stereotypes, among others a "kugel"—the South African (Yiddish) nickname for the materialistic, selfish, wealthy Jewish woman, better known in America as the Jewish

American Princess—and several leftists. The chief character is a Jewish girl, Hillela, who rejects her background and at school calls herself "Kim." Perhaps unconsciously mocking the Jewish leftist, and even underscoring the connection of the Jew and black, Gordimer has Hillela committing herself to the African struggle by relying heavily on her sexuality, and by marrying two black revolutionaries in succession.

The case of Jillian Becker is more transparent. Writing a decade after Gordimer's early work, she is the daughter of a wealthy family who felt themselves distanced from other Jews by their intellectual and cultural superiority.

On the surface Becker's 1967 novel *The Keep* is a satirical treatment of an upper-middle-class Johannesburg family. One subtext, however, is an icy rejection of all things Jewish. The family Leyton—the father a member of parliament, the mother a refined, bored lady with artistic pretensions—is based on the circumstances of Becker's own parents; and the consciousness of the narrator, the child, Josephine, is therefore close to her own.

With an exuberance which goes far beyond the dictates of the text, Becker constructs an ugly, fat, Yiddish-speaking aunt from whom the child recoils with disgust. Josephine admits that her "distaste" is irrational and "unfair" (34). However, since the author uses no satire or irony *against* Josephine, Josephine's point of view is endorsed. The mother, Freda Leyton, has similar attitudes: "[Freda thought] if only her aunts were thin ladies with white hands who smelt of lavender and wore pearls! When she had been a boarder at St. Catherine's School how she had wished on visiting days that her mother (bringing boxes of teiglach [sticky sweetmeats]) would not talk so loudly" (41). It would appear from the text that Freda desires a Gentile background and rejects her "fat" (implying "Jewish") aunts.

In assessing anti-Jewish bias, one must acknowledge that the main authorial attack is against Freda Leyton, who is treated throughout with sharp, even malicious, satire. It is she who, in the passage quoted at the beginning of the paper, fulminates against the Jews who visit Muizenberg. The hatred of Jews expressed by this central character might not necessarily correspond with that of the narrator, and, arguably, it cannot entirely be imputed to the author. It is partly a strategy used in devising a satirical portrait.

Nevertheless, in general in this text, the boundary between the attitudes attributed to the characters, that of the narrator, and Becker's own attitude are blurred. Perhaps, like Gordimer, she distances herself from the "dirty proletariat" in order to protect her own standing in the eyes of the community. The text powerfully expresses that aspect of snobbery of the more assimilated Jew for the lesser, the fear of being socially tainted, and the uncompromising campaign of dissociation which, since the time of the influx of

Eastern European immigrants, marked the relations between the two sectors of the Jewish community.

In other works by Jewish authors written toward the end of the twentieth century, Jews continue to be mocked and satirized.

Antony Sher is a South African who emigrated to London in 1968 at the age of nineteen to make a career on the stage. Having confessed in 1988 that he had been hiding "what I saw as my shameful South African identity,"[31] he publicly admitted in 1990 that his sense of shame had been reinforced by having to contend with two other painful areas—being gay and being Jewish. These, he confesses, "were all aspects of myself that I tried desperately to escape from and have had to come to terms with."[32]

Sher's sense of marginality—endorsed in three different ways—would seem to inform his 1988 novel *Middlepost,* loosely based on the facts of his grandfather's emigration to South Africa from Lithuania at the beginning of the twentieth century. The central character is a Jewish immigrant from Lithuania, a simpleton named Smous. This is an ironic allusion to the *smous* (pedlar) who features in much South African Jewish historiography and mythology. Peddling was an occupation taken up by large numbers of newly arrived Eastern European Jewish immigrants.

Smous's only companion in South Africa is a San woman (i.e., a black woman), again underscoring the felt connection between the Jews and the black population.

Sher's Smous is relentlessly shown as physically repulsive and intellectually damaged. His entire family in Lithuania is unsavory. A brother, Elie, had "started to wear a smudge of coal dust on the end of his nose to shorten its hooked shape and so de-Jew himself" (44), and mocks Yiddish expressions and Jewish customs such as circumcision and ritual slaughter. Significantly, Sher's Elie, Millin's Saul Nathan, Gordimer's Hilella and Becker's Leyton family, are all portraits of self-hating Jews. It is as if the writers have felt compelled through their own creativity to exorcise their own dilemmas.

In his second novel, *The Indoor Boy,* published in 1991, South African Jews are once again ugly, ridiculous or stupid. They are presented in terms of gross distortion. Judaism is associated with obscenities. Synagogue worshipers are "a raggedy old crowd, scourged by strokes or booze. Purplish drowned faces, or yellowy with winter tans. The men are bald and have damp moustaches. The women wear wigs or hairdos like ice sculptures, with turquoise daubed round their eyes, and smudged carmine on their lips. Their necks and wrists are bound in platinum, ivory, bone and plastic; and huge rings bulge on knuckly fingers" (194–95).

None of Sher's characters are convincing. They are "actor's" characters—

grotesques, as caricatured as those found in any Nazi propaganda. His novels can be read as case histories of that identity problem of shame and repudiation of the Other in oneself, which Erving Goffman has identified as a "spoiled identity."[33]

Sher made this clear when in 1991 he told an interviewer that he wrote at "a time of me facing up to my background; and through the medium of art, of writing, confronting the question of roots and cultural identity." He explored the Jewish aspect of his background at some length: "I suppose my first consciousness of being an outsider in any sense, was as a Jew. You know, just in the banal ways in that at school you're aware that you're having other holidays than the majority of kids." More profoundly shocking to him was the time spent in the South African army, where he was taunted as a *"Jood, vokken Jood."* It was an experience of being aware that "*racially* you were not the right thing" (emphasis added).[34]

Much earlier, Sarah Gertrude Millin had identified all these symptoms of Jewish self-consciousness. She had written: "the Jew is tortured by the knowledge that he does not belong. . . . The Jew *is* a peculiar person. . . . He simply cannot get on with his life . . . because he is so distracted with thinking about his Jewishness."[35] What Millin underscores is the slippery nature of Jewish identity formation, which becomes compounded by factors such as sexual identity and the negative labelling of a state obsessed with racial difference.

CONCLUSION

At the end of the twentieth century many Jews in South Africa continue to carry a burden of self-consciousness, sometimes developing into a form of hostility turned against the self. The origins of this condition have been traced to diverse sources: the worldwide phenomenon of Jewish marginality and self-hatred, the dynamics of Jewish immigration to South Africa during the nineteenth and early twentieth centuries, and the social and political circumstances of the host country. The fact that it emerges in the guise of literature is deplorable. It would seem that Jewish authors are weary of their position perpetually on a frontier. In an attempt to ingratiate themselves with the majority culture, to distance themselves from their origins and thereby to travel from the periphery of society to its center, they may well continue to set up and attack images of those whom they perceive to betray their origins—images of their parents and grandparents. In pandering to the worst side of human nature that derides and mocks the Other, these writers will create new icons of anti-Semitism which will surely contribute to the perpetuation of the very conditions from which their own identity problems arose.

On the other hand, developments in recent South African history, and the need to formulate a new, inclusive national identity would seem to dominate over the consciousness of division characteristic of earlier times. An examination of recent South African fiction reveals that these trends have indeed infiltrated the realm of fiction. For example, the Jewish characters in Nadine Gordimer's 1994 novel *None to Accompany Me* are unimportant and though not fully developed are mere shadows of stereotypes. It is to be hoped that Jewish writers will no longer seek out the enemy within, and that their sense of alienation at the margins of society will give way to a more fundamentally integrated concept of identity.

Notes

Sources for the chapter epigraphs are: S. G. Millin Papers, A539/M2, Manuscript Collection, University of the Witwatersrand Library, 1–2; "The Defeated" in *The Soft Voice of the Serpent* (London: Victor Gollancz, 1953), 198; and *The Keep* (London: Chatto and Windus, 1967), 104.

1. Sander L. Gilman, introduction to this volume.
2. Milton Shain, *The Roots of Antisemitism in South Africa* (Charlottesville: University Press of Virginia, 1994), 23.
3. *Critic's* "Diary" cited in ibid., 27.
4. J. Sherman, "The Shifting Frontier: Defining Immigrant Jewish Identity in Racist South Africa" (paper delivered at the conference on "Jewries at the Frontier," University of Cape Town, Cape Town, South Africa, Aug. 11, 1996), 5, 13.
5. Ibid., 5, citing B. M. Titlestad, "Eating-Houses on the Witwatersrand, 1903–1979" (M.A. thesis, University of the Witwatersrand, 1991), 135.
6. C. van Onselen, *New Babylon: Studies in the Social and Economic History of the Witwatersrand, 1886–1914*, 2 vols. (Johannesburg: Ravan, 1982), 1:109–11.
7. J. H. Munnik, cited in Shain, *Roots of Antisemitism in South Africa*, 28.
8. *Owl*, Jan. 23, 1897, cited in ibid., 32.
9. Gilman, introduction to this volume.
10. A. R. JanMahomed, "The Economy of Manichean Allegory: The Function of Racial Difference in Colonialist Literature," *Critical Inquiry* 12 (Autumn 1985): 63.
11. S. L. Gilman, *Jewish Self-Hatred: Anti-Semitism and the Hidden Language of the Jews* (Baltimore: Johns Hopkins University Press, 1990), 6–7.
12. S. L. Gilman, *Difference and Pathology: Stereotypes of Sexuality, Race, and Madness* (Ithaca, N.Y.: Cornell University Press, 1985), 34–35.
13. P. J. Furlong, *Between Crown and Swastika: The Impact of the Radical Right on the Afrikaner Nationalist Movement in the Fascist Era* (Johannesburg: Witwatersrand University Press, 1991), 63.
14. G. Shimoni, *Jews and Zionism: The South African Experience, 1910–1967* (Cape Town: Oxford University Press, 1980), 112.
15. Gilman, introduction to this volume.
16. See P. Rock, *The Making of Symbolic Interactionism* (London: Macmillan, 1979),

129–32; E. E. Jones et al., eds. *Social Stigma: The Psychology of Marked Relationships* (New York: W. H. Freeman, 1984), 32–36; H. Tajfel, *Human Groups and Social Categories: Studies in Social Psychology* (Cambridge: Cambridge University Press, 1981), 254–56; J. Katz, *Jewish Emancipation and Self-Emancipation* (Philadelphia: Jewish Publication Society, 1986), 131; J. Katz, *Out of the Ghetto: The Social Background of Jewish Emancipation, 1770–1870* (Cambridge, Mass.: Harvard University Press, 1973), 6.

17. For evidence that this view is still current, see the discussion of Millin's attitudes in F. Hale, "The Evolving Depiction of Indians in South African Fiction," *Quarterly Bulletin of the South African Library* 50.4 (June 1996): 176–82. This was kindly brought to my attention by John Simon.

18. L. Braun, "Not Gobineau but Heine—Not Racial Theory but Biblical Theme: The Case of Sarah Gertrude Millin," *English Studies in Africa* 34.1 (1991): 27–38.

19. Unpaginated notes, S. G. Millin Papers, A539/9, Manuscript Collection, University of the Witwatersrand Library; quoted by Braun, "Not Gobineau but Heine," 29.

20. S. G. Millin Papers, MS 188, box 29, The Brenthurst Library, Johannesburg, 6a–7.

21. Ibid., 21.

22. "The Right to Be Ugly" (1933), S.G. Millin Papers, A539/M2, Manuscript Collection, University of the Witwatersrand Library, 2.

23. S. G. Millin, *The Night Is Long* (London: Faber, 1941), 309–10.

24. In *The Lying Days,* for example, she describes the industrious blacks: "The gramophones from the stores made music and there was gossip and shouting above the tiny hammering of a man who sat cross-legged beating copper wire into bracelets. . . . a boy sat with a sewing machine, whirring the handle with his vigorous elbow jutting" (23).

25. S. Clingman, *The Novels of Nadine Gordimer: History from the Inside* (Johannesburg: Ravan, 1986), 222.

26. N. Gordimer, "A South African Childhood," *New Yorker,* Oct. 16, 1954, 111–16.

27. "On Freedom, Communism, and Judaism: A Conversation between Nadine Gordimer and Natan Sharansky," *Jerusalem Report,* Oct. 24, 1991, 5–7.

28. Sherman, "Shifting Frontier," 2.

29. Clingman, *Novels of Nadine Gordimer.*

30. L. C. Pogrebin, *Deborah, Golda, and Me: Being Female and Jewish in America* (New York: Doubleday, 1991), 228–31.

31. *The Guardian,* Sept. 2, 1988.

32. "*Middlepost:* Antony Sher," *Business Day,* Nov. 14, 1988.

33. E. Goffman, *Stigma: Notes on the Management of Spoiled Identity* (1973; Harmondsworth, U.K.: Penguin, 1979).

34. H. Bernstein, *The Rift: The Exile Experience of South Africans* (London: Jonathan Cape, 1994), 359–61.

35. S. G. Millin Papers, A539/M2, Manuscript Collection, University of the Witwatersrand Library, 3.

11 From the Brotherhood of Man to the World to Come: The Denial of the Political in Rabbinic Writing under Apartheid

CLAUDIA B. BRAUDE

"Claudia Braude challenges Rabbi Akiva Tatz to a public debate on is there a role for a pre-egalitarian Judaism in a post-apartheid South Africa?" This appeared in 1989 in the Community Notices section, mostly dedicated to shul and other activities of interest to the Jewish community, of *The Star* newspaper. Tatz, guru of the Ohr Sameach community, reportedly threatened to leave the country, the phone rang the whole night with people asking what I meant, and, when I denied placing the ad, if I had an enemy who would do such a thing to me. I don't. I knew who placed the ad. It was my brother Jake, as a prank, using my name as a foil for some of his own anger at the establishment Jewish community. (Conscripted into the South African Defence Force, Jake had served as an army chaplain, administering to the needs of the Jewish soldiers. He came, in my opinion, sharply up against the corruptions and contradictions, and got burnt. He has the distinction of having been thrown out of the chaplaincy, which I continue to congratulate). I wish, though, that I could claim the ad, and had challenged Tatz, and his rabbinic and secular counterparts leading the South African Jewish community, to debate what remains one of the only real theological—and indeed political—questions confronting the South African Jewish community: what role does pre-egalitarian Judaism continue to have in South Africa in the 1990s, with its nonracist, nonsexist constitution, in an environment where group separatism is no longer deemed okay, and where a third of the people participating in government are women? Jake's question has a reverse side, which we can start to unravel since its initial formulation: what role did nonegalitarian Judaism play in apartheid South Africa? What was Jake responding to in framing the question in the first instance? What role does it continue to have, and is this still appropriate?

This essay addresses these questions. It examines the development of rabbinic writing over seventy-five years, including nearly half a century under apartheid, to evidence the impact of Afrikaans nationalist rule on South African Jewish consciousness. Rabbinic textual output serves as a case study of the suppressed dynamic whereby South African Judaism (and particularly its Orthodox versions) and Jewish expression responded to Afrikaans nationalist succession to power in 1948 by becoming increasingly interpreted and represented as an apolitical concern. It incrementally shed reference to historical concerns, particularly to issues of class and race. Instead, it became devoid of capacity to say anything relevant about the political, national circumstances of racist life under apartheid. Through close examination of key and select rabbinic texts, this essay demonstrates that it was not an arbitrary shift, but one that evolved in response to hegemonic white supremacist rule. It was the response of a Jewish minority under the rule of Afrikaans nationalists, with its strong pro-Nazi history. This essay consequently traces both Jewish responses to fear of Afrikaans nationalists, including their anti-Semitism, and the impact of these fears on South African rabbinic writing and understanding of history. It demonstrates the specifically South African nature of this shift. In so doing, it counters the argument that South African Jewish life was no different to life elsewhere in other historical periods or places.

Responding to this essay, for instance, Israeli historian Ezra Mendelsohn argued it was inevitable that South African Jews responded as they did, given their typical diaspora minority status.[1] In an edition of *Jewish Affairs* (the mouthpiece of the South African Jewish Board of Deputies) dedicated to "Jews and Apartheid," Hanns Saenger and Joseph Sherman adopted this ahistorical model of Jewish history, asserting essential continuities in Jewish life in the diaspora irrespective of geographical location or historical period: "Apologies can no more be made for the complex motivations that governed the decisions of previous [South African Jewish Board of Deputies] Executives than for the decisions of generations of Jewish leadership elsewhere in the Diaspora."[2] They were responding in part to my article published in the *Mail and Guardian* newspaper in which I examined the relation between Jewish fear of Afrikaans nationalist anti-Semitism and pro-Nazism and Jewish collusion with apartheid, through the life of Percy Yutar, a prominent figure in the Jewish community and the state prosecutor in the Rivonia treason trial that sentenced Nelson Mandela to life imprisonment.[3] Such efforts (past and present) to suppress the impact of Afrikaans nationalism on

South African Jewish life by affirming continuities with life elsewhere as an explanation for the motivations of South African Jewish history service that history itself. Seemingly paradoxically, these efforts evidence the influence of South African conditions and ideologies. An ahistorical model of South African Jewish history services precisely South African issues of relations with Afrikaans nationalism, and South African race relations, obscuring memory of specific South African influences. Rather than ahistorically asserting essential continuities in Jewish life in the diaspora irrespective of geographical location or historical period, I analyze this relation between South African Jewish history and the context in which it evolved. Rather than reading South African Jewish theology in ahistorical terms, I have analyzed the specific historical conditions of life under apartheid. This essay consequently traces both Jewish responses to fear of Afrikaans nationalists, including their anti-Semitism, and the impact of these fears on South African rabbinic writing and understanding of history.

I will begin with a discussion of aspects of Jewish mysticism in the popular writing of Rabbi Akiva Tatz, whose formulation for "living inspired" is emblematic of the ahistorical nature of South African Jewish self-expression under apartheid. I discuss the otherworldly emphasis placed by Tatz in his interpretation of the role of the Sabbath in the Jewish calendar. Through discussions of Landau, Rappaport and Rabinowitz, I examine earlier treatments of the role of the Sabbath as promoted by these rabbis serving South African Jewish communities. The Sabbath represented to them, in different ways at different times of their own rabbinic careers, the brotherhood and equality of man within the social historical sphere. The distance (spanning three-quarters of a century) between Landau and Tatz, most evident in their respective readings of the significance of the Sabbath, is striking. Landau's affirmation of the economic and political life of the nation contrasts with Tatz's spiritual, otherworldly focus. This distance is evident in Tatz's replacement of Landau's notion of equality and the brotherhood of man with an affirmation of and guide book to the world to come. This shift directly mirrors the development of other aspects of South African Jewish life and responses to apartheid. The rest of this essay considers how this shift came about, and with what results, through a reading of certain key rabbinic texts in the intervening years. I consider Rabinowitz's application of assertions of the equality of all people in discussions of racial discrimination and apartheid, and the difficulties he experienced in promoting the equality of all people in face of the policy of political noninvolvement promoted by the South African Jewish Board of Deputies in their efforts to maintain cordial relations with the apartheid regime. The writing of Solomon Rappaport serves as a textual bridge between the political outspokenness of Rabinowitz and the political quietism of Tatz. I trace the shift, internal to his writing over several decades, away from an insistence on the need for Jews to challenge the racial status quo in South Africa to support for apartheid. The shift in Rappaport's writing is contrasted with the 1956 expulsion from South Africa of Rabbi Andre Ungar, an uncompromising and vocal critic of apartheid. Distanced by the leadership of the Jewish community, his expulsion further intimidated the Jewish community into both tacit and active support for apartheid. This section concludes with discussion of both forms of support within rabbinic writing. I then autobiographically and cursorily consider the impact of this shift in other arenas of South African Jewish communal life.

This essay was written and researched during the course of the Truth and Reconciliation Commission (TRC) concerned with accessing aspects of the past which were obliterated by apartheid historiographical impetuses. It is consequently deliberately positioned on the cusp of a combination of autobiographical and national memory regained. Informed by the imperatives of the TRC, I have sought to trace the influences of apartheid which, while concealed, continue nonetheless to shape the South African present. I have necessarily drawn on a personal journey and on autobiographical markers to indicate a narrative far bigger than the lives in question, in order to comment on and restore memory to the impact of the policies of South African Jewish leadership under apartheid on the construction of South African Jewish knowledge, consciousness, and social and political organization. By tracing the impact of Afrikaans nationalist hegemonic rule on Jewish self-expression, the necessity of Jewish engagement with the apartheid past becomes uncomfortably apparent. I conclude by posing a series of questions that will need to be addressed by future generations of scholars of South African Jewish history.

AKIVA TATZ: TRAUMA AND APARTHEID

The writing of Akiva Tatz is a good place to start. Tatz, an ex–South African doctor, who was conscripted into the South African Defence Force (SADF) where he fought in South Africa's cross-border wars in Angola, currently lives in Israel. In many ways, his book, *Living Inspired,*[4] which was "developed and refined"[5] during his time in Johannesburg in the 1980s, epitomizes the direction rabbinic output assumed under apartheid. Tatz's mission was to provide a "Torah-based" formulaic inspirational guide to living with anxiety and terror. He attributes this terror to an existential "lack of sense of purpose and direction."[6]

Tatz was working and writing in South Africa, giving regular blockbuster lectures and seminars to members of Ohr Sameach and the Jewish public, under the State of Emergency imposed by former President P. W. Botha in the mid-eighties, in an effort to destroy increasing resistance to apartheid. These were bad years, during which tens of thousands of South Africans were being detained without trial. Many people were tortured, died in detention or disappeared mysteriously. The men in Tatz's community were liable for two years conscription into the South African Defence Force to maintain the apartheid system in townships and across South Africa's borders. Tatz, however, failed to indicate, even momentarily, the impact of life under the apartheid regime in the emotional and spiritual lives of members of his community. His writing does not reflect the political source of the anxiety, terror and doubt he witnessed and sought to heal. Confronted by a Johannesburg community whose "inner life" he recognized to be "built on emotional and mental quicksand,"[7] he interpreted as existential the anxiety and uncertainty to which his writing testifies. Rather than the consequences of life in a racist police state, he attributed "the energy-sapping"[8] "human difficulties"[9] arising from this existential tension to doubt to "not knowing with full confidence what one's direction should be";[10] and to ignorance about the "Torah definition of the pattern of the world."[11] He prescribed "Torah" as the cure for a world which "seems haphazard and arbitrary, and [in which] one cannot generate any semblance of inner peace, let alone serenity."[12]

Unable to acknowledge or even refer to the material realities in his community, Tatz offered spiritual solutions to the psychological trauma resulting from life under apartheid (albeit within the privileged end of its social spectrum). His spiritual model of inspired living relied on the Kabbalistic mystical tradition. Tatz offered the possibility to change one's life and thereby alleviate existential anxiety through *Emunah,* in "faith in the overriding Unity of reality"[13] and in belief that "everything Hashem [God] does is good."[14] Tatz offered the possibility of reconstructing lives experienced as damaged and incomplete through references to the Kabbalistic notion of *shevirat ha-kelim,* the broken vessels: "We must use the 'broken pieces' available to us and painstakingly reconstruct them—in our personalities, our relationships, our prayers, our blessings, our lives. We must bring the light of original Creation, original inspirations, into the darkness so powerfully that it ceases to be dark. That is life; that is living inspired."[15]

"Living inspired" involves "liv[ing] in the darkness and ris[ing] above it."[16] Referring ostensibly to the challenge of establishing a spiritual life in an imperfect material world, of harnessing the divine with the realm of the mundane, the darkness of which Tatz speaks refers also to the oppressive reality of apartheid's states of emergency. Tatz uses the Jewish mystical tradition to interpret and give meaning to Jewish life in South Africa under apartheid. The images of catastrophe and doom central to the Kabbalistic imagination resonate with similarly popular apocryphal understandings of South African history—emigration or death at the hands of "black savages." Tatz, however, does not refer to this reality. Instead, he sought to inspire his community to bring about change in their lives, to repair the world, not by joining the struggle against apartheid, but by reconstructing the mystical shards. Thus, present in his writing is another central feature of Kabbalistic mythology, namely *Tikkun olam,* repairing the world. *Tikkun* encapsulates Kabbalistic belief in the possibility of changing conditions in the world, of changing God's intended course of actions, through religious activities including prayer and observance of the Sabbath.

These two mechanisms of Kabbalistic change—observance of the Sabbath and prayer—are seminal in his formulations of "inspired living." Consistent with the Kabbalistic tradition, he promoted the Sabbath as "*me-eyn olam ha'ba*—a small degree of the experience of the next world." Thus, "*Shabbos* rest is an opportunity for introspection. . . . Stocktaking; facing up to oneself honestly. This is itself a faint reflection of the eternal facing up to oneself which is of the essence of the next world."[17] It is through observance of the *Shabbath,* asserted Tatz, that moments of divinity are captured within the mundane. Similarly, consistent with Kabbalistic teachings, Tatz asserted that prayer is "not just a meditation" but is "intended to produce results too."[18] Prayer offers the opportunity to "make some change in the world or our situation in it."[19] Tatz's formulation of the kind of change that can be achieved through the religious activities of observance of the Sabbath and prayer in order to remove existential anxiety is personal and insular: "Prayer is *not* directed at changing Hashem [God] at all; it is directed at changing *you.* The idea is that the work of *tefilla* . . . is work on the self; the effort to change the personality."[20] Tatz's spiritual model of inspired living offers change, *Tikkun,* within the individual. These changes are presented as having the potential to change God's course of actions, but only in ways that make a difference to the individual who has brought about change within his or her emotional and spiritual frame:

> The reason we hope to achieve a result through *tefilla,* to make some change in the world or our situation in it, is as follows. We certainly cannot convince Hashem that we need some or other particular thing if He knows otherwise. However we can change ourselves to the point that the object of our request has a different meaning if a person wants wealth, for example, and is being

> refused that request because *it would not be good for him* (wealth can be a great ordeal), no amount of pleading will change that. But working on oneself until one reaches a refinement, an insight into the purpose of life and the correct perspective on wealth could result in a situation where that gift may now be *good* for that person! In other words one *can* change the dispensation granted to one by changing oneself.[21]

While drawing on the Kabbalistic imperative to work for change in the damaged world, for *Tikkun Olam,* Tatz robs these of their social orientation. Standing in a relation of continuity with existing Jewish mystical and theological traditions, Tatz's use of the Jewish mystical tradition links only with its conservative elements. The kind of change that prayer can bring about is concerned, in Tatz's scheme, with the well-being of the individual. In spite of the mystical nature of his writing and its sources, the example of change used by Tatz is deeply materialistic, and reflects the concerns of his Yuppie community. Similarly, the kind of change Tatz offered through the observance of the Sabbath is not concerned with changing the world of history (as it is in other Kabbalistic philosophies and systems), but with introducing aspects of the future world of *Olam Haba* into the world of history. He explains the Kabbalistic notions of *Tikkun Olam* and *shevirat he-kelim* as occurring within the individual, rather than within the historical domain. *Tikkun* is a private, noncommunal affair. Tatz's writing is not influenced by the Kabbalistic activist trends that promise redemption of history. Instead, he combined the Kabbalistic promise of the possibility of change with a quietist attitude to history. In his scheme, change can happen but only on an individual level. He formulated an ahistorical mysticism, devoid of any reference to the historical and political world taking place around him, to give meaning to life under apartheid. Consistent with certain Kabbalistic traditions, and disregarding of others, Tatz uses particular aspects of existing Jewish traditions to respond to South African Jewish life under apartheid.

JUDA LANDAU: THE BROTHERHOOD OF MAN, SOCIALISM, AND EQUALITY

That Tatz's apolitical inward-looking mystical response to life epitomized the development of South African rabbinic writing under apartheid, and mirrors the development of Jewish consciousness in general under apartheid, becomes clearer when read against the writing of Rabbi Juda Leib Landau half a century before. Landau came to South Africa in 1903, and served as rabbi of the Johannesburg Hebrew Congregation till 1915, when he became chief rabbi of the United Hebrew Congregation. He remained chief rabbi till his death in 1942. Landau was professor of Hebrew at the University of the Witwatersrand, to which he donated his library. Landau had an entirely different take on the significance of the Sabbath within the Jewish calendar to that of Tatz. Rather than a sojourn into an otherworldly sphere, the Sabbath epitomized for Landau the brotherhood and equality of man within the social, historical sphere. He presented these ideas in 1923 in a lecture entitled "The Sabbath," to the Working Men's Educational Union in Johannesburg.[22] In this lecture Landau compared the Sabbath, as the seventh day of the week, with Yovel, the jubilee year in which, according to the Bible, all slaves are to be set free. Landau interpreted these calendrical markers to signify equality between all people:

> It is thus clear that the main object of the Sabbath as of the Sabbatical year [Yovel] was to impress every Jew with the idea of personal freedom, of his higher mission as a member of the human race, and thus also with the idea of the equality of all men. . . . Needless to say that the Sabbath was instituted for all men alike, that the law makes no distinction between the rich and the poor, but it cannot be denied that it mainly benefits the working man [and] the labourer . . . who alone are able to appreciate a whole day devoted to rest, rest of body and mind. They are thus enabled at least once in seven days to give some thought to the nobler duties and ambitions of man.[23]

Landau considered the religious day of rest, and its secular form in the weekend, to be a "great boon and blessing to the working classes."[24] He understood the Sabbath to epitomize the equality of all men, and to be an "idea which has revolutionised modern society."[25] In "The Jewish Conception of Labour,"[26] another address presented to the Working Men's Education Union in 1923, Landau directly argued that all men are equal, irrespective of their class status:

> All those laws of justice and kindness sprang from one source, from the Biblical doctrine, that all races and all men trace their origin from one and the same parent, and that all were created in the image of God, that all bear upon their foreheads the stamp of a higher being, destined to be free. The prophet Malachi, who lived in the fifth-century B.C.E., expressed this idea very clearly and emphatically in the well-known verse, "Have we not all *one* father. Hath not *one* God created us? Why do we deal treacherously every man against his brother?" The ancient constitution of Judea, therefore, knew nothing of social distinctions. All tribes, and all members of each tribe, were equal before the law.[27]

Seminal in Landau's writing is an assertion of the Jewish belief in the origins of all people from one source. This idea informed his interpretation, most evident in his essay on the socialist revolutionary Ferdinand Lassalle,[28] of Judaism as a revolutionary religion. Landau treated Lassalle "from a Jewish point of view,"[29] not because he was "a son of the Jewish race"[30] but because, he argued, his attempt to "break a lance on behalf of wronged justice" was "chiefly Jewish."[31] Landau saw Lassalle's fight for freedom and social reform, for equal civil rights and inviolable social privileges, as an essentially Jewish one, such that "in him the ancient spirit of the Jewish prophets manifested itself in a new form, according to the changed conditions of history."[32] As Lassalle was the promoter of the brotherhood of man, argued Landau, he was the modern disciple of the prophet Samuel who had himself raised the battle cry against slavery. Landau's reading of Samuel into Lassalle demonstrates his profound awareness of and support for the struggle for socialism. Landau brought his affirmation of Lassalle's socialist imperative to bear on his reading of the role of the Sabbath in society. In a system affirming the equality of all men, irrespective of class, the Sabbath, argued Landau, served as the calendrical marker of social equality: a temporal leveling of class-based playing fields.

LOUIS RABINOWITZ: THE BROTHERHOOD OF MAN AND THE POLITICS OF RACE

The obvious political and social implications of Landau's theological teachings of social equality for questions of race politics would become significant in 1951, with the publication of *Out of the Depths,*[33] a collection of sermons by Chief Rabbi Louis Rabinowitz, delivered from the pulpit between 1945 and 1951, including the early years of apartheid. Two are particularly interesting for a discussion of the development of rabbinic writing under apartheid. Rabinowitz brought Landau's assertion of the oneness of all people directly to bear on South African race politics. Where Landau had spoken in the context of class politics, Rabinowitz responded to the pressing race politics of the day by speaking in terms of racial equality. He developed Landau's emphasis on social equality to speak out against the system of racial inequality being legalized in South Africa under the new Afrikaans nationalist government. Drawing on Jewish teachings, he discouraged his community from colluding with the racism of apartheid. Rabinowitz asserted Judaism's belief in racial equality and the brotherhood of man through discussion of a debate between the two talmudic figures, Rabbi Akiba and Ben Azzai. According to Rabinowitz, Rabbi Akiba's argument that "Thou shalt love thy neighbour as thyself" was a more useful statement for teaching the Brotherhood of Man than Ben Azzai's statement that "This is the Book of the Generations of Man; in the day that God created man, in the likeness of God made he him."[34] Ben Azzai argued that the former statement was open to misinterpretation, since people could conclude that the Hebrew word for "neighbor" signified "a fellow Israelite" rather than "a fellow man."[35] Rabinowitz affirmed Ben Azzai's position: "history and theology and polemics have shown the weakness in the verse of Rabbi Akiba," he preached,[36] and proceeded to expound a lesson for his South African community:

> The Afrikaner has only to say, "Afrikaners are my neighbours and my duty to love my neighbours apply only to them, but not to other nationals"; the Jew can say, "Jews I regard as my *re'im* but not non-Jews," for the whole point of the "fundamental principle" to be blunted and rendered meaningless. . . . [Ben Azzai's verse] reminds us that all human beings are of common descent, that every man is formed in the image of God. As our Rabbis beautifully put it, "Why was man created singly (in contrast to the animals which are not)? In order that no man should be able to say to another: My father is greater than thy father, i.e., I can claim a more noble descent than thee." *All men are equal, black and white and coloured, all hark back to one common origin, all are endowed with the spark of God's spirit.* That is the fundamental teaching of the Torah. . . . Living as we do in an environment which is powerfully tainted by a widespread denial of the truth of this doctrine, it is urgently incumbent upon us that we arm ourselves spiritually against its contamination, that we assert and act upon the Jewish doctrine—that doctrine which says, "Thou shalt love thy neighbour as thyself" is a great doctrine, but "This is the Book of the Generations of Man; in the day that God created man, in the likeness of God made he him" is even more fundamental, since it teaches beyond all cavil and doubt that all men are equal before God, that the spirit of God is divided in equal measure among his children.[37]

Here, Rabinowitz drew on Jewish traditions to speak out against Afrikaans nationalism and racism, and to discourage his community from internalizing its worldview. Rabinowitz promoted the need to identify with "the oppressed and the suffering" which, in the South African context, clearly meant those suffering racist, apartheid oppression. According to Rabinowitz, people concerned with the teachings of Moses were required to pursue justice. He was clear about the need for social justice, and about the role of rabbinic leadership in promoting it. On another occasion, he referred to the biblical figure of Moses in preaching the Jewish imperative of absolute social justice, including the pursuit of justice for others, even at the expense of their own security and self-interest: "A justice which knows no bounds and no limitations, a passion in whose white heat every other consideration wilts and melts away, justice absolute and justice universal, justice whether between Jew and non-Jews, whether between Jew and fellow Jew, whether between non-Jew and non-Jew, justice at the expense of security and self-interest; the taking of the part of the weak against the strong, even down to animal creation."[38] Rabinowitz's explicit opposition to apartheid made him "something of an exception"[39] among his rabbinic colleagues and Jewish leadership in general, as historian Gideon Shimoni has demonstrated. Rabinowitz's insistence on pursuing justice for all, even at the expense of Jewish security and self-interest, flies in the face, not only of Afrikaans nationalist ideology. In preaching against self-interest, Rabinowitz spoke out against prevailing sentiment within Jewish leadership as well.

JEWISH BOARD AND THE POLITICS OF POLITICAL NONINVOLVEMENT

Shimoni has indicated the "discretionary influence" of the Jewish Board of Deputies over the South African rabbinate.[40] The JBD was the body concerned with representing Jewish interests to the government. Formed in 1910, it was consistently concerned with the position of the Jew in South Africa. From the outset, it adopted a position of political noninvolvement in areas that did not affect Jews as Jews. This was a direct response to the history of South African immigration law. The dubious racial status of Jews, seen for the most part as not quite white, threatened Jewish access to the country from 1902 to the 1930s. While South African Jewish historiography consistently presents Jews as white, their belonging within white society was only guaranteed, ironically, with the introduction of apartheid. This position would assume a particular form under apartheid, after 1948, when the Afrikaans National Party came into power. Many opponents of the NP government were, in historian Patrick Furlong's words, "convinced that successors of the Nazis were now ensconced in Pretoria."[41] There is no doubt that the Jewish community, while not articulating this fear, were fearful of potential Nazi-like anti-Semitism. Stephen Cohen argues that "because of the National Party's views on Jewish immigration and its opposition to the Union's involvement in the war, Malan's electoral victory filled South African Jewry with trepidation."[42] In 1948, in the run-up to national elections, the NP were silent about the Jewish Question, and did not ground their campaign on an anti-Semitic platform. On coming to power in 1948, anti-Semitic sentiment of Afrikaans nationalists was muted. A delegation of the JBD to

D. F. Malan, Prime Minister, in 1948 met with a denial of his party's anti-Semitism. To this extent, Jews were not to be treated the way the NP had several years earlier assured they would be, nor the way non-whites were to be treated under apartheid. That South African Jews were not to be discriminated against meant they were to be treated like white South Africans. Jews became white. They were, however, still not invited to become members of the NP in the Transvaal. This ban on Jewish membership was justified by J. G. Strydom, chairman of the party in the Transvaal, on the grounds that Jews could not be part of the development of Christian National culture. Strydom denied that this undermined "Jewish entitlement to full and equal rights of citizenship under a Christian National regime."[43] Sounding something like Groucho Marx, Strydom had earlier said that "decent Jews would not want to join a Christian party [like the Herenigde National Party] and such Jews as had so little decency as to want to join it—they did not want as members."[44] By 1951, however, Jews were entitled to join the National Party, and Malan put forward a definition of the pluralism of white South African society that included a place for Jews. Jews were no longer considered unassimilable into white South African society. In return for introduction into white South Africa, Jews were expected to understand Afrikaans inspiration and preservation of identity as a *volksgroep* (national group). Given this pro-Nazi history of the NP, and close to fifty years of activities designed by the JBD to secure a place of belonging for Jews already seen as not quite white (if at all), it is not surprising that the primary concern of the JBD in responding to the NP's election success in 1948 was to create a cordial relationship between the Jewish community and the Afrikaans nationalists, in order to secure Jewish interest.[45] The JBD responded to Jewish uncertainty of belonging within white South African society by actively discouraging Jews from criticizing government policy of opposing apartheid. This resulted in the denial by the leadership of the Jewish community in the possibility of a Jewish response to racism and apartheid.[46] The JBD referred back to their existing position of political noninvolvement to assert that Jews had no right as Jews to comment on politics, and that Jews who spoke out against the apartheid regime did so in their individual capacity only, and not as members of the Jewish community. The board, at its 1956 Congress, distanced itself from Jews who were politically engaged in opposing apartheid. They argued they were neither able nor willing to control the political freedom of the individual Jew, and that the Jewish community should also not be held responsible for the actions of individuals.[47]

Rabinowitz's discomfort with the attitudes of Jewish religious and secular leadership and the restraints these imposed on his own position is clear from a letter he wrote to the *Jewish Chronicle* of London, in which he explained his position within the South African Jewish community:

> In an atmosphere such as this the position of the rabbi becomes one of peculiar difficulty, which is well-nigh intolerable. No matter how rigidly he confines himself to the purely ethical and religious implications of the prevalent racial policy, the moment he utters a word which can be construed as a criticism of that policy he is immediately charged with "preaching politics." . . . The official policy of the South African Jewish Board of Deputies, which is that the Jewish community as such cannot express any view on the political situation since Jews belong to all parties, generously concedes the right of the rabbi to speak on its ethical aspects. In effect, however, this is widely interpreted not only that he should confine himself to pulpit utterances but that such pulpit utterances should not receive any publicity outside the pulpit. When, therefore, as often happens, the daily press finds a sermon on the political situation of sufficient general interest to warrant publication, there is a vague feeling that the rabbi has gone too far.[48]

A key strategy adopted by the leaders of the establishment Jewish community, in their efforts to establish cordial relations with Afrikaans nationalists, was the active and deliberate marginalization of Jews on the left, opposed to apartheid. These Jews, including people like Rabbi Andre Ungar (whom I discuss further on), and other antiapartheid figures such as the trade unionist Solly Sachs, and Communists Joe Slovo and Ruth First, could not be acknowledged as part of the Jewish community colluding with apartheid in the name of survival and economic privilege. Their activities were marginalized as private, outside of communal acceptance, as Rabinowitz makes clear: "There are some Jews in the community who do attempt to do something . . . and when, as a result, they fall foul of the powers that be the defence put up by the Jewish community is to prove that these are Jews only by name, that they do not belong to any synagogue," said Rabinowitz.[49] "Have Jewish ethics ever descended to a more shameful nadir?" he asked.[50]

Under the influence of the JBD's policy of political noninvolvement, Jewish history and theology became increasingly articulated through the prism of Afrikaans nationalism and racial domination. This is evident from South African Jewish literature, ranging from the historiography through to the fiction (both beyond the scope of this essay) as well as from the strength of South African Zionism and the parallels drawn by some between Jewish and Afrikaans desire for national independence and self-determination. Rabinowitz expressed his dissatisfaction with the Jewish Board of Deputies' policy of political noninvolvement, "insofar as it implied a denial of any collective view even on the purely moral dilemmas inherent in South African society" (282). His outspokenness won him strong disapproval, both within and without the Jewish community. The *South African Observer,* a pro-government newspaper, warned that "in using the synagogue to intrude Judaism's doctrine of 'absolute equality' into South Africa's political affairs," the rabbi was treading on dangerous ground, because it "appears to give the sanction of Judaism to the activities of the many Jews prominently associated with liberal, socialist and communist movements—the common denominator of all of which is 'absolute equality.'"[51] Shimoni has evidenced, also, the negative response of Rabinowitz's rabbinic colleagues, particularly that of Rabbi M. Kossowsky, himself leader of the Mizrachi Zionist Party, who "publicly dissociated himself from Rabinowitz's actions"[52] in a sermon delivered to his own congregation: "I thoroughly disapprove of involving the Synagogue and the Jewish community as a whole in activities which in any way bear a political character," he said.[53] "No political labels must be stuck onto our holy prayers. The pulpit as well as the Synagogue must be kept out of the political struggle."[54] Kossowsky internalized, within his sermonizing, the JBD's discouragement of Jewish political activity. It was attitudes like his that made Rabinowitz's position increasingly difficult, and he left South Africa in 1961. While Rabinowitz's active Zionism made emigration to Israel an obvious decision, there can be little doubt that the frustration he describes with South African Jewish leadership was a contributing factor. At any rate, he left before his insistence on social justice and the brotherhood of man could be fundamentally sullied by the prevailing sentiments of Kossowsky and his ilk.

RAPPAPORT: SHIFT FROM POLITICAL TO APOLITICAL, 1951–85

The same, however, cannot be said for another rabbi who, like Rabinowitz, insisted in the early 1950s on Judaism's belief in racial equality, and the need for rabbinic leadership to provide a message of justice to their communities. The writing of Rabbi Dr. Solomon Rappaport (1905–86) offers the best example of the impact of the influence of Afrikaans nationalism on South African Jewish consciousness, and serves as a textual bridge between the political outspokenness of Rabinowitz and the political quietism of Tatz. Rappaport, whose grandfather was Rabbi Solomon Juda Rappaport, founder of the Judische Wissenschaft,[55] grew up in Vienna, leaving Austria when the Nazis came into power in 1938. He served the South African Jewish community for over thirty-five years, during which time his preaching underwent significant change, along the lines of the "discretionary influence" of the JBD.

His *Rabbinic Thoughts on Race,*[56] written during the same period as Rabinowitz's "Brotherhood of Man" sermon, stands out in religious Jewish writing in South Africa as the most coherent and overt rabbinic condemnation of the ideology and politics of apartheid. Indicating that "the intricate problems of inter-racial adjustment, resulting from difference in colour is a comparatively new experience in Jewish life,"[57] Rabinowitz was unequivocal that "the teachings of Judaism leave no doubt that a pattern of race relations based on the theory of an ineradicable biological inferiority of one race is out of harmony with the ethical traditions of Biblical-Rabbinic doctrine."[58]

Like Rabinowitz, Rappaport spoke in terms of racial equality, unashamedly rejecting any differentiation between people on the basis of racial descent and biology. Another piece, published three years later, is equally important. "Judaism and Race Relations" appeared in 1954.[59] Addressing Jewish ministers, Rappaport reiterated his rejection of racism. All men, he said, are "equal in their spiritual essence, in the infinite wisdom of their individual souls and their relations to their Maker";[60] and "the value of a human being is not predetermined by birth, the individual is not valued according to race, sex, or social status."[61] Judaism was about religion and ethics, rather than blood and heritage. The seed of Abraham was a spiritual rather than biological category, and historical Jewish group-pride was not based on feelings of racial superiority, but on "the exalted consciousness of religious excellence."[62] Like Landau and Rabinowitz, Rappaport asserted the notion of the brotherhood of man as a fundamental Jewish precept: "It is fundamental Jewish teaching" he said, "that all men are descended from one ancestor and consequently no people or family can claim hereditary superiority over any other."[63] Bringing the notion of the brotherhood of man to bear on the political relation of the Jew, Rappaport argued that "Jews above others, should disdain the common *Herrenvolk* attitude of their environment": "Jews in general and representatives of Judaism in particular, should bear personal witness to the Hebraic belief that One God is the Father of all men who, beyond all differences of creed and race, partake of the same divine nature and human intelligence. Such an attitude is an unavoidable ethical consequence of the central religious teaching of Judaism: the belief in One God of Justice."[64] Rappaport's affirmation of the equality of all people, like that of Landau and Rabinowitz, involved an affirmation of the political, socially-oriented nature of Judaism. Of the three, he is perhaps clearest in his assertion of the Jewish imperative for social action, arguing that Judaism was a "total religion" which dominated the whole of individual and collective life. Introducing the essay with a quote from William Blake ("Are not Religion and Politics the same thing? Brotherhood is religion"),[65] Rappaport denied there could be a separation between religion and politics, and consequently between religious practice and the political pursuit for social justice:

> There may be in Christianity a case for separation between religion and politics, according to the verse: "Render unto Caesar the things which are Caesar's, unto the God the things which are God's." Judaism, however, has been emphatically concerned with the affairs of state and society, with a just social and economic order. In the Torah civil enactments are part of the Divine Law, which the prophets of Israel did not hesitate to rebuke kings and nobles for their social and political transgressions.[66]

The observance of Judaism, in Rappaport's scheme, necessitated active involvement in shaping society and economic conditions. Like Landau several decades earlier, Rappaport affirmed the socialist political forces which promoted conditions of justice and equity demanded by Jewish religious tradition. Like Rabinowitz, he brought the denial of a distinction between religion and politics directly to bear on the position of the Jew in racist South Africa: "The modern Synagogue can therefore not remain indifferent to the question of civil liberties, of wages and housings, of squalor and ill-health, of poverty and insecurity. Any religion worthy of survival in the modern world must have an attitude to all matters affecting the moral foundation of society; it is in duty bound to take the side of the under-privileged, and the disenfranchised, and demonstrate that nothing can be politically sound unless it is also morally right."[67] Rappaport challenged his rabbinic colleagues to engage with local problems of race. He denied that the absence of colored and non-European Jews in South Africa should preclude Jewish ministers from looking beyond the Jewish group, in order to define its attitude to race and to apply the teachings of Judaism to the question of racial equality.[68] It was the duty of the synagogue, he argued, to bring Jewish moral teachings to bear on all social issues, in order to improve the moral climate of the broader society. The Jewish minister had a duty to shake up Jewish complacency, and to make Jews "feel uncomfortable in their ready assimilation to the current racial attitudes of the dominant society."[69] The Jewish minister should encourage his community to participate in developing a just society, and to identify with "the struggle against injustice, ignorance, social and economic discrimination."[70]

The 1954 article was included in *Jewish Horizons*,[71] a collection of Rappaport's writing published in 1959. The book was reviewed in the *Sunday Express* newspaper in the middle of that year.[72] The review, running under the title "No strict Jew can be a Nat.—Rabbi," said that, "strictly speaking, no Jew should ever dream of applying for membership of the Nationalist Party, according to a distinguished Rabbi in a newly published book." Nervous perhaps at the fact of a wider audience than *Jewish Horizons* might have attracted, Rappaport lost little time in replying to the article. He objected to the "impression [it conveys] that in my recently published book I expressed opinions on the desirability or otherwise of Jews not joining one of the political parties of South Africa. In the interest of objective truth I wish to point out most emphatically that I nowhere express such opinions."[73] Emphasizing the part of the essay concerned with staying detached from the sullying influence of party politics, Rappaport succeeded in undermining the thrust of his essay, correctly highlighted by the reviewer, that Jews should avoid the racist politics of the National Party. This was entirely consistent with the JBD's denial that there could be a political Jewish position. Rappaport's early promotion of the brotherhood of man was visibly influenced by the internalizing of the JBD's denial of a Jewish response to apartheid, resulting in the privatizing of Judaism, and the shrinking of the space of the political in relation to the religious.

While this shift generally characterizes rabbinic writing under apartheid, as argued, it is most stark in Rappaport, whose career explicitly embodies the shift. And in the retrospective gaze of this reader, it was downhill from there. The fundamental shift in position characterizing his response becomes manifest several years later. Unnerved by developments in independent African countries in the sixties, Rappaport affirmed white supremacy in South Africa. According to Shimoni, he cautioned any rabbi who contemplated coming out to South Africa that he "will be unable to allay the anxieties of his flock by delivering sermons on the Fatherhood of God and the Brotherhood of Man,"[74] and noted that "while Jews wanted to keep their community separate, they could not deny this same right to the Afrikaner."[75]

In his 1966 High Holy Day sermon[76] to his Johannesburg congregation Rappaport eulogized Hendrik Verwoerd, architect of apartheid and prime motivator of the *Herrenvolk* mentality which Rappaport had not too long ago condemned. He again favorably compared Jews and Afrikaners, referring to them as "two small but indomitable nations"[77] which had tried to maintain their identity "in the face of superior numbers and more powerful cultures."[78] He compared Mount Herzl in Jerusalem with Heroes-Acre in Pretoria, describing them as mutually symbolic of the Afrikaans and Jewish "unquenchable longing for national independence."[79]

Rappaport's writing after this ceased to be characterized by his unequivocal emphasis on the relation between the political and the religious. Subsequent references to issues of social justice, like this one, are couched in ahistorical and biblical terms, their previous political resonances becoming increasingly rarified and abstruse. Writing, for example, in the middle of the State of Emergency, with the harshest government clampdown (at about the time Tatz was producing his illuminations), Rappaport preached a New Year's address, devoid of the outspoken, direct, politically charged tone of his earlier writing: "But the Hebrew prophets' attack on social injustice is much more direct, like Amos' condemnation of the rich who say, 'I will build me a wide house and spacious chambers, and it is sealed with cedars and painted with vermilion,' or of the businessmen who say, 'When will the new moon be gone, so that we may sell corn, and the Sabbath that we may set forth wheat, making the ephah small, and the shekel great, and selling the refuse of the wheat?'"[80]

In place of his earlier outward-looking emphasis on addressing immediate social inequalities and injustices is a self-referential frame of reference devoid of mention of the political chaos happening around him. The intricate relation between religion and politics asserted in the 1950s is replaced, such that religion is a necessary antidote to the turmoil produced in the social and political arena: "Men cannot live long without religion. In its absence a mood of disquiet and pessimism becomes common."[81] Like Tatz, Rappaport now offered religion as a solution to inner, existential, personal difficulties. Thus, Rappaport's views on the relation between religion and politics, and consequently of the role of Jews in challenging the racial status quo in South Africa, underwent an about-turn.

UNGAR AND SOUTH AFRICAN JEWISH MORAL ABDICATION

That this change was not spontaneous, but took place under and reflects the influence of South African Jewish communal politics fearful of a clampdown on the Jewish community by the Afrikaans nationalist government, is evident when considering Rappaport in relation to the story of another rabbi who had escaped Nazi Europe, and served a South African Jewish community. Rabbi Andre Ungar, a Hungarian, came to South Africa in 1955 to serve as rabbi of the Reform Congregation in Port Elizabeth. His political outspokenness and criticism of racist government policy soon got him embroiled with the Jewish community. Like his Orthodox colleagues Rabinowitz and Rappaport, Ungar was clear about the Jewish ministerial need to speak out from the pulpit against racism: "I consider it the duty of all men, especially of ministers of religion, to fight against prejudice, oppression and man's inhumanity to man wherever they are," he said in 1956.[82] And, indeed, Ungar spoke out strongly against apartheid. For instance, he criticized the government's refusal to issue a visa to a black student, Stephen Ramasodi, to take up a bursary to study in the United States:

> A young man, almost child, had his dreams of entering what, in his circumstances, must be the nearest equivalent of entering the Promised Land, most cruelly shattered. . . . The refusal came to Moses as a punishment for a sin he had committed. Ramasodi is innocent: unless it is a crime to be born dark-skinned. Moses had the comfort in his distress of knowing that this decree came from an all-wise and merciful God—the harsh verdict over this young man was passed by arrogantly puffed up little men in heartless stupidity.[83]

Interpreting South African race politics through reference to Jewish text (Deuteronomy 3:26), he compared the plight of Ramasodi, refused entry into the United States, and his future, with that of Moses, refused entry into the land of Canaan. On another occasion he interpreted it through reference to Jewish history, by criticizing the introduction in 1956 of the Group Areas Act, the cornerstone of apartheid legislation which segregated people's living space on the basis of race. Ungar compared the removal of communities from their homes into group areas with the construction of ghettos for Jews by the Nazis, including those in Hungary. He said that "Hitler is again on the march."[84] This sermon was described by the Afrikaans nationalist press as "'one of the most venomous attacks' made against the Group Areas plan."[85] Ungar was ordered by the minister of the interior, T. E. Donges, to leave South Africa. While he was already planning to leave, and while no reasons for the expulsion order were provided, Ungar interpreted the order as a response to his criticism of apartheid,[86] and consequently as an attempt to intimidate the Jewish community into silence.[87] Editorial opinion in newspapers around the country echoed these views.[88] The *Evening Post* suggested the expulsion was a warning to churches in general, and the Port Elizabeth synagogue in particular, that criticism would not be tolerated.[89] Ungar's criticism of apartheid policies elicited a strong and ugly response from members of the Jewish community who sought to dissociate themselves from his Jewish attack on the government.[90] "Jewish Reader," in a letter published in the Afrikaans *Die Oosterlig* newspaper, responded to his criticism by denying that his opinions represented those of South African Jews,[91] be they Reform or Orthodox. A. M. Spira, the chairman of the Eastern Province Committee of the Jewish Board of Deputies, immediately responded to the *Evening Post*'s editorial by denying that Donges's order was an intimidation of the Jewish community. He said that opinions in the Jewish community were diverse. Arguing along the lines of "Jewish Reader," he distanced the Jewish community from

Ungar's views. Ungar "spoke entirely as an individual—neither for his congregation nor for South African Jewry as a whole,"[92] he said. A letter carried in the *Jewish Review,* the newsletter of the Eastern Province Jewry, said Ungar's departure would be welcomed "with a sigh of relief."[93] S. Kluk, writing in *Die Oosterlig,* branded Ungar a "Communist" and a "false prophet," and claimed that the majority of South African Jews, irrespective of political affiliation, "loyally support the Government in its efforts to secure the future for the European minority in South Africa."[94] All these responses reflect the JBD's denial of a political position for Jews, the fear underlying their efforts to establish cordial relations with the National Party government, and their marginalizing of any Jew who spoke out against the apartheid regime. This involved the privatizing and individualizing of a political response.

"RESPONSIBLE LEADERSHIP": TACIT AND ACTIVE SUPPORT FOR APARTHEID

The Board's insistence on political noninvolvement, and the need for what they deemed "responsible leadership" that wouldn't rock the boat is strongly evidenced in the writing of Rabbis Bernard Casper (1917–86) and Nochim Leib Marcus (1915–86). Casper's book, *A Decade with South African Jewry,*[95] provides an illuminating text with which to consider the shift in rabbinic thoughts on race and the religious and general role of Jews in South Africa. Casper had moments of political outspokenness. In 1970, for instance, he delivered an address on the question of detention without trial, and defended the rule of law, at a public meeting organized by the Christian Church Council. While the speech is interesting in and of itself for its criticism by a rabbi of government policy, it serves to highlight even more strongly the absence of political vision in any of his other writings. It suggests that politics were kept within the sphere of public meetings and were entirely removed from any religious context. This is a marked shift from understandings of the relation between religion and politics in the writing of Landau and Rabinowitz, and the earlier writing of Rappaport.

Speaking in 1964 on the occasion of the Golden Jubilee of the Great Synagogue in Johannesburg, Casper outlined the achievements and goals of the South African Jewish community, including the work of the JBD, the Board of Education, the Zionist Federation and the Beth Din. There is a singular absence of reference to or mention of any reality prevailing in the country outside the parochial, self-referential bounds of the Jewish community. Instead he is thankful for the "daylight of liberty and tolerance and opportunity that have attended the Jew in this land."[96] Landau's assertion of the religious need for social and political engagement was replaced by an insular, inward-looking, self-satisfied Jewish community. Instead, the only role for Jews, according to Casper, was a religious one, in a framework devoid of any reference to a political arena. He, like the JBD, dismissed any Jew concerned with activities not defined as Jewish, that is, religious. Casper maligned any attempt by Jews, of which there were many, to move beyond the narrow bounds of the Jewish community. Those Jews become the "keepers of the vineyards' of others."[97] Not only must Jews not get involved in any other arena, including that of political opposition to racism and apartheid, he argued, but they must take advantage of the ethnic separatist circumstances in South Africa to strengthen Jewish life: "When we think of the superhuman efforts made by Jews in Russia to preserve some part of our heritage, some link with our history and literature, are we not doubly beholden to take advantage of the conditions of religious freedom we happily enjoy in this country to practice the faith of our father and ensure that it be also the faith of our children?"[98] Thus, Casper affirmed the promotion of Jewish group preservation under the ethnic separatist conditions of apartheid. Not only did he discourage Jewish criticism of its racist philosophy and consequences, but he affirmed their impact on Jewish life.

Similarly, the theology of Rabbi N. L. Marcus, in *Around the Tents of the Torah,*[99] is informed by group interest promoted by apartheid, and evidences the Jewish internalization of apartheid discourse and ideology. Like Casper and the JBD, he actively marginalized Jews opposing the state: "We have had many Jewish revolutionaries and fighters for freedom and justice, but they have used their energies and capabilities to free and liberate other nations. Their own race and people they ignored completely. They have brought sacrifices on the altars of nations, who later rejected them, but have intentionally forgotten their own cause and future."[100] Adopting the language and logic of apartheid's "own affairs," Marcus dismissed the Jewishness of people pursuing social justice for "other nations," which in the South African context referred to the antiapartheid pursuit of justice on behalf of black South Africans. Gone is Landau's praise for Lassalle as a Jewish revolutionary fighting for social justice; and Rabinowitz's, Rappaport's and Ungar's promotion of social justice for all irrespective of race. Elsewhere Marcus actively encouraged support for the apartheid police state, pursuing a policy of law and order by oppression of the black majority:

> "Judges and officers shalt thou make for thee." The expression "for thee" may be explained as "for your benefit." Meaning that if you will appoint the cor-

> rect judges then you will live in peace and happiness; order and discipline will prevail in the land. Our Rabbis state (Ethics 3–2)—"Pray for the welfare of the government, since but for the fear thereof men would swallow each other alive." The proper duty of the police is to restrain and if necessary punish the criminals. . . . "Which the Lord is giving to your tribes." The verse continues in the singular, to emphasise that each tribe has to consider himself a partner in the establishment, welfare and security of the country.[101]

Jews, as a "tribe," must pray for the welfare of the apartheid government, rather than oppose its racism and brutality. Here Marcus speaks the language of paranoid white South Africa, supporting state oppression of the black majority in the name of law and order. Put simply, Marcus's sermon must be read as an Jewish apology for apartheid's protection of white, minority interests and privilege.

The JBD's denial that there could be a communal response to apartheid, formulated and promoted in response to the NP's history of anti-Semitism, resulted in the increasing interpretation of Judaism as having no message for South African politics. Landau's assertion of the inextricable relation between religion and politics, and of the brotherhood of man, became meaningless. The shift in Rappaport's writing is the clearest example of this. Rappaport had started out by affirming both the need for political engagement and to oppose racism and discrimination in South Africa. He, like Casper, Marcus and many others not mentioned here, ended up actively supporting the ethnic separatist ideology of Afrikaans nationalism and, through his silence on the political travesty taking place around him, implicitly supporting the apartheid regime. The shift took place within a short time, between the first publication of his 1954 essay and the review of its second publication five years later. In the intervening years, Rabinowitz quit, Ungar had been thrown out of the country, and the JBD, in establishing cordial relations and securing Jewish communal with the previously pro-Nazi National Party, had denied the possibility of a communal response to apartheid. The shift in Rappaport's writing consequently mirrors the JBD's position of cordial relations with the apartheid regime, and of political noninvolvement. It evidences the impact of these positions on South African Jewish cultural and religious expression. This impact on communal Jewish South African expression resulted in and is epitomized by Tatz's mystical, apolitical formula for living with the anxiety produced by life under apartheid.

While there are many South African rabbis unconsidered in this essay there is one whose life profoundly touched mine. Rabbi Norman Bernhard, of Oxford Shul in Johannesburg, came to South Africa from America in 1965. Bernhard believes himself, in spite of pressure from the state, to have been a strong and consistent critic of the National Party and of apartheid: "Several visits by the security police, who I knew were monitoring me, and even being twice ordered to leave the country, did not intimidate or inhibit me, and brought about no changes whatsoever in the tone or direction of my antiapartheid sermons or talks,"[102] he recently asserted. The truth, for complex reasons, is much less clear than that. Benjamin Pogrund, journalist and antiapartheid activist, initially in an unpublished interview with this author and subsequently in the course of the extensive correspondence responding to my *Mail and Guardian* article, attributes the demise of his friendship with Bernard to the latter's acceptance of government intervention: "Months later, I met him by chance and he explained his mysterious disappearance from my life: his work permit had been withdrawn, and he had learnt from government officials that it was because of his sermons against apartheid and his friendship with me."[103] Pogrund describes sitting on one side of Oxford Shul, with Percy Yutar on the other. Yutar, an observant Jew, was treasurer and president of the United Hebrew Congregation of Johannesburg.[104] He was also, at one point, president of the South African Jewish Education Fund Drive. In this context he said that "he firmly believed the survival of the Jewish community depended largely on the soundness of the Hebrew and Jewish education of its youth."[105] In 1966 the United Hebrew Congregation helped to establish a new Jewish day school. Located on the grounds of Oxford Shul, Bernhard was its director. On the school's tenth anniversary, in 1976, Bernhard thanked the United Hebrew Congregation, including its "past and present leaders and office staff," presumably including Yutar, for facilitating the establishment and running of the Menora Primary School,[106] "perhaps just to humour me, but by now because they have long since come to be proud of the Menora Primary School as the most vivid fulfillment of the Congregation's highest constitutional aims and purposes."[107] Presumably Yutar—both an active member of Bernard's congregation, and involved with developing Jewish education as a survival strategy for the Jewish community—was supportive of the establishment of the Menora Primary School.

I was one of children enrolled at the school, from 1972 to 1979. I was nine years old when the school turned ten in 1976, a year better remembered for the Soweto riots when people at the same age were active in the student uprising against apartheid education, in which they were taught in Afrikaans. Many kids were killed. Others soon went into exile and joined UmKhonto We Sizwe, the armed wing of the ANC, where they fought and many died. I, on the other hand, was studying *chumash* (Bible). Apart from the phone call from an uncle in England (who had emigrated years before) asking if we were okay, as it looked, on the BBC, like Johannesburg was going up in smoke, and apart from the subliminal fears, I was clueless as to what was going on. My mind was full of obscure, biblical bits of information and methodology (some of which has stood me in good, textual stead, so can't be entirely regretted). It was presented as everything, as all-consuming world reference. Turn it over and over for all is in it. Well, not quite, as it turns out. My *chumash* notebook from Standard Three, in 1978, is oddly illuminating. It tells several quirky stories, but none I expected to encounter one evening recently when my brother Hillel and I looked at them for a playful insight into what our heads were being filled with. Rabbi Warshawsky was my *chumash* teacher. Sometimes he'd play his accordion, and sing with zeal; other times he'd cane Davey B. and Michael H. for picking fights with his daughter Chana (she could fend for herself—one day she got rid of a burglar in the house by brandishing a bread knife in his direction). Warshawsky set a weekly *chumash* test with revealing questions like, "What were the two reasons that Yisro didn't want to go with the Jews to Eretz Yisroel [the land of Israel]?" The notebook documents my (apparently correct) answer: "1. He wanted to go to his land to sell his property. 2. He wanted to go to his birthplace to convert his family." And, "The *Aron* [ark] went ahead three days 'to fix for them rest.' What does this mean?" And the answer: "It means to make the place ready for the Bnei Yisrael so they won't have to work to get things organised," not an insignificant response, given white South African dependence on black domestic help.

The notebooks are old, the paper glue past its due date, crumbling off the page. I play with the sheet fallen out, till my eyes focus on the back of the page. An Oxford Shul letter. The school shared facilities, and the *chumash* test was printed on paper recycled from the shul: "Bnot Oxford invites you to a stimulating and thought-provoking lecture and discussion by Tammy Wolpert Psychologist. Topic: Communication: Parent/Child Relationships. Leading to Jewish and Afrikaans Youth—Similarities and Differences. To take place in the Minor Hall, Oxford Synagogue, on 23rd August 1978 at 8.00 pm. Tea and cake will be served." On the flipside of the page. Same sheet of paper. On the one side the minutiae of self-referential biblical studies, devoid of any reference to anything historical, let alone political. On the other side the real story: the similarities and differences between Afrikaans and Jewish youths. The ethnic separatism and group consciousness implicit in the question and the comparison becomes pedagogical pursuits on the other side of the page. In other words, my Jewish education was the direct product of the desire of the apartheid state to promote ethnic separatism. In spite of assertions of critical distance from the pressures and imperatives of the apartheid state, the South African Jewish establishment, like much of white South Africa, internalized the values and ideology of apartheid and ethnic separatism. The terms and discourse of apartheid fast became appropriated within all areas of Jewish life and consciousness. This is as true for the rabbinic output of Tatz as it is for the Jewish education at Menora Oxford. Both were equally and similarly (and invisibly) the result of a fearful confrontation with Afrikaans nationalism. The more Judaism and Jewish life were interpreted as apolitical, devoid of any critical response to racism and social inequality, the more they responded to and were influenced by apartheid. In other words, the less visible their contact with the political realities and ideology of Afrikaans nationalism, the stronger their connection.

This examination of South African rabbinic writing, by no means exhaustive, serves as something of a case study for South African Jewish history and consciousness as it encountered Afrikaans nationalism, an encounter of a (Jewish) minority among a (white) minority. The shrunken space of the political within the religious sphere, as traced in this essay, was a consequence of the active discouraging of Jews from opposing the racist policies of the National Party, in an effort to secure a cordial relationship with the apartheid government. It can be seen as a "Zionist" model of rabbinics, in the way it directly parallels the denial of a politically meaningful space for Jews in the Diaspora, including South Africa, both in the deferral away from South Africa to Israel (as by Kossowsky) or to an otherworldly sphere (as by Tatz). A deferral motivated not so much by Jewish theology per se, as by fear of reprisal from the Afrikaans nationalist government. Thus, even Zionist expression in South Africa was motivated, in part, by the encounter with Afrikaans nationalism. Shimoni has demonstrated the close relationships that existed between the JBD, concerned primarily with issues of local concern, and the South African Zionist Federation, focussing on issues of Zionist concern. This closeness was premised on the sympathy of the JBD to the Zionist cause, a sympathy not only motivated by interest in the growth and affairs of the Jewish state. It also coincided exactly with the Board's refusal to get involved in matters of South African concern, for reasons not dissimilar to those that motivated belief in Zionist ideology. The JBD, which did not necessarily promote Zionism, nevertheless functioned within a similar frame of reference, such that the only cure for anti-Semitism in South Africa was keeping the low kind of political profile deemed suitable to the vulnerable position of Jews in the Diaspora. So while it wasn't overtly Zionist, the political assumptions on which it was founded were closely related, and had much the same consequence for the self-perception and expression of South African Jewry. Zionism didn't offer a viable alternative to life in South Africa. It did succeed in providing a "political dimension of cultural life, in the form of the political party divisions within Zionism."[108] Thus, South African Jewish communal activity was channeled in a Zionist direction, rather than engaging with local politics, of which there was no shortage. While ostensibly strong, South African Zionism was deeply ambivalent, caught between the notion of *aliyah* (emigration to Israel) as its ultimate goal, and the daily reality of a good and comfortable life in South Africa.[109] South African Zionism was often less about living in Israel than it was about denying a political life in South Africa. As such, it was arguably one collusional tool in Jewish consciousness under apartheid. It functioned to discourage South African Jews from opposing the racist policies of the National Party and the government. In promoting the belief that Jews in the Diaspora live under the watchful hospitality of their gentile hosts, South African Jews were actively discouraged from feeling the kind of belonging that could accommodate criticism, including criticizing the politics of the apartheid regime.

My reasons for referring to my brother Jake at the beginning of this paper are not entirely autobiographical. Jake has a soulmate in Kinky Friedman, working in a white supremacist environment in Texas, asserting, as Seth Wolitz argued in his contribution to this volume, the egalitarianism of a third-generation Jew operating in the broader cultural life of a state and nation. Like Jake, being myself fourth-generation, I believe in the need of a public-oriented representation, rather than the invisibility affirmed by my parents' and grandparents' generations. As in the life of South Africa generally it is time for the skeletons to come out the closet, in order for there to be an assessment of the location of Jewish identity within broader post-apartheid South African identity. A truly post-apartheid Jewish identity will be one that no longer looks over shoulders, but that feels secure enough to confront the unspoken fears of the past, and to participate fully in the life of the new South African nation. For this to be possible it will be necessary to interrogate the surface facts that constitute the collective memory of the South African Jewish community. It will require something of an internal Truth and Reconciliation Commission, motivated by the desire for self-insight that comes with truth, knowledge and understanding, as is happening elsewhere in South African society. It will be necessary to examine what role the Jewish community played in participating in and benefiting from life under apartheid, and how Judaism, Jewish history, and Zionist ideology were used to this end. It will be necessary to examine how Judaism was affected by apartheid, what interventions were made that resulted in the theological shifts I have demarcated, and who was responsible for these. It will be necessary to know how educational policy was informed by desires to toe the ethnic separatist line, including the role played by Jewish Studies at a tertiary level; and why some aspects of South African Jewish literature, history and politics were promoted while others were silenced in the production of South African Jewish knowledge. It will be necessary to know what deals were cut with the apartheid regime; what role the Zionist Federation played with regard to military links between South Africa and Israel; what role kosher kitchens and Jewish units served in the South African Defence Force; how Afrikaans nationalism interacted with Jewish nationalism to produce right-wing Zionist youth movements; what the role of the Jewish press was. Like South African society in general, the contemporary Jewish community needs to understand its origins. It needs to restore memory to the hidden fear of Afrikaans nationalism that informed the development of South African Jewish consciousness and social organization. It needs to understand why the only successful South African Jew is one who lives in Jerusalem or Sydney or Chicago; and why some members of the Jewish community are more right-wing, sexist, and homophobic than your average white South African; why it's still acceptable in some circles to talk about the "shochs" and the "schwarzes,"[110] and why it ever was. It will be necessary also to celebrate the demise of white supremacy that continued to query in subliminal and complex ways the right of Jews to belong. Taking the debate beyond the careers and perceptions of one or two prominent leaders of the South African Jewish community (Yutar, Bernhard) in order to examine the systemic nature of the impact of the fear of Afrikaans nationalism is necessary to arrive at a truth that will allow real integration into a society based on nonracism and a Bill of Rights culture, uncluttered by a continued investment in dynamics and concerns given life under a white supremacist state.

There are hopeful signs that the tradition of Landau, Rabinowitz and Ungar is being reinvigorated in South Africa. The writing of Rabbi Cyril Harris[111] offers the first indication of a post-apartheid rabbinic position. He himself offers a Judaism distanced from its apartheid treatments, which he characterizes as concentrating on interpretations of Jewish tradition which "stress the disharmony between Jew and non-Jew."[112] The deemphasis during the apartheid era of Jewish teachings concerned with "the duties towards fellow human-beings,"[113] with the brotherhood of man, resulted in disillusionment on the part of "a significant number of young Jews with a social conscience,"[114] says Harris: "It is therefore essential in the post-apartheid era that the Jewish ideological vision, urging input towards social development, be forthrightly stated. How Jewish teachings concerning involvement in the well-being of the non-Jew can be applied in positive manner in our own times, must become the focus of urgent and frank debate in our own community."[115]

Notes

1. Similarly, politician Harry Schwarz, writing subsequently about Jews and apartheid, said "the attitude of Jews was reflected in their communal stance and their official pronouncements, which seemed to return to the principle that had characterised their conduct during the Middle Ages—to keep on good terms with the rulers" ("Jewish Modes of Opposition," *Jewish Affairs* 52.1 [Autumn 1997]: 38).

2. Hanns Saenger and Joseph Sherman, "Shouting from the Grandstand: By Way of an Afterword," *Jewish Affairs* 52.1 (Autumn 1997): 82.

3. As editor of *Jewish Affairs*, Sherman was implicitly justifying his rejection of my essay, which had been written for *Jewish Affairs*. I subsequently resigned from the editorial board of the magazine.

3. Akiva Tatz, *Living Inspired* (Michigan: Targum Press, 1993).

4. Ibid., acknowledgments.

5. Ibid., 11.

7. Ibid., 110.

8. Ibid., 51.

9. Ibid.

10. Ibid.

11. Ibid., 110.

12. Ibid.

13. Ibid., 12.

14. Ibid., 38.

15. Ibid., 208–9.

16. Ibid., 208.

17. Ibid., 170–73.

18. Ibid., 102.

19. Ibid., 101.

20. Ibid.

21. Ibid., 101–2.

22. In J. L. Landau, *Judaism in Life and Literature* (London: Edward Goldston, 1936).

23. Ibid., 36–39.

24. Ibid., 44.

25. Ibid., 39.

26. In Landau, *Judaism in Life and Literature.*

27. Ibid., 127.

28. In Landau, *Judaism in Life and Literature.*

29. Ibid., 264.

30. Ibid.

31. Ibid.

32. Ibid., 290.
33. Louis Rabinowitz, *Out of the Depths: Sermons for Sabbaths and Festivals* (Johannesburg: Eagle Press, 1952).
34. Ibid., 12.
35. Ibid.
36. Ibid.
37. Ibid., 12–13 (emphasis added).
38. Ibid., 68–69.
39. Gideon Shimoni, *Jews and Zionism: The South African Experience, 1910–1967* (Cape Town: Oxford University Press, 1980), 282.
40. Ibid., 277.
41. Patrick Furlong, *Between Crown and Swastika: The Impact of the Radical Right on the Afrikaner Nationalist Movement in the Fascist Era* (Johannesburg: Witwatersrand University Press, 1991).
42. Marcus Arkin, ed., *South African Jewry: A Contemporary Survey* (Cape Town: Oxford University Press, 1984), 10.
43. Quoted in Shimoni, *Jews and Zionism,* 211.
44. Ibid.
45. Ibid., 224.
46. *Jewish Affairs* (June 1958).
47. Shimoni, *Jews and Zionism,* 276.
48. Quoted in ibid., 283.
49. Ibid., 283–84.
50. Ibid.
51. Ibid., 282.
52. Ibid., 283.
53. Quoted in ibid., 283.
54. Ibid.
55. *South African Jewish Times,* Apr. 14, 1949.
56. S. Rappaport, *Rabbinic Thoughts on Race* (Johannesburg: Electric Printing Works, 1951).
57. Ibid., 38.
58. Ibid.
59. "Judaism and Race Relations," in *Hashachar: A Collection of Addresses, Essays, and Articles,* ed. L. I. Rabinowitz (Johannesburg: South African Jewish Ministers' Association, 1954).
60. Ibid., 65.
61. Ibid., 66.
62. Ibid.
63. Ibid.
64. Ibid., 69.
65. Ibid., 61.
66. Ibid., 61.
67. Ibid., 63–64.
68. Ibid., 61–62.
69. Ibid., 69.
70. Ibid.

71. Solomon Rappaport, *Jewish Horizons* (Johannesburg: B'nai B'rith, 1959).
72. *Sunday Express,* Aug. 12, 1959.
73. *Sunday Express,* Aug. 30, 1959.
74. Quoted in Shimoni, *Jews and Zionism,* 285.
75. Ibid.
76. *Zionist Record,* Sept. 28, 1966.
77. Ibid.
78. Ibid.
79. Ibid.
80. Combined New Year annual issue of *Zionist Record* and *South African Jewish Chronicle,* Sept. 6, 1985.
81. Ibid.
82. *Eastern Province Herald,* Dec. 10, 1956.
83. *Eastern Province Herald,* July 30, 1955.
84. *Evening Post,* Dec. 10, 1956.
85. Ibid.
86. *Cape Times,* Dec. 10, 1956.
87. *Evening Post,* Dec. 10, 1956.
88. See *The Star,* Dec. 10, 1956; *Evening Post,* Dec. 10, 1956.
89. *Evening Post,* Dec. 10, 1956.
90. Letter to *Die Oosterlig* from "Jewish Reader," Aug. 3, 1955, copy in JBD Archives, Johannesburg.
91. Ibid.
92. *Evening Post,* Dec. 14, 1956.
93. *Jewish Review,* Dec. 1956.
94. Letter from S. Kluk, *Die Oosterlig,* Jan. 22, 1957.
95. Bernard Moses Casper, *A Decade with South African Jewry* (Cape Town: Howard Timmins, 1972).
96. Ibid., 63.
97. Ibid., 121.
98. Ibid., 121–22.
99. N. L. Marcus, *Around the Tents of the Torah: Commentary on the Bible* (Cape Town: privately published, 1973).
100. Ibid., 138.
101. Ibid., 154–55.
102. Letter from Norman Bernhard, *Mail and Guardian,* Apr. 11–17, 1997.
103. Letter from Benjamin Pogrund, *Mail and Guardian,* Apr. 18–24, 1997).
104. Leon Feldberg, ed., *South African Jewry, 1965* (Johannesburg: Fieldhill Publishing Co., 1965), 415.
105. *South African Jewish Times,* Nov. 21, 1958.
106. Menora Oxford Primary School, tenth anniversary volume, author's private collection.
107. Ibid.
108. Shimoni, *Jews and Zionism,* 34.
109. Ibid., 267.
110. Pejorative Yiddish names for people of color.

111. Rabbi C. K. Harris, *Jewish Obligation to the Non-Jew* (Johannesburg: Tikkun Publications, 1996).
112. Ibid., 3.
113. Ibid.
114. Ibid.
115. Ibid.

12 Writing Oneself at the Frontier: Jewishness and Otherness in Albert Memmi's *La Statue de Sel*

HEIDI GRUNEBAUM-RALPH

In the light of Sander Gilman's theorization of the frontier as a conceptual model for the examination of Jewish identity and history, I would like to precede the introduction to my subject proper with a meditation on the project of the Truth and Reconciliation Commission (TRC) in South Africa. Although the present article examines representations of identity, writing, and the colonial experience, my gesture to the public memorial process symbolized by the TRC in South Africa calls attention to a different context, although a no less symbolic threshold, against which this present meditation was formulated. In South Africa, the Commission's tasks represent the beginning of an endeavor which seeks to listen to the impact of colonial rule on the emerging stories of personal and collective histories of violence, oppression, torture, shattered lives, and survival which are being constituted at a new narrative frontier within the country. This is significant because central to the forging of a public discourse on memory and history—initiated within the space of the Truth and Reconciliation Commission—is the question of self-representation. Thus, the powerful symbolism of the frontier, as formulated by Gilman, contextualized as a site where memory-work is consecrated, can hardly be lost at a moment of rethinking the way that people imagine themselves and one another, of reexamining the impact of the colonial experience on the imagination of identity and its sociocultural constructions.

Written against the backdrop of an ongoing involvement with the historical process of a post-apartheid recovery of historically silenced voices, this article examines the way that a double consciousness of identity, legacy of the colonial encounter, informs Albert Memmi's autobiographical text, *La statue de sel.*[1] To examine how Memmi imagines himself without placing the reading of his text within a context which has impacted on understandings of the production of personal histories is to ignore the complex relationship between identity, memory, self-representation and the politics and history of a writing and a reading; a relationship which the text itself bears out.

Memmi's text emerges from a vision of the personal in relationship and engaged with the world. In this case, interrogating the discursive boundaries of identity becomes inextricably linked to interrogating the ways that these boundaries are historically constituted. Moreover, the symbolic location of this examination—at the intersection of the conceptual frontiers of the personal and collective—reflects the reciprocal impact and profound embeddedness of the individual within their social, political, cultural, and historical context and how these contexts affect the way that knowledge (self-knowledge, in this case) is produced. Indeed, in the preface to *La statue de sel,* Albert Camus goes as far as to suggest that the inner turmoil reflected in Memmi's formulation of identity mirrors the contradictory social and political realities of North Africa (10).

"I cannot know *who* I am," Memmi has written, "[but] through successive accumulations, I could know *how* I am."[2] It would seem, then, that in order to examine *how* Memmi's narrative reveals a specific self-understanding of Jewishness in a colonial society, it is imperative to examine these expressions as they are historically subjected to, constituted by, and reflective of the dominant discursive models; the same conformations set up within South Africa, for example, by race-obsessed discourse.[3] As Claudia Braude demonstrates, the discursive formations of "race" have directly impacted on Jewish self-representation and self-understanding and are therefore central to the way that these self-representations are constructed within a South African context. Whereas Braude locates her concerns within that context, the focus of the present article shifts to North Africa, to Tunisia, where the colonial encounter, with the its projections, fantasies, and scandals of difference, underpins Memmi's literary search for an essentialist identity. Through its examination of the construction and interpellation of identity in *La statue de sel,* this article aims to explore whether Africa—designated as a historically problematic site of Otherness by colonial and neocolonial discourse—can be examined as a conceptual framework which impacts on the reading of texts by Jewish writers who interrogate their origins and identities, and who write in Africa and in relation to that space.[4]

MEMMI'S FRONTIER: SHIFTING BORDERS, DISTORTING MIRRORS

Briefly, Memmi's autobiography is formulated as a historically chronological flashback presented as a meditation while sitting for a philosophy examination. At the threshold of this symbolic rite of passage, he calls his identity and its production into question. Each narrative segment is organized around an anecdote which becomes a metaphor for memory and the processes of its narration. Through its recollections of childhood and adolescent memories, this autobiographical novel traces the vicissitudes of the protagonist (fictionally named Alexander Mordechai Benillouche) in Tunisia from early childhood, living, significantly, on the borders of both the Jewish and Muslim quarters at a cul-de-sac on the Rue Tarfoune. It describes his education at the Alliance Israélite of Tunis and his family's material poverty; his intellectual formation, academic achievements and ambitions; the experience of his emerging sexuality; the rejection of his family and their traditions. It recounts his perceptions of the dichotomies of colonial society as a victim of both colonial and anti-Semitic racism: the witnessing of anti-Semitic pogroms in Tunis; his detention in and escape from a Tunisian labor camp during World War II; the rejection by the Free French government of his voluntary conscription because of his Jewish name. The narrative closes when the first-person narrator decides not to complete the philosophy examination and ends when he departs from Tunisia for Argentina.

By writing literally "out of Africa" as a way of looking back and of tracing the origins of an identity in crisis, Memmi writes Africanness, Arabness and Jewishness into his text as effaced identities. Indeed, it is through Memmi's retrospective gaze that North Africa, itself, is shown as a "non-space," a silence resisting the inscription of the text through a narrative which simultaneously presents its protagonist as progressively dispossessed of all identity.

Within the colonial paradigm the layers of subjective voices which inform identity are bound to be formulated in terms of the power-relations generated by the politics of identity; hence, subjectivity in this text is formulated in terms of binary oppositions. By representing these binaries as mutually exclusive dichotomies, such as when Memmi states that "between the Orient and the West, between African beliefs and philosophy, between *patois* and French, I had to choose" (247), he emphatically banishes the possibility of the reconciled, idealized difference of hybrid (and hyphenated) identities. In this interrogation of the origin of ontological alienation—within an already problematized discourse of linguistic, ethnic and cultural identities of the referential site of Africa—the search for subjectively constructed identity emerges rather as perpetual displacement. Thus, read against Gilman's assertion that the frontier model of Jewish history becomes the space of confluence and separation, where multiple discourses emerge and "the complex interaction of the definitions of self and Other are able to be constructed," Memmi's text finds particular resonance. Here, the paradigms of racism, of anti-Semitism, cast through the optic of colonial experience, are inscribed in and reinscribe definitions of self and Other in a narrative which constantly repositions and displaces these two categories. In this way the writing project itself becomes a writing of the perpetual dislocation which the (post)colonial condition has come to represent. Identity as radical displacement is manifested through a narrative genre which traditionally claims a stable and linear identity for its subject: autobiography. In this instance, however, generic form shapes crisis and threatens this endeavor of self-representation. As such, in Memmi's attempts to trace the origins of an identity in conflict, his text testifies to a sustained displacement enacted in the very description of that identity. Such a crisis is played out through the subversion of autobiography as a project of symbolic recovery of a stable relationship between the experience of one's subjectivity and its representation. Memmi rewrites Livia Käthe Wittmann's assertion in her contribution to this volume that to "[live] with the differences within, that is, accepting multiple discourses shaping one's subjectivity and giving meaning to one's multiple identities, is one thing, while living comfortably with socially inclusive or exclusive cultural representations defined by others is another." In *La statue de sel,* identity is primarily formulated in terms of those inclusive or exclusive representations which are defined by others. That formulation is, in turn, the meaning-producing determinant of the multiple discourses which underscore identity. It is in the *writing* of the contradictions of identity, defined elsewhere and constituted within the colonized space of North Africa, that the complexity of this predicament comes to be highlighted, since within the dichotomizing oppositions of anti-Semitic and colonial discourse it is the successive representations of subjectivity as the oppressed, colonized North-African, Arab, Jewish Other followed by a rejection of these internal categories which characterizes Memmi's text. In this way, the text constructs an impossible formulation of personal identity based on successive rejection, revolt, recuperation, and rejection, so that when definitions of identity reject the corresponding inscription of the Other the narrator describes this experience of split consciousness as a wounding: an "irremediable mutilation" (42) of Self and a "strangeness of being" (25).

AUTOBIOGRAPHY, PATRIARCHY, AND DISPLACEMENT OF THE NAME

The narrative emplotment which traces the narrator's rejection of his family, environment, culture, and tradition, followed by his embrace and internalization of a Western European cultural model and then his rejection of this model functions as an attempt to restore a specifically patriarchal model of memory. Here, autobiography becomes a recovery of personal history which is signified by the displaced memory of the Father. Indeed, the text is even dedicated to Memmi's father, to both the real and symbolic Father. It is as the story of the narrator's name that this project of paternal recuperation is narrated.

Referring to the symbolic and physical topographical border where the narrator passes his childhood, the first section of the text, which is entitled *L'impasse* (cul-de-sac or dead end), sketches the family-life and childhood spent at the border of both Jewish and Muslim Arab quarters. This particular topography is significant in that it symbolizes the multiple straddlings which will characterize the narrator's life. Home and birthplace at the cul-de-sac, a border space in Rue Tarfoune, are significantly designated metonymically throughout the narrative as *L'impasse.* Interestingly, it is the proper name of the first-person narrator which is revealed as the symbolic site of dislocation. The impasse of the birthplace is prefigured by an impasse of the patrimonial legacy, the name: sign and signature which here places the individual within a patriarchal tradition, a male narrative, and which announces the reciprocal inscription of the individual within language, culture. Within the text, the central chapter bearing the name of the protagonist is structurally and conceptually the turning point. It is this name which locates and symbolizes the fracture of his identity, an observation which is echoed by the narrator's claim that "if I believed in signs, wouldn't I be able to say that my name already contained the meaning of my life? How could I create a synthesis, as refined as the sound of a flute, from so many disparities?" (109).

Identity uttered in the internalized terms of the Other, that is, in terms of a perpetual provisionality—the enacted marginalization of difference—is signed by the name, mark of origin par excellence. If the name is the symbolic frontier of identity formulation, an examination of the etymology of the autobiographical narrator's name, Alexander Mordechai Benillouche, bears this out:

> My name is Mordechai, Alexander Benillouche. . . . At the Impasse, at the Alliance, I ignored that I bore such a ridiculous, such a revealing name. . . .
>
> Alexander: resonant, glorious, was given to me by my parents in homage to the prestigious West. To them, it appeared to translate the image which they had of Europe. The students sniggered, making Alexander burst out like a trumpet blast: Alexan-nder! Then, I hated my first name with all my heart and my fellow students as well. I hated them and I thought them right, and I resented my parents for this stupid choice.
>
> Mordechai, Mridach in diminutive, marked my participation in Jewish tradition. That was the fearsome name of a glorious Maccabbee, as well as that of my grandfather, frail old man, who never forgot the terror of the ghetto. . . .
>
> Mordechai, Alexander, Benillouche, Benillouche finally, Ben-Illouch or the son of the lamb in berber-arabic patois. From which highland tribe did my ancestors come? In short, who am I? (107–9)

In this quest for a genealogy which would confer the desired metanarrative of self-definition, a subtext of ontological anxiety emerges. This subtext is clearly shaped by the internalized conflict perpetually played out within the ordering of the colonial paradigms: between dichotomized positionings of language, culture, and ethnicity. By juxtaposing the family name as the subverted patriarchal referent of ontogenesis ("son of the lamb"), with the interpositioned Jewish name and with "Alexander," symbol of conquest, indelible trace of Europe on Africa, identity is literally "named" as a destabilizing representation of difference. Interestingly, *louche* (French word meaning suspicious, dubious or fishy), contained in the berber-arabic patronym Benillouche, confirms the narrator's double-edged anxiety regarding his name which represents him as Other to others (and to himself) as well as the very project of self-portraiture which attempts to represent identity as fixed, and fixable. Indeed, Memmi confirms this anxiety when he asserts elsewhere that "all identity is and remains doubtful" (24). At the same time this translational wordplay attests to the problematic relationship between language, culture and ethnicity by indexing the inescapable power relations set up within the psychosocial space of the colonial encounter.

Clearly, as Mordechai designates the narrator's Jewish heritage, the extract also demonstrates how the name of the individual is inserted within a historically, culturally and ethnically defined genealogy. In the Jewish memorial canon Mordechai may well refer to the heroism of the eponymous warrior, yet it also evokes the more recent "terror of the ghetto," the anti-Semitic pogroms in Tunisia. In this way attempts to represent identity as a tracing of crisis in self-representation can also be seen to signpost the way that Jewish identity both destabilizes and reshapes dichotomies of difference within the colonial context.

Perhaps a clue to the question as to why Memmi creates a fictional name for his autobiographical protagonist lies in a story of his nonfictional name, Albert Memmi, in his essay entitled "Le Moi, cet inconnu" (The Me, This Stranger). In this essay, Memmi recounts why he should have been named Abraham (his grandfather's name)—symbol of Jewish history, memory, and patriarchal transmission—and why, instead, he is Albert:

> When my father, happy and proud to announce, to whomever would like to listen, even to a Muslim employee at city hall, the birth of his first male offspring/descendent, the employee, being in a bad mood that day, or finding the chance to humiliate a Jew, made it absolutely clear to him that he would have to make do with Albert, approximate equivalent of Abraham, not much is known why. A bureaucrat of the administration, whether he be Muslim, regardless of his rank, was a considerable persona, for my father, an artisan harness-maker. Humiliated in effect, troubled, especially worried by the unforeseeable consequences of this symbolic mutilation, he deferred without commenting.[5]

Read alongside *La statue de sel,* this account would suggest that the invented name functions as a reinstating of the (historically displaced) patriarchal control over naming progeny. As such, the fictionalized name attempts to recover the autonomy of the Father's authority which has been displaced by the colonial system and which is represented here by the "bureaucrat of the administration." Clearly then, recalling the "bastardization" of the nonfictional name—placing patrimony in doubt—signifies the colonial administration's intervention in and rewriting of the history of the colonized Father. So, while symbolizing the legacy of colonial history, the fictional patronym writes back into that history the expropriated authority and autonomy of the Father as progenitor of a defined history and memory.

The authorial restoration of the Father's authority masks another displacing mechanism which emerges through unraveling the authorial patronym itself: Memmi.[6] In French, Memmi condenses two signifiers which underlie representations of identity and identification, markers of sameness and difference: *même* (same or identical) and *mi* (half), therefore "half-same." Jon Stratton, in his discussion of the cultural representation of the Jew in Australia, cites Homi Bhaba's formulation of the "*almost the same, but not quite*" construction of colonial mimicry. As this reading of the name demonstrates, Bhaba's "*almost the same, but not quite*" gesture to the slippage from which Otherness emerges finds particular resonance. If the name *Même-mi* is an announcement of subjective presence, it now becomes a trope of the colonial subject's lack, a presence marked by the absence of the half: the Self is "almost the same" and therefore irremediably Other. The threat of instability, of cleavage which pervades the fictional narrator's subjectivity, is now made symbolically immanent. This is underscored further by the phonemic doubling of the central *m* of the name: mirror-like inscription operating the splitting mechanism of duplication. Through this *dédoublement* at the center of the authorial name, the authorial signature becomes a metaphor for the entire narrative project of Self-representation.

LANGUAGE AND THE DISTORTED TONGUE OF THE (M)OTHER

In important studies on language as marker of difference, representations of language within colonial and anti-Semitic discourses are shown to set up reifications of race and ethnicity—such as blackness, Jewishness, Arabness—which are fixed as immutable, natural, deterministic and which become internalized and reproduced as such.[7] That language is positioned as both subject and object of the inscription of the dominant discourse on the other as Other and of the internalization of that designation is central to any interrogation of contested representations of identity. Indeed, that Memmi writes in French, "beautiful language," while he presents his mother-tongue, "Tunisian patois" (43), as a distorting, deformed, and limiting tongue, attests to his positioning of language in self-representation as well as to its metonymic function in that representation. The determinant role of language within a contested referential site of difference—that is, where identity as an Other is designated as ethnically, culturally, and ontologically inferior within colonial Tunisian society—and Benillouche's internalization of these designations resonates throughout the text. This is clearly demonstrated when Benillouche describes his mother-tongue, judeo-arabic patois,

> which I spoke with the accent of the ordinary Muslims of the quarter and of the coarse customers in the shops. The Jews of Tunis are to Muslims what the Viennese are to the Germans: they drawl over their syllables, they sing, softening or weakening of the guttural speech of their fellow citizens. My relative correction of this merited the mockery of everybody: my fellow Jews did not approve of this difference or believed it to be an affectation while the Muslims suspected that I was mocking them. (43)

By employing a trope which implicates the group as the embodiment of their language, the narrator presents his mother-tongue as a language which is neither "possessed" nor inhabited by the Jews. At the same time the language is represented as deformed when it is articulated by Jewish speakers whose "weakening" and "softening" of the language of their "fellow citizens" is seen as a contamination of that language. "The relative correction" of the narrator's speech reflects the internalization of a deep shame of the stigmatized self marked by his or her language inscribed by the other.[8] In an image which becomes a metaphor for representation of language responding to the internalized antipathy of the other as a social and cultural pathology of self-definition, the narrator describes how his language is once again mocked for being marked by the accent of the ghetto, not by the inhabitants of the ghetto, as before, but by the "rich Jewish students, of second-generation Western culture" (43) with whom the narrator comes into contact for the first time when he goes to the high school.

Predicated on the parallel logic of the "race" constructions of colonialism and anti-Semitism and the representation of these paradigms in language, this group (the rich Jewish students) is in turn stigmatized by the narrator because they do not know "how to pronounce that impossible French *r* which Paris has imposed on France" (43). In terms of the colonial paradigm his patois is already a distorted language, reflecting the degree to which its speaker is marked as assimilated and acculturated or, conversely, as unassimilable within colonial society. The internalization of the value-producing models of sameness and difference in the text therefore enacts an eternally doubled rejection of a subjectivity experienced as an "irremediable mutilation of self" (42). In an extract where this metaphor of wounding becomes conflated with the mechanics of speaking, the narrator notes: "I tried, I resolved a countless number of times to use the guttural Parisian *r* constantly until it sounded correct. But when I watched my language, I lost my train of thought and so I was soon obliged, when formulating a complicated idea, to leave my language alone in order to think" (120).[9] By locating "mutilation" as a phonetically, phonemically enacted splitting (between thought and language), the narrator underscores the materiality, the physicality of experiencing identity as fragmented. Premised on a Fanonian "splitting" of the colonized Self effected by the internalized, fixing gaze of the colonizer, a splitting is enacted as the literal rupture between thought and its representation in language within the site of the phoneme *r*, primary unit of a meaning-constituting relationship in language. The rupture of such relationships, which is echoed as the experience of identity as "mutilated," constructs, in turn, a powerful metaphor of the dialogic rupture, of the incommunicability between Self and Other within specific historical contexts of contested identities.

That the narrative represents an endeavor of self-definition which is contemplated during the duration of a philosophy examination testifies to the dualistic positioning of language in the construction of epistemological discourse which is both reflective and constitutive of the dominant power/knowledge regimes of the moment. For the narrator, language and philosophy represent the site of making anew, a tabula rasa of the Self and its reinvention in the wished-for image of the other. Thus, the narrator proclaims that "I would not be Alexandre Mordechai Benillouche. I would leave myself and I would go towards the others. I was neither Jewish, nor oriental, nor poor, I did not belong to my family nor to their religion, I was new and transparent: I was to be made, I would be a philosophy teacher" (248). Clearly, the internalized antipathy of the other as the self-hating impulse, par excellence, is played out as the desired reinvention of a subjectivity reinscribed by and through French language and its philosophical discipline as both subject and object of the language. Thus, the agency of language—incarnated through the intellectual application of the philosophy teacher, the earnest engagement of the writer, the flawless articulation of the speaker—is highlighted through its representation as magical: language becomes the site of transformation. It is therefore no coincidence that the benefactor who sponsors Benillouche's education and who facilitates his fervently desired transformation in the narrative is a pharmacist who is aptly named Monsieur Bismuth. Thus, bismuth, a transmutable metal found in alloys, functions as a symbolic referent of transformative agency. Clearly the very name of his benefactor resonates with the powers of potential transmutation represented by the character himself. As the material agency of change, French language is therefore invested with potent power, alchemic properties, and it is this assignment of magical agency to language which prompts the narrator to claim that "language participated directly in things, it had their density," and that he "has never been able to rid [him]self of this magical bewitchment of language" (45). Through acquiring this "beautiful language" of the other, Benillouche desires becoming the "thing"—a Frenchman—like the principal of the Alliance Israélite who "impressed us with his perfect diction and polished manners, who represented in our eyes a true Frenchman, a Frenchman from France, a status whose prestige remained untouched" (93). As the shifting, conflating boundaries of identity and identification are played out in this colonial space, the principal's "perfect diction" and "polished manners" come to metonymically represent the Alliance as the formative space for the transmission of Jewish culture as well as the institutionalized colonial site of French cultural imperialism.[10]

A WAY OUT OF THE IMPASSE: SELF-EXILE

The third part of the narrative, entitled *Le monde* (the world), sets the scene for the impossible double-bind in which the narrator finds himself. Two events are recounted by Benillouche which insist on his Jewishness and which catalyze a procedure of systematic rewriting and reanalysis of his identity and its reifications. When the narrator maintains that "it was necessary for the West to betray me twice before I would stop locating the sense of my life within it. And I had already broken off with the East" (279), he prefigures a breakdown in the project of self-representation. Initially, this is echoed in the rejection of the race-biology discourse of prewar Europe, its anti-Semitic doctrines, and its epistemological legitimations, when Benillouche exclaims, "At the price of much struggle I had chosen the West and rejected the East within me! Now I was beginning to doubt what had appeared to be the essence of the West: its philosophy" (290). It is the outbreak of anti-Semitic pogroms in Tunis followed shortly by the eruption of World War II which precipitates a break from the impasse which culminates in Benillouche's ontological crisis; and it is the question of Jewish identity which catalyzes this break. As subject of a French protectorate, Benillouche's Jewishness defines him as an enemy of both the German occupiers as well as of the French authorities. Following his escape as an intern—because he is Jewish—from a forced-labor camp and return to Tunis, Benillouche falls ill with a fever.

In the account of feverish illness the final significant subversion of self-definition is operated and, hence, it is during illness—narrated as an imaginary response to the rumors of the Nazi extermination of European Jewish communities and the betrayal of the Jews by the Vichy government—that Benillouche articulates his rejection of the European paradigm as a direct consequence of his Jewish identity. Yet again it is the search for essentialist identities which enacts displacement. Having effectively rejected all paradigms which inform representation of subjectivity, and having discovered that his Self remains unrepresentable outside of the designation of the other, Benillouche now seeks a way out of the aporetic abyss to which his double consciousness has led: "In the confusion of the buzzing in my ears, in the fire which embraced my cheeks and my brain, the only thing I was certain of was that I had to finish off the whole and conclude. Besides, would I have the strength to continue living in this unstable equilibrium?" (344). Because this project has proceeded from a dialectical operation—examination, consideration and rejection of binary oppositions—the logical conclusion of this quest should be equilibrium, synthesis or closure. However, when Benillouche discovers that identity is inscribed as a fixing of a preestablished meaning despite his endeavor to the contrary, he cannot find a stable internal referent from which to respond. It is at this moment that a dream of the narrator's own death is narrated. As subconsciously willed presentation of a narrative ending to this existential impasse, the death-dream represents a break from the autobiographical enterprise and the removal of that enterprise from the scene of language, of writing.

When the narrator wonders if, "like Lot's wife who God changed into a statue, am I still able to live beyond my gaze?" (368), he is expressing the doubt raised by the dream as to whether identity can be nonreflective and nonreflexive in the context of a writing of that identity. Effecting a symbolic death, Benillouche burns his journals, precisely in order to live beyond the gaze, to leave the mirror held up by the gaze. As a project of inscription, this immolation ironically represents a renunciation of the autobiographical quest for self-definition and this is why Benillouche leaves Tunisia for a new world: significantly, for Argentina. By anticipating closure as a way out of the paralysis of self-definition, Benillouche quits the scene of Africa and its symbolic, specular position. Self-expropriation enacts a metaphorical closure which writing does not achieve.

THE PILLAR OF SALT: THE JEWISH GAZE AND LOOKING BACK

Self-representation is anticipated as a problematizing endeavor by the very title of the novel, *La statue de sel,* which is, in turn, echoed by the epigraph, a biblical citation: "*Lot's wife looked back and she became a pillar of salt. Genesis, 19, 26.*" By naming after, citing from, and referring to biblical text, to Jewish canon, Memmi writes his preoccupation with Jewishness and its definitions into his text as the reference point of his narrative. The biblical reference to the account in Genesis when Lot's wife's retrospective gaze—forbidden under divine injunction—causes her to be transmogrified into a pillar of salt is highly significant. In Memmi's text, the biblical legend becomes an allegory for the individual witnessing their past. Clearly, the biblical anecdote suggests that inherent in the writing of one's Self, in the examination of one's identity which is the self-objectifying gaze, is the threat of being immured by that very writing; so when the autobiographical narrator observes that in his quest to know himself death presents itself as an issue of that quest, he preempts the very act of narrating this looking-back as specular, problematizing, and menacing. In turn, the displacement and alienation implicitly present in this metaphor of the gaze highlights the complex relationship between autobiographical representation, memory, and the politics of identity. Hence, the gaze of the self-defining subject becomes the metaphor for a witnessing of displacement and alienation enacted by a perpetually contingent identity.

It is this metaphor of the internalized gaze of colonial Self/colonized Other and its inscription of rupture which, significantly, echoes Franz Fanon's examination of the appropriating and constituting gaze of the colonizer.[15] Indeed, Memmi's text resonates with images of the narrator's experience of alienation under this fixing glance of the internalized Other, signified here by the individual looking in the mirror. In his text, the fixing gaze which stares out is reflected back again and out again, ad infinitum, in a sustained encounter of non-recognition. In this way, the image of the reflected Self in the mirror comes to symbolize a double rupture, a *mise en abîme,* the specular site of perpetual displacement in this account of shifting and irreconcilable self-definitions: "I was myself and yet I was a stranger to myself. This was a mirror which covered an entire wall, so clear/transparent that it was difficult to make it out as mirror. More and more, I was becoming a stranger to myself. I had to stop looking at myself, I had to get out of the mirror" (247). Clearly the image of the reflected gaze suggests that subjectivity is estranging, it is paralyzing, and it is threatened with fragmentation. This threat is inherent in the very formulation of subjectivity; a proposition which prompts Memmi to suggest that one is always near the point of dividing, of splitting, and hence "the unsettling ambiguity of the mirror, . . . its cruel honesty and enigmatic resonances" (25).

BEYOND THE GAZE

Memmi's exposition and critical analysis of colonialism as predicated upon a binary structure of oppositional relationships fixed by dominant power discourses—signified by the coupling of self/other, oppressor/oppressed, colonizer/colonized, European/African, and European/Arab—is expressed in *La statue de sel* in terms of an ahistorically and psychoanalytically framed interiority. Initially, self-representation insists upon the oppositional borders of Otherness as binary: "Jewish, not Moslem; a townsman, not a highlander . . .; African, not European . . .; native in a colonial country" (109). It is only when the implications of each construct are examined within its historically located moment that its representations are shown to be forged in eternal relation to another and to an Other, and that the limits of difference set up by these constructs shift with the interpositioning of a Jewish identification.

According to the logic of Memmi's text, identity is provisional. It is contingent upon the writing out of difference as displacement and the representation of the history of Self as conditionally constitutive. Thus, Jewishness is consistently characterized by alienation, menace, incommunicability. Indeed, for Memmi, "the pervasive themes of the Jewish condition [are] the stranger, the impossibility of communication, the disorientation, the danger, etc."[12] Elsewhere Memmi has outlined and insisted upon the negativity of this "Jewish condition" whose difference and separation is inextricably bound to its historical oppression.[13] Following an almost Sartrean formulation of Jewish identity,[14] the notion of a Jewish identity constructed as an ahistorically constituted negativity and, by extension, as relative, is problematic not least because it is predicated upon the converse proposition of a *dejudaized* definition of Jewish identity. Such a proposition implies that liberation lies in sameness and assimilation, in universalized notions of difference, and in essentialist formulations of identity. By narrating identity or, rather, what becomes a nonidentity, through the image of the retrospective gaze of narrated memory, Memmi effectively covers over the Jewish, African, Arab, Berber voices which inform his subjectivity. Africa, the encountering space of difference, and subjectivity as Other are silenced in the interplay of continuously repositioned identities. As difference is scandalized, identity is progressively and tragically represented as absence. Even Albert Camus's description of Memmi in the preface to *La statue de sel* is framed in terms of a relative negativity, an absence. Camus writes that Memmi is "a French writer from Tunisia who is neither French nor Tunisian. He is scarcely Jewish, since, in a sense, he would not like to be" (9).

I would contend, then, that it is precisely by writing back into Africa—topos of symbolic frontiers—that any possibility of a universalized, transcendental, and independently produced Jewish identity which is unaffected by the problematizing categories of "race" (and color), ethnicity, and culture constructed within dominant power/knowledge regimes is placed into question. This is indexed by Memmi's own arbitrary use of the terms "African," "Muslim," "Arab," "Jewish," and "Jew" to signify interchangeably and unproblematically religion, culture, ethnicity, and national identity throughout the text. When Guy Dugas therefore observes and comments on the evolution of an increasingly problematic *judéité* in Memmi's oeuvre, I would say that it is a direct function of the colonial encounter's power/knowledge discourses which have historically problematized all formulations of identity.[15]

Framed by new positionalities of memory and history, emerging interrogations of multiple identities, of differences, are placed necessarily at both real and symbolic frontiers of recovery. Hence, it is simultaneously the universal as well as the specific concerns represented by the current project of recovering memory in South Africa—a new frontier in interrogations of colonial pasts—which provide a context in which to read Memmi's autobiographical narrative. The concerns of such a project exert demands for rereadings of representations of identity; for beyond its legalistic casting, the Truth and Reconciliation Commission has come to represent one of the most important contemporary interrogations on the politics and ethics of representing the Self, representing the past, uncovering memory, and witnessing the materiality of oppression.[16] I would argue, then, that such concerns inform new readings of Jewish writing—in northern or southern Africa—in order to interrogate the ways in which ethnicity, language and historical/cultural practices simultaneously shape and are shaped by these texts.

Notes

1. Albert Memmi, *La Statue de sel* (The pillar of salt) (Paris: Gallimard, 1966). All translations of extracts from Memmi's texts are my own. Further parenthetical page references to this work are made in the text.

2. Albert Memmi, *Ce que je crois* (Paris: Bernard Grasset, 1985), 32.

3. In the light of this assertion, I would not read Anthony Sher's novel *Middlepost* as being symptomatic of an internalized radically anti-Semitic discourse and expressed as a self-hating representation, as Marcia Leveson suggests. I would say, rather, that Sher's text, which is saturated by an excess of stereotypes in its representations of *all* its characters, uses grotesque parody to call attention to the absurdities inherent in the constructions of culture, race, ethnicity, gender, sexuality, and language in the referential assumptions that underlie all stereotypes. As such, Sher's text presents Jewish identity as subjected to, represented through, and literally deformed by the same South African discourses of race and difference as any other representation of identity that is located in South Africa would be.

4. The location of this examination of identity in the culturally, ethnically, and topographically undifferentiated space of Africa follows from my reading of the epigraph in the preface of Memmi's *Portrait d'un juif* (Paris: Gallimard, 1962). The preface is entitled "Why this book . . . ," and the epigraph is, in fact, a passage from *La Statue de sel:* "Could I be descended from a Berber tribe when the Berbers themselves failed to recognize me as one of their own? I was Jewish, not Moslem; a townsman, not a highlander. Even if I had borne the painter's name, I would not have been acknowledged by the Italians. No, I am African, not European. In the long run, I would always be forced to return to Alexander Mordechai Benillouche, a native in a colonial country, a Jew in an anti-Semitic universe, an African in a world dominated by Europe."

By inserting a quotation from his autobiographical novel into the preface of *Portrait d'un juif,* Memmi suggests that the textual "portrait" of a Jew that he will attempt to construct is closely connected to his own attempts to grapple with the difficult definitions of Jewishness. In fact, the first sentence in the preface which follows the epigraph states that since the book "is to a great extent a self-portrait it is fitting that I should briefly recall who I am." Clearly, then, the location of subjectivity on the axis of Jew/African/Berber/Arab/colonized will underpin the concepts of *judäisme, judäicité*, and *judéité*, terms that attempt to articulate the religious, sociocultural, and ethnic dimensions of Jewish identity, in *Portrait d'un juif*. Conversely, the location of subjectivity on this axis produces a reading of *La Statue de sel* that highlights the difficulties of articulating identity when all terms of definition are problematized. See also V. Y. Mudimbe's discussion of Africa as undifferentiated space in *The Invention of Africa* (Bloomington: Indiana University Press, 1988).

5. Albert Memmi, *Ce que je crois* (Paris: Bernard Grasset, 1985), 23–24.

6. I would like to thank Jean-Louis Cornille for his comments and suggestions regarding readings of Memmi's name.

7. See, for example, Sander L. Gilman, *Jewish Self-Hatred: Anti-Semitism and the Hidden Language of the Jews* (Baltimore: Johns Hopkins University Press, 1986), and Franz Fanon, *Black Skin, White Masks* (London: Paladin, 1970).

8. See Ngugi wa Thiong'o, *Decolonising the Mind: The Politics of Language in African Literature* (London: James Currey, 1986), chap. 1; and Fanon, *Black Skin, White Masks*, chap. 1.

9. Compare this extract with Fanon, *Black Skin, White Masks:* In a powerful description of the placing/displacing structures of the colonial paradigms of language, it is the "embroidered" correction of the vocalization of Memmi's "impossible *R*" from which the profound shame of one's language emerges. Hence, the "Negro arriving in France will react against the myth of the *R*-eating man from Martinique. He will become aware of it, and he will really go to war against it. He will practice not only rolling his *R* but embroidering it. Furtively observing the slightest reaction reactions of others, listening to his own speech, suspicious of his own tongue" (16).

10. Guy Dugas, *Littérature Judéo-Maghrebine d'expression française* (Paris: L'Harmattan, 1990), 30.

11. This is powerfully illustrated when Fanon (*Black Skin, White Masks*, 77) likens the colonizer's gaze to being "sealed into that crushing objecthood." The description continues: "The movements, the attitudes, the glances of the other fixed me there in the sense which a chemical solution is fixed by a dye. I was indignant; I demanded an explanation. Nothing happened. I burst apart. Now the fragments have been put together again by another self" (77)

12. Albert Memmi, "Qu'est-ce que la littérature juive?" *Les Nouveaux Cahiers* 2 (May–July 1965): 36–37.

13. See, for example, Memmi, *Portrait d'un juif*.

14. Jean-Paul Sartre, *Réflexions sur la question juive* (Paris: Gallimard, 1962).

15. Dugas, *Littérature Judéo-Maghrebine d'expression française*, 60.

16. For my discussion on memory, testimony, and the TRC, see Heidi Grunebaum-Ralph, "Saying the Unspeakable: Language and Identity after Auschwitz as a Narrative Model for Articulating Memory in South Africa," *Current Writing* 8.2 (Oct. 1996): 13–23.

PART 3 Conflict

13 The Color of Jews: Jews, Race, and the White Australia Policy

JON STRATTON

There has been much very good social and political history written about the Jews in Australia.[1] However, none of this work sets this history within broader ideological understandings of Jews in the West, or in the context of the complex interrelationship of ideas about race and the nation-state which have been central to the development of the Australian nation-state. Conversely, in histories of migration to Australia and discussions of population policy, Jews get mentioned hardly at all—not at all in Stephen Castles et al.'s justly well-known *Mistaken Identity: Multiculturalism and the Demise of Nationalism in Australia,*[2] and three pages, one of which is a quotation, in Geoffrey Sherington's standard text, *Australia's Immigrants 1788–1988.*[3] In this article I want to bring Jewish history in Australia out of its isolation and begin an examination of the cultural construction of Jews in the context of the evolution of the White Australia policy and its corollary, the idea of assimilation as the central plank in the formation of the Australian nation-state.

CONCEPTUALIZING AMBIVALENCE

The most useful way to theorize the situation of Jews as a category in Australia is through the concept of ambivalence. That Jews are hardly mentioned in the standard histories of migration to Australia or, for that matter, in the three major books written on the White Australia policy during its operation should not surprise us when we realize the extent to which the ambivalent situation of the Jews in the context of the Australian nation-state could have unsettled and laid bare the discursive assumptions on which that policy was founded.[4] There have been two recent theorizations of ambivalence, both of which, in different ways, help to illuminate the subject at hand. Zygmunt Bauman argues that what characterizes the modern is that "it contains the *alternative* of order and chaos."[5] He suggests that the primary drive of modernity is the establishment of order. Applied in terms of society: "There are friends and enemies. And there are *strangers.*"[6] Friends are those who are characterized as like—in the sense of more or less the same as—us, enemies are those who threaten our order. Reworking Georg Simmel's notion of "the stranger," Bauman describes the stranger as one who "comes into the life-world and settles here, and so—unlike the case of mere 'unfamiliars'—it becomes *relevant* whether he is friend or foe."[7] For Bauman, the stranger is "ineradicably *ambivalent,* . . . blurring a boundary line vital to the construction of a particular social order or a particular life-world."[8] Taking ambivalence and its eradication as the founding problem of modernity leads to a certain reification in Bauman's important discussion. He writes that, "*The nation-state is designed primarily to deal with the problem of strangers, not enemies.*"[9] It is more useful to describe the nation-state as a machine which produces strangers as it produces friends and enemies. From this point of view it is not that the stranger "threatens the sociation itself—the very *possibility* of sociation,"[10] but, rather, that he or she threatens the integrity, the homogeneity, of the nation by calling into question the assumptions through which the nation constructs itself.

There is a confusion in Bauman's theorization. On the one hand, the stranger has come from elsewhere, he or she is, we might say, Other. On the other hand, the stranger blurs boundaries; they are, it would seem, in some sense "the same as" us. In order to understand what is at stake here, and what is so important in Bauman's understanding of ambivalence, we must turn to Homi Bhabha's work. In a now well-known article, "Of Mimicry and Man," Bhabha describes colonial mimicry as "the desire for a reformed, recognizable Other, *as a subject of a difference that is almost the same, but not quite.* Which is to say that the discourse of mimicry is constructed around an *ambivalence;* in order to be effective, mimicry must continually produce its slippage, its excess, its difference."[11]

Bhabha's starting point is a discussion of British colonialism, particularly in India. He argues that colonial practice—certainly that of the British in India—was to take the Other and educate him or her in the ways of the colonizer while continuing to mark him or her as Other. In this way the Other is reformed as ambivalent, in some ways the same as the colonizer but, in the end, always excluded and constructed as a mimic.

What is at stake in a comparison of Bauman's and Bhabha's theorizations of ambivalence is the status of the stranger and Other who produces the ambivalence. In Bhabha's work the Other always remains Other, ultimately formed as such along the faultline of race: "Almost the same but not white."[12] The ambivalence in this case always in the end falls back into the binariness through which the colonizer constructed the colonized as Other in the first place. In Bauman's case, while the stranger he describes would seem to be Other, the description that Bauman provides of ambivalence suggests a much greater degree of ambiguity. From this description the stranger would seem to be thought of as, partly, the "same" as the members of the nation. We might say that, rather than being "almost the same but not white," these strangers are both white and not-white, the same and yet also Other. It is, then, no wonder that the group who Bauman has in mind for his modern strangers are the Jews: "The Jews have been the prototypical strangers in Europe split in nation-states set on annihilation of everything 'intermediate,' underdetermined, neither friendly nor inimical."[13] In the case of Australia, a settler-state where the nation itself had to be brought into existence, the ambivalent situation of the Jews was precisely played out through the processes employed to define and form the Australian nation.

It is no wonder that general discussions of Australia's migrant-population history and policy have ignored the Jews. The Jews, as a category, transgress the two major discourses on which Australian population policy has been constructed: race and nation. In Australia the discourse of race was used to demarcate the cultural limits of the nation as it was being formed in order to produce that culturally homogeneous nation which was the classical form of the nation during the modern period. As Ien Ang and I have argued elsewhere, "the White Australia policy was, in the first instance, a *nationalist* policy and reflects the new nation-state's search for a national identity in a European culture and a British-based racial homogeneity (which inevitably implies the exclusion of racial/cultural Others)."[14] Through the period of the late 1960s, when Australia began to open its doors to those groups who had been most determinedly excluded in the era of the White Australia policy—"Asians"—the biologically essentialist rhetoric of race gave way to the cultural relativist rhetoric of ethnicity. At the same time, the practice of identifying migrants according to national background continued. In both these major eras, the times of assimilation and of multiculturalism, Jews have not fitted the categories used. For example, while Jews were increasingly racialized in popular, and sometimes governmental discourse, from the middle of the nineteenth century, the Australian census has consistently classified Jews by their religion. As a consequence, all estimates of the numbers of Jews in

Australia are dependent on those who give Judaism as their religious affiliation.

With the advent of ethnicity rhetoric and multiculturalism, the problem is compounded. Ethnicity is closely identified with culture and, in turn, is geographical in the sense that particular ethnic cultures are assumed to come from particular regions or nations. Today, under half of Australia's Jewish population has a background in Anglo-Jewry. Many of Australia's early Anglo-Jewish migrants were descendants of the Sephardis who had begun settling in England during the period of the Commonwealth in the seventeenth century. Probably over half of the total population has an Ashkenazi heritage coming from Germany or the Russo-Polish Pale in the years between 1930 and 1950.[15] Moreover, unknown numbers of Australian Jews have arrived by way of a generation or two in England or other countries that received Yiddish migration from the late-nineteenth century onward. Since the Second World War, as we shall see, an increased number of Indian-Sephardi, Iraqi-Sephardi, Egyptian-Sephardi and Oriental Jews have entered the country.

Jews, then, cannot be identified in terms of a single ethnic-cultural background, and cannot represent themselves as such at multicultural celebrations with "ethnic dancing," "ethnic clothing" or "ethnic food." As should also be clear, Jews are not a "national group" in the sense of migrating to Australia from an original nation-state. One thing that these continuities around the category of the Jew in Australia suggests is that the conceptual differences underlying the apparently very different policies of assimilation and multiculturalism are by no means as large as many Australians would like to think.[16]

In order to illustrate the points I want to make about Jews and the White Australia policy, I will focus on three particular moments: the mid-to-late nineteenth century, that is the period leading up to Federation in 1901; the late 1930s and 1940s, when there was pressure on Australia to take in Jewish refugees from Europe; and the 1940s and 1950s, when many Sephardim sought to migrate to Australia. In the first period we see the understanding of Jews in Australia being reshaped by the general Western racialization of the Jews. In the second, the pressures placed on Australia by the numbers of Jewish refugees helped to create an increasingly overt discriminatory attitude. This highlights the interaction between discourses of race and nation where there has been a tendency, all the more present in Australia's version of multiculturalism, for race to hide behind the rhetoric of nation. In the third moment we find the notion of the Jews as a single race breaking down in the face of a preoccupation over the color of prospective Sephardi migrants. Overall, this history shows how the ambivalent construction of the

Jews, using Bauman's theorization of ambivalence, was acted out in the context of the attempt to form a homogeneous Australian nation and a unitary Australian identity.

ASSIMILATION, RACE, AND THE NATION-STATE

With the nineteenth-century rise of the modern nation-state, Jews in Europe were gradually emancipated and expected to assimilate. The nation-state was founded on the notion of representation, identifiable in political theory discussions about the relation between the state and its citizens. In this structure, the citizen was thought of as an individual. As Jean-Paul Sartre puts it in his discussion of the democrat's attitude to the Jews: "He recognizes neither Jew, nor Arab, nor Negro, nor bourgeois, nor worker, but only man—man always the same in all times and in all places. He resolves all collectivities into individual elements. To him a physical body is a collection of molecules; a social body, a collection of individuals. And by individual he means the incarnation in a single example of the universal traits which make up human nature."[17] The trade-off for emancipation and equal rights was the loss of any collective distinctive difference which might threaten the idea of universal traits. At the same time the nation was thought of as a homogeneous entity made up of a single people sharing the same language, culture and, in its most essentialist formulation, the same race. Benedict Anderson's popular description of the nation as an "imagined community" suggests the importance of homogeneity in the experience of the nation.[18] Bauman's theorization of "friends" as an expression of a modern understanding translates, in terms of the nation, as a grouping of people with the same culture and, in terms of those who are not quite the same but who could be, a political emphasis on assimilation.

It was, in fact, the claimed homogeneity of the nation which enabled all of its members to be thought of in terms of the state as what Sartre describes as "a collection of individuals." In this context two divergent approaches were taken to the Jews in Europe. On the one hand, Jewishness was reduced to adherence to a particular religion, Judaism. In this way the ideal of assimilation involved the taking-on-board of the culture and language of the dominant national group. Judaism could be tolerated as a religion which, while not Christian, was nevertheless the antecedent to Christianity. On the other hand, as an endogamous group whose presence in Europe preceded that of the nation-states, Jews were progressively racialized and often subjected to a political anti-Semitism aimed at excluding them from membership of the modern states in which they found themselves to be living.

Leon Poliakov argues that it was Gregorius Hornius, in 1666, who first associated race with color, claiming that there were three basic racial groupings in the world, each descended from one of Noah's three sons, Ham, Shem and Japheth. For Hornius, "the Japhethites became whites, the Semites were the yellow races, and the Hamites became Negroes."[19] Up until the mid-nineteenth century, Jews were usually regarded as a part of the white race. As George Mosse puts it: "The Jews were either ignored by anthropologists during much of the eighteenth century or considered part of the Caucasian race [the category devised by Blumenbach (1752–1840)], and still considered capable of assimilation into European life. . . . Ideas of cosmopolitanism, equality, and toleration operated for the Jew as they could not for the Negroes; after all, the Jew was white."[20] It was the French writer Arthur de Gobineau, in *Essai sur L'Inégalité des Races Humaines* (1853–55), who was one of the first to identify the Jews as a separate race. Gobineau also popularized the idea of the white race as being Aryan, and having an origin in northern India. Subsequently another Frenchman, Ernest Renan, began to identify the Semites with the Arabs and Jews and, increasingly, with the Jews alone. In this way there was produced the basis for the dominant system through which the Jews were racialized in continental Europe in the late-nineteenth and twentieth centuries, that of Aryan versus Semite, a distinction founded in the first place on the claimed geographical origins of these two groups. For the purposes of discussion of the racialization of Jews in Australia it is important to note a distinction between racialization by color and racialization by claimed historical geographical origin and physical type. In Australia, as in other English-speaking countries including the United States, racialization of the Jews has always been marked by ambiguity about their color-status. One reason for the lack of usage of the Aryan/Semite racial distinction in Australia may be that, being a settler-state, the Jewish presence was never allowed to reach a point where such a clearly discriminatory distinction against a "European" people would have been useful. At the same time, unlike in Europe, distinction in terms of color—that is, the classification of "non-European" peoples—was of much greater importance in excluding those not considered appropriate to the Australian national project.

As an essentialist collective category race was a useful way for Enlightenment Europe to limit its universalist claims about the traits that make up human nature. In this way, "white," or "Caucasian," could be used to distinguish Europeans from Others. As national claims developed in tandem with the establishment of nation-states, so race also began to be used as a way of describing the legitimacy of national groupings. In this way, during the last half of the nineteenth century, writers like Matthew Arnold (1822–88) and Rudyard Kipling (1835–1936) began talking about an "English race." It is during this period, with the upsurge of national claims, that Jews began to be racialized. In *Imagined Communities,* Anderson argued that "dreams of racism . . . have their origin in ideologies of *class,* rather than those of nation."[21] Certainly racism and anti-Semitism can be used to establish or preserve class difference, but their development in Europe was very deeply associated with the establishment of the discourse of nationalism. This is nowhere more clearly demonstrated than in the construction of the Jews as the internal Other to the development of European nation-states during the nineteenth century. The most important example here is Germany and, in particular, the career of Wilhelm Marr, who is credited with inventing the neologism "anti-Semite" in the years around 1880. Marr started out his political life as a radical, enthusiastically supporting internationalism and the emancipation of the Jews. By the 1870s Marr had become a firm supporter of German nationalism and was publishing diatribes against the presence of Jews in Germany. During this time there was a movement toward German unification which culminates in 1871. In 1879 Marr published his most well-known book, *Der Sieg des Judenthums über das Germanenthum* (The Victory of Jewry over Germandom).[22] In Marr's career we can see how the shift to supporting German nationalism also led to the development of anti-Semitism as a racial ideology. Marr's fear of the Jews, indeed his claim that the Jews had already taken over Germany, was linked to a perception of the Jews as having no national home and, consequently, as internationalists who, in practice, would thwart any national struggle. Such a fear is played out in the anti-Semitic propaganda, *The Protocols of the Elders of Zion.*

In the nineteenth century Australia was not yet a nation-state in its own right. It was a collection of colonies which were ruled individually from London. In Europe the Jew was constructed as the internal, and partial, Other to particular nations which claimed to have an immemorial existence and the right to a particular area of land. In Australia, as in other settler-states, national identity could not, in the first place, grow out of a claim about the national group's relationship with the land. Here, the Jews and the other, mostly British and Irish, migrants were all displaced. Moreover, the Jewish convicts and migrants had mostly come from Britain where the bourgeois Jews, at least, had been very much assimilated. Unlike in Europe where political anti-Semitism could construct Jews as displaced interlopers in a national territorial community where they had no right to be, in Australia the Anglo-Jewish migrants came from a highly assimilated community and had as little national claim to the Australian land as any other migrant. At this point we need to emphasize the extent of that assimilation. As Charles Price notes: "That which came to be called the Anglo-Jewish way of life ('orthodoxy and efficiency, piety and dignity, modernity of method with strict adherence to tradition') was worked out in England during the half century before 1880, largely under the influence of the German-born Chief Rabbi, Dr. Nathan Adler."[23] In England the influx of Eastern European Jews in the decades after 1880 produced a crisis in the situation of Anglo-Jewry[24] and led the British government to enact its first legislation to control immigration, the 1905 Aliens Order. In Australia, the refugees of the 1930s and 1940s produced a comparable crisis in Australian Anglo-Jewry. What the influx to England did, as the reports of a threatened influx at this same time did in Australia, and as happened in Australia in the 1930s and 1940s, was make the Anglo-Jews visible as a group through their alliance with the European Jews. In this way the Anglo-Jewish attempt to resolve the ambivalence of their situation by assimilating in British society culturally while retaining Judaism as a religion and endogamy was placed in question.

In comparing the situation in the Australian colonies with that in Britain we find an anomaly that speaks volumes for an understanding of the situation of Jews in the European nation-states. As Israel Getzler puts it: "If in England from the 1830s onwards Jews, as before them dissenters and Catholics, had to struggle for equal civil and political rights—especially the right to enter Parliament—this was far less the case in the British colonies. . . . By offering religious tolerance and rights of citizenship to all prospective settlers except Catholics, Britain encouraged the immigration of dissenters, European Protestants and Jews into its colonies."[25] Unlike Britain, where Jews were gradually emancipated through Parliamentary Acts in 1854, 1858 and 1866, when Jewish peers finally gained the right to sit in the House of Lords, "In the Australian colonies Jews appear from the beginning to have enjoyed full civil and political rights: they acquired British nationality, voted at elections, held commissions in the local militia, were elected to municipal offices and were appointed justices of the peace."[26] In other words, Jews were fully integrated into the political and administrative structure of the colonies *because* they were colonies and did not have the status of national entities. At the same time, this being before the late-nineteenth-century racialization of the Jews, in the Enlightenment tradition, Jewish identity was officially understood as a function of religion. Getzler's book documents what was considered by the Jews of the various Australian colonies to be the one impediment to complete equality, that the Jewish religion was not of an equal official status to Christianity.

RACIAL EXCLUSIVITY AND THE FORMATION OF THE AUSTRALIAN NATION-STATE

Where, for the European nation-states, the biggest threat to a homogeneous nation was always internal, and typified in "the Jews,"[27] in the Australian colonies through the second half of the nineteenth century the threat to a homogeneous nation was external, that is to say it was an effect of migration, and was embodied in the Chinese. Chinese males began arriving in numbers in the 1850s, when gold was discovered in Victoria, and by 1859 "made up almost 20% of the male population in Victoria, although only 8% of Victoria's total population and about 3.3% of the total population in the Australian colonies in 1861."[28] In June 1855, the first of many restrictive acts was passed, the Victorian "Act to make Provision for Certain Immigrants."[29] This limited the number of Chinese passengers that could be brought in any vessel to one for every ten tons of registered tonnage and introduced a head tax. With the Chinese simply shifting their port of entry to South Australia, the entry limitation was lifted. In 1857 Victoria introduced a monthly license fee on the Chinese of £1, later reduced to £1 every two months.[30] In 1857 South Australia introduced an act almost identical to Victoria's 1855 act, and in 1861 New South Wales passed the Chinese Immigration Restriction Act which, again, was practically the same as the 1855 Victorian Act.[31] Over the next twenty years the various colonies, independently of each other, varied their laws in response to the local situation. Finally, in 1880 in Melbourne and continuing in early 1881 in Sydney, an Intercolonial Conference with delegates from all colonies decided that, in the face of the possible consequences of large-scale Chinese migration, the colonies needed to coordinate their legislation. In 1888, at another Intercolonial Conference, the delegates proposed a uniform legislation which limited Chinese passengers on vessels to one per 500 tons of ship's cargo.[32] By 1890 the Australian colonies had in place more or less consistent legislation limiting the entry of Chinese. Standardizing laws protecting the colonies from Chinese migration was an important spur to Federation.

Throughout this period the Chinese were perceived as racially Other and as unable to be mixed in with the white, British stock of the colonies. Their very numbers made them a threat. In 1857 Sydney's newspaper *The Empire* described them as "a swarm of human locusts."[33] Richard White argues that, "during most of the nineteenth century, it was generally accepted that Australia had a clear political and cultural 'image' which was considered neither particularly British nor Australian. Australians saw themselves, and were seen by others, as part of a group of new, transplanted, predominantly Anglo-

Saxon emigrant societies."[34] The reason colonial Australians were not concerned with themselves as either British or Australian was that the colonies did not think of themselves in national terms. Instead they thought of themselves racially as Anglo-Saxon. In this thinking, the Jews were invisible as a separate race. However, the idea of Australian identity as "a tug-of-war between Australianness and Britishness . . . became common towards the end of the nineteenth century"[35] as the colonies began to think of themselves in national terms. By this time, the Chinese were seen as a threat to the British civilization of the colonies. In 1877 the *Sydney Morning Herald* quoted the premier of Queensland at the time when Queensland's 1876 Act, which legislated on "Asiatic and African aliens," was withheld royal assent pending changes. He said, "We fear that both our rights [of self-government] and our civilisation may be compromised, and that our social and political system may be imperilled, if on any plea whatever a Chinese immigration is forced upon us against our wishes and against our interests."[36] As we shall see, it was in the latter part of the nineteenth century, concurrent with the rise of Australian nationalism, that the first major wave of anti-Semitism spread through the colonies.

Up to around 1890 the focus of the Australian colonies' concern was specifically with the regulation of Chinese migration. After this the concern became much more directly racial in its form, aimed at excluding nonwhites. Andrew Markus describes this transition very well. He writes: "There was considerable development of racial consciousness in the period 1850–90 and this is particularly apparent in legislation directed at the Chinese. With reference to the definition contained in legislation, there is a change from a territorial emphasis to one specifically couched in the terminology of race."[37] Willard gives the main reason for this: "In the fifties this primary reason [of national self-preservation] for [the colonies'] policy found expression in the resolve to maintain the British character and institutions in the Australian Colonies; toward the end of the century, however, it was expressed in terms of Australian nationalism."[38] The consequence was a shift from a dichotomous construction of Anglo-Saxon/British versus Chinese to a general opposition which instantiated whiteness self-consciously and took the British as the type of "whiteness," and opposed it to a general category labeled "coloured." Willard argues that around the early 1890s there was an increasing consciousness in the Australian colonies of other "Asian" migrants, mostly Indians and Ceylonese.[39] By the mid-1890s this concern was extended to the Japanese, small numbers of whom had been arriving in Australia. What concentrated the minds of the Australian colonies' legislators, however, was the 1894 Anglo-Japanese Commercial Treaty which enabled free travel of nationals of both countries to either country. The Australian colonies were given the opportunity to ratify the treaty.[40] They did not do so.

There was a push to extend the laws regulating Chinese migration. In 1896 another Intercolonial Conference met and decided to extend the 1888 Restriction Bill "to all coloured races," including those people who were British subjects.[41] The bills to this effect sent to London by New South Wales, South Australia and Tasmania for assent were all reserved. In a speech to the Australian representatives at the Imperial Conference of 1897, Secretary of State for the Colonies Joseph Chamberlain made very clear that Her Majesty's government, while accepting the need of the colonies to keep out undesirable immigrants—such as those who are dirty, ignorant or paupers—would not sanction exclusion "by reason of . . . colour, or by reason of . . . race."[42] Instead, Chamberlain recommended an act along the lines of that of Natal which was an education test, requiring prospective migrants "to write out and sign in a European language an application to the Colonial Secretary in a form set out in a Schedule to the Act."[43] Chamberlain's speech was certainly strategic. He did not want either Japan, with whom Britain had recently signed a commercial treaty, or India, the most populous and economically important country in the Commonwealth, to think that Britain condoned racism. On another occasion Chamberlain affirmed his personal view: "I believe in this race, the greatest governing race the world has ever seen; in this Anglo-Saxon race, so proud, so tenacious, self-confident and determined, the race which neither climate nor change can degenerate, which will infallibly be the predominant force of future history and civilisation."[44] Willard notes that the phrase "White Australia" was being "frequently used as early as 1896 to denote the Australian policy."[45] As the colonies moved toward federation and an increasing independence from Britain, race became the crucial marker of the nascent Australian identity, the signifier of both inclusion and exclusion. In the first instance "white" indicated British national origin—with the presumption that the British were racially homogeneous—but other northern Europeans were acceptable. Within this context, as I shall now demonstrate, Jews were acceptable up to a point, being thought of ambivalently, as I discussed at the outset, as both white and nonwhite.

During the nineteenth century there was an undertow of everyday anti-Jewish feeling feeding on European stereotypes of Jews. As *Free Lance* put it in 1896, the Jew in Australia was known as "a financier, a lawyer, a bookmaker, a pawnbroker or dealer in second-hand goods."[46] Cartoons of Jewish men portrayed them as fat, unshaven, hooknosed and speaking with an Anglo-Yiddish accent. Contrary to this stereotype, Australia's Anglo-Jewry was highly assimilated with only a small presence of Jews from Eastern Europe.

In the 1890s there was an upsurge in anti-Jewish feeling, indeed in what we can begin to call anti-Semitism. One of the most important characteristics of anti-Semitism, the defining feature of its modernity, lies in its association with nationalism. As a settler-society, the first form the racialization of the Jews took was a preoccupation with Jewish immigration. The catalyst for the upsurge seems to have been a report in an English newspaper, taken up by Australian newspapers in early 1891, that the Jewish philanthropist, Baron Maurice de Hirsch, was considering sending 500,000 pauperized Russian Jews to Australia to form an agricultural settlement.[47]

As it happens the report was inaccurate, but this is beside the point. The consternation caused in both Australian Gentile and Australian Anglo-Jewish circles was considerable. Most of the outcry over the report came in terms of fears of the new migrants taking Australians' jobs, lowering wages and therefore the standard of living. However, it is clear that the Jews were beginning to be racialized. A member of the New South Wales Legislative Assembly talked awkwardly of "the Jewish people or the people of any religious denomination,"[48] but the *Bulletin,* which carried on its masthead the slogan "Australia for the White Man," was much more forthright. It wrote: "Even the Chinaman is cheaper in the end than the Hebrew, . . . the one with the tail is preferable to the one with the Talmud every time. We owe much to the Jew—in more senses than one—but until he works, until a fair percentage of him produces, he must always be against democracy."[49] The claim that the Jew does not work at laboring jobs is a part of the modern stereotype of Jew. It is a transformation of the image of the Jew as a usurer. In capitalist society, as Karl Marx argued, integration into the society is gained by one's selling of one's labor-power or one's owning of the means of production. To not work signifies that one is in some sense not a member of the society. In Australia, working-class anti-Semitism has always been strong and closely linked with labor politics and radical nationalism.[50] Fears of Jewish workers taking Australian jobs, or Jewish entrepreneurs employing only Jews or else employing Australian labor at low wages, were translated into an assertion of a homogeneous British-based, Australian national identity. In this extract from the *Bulletin,* we can see how this operates by way of racializing the Jew, implying a racial equivalence with the Chinese—though the Chinese is preferable as a worker. Here, then, both Jews and Chinese are racialized and in this way Othered equally, with the intention that both should be excluded from a racially and culturally homogeneous white Australia.

That this comparison is not simply idiosyncratic can be demonstrated by a quotation from an 1891 letter to the London *Jewish Chronicle* written by the Australian Anglo-Jew, Walter D. Benjamin, who feared an influx of Russian

Jews. Benjamin explained that the penniless Russian Jew "would be regarded every whit as unfavourably as the Chinese cook, the Hindoo hawker, the Kanaka plantation hand, the Tamil servant, or the Lascar sailor," and he even compared "the hypothetical mass Russian Jewish migration to Australia with America's 'Negro problem.'"[51] Here we have again the suggestion that Gentile Australians—and even Australian Anglo-Jews, as Benjamin's letter suggests—would equate *Russian* Jews with Chinese. The addition of "Hindoo," "Tamil" and "Lascar" brings us to the assumption informing the comparison: that these Russian Jews will be thought of as "Asiatic." Given the European orientalizing of European Jews in the second half of the nineteenth century and the perception in Australia that Russians in general were "Asiatic" rather than "European," this is understandable.[52] It also points to the fear which may well have stimulated Benjamin's letter, that Australia's Anglo-Jews might themselves become racialized as "Asiatic."

Against this, Benjamin's second rhetorical move is to racialize the Russian Jews so as to emphasize, by contrast, the Britishness of Anglo-Jewry. If the unassimilable Russian Jews are, by implication, "black," then the assimilable Anglo-Jews must be, like the British, "white." The implication of the blackness of some Jews was not idiosyncratic. It is of a piece with an important European tradition, which precursed their orientalization—their "Asianization" in Australian racial terms—as Semites, which colored the Jews as black. Sander Gilman writes that, "The general consensus of the ethnological literature of the late nineteenth century was that the Jews were 'black' or, at least, 'swarthy.'"[53] Through the nineteenth century, "black," as a term of racial coloring, was used by Europeans to define Otherness. For example, in Britain the Irish were described as "black."[54] In this way the position of the Irish as a colonized Other was expressed, putting them on a par with Africans.[55] It is important to note here that, in Australia, the highly assimilated Anglo-Jews were thought of as "white."

Hilary Rubenstein describes how the Jewish "communal shock at the anti-Semitism of the 1890s was consolidated by populist anti-Semitism in the decades to come."[56] In Australia, the racialization of the Jews took place in the context of the nationalism which led to the establishment of a federated Australia and the White Australia policy. The persistence of a racial anti-Semitism was linked to the Australian nationalist desire for a homogeneous white nation. From this time on, the fear for Australia's assimilated Jewry, caught in the ambivalence of their white/nonwhite status, was that any increased visibility for the Jews, any signs of racial/cultural difference, would mark them as a threat to the homogeneity of the nation.

In 1901 the colonies of Australia federated. The first act passed by the new

Commonwealth government was the Commonwealth Immigration Restriction Act. Modeled on the Natal Act as recommended by Joseph Chamberlain, it "prohibit[ed] the entry into Australia of any person who, when asked to do so, fail[ed] to write out at dictation, and sign in the presence of an officer, a passage of 50 words in length in a European language."[57] In 1905, after representations from the Japanese, the act was made to seem even less racist by the dropping of the requirement that it should be a European language. In fact, in this act, language operates as a substitute for race. In racialist discourse, race is able to be exclusionary because it is claimed to be an essential attribute of the person. Languages, on the other hand, are learned. However, in this instance, the choice of language used in the test was up to the discretion of the immigration officials with the consequence that the test could, in fact, be used as an exclusionary device. The use of language in this way has other implications. The modern nation-state had, ideally, a single, uniform language for its homogeneous national population. In Australia the use of English is not simply functional, it has important national and "racial" significance as the language of white Australia's British heritage. It is, therefore, not surprising to find that "in its first draft the dictation test was to be administered in the English language."[58] This was changed as a consequence of the worry that it would offend European countries although, ironically, the greater the choice of possible language the greater the insurance that someone who was not considered desirable would be kept out. Nevertheless, the choice of European languages signals what was considered to be the limits to "whiteness" and where "coloredness" began.[59]

The justification for the White Australia policy was put forward by Alfred Deakin, the first attorney general, in the debate on the Commonwealth Restrictions Bill. He argued that: "A united race means not only that its members can intermarry and associate without degradation on either side, but implies one inspired by the same ideals."[60] In practical terms Jewish endogamy has been one of the key stumbling blocks in the process of Jewish assimilation in the modern nation-state. It is significant that Deakin should single out intermarriage as the exemplary form of social integration in the modern state. In essentialist terms racial difference ideally operates as a bar to marriage, the children of such unions often thought to be retarded or themselves sterile.[61] From this point of view the acceptance of intermarriage signifies a lack of racial difference. Jews were thus caught on the horns of a dilemma. If they were accepted as marriage partners by Gentiles, this was a crucial step in the process of national assimilation, but, in doing this, they destroyed the endogamous basis of Jewish particularity—not just a religious grouping but something more.

The high level of assimilation of Anglo-Australian Jewry, and the general lack of regard of Jews as a race, was reflected in the high levels of intermarriage through the nineteenth and the first half of the twentieth century. In 1911, 27 percent of Jewish husbands in Australia had non-Jewish wives and 13 percent of Jewish wives had non-Jewish husbands. In 1921 these figures had increased to 29 percent and 16 percent, respectively.[62] However, by the 1991 census the figure had declined to an overall rate of 10–15 percent.[63]

With the nationalist rhetoric around federation, new pressures were put on the Jews to assimilate into the new nation-state. In this situation, where Jewish identity was already thought of primarily in terms of religion rather than race, it is no wonder that the rate of intermarriage rose. What brought it down again, and reasserted a distinctive Jewish identity, was the influx of German, Polish and Russian refugees before and after the Second World War. Simultaneously, it was these Jews that heightened the racialization of Australian Jewry precisely through their reassertion of a Jewish cultural identity.

Apart from the gradation of white to colored, race was complicatedly mixed in with language and with culture. Premised on an Australo-British norm that combined visual discrimination, with the valorization of the English language and Anglo-Australian cultural practices, assimilation was considered to be possible only for those who did not vary too much in any of these three categories, where difference in any one suggested difference could be found in the other two. Thus, for example, in the 1930s, in spite of being Europeans, Italians, and especially southern Italians who were considered similar enough to the British/European norm to be let in by the government, were not so considered by the general population. They had a different language, some very different cultural practices, such as their version of Catholicism and the using of garlic, and they were considered to be dark enough to be called "colored." In 1934 "there were 'anti-dago' riots at Kalgoorlie, in which several people were killed."[64]

By the 1920s,

> the general impression was that "good Jews" were those who were Australian or British, conformed with the norms of the Anglicised Australian community, spoke English without an accent, engaged in "respectable" business practices and in no way stood out from the great anonymous mass of other Australians. "Bad Jews" were the opposite. They were foreign, exhibited different customs and modes of behaviour, rarely spoke English without an accent (and employed a syntax which held them up to derision), and had business principles derived from the eastern European village or market town rather than the local shop in the high street.[65]

Eastern European Jews had two of the three markers of difference. With any other group, such as the Italians, this would have been enough to have them classified as racially different. On the other hand, in the color typology of race, Jews in Australia tended to be thought of as white. This assumption began to be destabilized in the 1930s when there was an increasing number of applications to come to Australia from German and subsequently Eastern European Jews.

THE RACIALIZATION OF EUROPEAN JEWS IN AUSTRALIA

From the early 1930s the racialization of the Jews as Semites was becoming the dominant ideology in Germany with the Nazi rise to power. In June 1933, a cabinet memorandum was prepared for the minister of the interior concerning an application from an Australian resident for permission to bring to Australia his brother and wife and child, who "are of the Jewish race."[66] Here, it would seem, "race" follows the Nazi usage. As the 1930s progressed, the Australian government became more and more worried about the number of Jews applying to come to Australia. In 1936, Assistant Secretary T. H. Garrett of the Ministry of the Interior opined that, "Jews as a class are not desirable immigrants for the reason that they do not assimilate; speaking generally, they preserve their identity as Jews."[67] Here, it is unclear what is meant by "their identity as Jews." Not, in all likelihood, their religious identity alone; could it be their cultural identity? And, if so, then what must be meant is *Yiddishkeit,* not a Jewish cultural identity per se, but a *particular* Jewish language and culture which, in Australia as in other English-speaking Western countries, had begun to be inflected among the Gentile populations as "Jewish culture." Perhaps the best example of this is the still-current tendency to identify a Yiddish-English accent as a Jewish accent.

By 1938, the official specifying of Jews was becoming clearly racially-based. In altering the rules for Dutch migrants, it was established that the new leniency "would not apply to persons of Jewish race."[68] During the same year the British passport control officer in Budapest, V. C. Farrell, wrote to the secretary of the Australian Department of the Interior that "99% of the applications are from persons of the Jewish race."[69] The same year a Department of the Interior memorandum was sent to the cabinet which recommended a specific quota be decided upon for Jews. It finished: "The adoption of the suggestion to limit the number would mean the establishment of a quota for Jews, who are a separate race as distinct from a nationality."[70] This precisely lays out the problem.

If Jews cannot be understood as a religious group, and from an Australian perspective the cultural and linguistic differences of some Jews, coupled with their endogamy, mean that this is not (wholly) possible, then how can Jews be classified? In the discursive system of modernity there were two other possibilities, race and nationality, which, as we have seen, overlap with race sometimes to essentialize nationality. Jews cannot be a nation in the modern sense of the word because, first of all, they do not have a nation-state, but, more profoundly, they do not occupy, or claim to have historically occupied, any particular piece of land—Zionist claims about Palestine aside—which could provide the site for a unitary origin. And yet, in some sense, the Jews from different nation-states claim some sort of connection. The only solution had to be that the Jews are a race. This is what enables them to be thought of as a specific group in their own right. Yet again, this did not seem quite right because some Jews, Anglo-Australian Jewry, appeared able to assimilate. These Jews must, therefore, be "white." Once again we find Jews being constructed as the source of ambivalence, blurring the racial boundary that was being used to help construct the Australian nation. Jews, in other words, were being thought of as both "white" and "nonwhite."

While the weekly *Truth* was describing the Jews as a race, asserting in 1938 that, "As a racial unit they are a menace to our nationhood and standards. As an inflow of migrants, they are a menace to employment,"[71] the highly assimilated Jewish community was affirming also in 1938 that it "does not consider that any sudden large influx is in the interests of the immigrants themselves," and that, "The newcomers must be Australianized as soon and as completely as possible."[72] Here we have the worry about cultural difference and visibility, differences which, in the Australian context where race patrolled the cultural homogeneity of the nation, could lead to charges of racial difference such as those expressed by *Truth*.[73]

Tensions between the new Jewish arrivals and Australian Jewry reached a point by 1944 that A. Masel, president of the Victorian Jewish Advisory Board, wrote: "It must be admitted that many Australian Jews have maintained an aloof, patronizing, even hostile attitude towards newer arrivals. . . . I am convinced that many Australian Jews still look upon the new arrivals as aliens, not as fellow Jews."[74] This shows well the other side of the problem, Australian Jews who were so assimilated that they had assumed the homogenizing values of assimilatory Australian national culture and thought of European Jews as different. Fifty years on, the position of Australian Anglo-Jewry seems to have been remarkably similar to that espoused by Walter D. Benjamin in his letter to the London *Jewish Chronicle* in 1891, suggesting that, as Australian Jews assimilated, thinking of Judaism as only a religion, then they also thought of themselves racially as "white."

The problem with describing the Jews as a race was that some were accepted as having assimilated, and having intermarried. If this was so then they must also be "white," in Australian racial terms. This ambiguity underlies the following comment, again from 1938, from the Commonwealth Investigation Branch: "In type, culture and economic standard these [German] Jews form an entirely different nation from the Jews who here have created some anti-Jewish feeling: the Polish and other Eastern Jews in Carlton [Melbourne] for instance. In looks and behaviour they are rather German than Jewish, [and] the same applies to their culture and business ethics."[75] Germans were one of the nationalities highly favored for Australian migration because they were thought to assimilate so well—they were, of course, also thought of as white. In this quotation, then, "nation" is used rather than "race" in order, first of all, to distinguish between the modern, assimilated German Jews and the premodern, Yiddish language- and culture-based Polish Jews. Secondly, it is used to suggest the assimilability of German Jews in Australia, something possible for other white nations but not for other races. What could happen, in the Australian version of modern thinking about the nation-state, if a group does not assimilate can be seen in a cabinet document of the same period which directed that migration preference should be given to "Austrian and German Jews because . . . on the whole they have become more assimilated in European ways, say, than the Jews of Poland where they have practically formed a State within a State."[76]

During 1939 the Australian government attempted a more formal method of identifying Jews. On Form 40, "Application for Admission of Relative or Friend to Australia," and Form 47, "Application for Permit to Enter Australia," it asked intending migrants to state whether or not they were Jewish and nominees to state if the person is or is not of Jewish race. It seems that the request to differentiate came originally from the Australian Jewish Welfare Society, though they did not specify in what terms differentiation might be made.[77] When the forms were issued, the A.J.W.S. complained about the use of the word "race." The secretary of the A.J.W.S. wrote to the Department of the Interior requesting a change, saying that the Society "had received numerous protests from members of the Australian Jewish Community in Victoria and New South Wales, who have taken great exception to the words 'JEWISH RACE.' They are most emphatic in their protests and wish to point out that they are BRITISH SUBJECTS of JEWISH FAITH, and the word 'RACE' especially, is most obnoxious to them."[78] The Department immediately agreed and the word "race" was dropped. Aside from the Nazi, genocidal, connotations of the idea of a Jewish race—which was itself bound with German nationalism as the earlier brief discussion of Wilhelm Marr suggests—it should by now be clear why the Australian Jewish community would much rather have Jews defined in religious rather than racial terms. The insistence on Australian Jews being British subjects—as all Australians were at this time—suggests the connection between race and nationality. Religious difference, especially within Christianity, was tolerable in Enlightenment thought.[79]

The Nazis racialized all Jews, starting with the highly assimilated Jews of Germany and Austria, and moving on to the unassimilated and nonmodern Yiddish Jews of the Pale. The Australian government's racialization of the Jews in the second half of the 1930s took place ambivalently and in the context of migration. Here the general Nazi racialization connected in complex ways with the Australian inflection of the discourse on race in which race marked those who, it was considered, could (be) assimilate(d). At the same time, the recognition in Australia that Jews continued to preserve a degree of separate identity led to an interest in limiting the numbers entering Australia. From this perspective we might take the relatively static figure for the proportion of Jews in the Australian population, between 0.4 percent and 0.5 percent over almost all of Australia's existence as a nation, as an index of Australian tolerance of the nonassimilation of those considered assimilable during the roughly sixty years of the White Australia policy. One impact of Nazi expansionism was to cause the Jewish refugee crisis to involve Jews of many nationalities. Since the Australian government considered the modernized Jews of Western European countries, who were often already assimilated in various ways, more assimilable than the Yiddish, Polish and Russian, Jews of the Pale, and since they wanted to limit the numbers of Jews entering Australia anyway, the government was gradually forced toward a rhetoric of race. However, the Jews of concern were European and Eastern European. In Australian racial discourse European Jews were thought of as white and Eastern European Jews were also, if more ambivalently, white. As a consequence, while the Jews were strategically racialized they seem to have not been colorized, suggesting once again, in the context of Australian racial discourse, that Jews were both "white" and "nonwhite." Turning to a discussion of the post–Second World War attempts of Sephardim to migrate to Australia we find, for the first time, an attempt to distinguish "white," "European" Jews from "colored," "Asiatic" Jews. In this process the racialization of some Jews as "colored" and others as "white" threw into question the basis for describing the Jews as a unitary group.

THE PROBLEM OF NON-EUROPEAN JEWISH MIGRATION

In the decade following the Second World War, the identification of Jews posed a quite different problem for the Australian government. This involved the Sephardim and other non-European-based Jewish groups, some of whom wanted to migrate to Australia from countries such as Egypt, Iraq and India. The reasons for this new push by Sephardi and Oriental Jews in the postwar period are diverse: the unsettling of Jewish groups in the "East" as a consequence of Japanese invasion, the establishment of Israel and the allied change in attitude toward Jews in the Arab countries, and the independence of India were all important.

In the organization of the world according to the White Australia policy, "Asia" began where "Europe" ended and people got more "colored" the further away they were from Britain. Australia was, therefore, a "white" nation-state among "Asiatic" peoples. Given that the majority of European Jews are Ashkenazi and the majority of non-European Jews are Sephardi and Oriental, we can see how the set of preferences translates into a privileging of Ashkenazi Jews over Sephardi. Although the question posed for the Australian government by these Jews from outside of Europe was, in itself, very simple—can they be considered "white"?—answering it was highly problematic. In this case the boot was on the other foot. For Jews living outside of Europe it was, ironically, much better to claim Jewishness as in some sense a racial quality, or at least to affirm the practice of endogamy, and to allow Australians to continue to think of Jews as in some sense "European," and therefore "white," people. Of course, this produces a very unusual history of the Jews as, in some way, originating from Europe, but it is not one that ever seems to have worried either the Australian people—except certain anti-Semitic groups—or the Australian government. Perhaps one reason for this has been the close historical entanglement of British and Anglo-Jewish migration.

In the first instance, Jews from the Middle East were considered to be "Asian" and were not to be allowed into Australia. In 1949, T. H. Heyes, the secretary of the Department of Immigration, sent a letter marked "Secret" to the Department of External Affairs stating the government's position: "The Minister holds the view that persons who are not of pure European descent are not suitable as settlers in Australia and it is his desire that those wishing to make their homes in this country be not granted the facilities to do so, even though they are predominantly of European extraction and appearance. 'Persons of Jewish race of Middle Eastern descent are not eligible, under the existing Immigration Policy, for entry to Australia.'"[80] Here Jews are classified as a race while a particular geographical/racial "descent"—which would make them "Asiatic"—is the marker to exclude a certain section of this race. The confusion of the Australian government over whether Jews should be classified by religion or race is demonstrated by comparing the above letter to an internal memorandum of the Department of Immigration written about the same time: "Non-British Europeans, who are born in the Middle East and are not Jewish, may be admitted provided they can comply with current immigration rules. It will be seen that there is a certain amount of discrimination against persons of the Jewish faith as the fact that they were eligible for admission prior to the decision of 1948 and not afterwards reveals that they are not rejected on racial or other grounds but solely because of their faith."[81] According to the logic of this memo it would seem that Jews born in the Middle East might be considered to be "Europeans," and therefore "white." That they are to be excluded from Australia must, therefore, be because they are of the Judaic religion. At this point we are returned to questions of religious tolerance. To follow the logic further, perhaps Judaism might be considered an "Asiatic" religion? Within the traditional European distinction between "Europe" and "Asia," where "Asia" began at the Muslim Ottoman Empire, this was the case. However, these possibilities were never developed as the problem of the Sephardim and Oriental Jews got played out in the mutual discourses of race and color.

In 1954 a confidential Department of Immigration document distinguished between "Jews who are British subjects and of European origin, [who] are permitted to enter Australia subject to the same conditions as any other European British Subjects" and "Jews of Middle Eastern origin."[82] As for these Jews, "it has been found that a proportion of them show distinct traces of non-European origin and their admission is generally restricted to the wives and minor children of residents of Australia. Applications for the admission of this class of persons, whether of British or alien nationality, should be referred, accompanied by evidence that they are at least of 75% European origin, as in the case of Eurasians who are not Jews."[83]

We can start here with the term "Eurasian." Given that the White Australia policy adhered to the European definition of "Asia"—that "Asia" began where "Europe" ended—"Eurasian" was defined, in the first instance, by its European, white, component. Once again, it seems, Jews are being considered as, in the first place, "white." This is of particular interest because, following from the assumed mythical history of Jews as "European," a hierarchy of Jews can be constructed out of the Australian government rulings which goes: Anglo-Jews, German and other northern European Jews, Polish and Russian Jews, non-European Jews. Russia was included in "Europe" and "Asia" began at the Dardanelles. In the censuses, Afghans, classified as a "non-European race," mark the latitudinal limit to Europe. Russians were not a desired migrant nationality and one suspects that, had many Russians wished, or been allowed by the USSR government, to come to Australia, the Australian government would have tried to distinguish "European Russians" from "Asiatic Russians."

This Department of Immigration document also makes plain how much "colored" ancestry a person can have and still be allowed into Australia. Anything more than 25 percent makes a person look too colored—too "Asian"—and suggests their unassimilability, or maybe the fact that the "white" Australian population would not let them assimilate. The general policy of 75 percent "European blood" for "Asian" applicants to migrate was put in place in October 1951.[84] One further assumption here is, again, that Jews are "white."

Later in 1954, Heyes wrote a further memorandum in which he announced that the 75-percent rule need not be strictly adhered to in the case of Sephardim.[85] Before the 75-percent rule and, it would seem, after it also, judgments on Sephardi migration applications were made according to a visual inspection of the applicant. In one case around 1950 of two brothers and two sisters, the younger brother was able to migrate. After being rejected, the sisters arrived in Australia on tourist visas. The immigration officer wrote that "Miss E. Aaron shows very little trace of colour and in my opinion is a quarter caste or less. Her sister appears dark but in my opinion is less than half caste."[86] The sisters were allowed to stay in Australia. Finally, after many attempts, the elder brother gained entry also.[87]

With this discussion of the Australian government's attitude to the "problem" of the Sephardim in the terms of the White Australia policy, we are returned to Australia's preoccupation with excluding the "Asiatic" as a cornerstone of the construction of a homogeneous white Australian nation based on British culture and speaking English. Racial difference was thought of in terms of people being more or less colored as they varied from the white, British norm. This operated as the basis for an inclusion or exclusion as national groups were thought to be more or less assimilable. Behind the discussions of national groups and their cultures lay a Social Darwinist view of race and an idea of superior and inferior civilizations. Thus, while the practical core to the White Australia policy was the attempt to construct a unitary national people, with one language and one culture, behind it lurked the idea of white, British, or at least European, superiority. Within this characteristically modern discursive system the Jews were difficult to categorize. In Enlightenment thinking they were neither clearly a religious group or a race, and certainly not a nation. In fact they are, in Bauman's terms, strangers, people whose "ineradicable ambivalence" blurs the boundaries of the modern nation-state and upsets the neat modern binary distinction between friends and enemies or, more relevantly, "our nation" and "their nation." As the new state of Australia struggled, in the modern tradition, to produce a homogeneous national body, so the Jews disrupted the very discursive categories on which this could be formed: "race" and "nation." From the 1911 census there were two classifications for Jews, "Jews" as classified by religion and "Asiatic Jews," a racial categorization which was used until 1966. Accepted as "white," in the main, by virtue of Anglo-Australian Jewry's colonial presence and high degree of assimilation, there was always the possibility that Jews in Australia would be racialized as "Asiatics" and excluded from the nation-state.

Notes

I would like to thank Ien Ang for her comments on an early version of this essay, which was written with the aid of an Australian Research Council Large Grant given to Ien Ang and me for a project entitled "Reimagining 'Asians' in Multicultural Australia." A shorter version of this essay previously appeared in *Journal of Australian Studies* 50–51 (1996): 51–65.

1. Most important and specifically related to my topic, P. Y. Medding, *From Assimilation to Group Survival: A Political and Sociological Study of an Australian Jewish Community* (Melbourne, 1968); Israel Getzler, *Neither Toleration nor Favour: The Australian Chapter of Jewish Emancipation* (Melbourne, 1970); Michael Blakeney, *Australia and the Jewish Refugees, 1933–1948* (Sydney, 1985); Suzanne Rutland, *Edge of Diaspora: Two Centuries of Jewish Settlement in Australia* (Sydney, 1988); Hilary Rubenstein, *The Jews in Australia: A Thematic History,* vol.1: 1788–1945 (Melbourne, 1991); Paul R. Bartrop, *Australia and the Holocaust, 1933–1945* (Melbourne, 1994); Paul R. Bartrop, "Indifference and Inconvenience: Jewish Refugees and Australia, 1933–1945," in *False Heavens: The British Empire and the Holocaust,* ed. Paul R. Bartrop (Lanham, Md., 1995).

2. Stephen Castles et al., *Mistaken Identity: Multiculturalism and the Demise of Nationalism in Australia* (Leichardt, 1988).

3. Geoffrey Sherington, *Australia's Immigrants, 1788–1988,* 2d ed. (Sydney, 1990).

4. Myra Willard, *History of the White Australia Policy to 1920* (Melbourne, 1923); A. C. Palfreeman, *The Administration of the White Australia Policy* (Melbourne, 1967); H. I. London, *Non-White Immigration and the "White Australia" Policy* (Sydney, 1970).

5. Zygmunt Bauman, *Modernity and Ambivalence* (Cambridge, Eng., 1991), 6.

6. Ibid, 53.

7. Ibid., 59.

8. Ibid., 61.

9. Ibid., 63.

10. Ibid., 55.

11. Homi Bhabha, *The Location of Culture* (London, 1994), 86.

12. Ibid., 89.

13. Bauman, *Modernity and Ambivalence,* 85.

14. Jon Stratton and Ien Ang, "Multicultural Imagined Communities: Cultural Difference and National Identity in Australia and the USA," *Continuum* 8.2 (1994): 141.

15. The 1991 census, which still classified Jews as a religious group, calculated the Jewish population at 74,186 people, which represents 0.44 percent of the total Australian population. William Rubenstein has analyzed the 1991 Australian census data on Jews in *Judaism in Australia* (Canberra, 1995).

16. For a discussion of Jews and multiculturalism in Australia, see Jon Stratton, "The Impossible Ethnic: Jews and Multiculturalism in Australia," *Diaspora* 5.3 (1996): 339–93.

17. Jean-Paul Sartre, *Anti-Semite and Jew* (New York, 1948), 55.

18. See Benedict Anderson, *Imagined Communities: Reflections on the Origin and Spread of Nationalism,* rev. ed. (London, 1991).

19. Leon Poliakov, *The Aryan Myth* (London, 1974), 143.

20. George Mosse, *Toward the Final Solution* (New York, 1978), 14.

21. Anderson, *Imagined Communities,* 149. Cf. Tom Nairn, *The Break-Up of Britain* (London, 1977).

22. On Wilhelm Marr's life, see Moshe Zimmermann, *Wilhelm Marr: The Patriarch of Anti-Semitism* (Oxford, 1986).

23. Charles Price, *Jewish Settlers in Australia* (Canberra, 1964), 15.

24. See, for example, Geoffrey Alderman's discussion "English Jews or Jews of the English Persuasion? Reflections on the Emancipation of Anglo-Jewry," in *Paths of Emancipation: Jews, States, and Citizenship,* ed. Pierre Birnbaum and Ira Katznelson (Princeton, N.J., 1995).

25. Getzler, *Neither Toleration nor Favour,* 10.

26. Ibid., 11.

27. Jean-François Lyotard discusses the discursive category of "the jews" in *Heidegger and "the jews"* (Minneapolis, 1990). Lyotard's formulation is more universalist than mine, seeing "the jews" as "the irremissable in the West's movement of remission and pardon" (22).

28. Sherington, *Australia's Immigrants,* 66.

29. Willard, *History of the White Australia Policy,* 21.

30. Ibid., 27.

31. Ibid., 33.

32. Ibid., 90.

33. Quoted in ibid., 19.

34. Richard White, *Inventing Australia* (North Sydney, 1981), 47.

35. Ibid., 47.

36. Quoted in Willard, *History of the White Australia Policy,* 47.

37. Andrew Markus, "Australian Governments and the Concept of Race: An Historical Perspective," in *The Cultural Construction of Race,* ed. Marie de Lepervanche and Gillian Bottomley (Sydney, 1988), 50.

38. Willard, *History of the White Australia Policy,* 189.

39. Ibid., 107.

40. Sean Brawley, *The White Peril: Foreign Relations and Asian Immigration to Australasia and North America, 1919–1978* (Sydney, 1995), 48–49.

41. Willard, *History of the White Australia Policy,* 109.

42. Quoted in ibid., 112. Willard quotes this important speech extensively.

43. Ibid., 113.

44. Quoted in White, *Inventing Australia,* 71.

45. Willard, *History of the White Australia Policy,* 99.

46. Quoted in Rutland, *Edge of Diaspora,* 95.

47. Rubenstein, *Jews in Australia,* 1:116.

48. Quoted in ibid., 1:479.

49. Quoted in Rutland, *Edge of Diaspora,* 95.

50. See, for example, Peter Love, "The Kingdom of Shylock: A Case-Study of Australian Labour Anti-Semitism," *Journal of the Australian Jewish History Association* 12.1 (1993): 54–62.

51. Quoted in Rubenstein, *Jews in Australia,* 1:117.

52. One discussion of the nineteenth-century European orientalizing of the Jews is Paul Mendes-Flohr, "*Fin-de-Siècle* Orientalism, the *Ostjuden,* and the Aesthetics of Jewish Self-Affirmation," *Studies in Contemporary Jewry* 1 (1984): 96–139. Mendes-Flohr also discusses how Polish Jews came to be described as *Halb-Asien* through the work of the popular Viennese Jewish novelist Karl Emil Franzos, "indelibly marking the East European Jews as non-European, semi-Oriental people" (102).

53. Sander Gilman, *The Jew's Body* (New York, 1991), 171.

54. See Anne McClintock, *Imperial Leather: Race, Gender, and Sexuality in the Colonial Conquest* (New York, 1995).

55. See Theodore W. Allen, *The Invention of the White Race,* vol. 1 (London, 1994).

56. Rubenstein, *Jews in Australia,* 1:483.

57. Willard, *History of the White Australia Policy,* 121.

58. Blakeney, *Australia and the Jewish Refugees,* 28.

59. It is interesting to note in this regard the importance in multicultural rhetoric of the designation "N.E.S." (Non-English Speaker), which has rapidly slipped into "N.E.S.B." (Non-English Speaking Background), thus introducing a notion of cultural difference between "English-Speaking Background" and "Non-English Speaking Background," in key ways an ethnic reworking of the White Australian Policy's essentialist, racist distinction.

60. Quoted in Willard, *History of the White Australia Policy,* 189.

61. See, for example, Robert Young's discussion of nineteenth-century theories about miscegenation in *Colonial Desire* (London, 1995).

62. Rutland, *Edge of Diaspora,* 141.

63. Rubenstein, *Judaism in Australia,* 43.

64. Castles et al., *Mistaken Identity,* 20.

65. Bartrop, *Australia and the Holocaust,* 16.

66. Ibid., 27.

67. Ibid., 31.

68. Quoted in ibid., 47.

69. Quoted in ibid., 48.

70. Quoted in ibid., 52.

71. Quoted in Rutland, *Edge of Diaspora,* 189.

72. Quoted in Medding, *From Assimilation to Group Survival,* 160.

73. As late as 1960, in a study of "social distance" attitudes carried out in Perth, Western Australia, Jews ranked sixth behind English, Germans, Dutch, Poles, and Italians on a combination of scales indicating acceptability. Below Jews came Malayans. These national categories—except for Jews, of course—are interesting for the way they express racial concerns. This study can be found in Ronald Taft, *From Stranger to Citizen: A Survey of Studies of Immigrant Assimilation in Western Australia* (Perth, 1965), 18–20.

74. Quoted in Medding, *From Assimilation to Group Survival,* 161.

75. Quoted in Bartrop, *Australia and the Holocaust,* 54.

76. Quoted in Rubenstein, *Jews in Australia,* 167.

77. Ibid. Just how sensitive the race issue still is can be gauged from Bartrop's description of Forms 40 and 47 as "another example of departmental anti-Semitism" (*Australia and the Holocaust,* 151), not knowing of the A.J.W.S.'s request.

78. Quoted in Bartrop, *Australia and the Holocaust,* 152.

79. It is worth remembering in this connection that the modern European nation-state was not, on the whole, secular. It was, in many cases still is, Christian. Thus, the push for Jewish religious equality in the Australian colonies in the second half of the nineteenth century had implications for the establishment of a Christian state, all the more so when England had the Church of England as its established Church. It is in this context that William Wentworth, then a member of the New South Wales Legislative Council, argued in 1853 that any religious group including, in his word, "Mohammedans," should be given religious equality while Jews had a particularly good claim because Christianity originated in Judaism. George Nichol, a former editor of the radical *Australian,* agreed with Wentworth about Judaism but would not go so far as to give religious equality to "Mohammedans" and "pagans." (My account of this debate is taken from Geltzer, *Neither Toleration Nor Favour,* 43.) Here we can see how close to exclusion from the modern nation-state Judaism was, and how defining Jews in terms of religion still opened up questions about their full membership of particular nation-states.

80. Quoted in Naomi Gale, "A Case of Double Rejection: The Immigration of Sephardim to Australia," *New Community* 20.2 (1994): 274.

81. Quoted in Rutland, *Edge of Diaspora,* 242.

82. Quoted in Gale, "Case of Double Rejection," 274.

83. Quoted in ibid.

84. Ibid., 280.

85. Ibid.

86. Quoted in ibid., 276. I have taken my outline from Gale's discussion of the case.

87. On the Jewish side, the Australian Anglo-Jewish/Ashkenazi establishment treated the Sephardi migrants in a very similar way to the way Australian Anglo-Jewry had treated the European and eastern European refugees. As Gale puts it: "The Ashkenazim at best displayed little interest in their co-religionists. Indeed, many seemed unwilling to recognise the Sephardim as Jews" (ibid., 283).

14 Ethnonationalism, Anti-Semitism, and Identity Politics: The North American and South African Experiences

MILTON SHAIN

In an insightful comparative examination of modern anti-Semitism in the West, Todd Endelman reminds us of the importance of "national context" when accounting for "the accents and stresses" of anti-Semitic thinking.[1] In particular, Endelman draws our attention to what he terms "illiberal anti-modernism," most evident in Germany and Austria from the 1870s. "In those states," he writes, "where the fundamental ideas of bourgeois liberalism (religious toleration, parliamentarianism, equality before the law, occupational mobility, laissez-faire capitalism) failed to attract widespread support, e.g., Germany and Austria, there was less willingness to tolerate the integration of Jews than elsewhere."[2]

Endelman's emphasis on ideology, and his deemphasis of Jewish particularism or behavior in the equation of anti-Semitism, is instructive.[3] If Jewish particularism, he argues, was a primary variable, anti-Semitism would have been most virulent in Great Britain and the United States. New York and London, he points out, had highly visible and alien Jewish communities. In both countries, however, Jews were not the recipients of sustained "public" or "programmatic" anti-Semitism.[4]

Endelman's stress on ideology is a salutary warning to those who, through an "interactionist" perspective, seek to locate anti-Semitism essentially in "rational" material or cultural clashes. Colin Holmes, for example, is quite comfortable in explaining British anti-Semitism at the turn of the century in terms of job shortages, housing crises and economic stringency.[5] Similarly, Albert Lindemann's comparative examination of the Dreyfus, Beilis and Frank Affairs highlights as a primary cause of anti-Jewish hostility the structural niche occupied by Jews in a modernizing world.[6] Anti-Jewish ideologies, in other words, have a "reasonable" basis and the role of Jews in the creation of anti-Semitism cannot be ignored. As Lindemann puts it, anti-Semitism needs to be explained in terms of "the experience of real people in the real world."[7]

While not wishing to ignore the importance of material and cultural clashes (especially at the time of the great Eastern European Jewish migrations), it is important to stress dominant ideologies or cultural patterns. These ideologies, generated beyond the Jew, although not necessarily unrelated to the Jew, are a key to understanding the potency and depth of anti-Semitism. Among such cultural patterns, antimodernism, as identified by Endelman, does seem to be an important factor. Ethnonationalism, at least in its nineteenth- and early twentieth-century form, is another essential ingredient. Very often it subsumes antimodernism and to a substantial extent depends upon the "other" in its genesis and success. In this sense, "the Jew," a symbol of modernity, provides a useful focus for attention, helping to elevate the insider at the expense of the outsider. This becomes apparent when looking comparatively at the experiences of Jews in America, Canada and South Africa.

In all three settings Jews were a conspicuous minority and, at certain times, the targets of abuse and vilification. Abuse, however, was most rampant, sustained and widespread during periods of nativism (an incipient form of ethnonationalism) in America, and unbridled ethnonationalism in Quebec and South Africa. Nativism and ethnonationalism are inclined (although they need not be) toward illiberalism and antimodernism. This was particularly evident in South Africa and Quebec in the 1930s and early 1940s, where anti-Jewish stereotyping was transformed into sustained anti-Jewish hostility with a mass base. The context was an exclusivist ethnonationalism: in the Quebec case, a Francophone hostility rooted in language and confession; in the South African case an exclusivist Afrikaner *volkisch* ideology, rooted in language and confession. In the former, Catholicism informed hostility; in the latter, Calvinism. Common to both contexts was an illiberal antimodernism, generated by what one scholar has referred to as the "Poor Whites of the British Empire."[8]

THE CONSTRUCTION OF AN ANTI-JEWISH STEREOTYPE

Although Jewish status in the period of early colonial settlement demonstrated some anomalies, all three countries were essentially postemancipation societies. That is to say they were products of the Enlightenment, at least insofar as European settlers were concerned. While this meant a softening of attitudes toward the Jew, it also meant the incorporation of age-old hostilities toward Judaism. These hostilities were deeply embedded in the western tradition and easily transferred to the colonial world. In Canada, "a steady stream of theological anti-Judaism ran throughout the pre-Confederation era,"[9] while in Colonial America, "the very word Jew evoked something negative in the minds of many, if not indeed most of their neighbours."[10] In South Africa, long before the arrival of Jews, the English explorer John Barrow described a certain exploitative element in the hinterland as "a kind of Jew broker defrauding the simple boors."[11] In an age of great migrations, the penetration of European ideas (including the deeply rooted anti-Jewish stereotype) was inevitable.

Nevertheless, settler minorities were by and large treated with Enlightenment liberality. In the United States, in particular, "the test of national origins, religion, social class, or region" played little role for entry into the American people.[12] In English Canada and in the two southern African British colonies—Cape Colony and Natal—the situation was similar, since Jews had achieved "effective civil, if not political, rights in England by the middle of the eighteenth century."[13] On the other hand, in French Canada the clergy held some influence, and religious confession influenced political rights. The Fathers of Confederation, writes Michael Brown, "envisaged a binational, bicultural, bilingual, bireligious, biracial state, not a pluralistic melting pot. That meant that Jews, who were neither Catholic nor Protestant, and for the most part, neither British nor French, were constitutional outsiders."[14] Much the same applies for the breakaway Boer Republics—the Orange Free State and South African Republic. Here deeply conservative and insular views meant an inextricable relationship between state and religion, and a concomitant marginalization of the Jew.[15] The constitutions of both these republics, established in the mid-nineteenth century, denied full rights to non-Protestants.

Marginalization informed perceptions of the Jew, especially the alien Yiddish-speaking newcomers from Eastern Europe who made their presence felt from the late nineteenth century. But even before the arrival of the Eastern Europeans, and well beyond the exclusive Boer Republics and Quebec, Jews were viewed with suspicion. This was best illustrated in the American Civil War when personal fears and frustrations, economic tensions and mass passions were projected onto the Jew, an ideal and convenient scapegoat.[16] While fundamentalist Christianity goes some way toward explaining hostility, the influence of incipient nativism in mid-nineteenth-century America cannot be ignored. Hostility toward Irish and German immigrants had at that time generated a nativist resentment expressed in the American Party or the Know-Nothings.[17] That sentiment sharpened ethnic boundaries and initiated a quest for the meaning of Americanism. In nativism one sees an embryonic ethnonationalism. Certainly in the American case, anti-Semitism and nativism were directly correlated.

Nativist sentiment, with its hostility toward the modern, also informed late-nineteenth-century anxieties in America,[18] especially in the rural Midwest, as exemplified in the Populist movement. While scholarly debate concerning the role or extent of anti-Semitism within the movement continues,[19] there can be little doubt that anti-Jewish motifs found their way into Populist rhetoric. Angry farmers castigated the unproductive middlemen, faraway bankers and conspiratorial urban plutocrats.[20] For many, the Jew fitted these categories. Agrarian anti-Semitism, notes Higham, looked back nostalgically to an earlier age, when power was not in the hands of Wall Street plutocrats and Jews.[21] Put simply, the "producing classes" pitted themselves against the "unproductive" speculators and monopolists.

Similar sentiments were articulated in rural Canada, where anti-urbanism and anti-industrialism operated. French Canadians, writes Brown, "waxed nostalgic about their past, a past without Jews. This was the *fin de siècle.* An old, quiet, pastoral Christian world was waning, giving way to a new one—commercial, industrial, urban and secular in character. Jews in French-Canada were part of this new world, in fact, its more potent symbol, since they had been absent from the old. As such, they became the target of considerable animosity, indeed, the scapegoats for people who viewed the present with distaste and the future with anxiety."[22]

Rural antagonism toward the Jew manifested itself in attitudes toward the smalltown trader and peddler. Banking records, utilized by David Gerber and Richard Menkis in their studies of Jews and credit rating in late-nineteenth-century America and Canada respectively, show how widespread antipathy was. Jews were not held in good repute and were seen to be risky and unreliable debtors. In short, they were to be avoided.[23] Much the same applies to South Africa, where Standard Bank Inspector Reports similarly questioned the integrity of Eastern European Jews. In considering advances to these newcomers, banks were asked to be especially vigilant. In commenting, for instance, on an advance to one Lazarus, the inspector noted: "For a country Jew shopkeeper, whose statement of position is verbal only, and whose character is admittedly bad, too much accommodation seems to be given to this party."[24]

Rural antagonism toward the Jew merged with evolving anti-Jewish sentiment in the large cities. Here the alien Jew was easily identifiable and the target of abuse. Hostility was "widespread and deep-rooted" in Anglo-Canada, where there was even talk of "inborn prejudice" against Jews.[25] French Canadians were even more hostile, with the French-Canadian nationalist, Olivar Asselin, decrying "the invasion of exotic babbling" Jews into Montreal.[26] "Scum," "offscourings" and other such appellations were regularly attributed to the newcomers who were accused of a range of evils such as vice and illicit liquor dealing.[27] In Atlanta, the Leo Frank Affair captured the animus aroused by the newcomers, in that case the penetration of Jews into the South.[28] In Quebec and South Africa there was an added dimension: Jews were associated with a hegemonic urban English culture and as such posed a threat to traditional French-Canadian and Afrikaner rural values.

While South Africa and Canada did not have the equivalent of an American Populist movement, many did associate the Jew with finance and, more specifically, with a network of international financiers.[29] In South Africa this association was reinforced by the conspicuous presence of Jews on the Witwatersrand, and by their disproportionate representation among the mining magnates. J. A. Hobson, Johannesburg correspondent for the *Manchester Guardian* and later doyen of the British liberal-left, argued that a ring of Jewish international financiers controlled the most valuable resources of the South African Republic. In his book on the Anglo-Boer War, Hobson postulated the notion of a war fought in the interests of a "small group of international financiers, chiefly German in origin and Jewish in race."[30] Clearly his accusations echoed rhetoric used by American Populists.

It is significant that hostility toward the Jew in South Africa at this time was rooted much more in economic competition than in nativist or ethnonationalist concerns. Certainly in the urban centers the unemployed and unskilled, not to mention the mercantile establishment fearful of competition, looked upon the Jew with suspicion and hostility. Most important, however, it was the parvenu Jew, a symbol of the city and finance, who fired the anti-Jewish imagination. For the impoverished farmer, hostile to change and a victim of modernization, the Jew was a symbol of greed, living by his wits and alien to all that was valued. He was rootless, scheming, and not given to manual work. In the early twentieth century, however, there was nothing like the American Populist movement, notwithstanding the rapidly emerging "poor white" problem.

Quebec was, as noted above, also infused with an antimodernism, welded by a militant religiosity which saw Jews as particularly unwelcome.[31] French Canadians were concerned with communal prerogatives, including race and religious homogeneity. It is instructive to note that English Canada was less hostile toward Jews than Quebec. Like America and Great Britain, a measure of pluralism and individualism was accepted. Concern with race and homogeneity—in essence ethnonationalism—compromises pluralism and broader rights. In America it took the form of nativism and informed the anti-Jewish lobby before World War I. Nativism would blossom in the postwar years and would also be evident in Quebec and in South Africa.

NATIVISM AND ETHNONATIONALISM

Extreme xenophobia characterized the postwar western world in the wake of the Russian Revolution. Jews were rapidly associated with Bolshevism, their threat aggravated by the continuous influx of Russian Jews to the new world. The "Red Scare" was widespread and informed perceptions of the Jew, particularly in the context of labor instability. The great steel strikes of 1919 in Canada[32] and America,[33] and the 1922 Rand Rebellion in South Africa,[34] ensured the association of Jews with subversive Bolshevism. Hatred and fear of the foreigner saw a refurbished Ku Klux Klan in America in the 1920s and the enactment of anti-immigration legislation in 1921 and again in 1924. Essentially informed by a galloping nativism, the legislation demonstrated vividly how Jews (not the only targets) were considered unsuitable immigrants. Eugenicist notions fed into xenophobic and nativist rhetoric, built upon earlier negative stereotypes.

Xenophobic and nativist hostility toward the Jew was best captured in Henry Ford's *Dearborn Independent,* an outrageous anti-Jewish newspaper backed by Ford's resources. Styled by Feingold as a "latter day populist," Ford attacked Jews for exploiting farmers' organizations and for their alleged control of Wall Street.[35] In much the same way as Johannesburg symbolized Jewish power in South Africa, so New York became a symbol of Jewish power in America.[36] For the anti-Semite, the Jew symbolized all that was evil in the modern world, a world nostalgically contrasted with an idealized past age of order and harmony.

In South Africa, regular appeals were made to maintain the "Nordic" character of the white population. Eastern European Jews were labeled "unassimilable," and perceived as immutably alien and inherently devious. The newcomers, mainly from Lithuania, were allegedly subverting the social order and values of the white population. Calls for exclusion, echoing American rhetoric, were heard throughout the 1920s, from both English- and Afrikaans-speaking whites, culminating in the Quota Act of 1930.[37] The act, modeled on American immigration legislation, put a virtual end to Eastern European Jews entering South Africa. Like its American counterpart, restrictive rationales were built upon eugenicist notions, with concerns about "nordic" stock and the "character" of the white population.[38] While much of the support for restrictive legislation was rooted in economic competition and a constant fear of Jewish upward mobility, Afrikaners were, in addition, driven by an emergent ethnonationalism. Here an exclusivist, backward-looking, *volkisch* and illiberal ideology began to operate. By 1930, one in five Afrikaners were classified by the Carnegie Commission as "Poor Whites." For these social and economic casualties of industrialization, the Jew symbolized the alien and inhospitable city and all its vices.

Canada also experienced a rise of nativism in the 1920s, incorporating calls to exclude immigrants, particularly Jews. Jews in Ontario were challenged for their failure to assimilate, and were accused of invading the public schools and threatening the social order.[39] In short, they were "the object of widespread paranoia and xenophobia."[40] In Alberta, Jews were a focus of the populist Social Credit movement, which built on the American Populist legacy.[41] It was in Quebec, however, where hostility was most marked. Inspired by the Catholic Church, Jews were characterized as middlemen, unsuited to the province's needs. Hostility was built upon the earlier negative stereotype, gaining strength (as in the case of Afrikaners in South Africa) with the emergence of Quebecois ethnonationalism. Nationalist emotion exploded in the 1930s, fueled by the trauma of the Great Depression. Quebecois ideology was exclusivist in orientation, illiberal in character and defensive in nature. The Jew was an alien symbol who, notes Pierre Anctil, stood outside the Canadian tradition.[42] Whereas Anglo-Protestants were at least Christian, the Jews were an aberration, threatening Quebec's religious character. Most important, Jews were associated with modernism and materialism. Their success in moving into occupations previously occupied by Gentiles and coveted by Francophones ensured an ethnonationalist response.

Canadian anti-Semitism expressed itself in opposition to Jewish involvement in educational governance, in the Achat Chez Nous movement in which French Canadians were urged to stay away from Jewish shopkeepers, and in the emergence of a range of fascist movements. Lita-Rose Betcherman and Esther Delisle have vividly captured the gross anti-Semitism of the period.[43] Delisle, in particular, has shown how mainstream Francophone nationalism in the 1930s (including the writings of Lionel Groulx, patron saint of modern Quebec nationalism) was infused with anti-Semitism which fed on European ideas and currents.[44] Jews were accused of both capitalism and communism, and blamed for all the evils of modernity. As in South Africa, they were perceived to be "unassimilable," upwardly mobile and a threat to the urban landscape. In addition, Jews were charged with corrupting the moral fabric of society. "By painting such a repugnant and malevolent portrait of the Jew," writes Irving Abella, "the nationalist could argue that a nativist movement would clear their society of its enemies, restore order and return to their over-eager hands the reigns of power. And all this could be done by getting rid of the Jew."[45] Pierre Anctil is correct when he points out that the Jew served as a "catalyzing impulse," a useful scapegoat upon which to pin all the social, moral and economic problems of Quebec.[46]

Fascist groups, such as Adrien Arcand's Parti National Social Chrétien, were at the forefront of scapegoating Jews. Besides highlighting the allegedly negative role of Jews in society, these extremists sought to redefine the nature of French Canada. The Jew was a useful means of bolstering a Francophone identity, rooted in confession and notions of race. As Abella explains, anti-Semitism became "simply an extreme form of nationalism," in which there was no place for the Jew. "Theirs was to be a country of homesteaders and farmers."[47] While the most difficult period for Jews coincided with economic hardship in the interwar period "when fears of foreign domination were pronounced in the province,"[48] the source of hostility lay in a hostile antimodernist ethnonationalism. Jews were an obstacle to the nationalist enterprise.

Anti-Semitism was also an important and influential component of the Afrikaner *weltanschauung* in the 1930s. It was particularly evident in the rhetoric and actions of the "shirt" movements, most notably the Greyshirts. Against the background of drought, depression, and rapidly increasing black economic competition, these fascist clones, with a marked preference for "the language and symbolism of Nazism," devoted themselves primarily "to attacking that oldest of scapegoats, the Jew."[49] Anti-Jewish ideas rapidly permeated the mainstream of Afrikaner nationalism. The groundswell of anti-Jewish feeling—especially demands for action, the boycotting of Jewish businesses, and threats against the Jewish community—prompted the ruling United Party to introduce stiffer educational and financial requirements for immigrants, culminating in the Aliens Act of 1937 which closed the loophole of German-Jewish immigration.[50]

The rhetoric of protest and opposition to Jewish immigration was riddled with racist assumptions and anti-Semitic generalizations. Jews were seen as aliens, disloyal, bent on exploitation, communists and inclined toward conspiratorial behavior. Most important, fringe sentiment was gradually integrated into the core of the political program of the opposition Purified National Party. By the late 1930s anti-Semitism had become an integral part of *volkisch* Afrikaner ethnonationalism. Many of the key theoreticians within the movement had, in fact, studied in Germany, where they imbibed ideas of the corporate state, an idealist worldview, and a sense of exclusivist nationalism.

These ideas propelled a powerful republicanism rooted in notions of divine election, a leitmotif within the Afrikaners' civil religion.[51] Like their European (and American and Canadian) counterparts on the right, Afrikaner nationalists were opposed to liberalism, Marxism, and laissez-faire capitalism.

As was the case in Quebec, anti-Semitism served an important function within Afrikaner society. The quintessentially alien Jew helped to consolidate an all-embracing Afrikaner identity, understood in terms of cultural unity, national roots, and opposition to the foreigner. In other words, anti-Semitism helped to cover over and blur class divisions and antagonisms within Afrikaner society. The Afrikaner's inferior status in white society and his poverty could be explained in racial or national terms. Moreover, by employing the discourse of "race" to exclude and denigrate Jews, the Afrikaner was in turn elevated. As Robert Miles notes in his critique of racism, "the act of representational exclusion is simultaneously an act of inclusion, whether or not Self is explicitly identified in the discourse."[52] It is therefore no coincidence that anti-Semitism continued to suffuse specifically right-wing Afrikaner political discourse and programs, despite the upturn in the economy from the mid-1930s. Of course, the illiberal and antimodernist nature of Afrikaner ethnonationalism during the 1930s also helps to explain why, in Endelman's terms, "public" anti-Semitism was essentially an Afrikaner phenomenon and why it had appeal across the whole spectrum of Afrikaner nationalist opinion.

In America, anti-Semitism in the 1930s built upon the nativism of the 1920s but never developed in the way it did in South Africa and Quebec. Notwithstanding the appalling economic conditions, anti-Jewish hostility threatened, but never took on, a mass base.[53] It was not part of a national agenda and the Jew was not needed as a symbol to enhance a national movement and to define its essence. The result was an absence of ideological coherence, despite a great outpouring of anti-Semitism from individuals, very often rooted in Catholic and Protestant fundamentalism.[54] Father Coughlin's rabid anti-Semitism rivalled the rhetoric of anti-Semites in Quebec and South Africa, but failed to resonate. He did not speak for an ethnonationalist movement in search of an identity. The same applies for William Dudley Pedley and his Silver Shirts, Fritz Kuhn's German-American Bund, the Reverend Gerald Winrod, George Sylvester Viereck, and the Reverend Gerald L. K. Smith. All appealed to individuals obsessed with Jews rather than to a "people" allegedly dominated by Jews. These individuals were at best leaders of small disaffected groups; they were not an advance guard of an ethnonationalist movement, attempting to mold a "people" by using the Jew as a classic "other."

Consequently, despite the intensity of anti-Semitism in the 1930s being greater than at any other time in American history, it was never an issue integrated into a wider political agenda. American anti-Semitism was not embedded in cultural battles, as was the case with Afrikaner and Quebecois ethnonationalism. It did lead, however, as in Canada and South Africa, to the restriction of Jewish immigration, an aloofness from the Jewish catastrophe in Europe, and a reluctance to receive Jewish refugees. But it was not part of a psychological liberation enhanced by its focus upon the Jew as an antitype. Hostility was more akin to Anglo-Canadian and South African English-speaking anti-Semitism. In Canada that involved calls for restriction, incidents such as the Christie Pits riots and the creation of "Swastika Clubs."[55]

Sustained attacks on the Jews in a programmatic sense were, however, absent. Where there were indications of sustained hostility in Anglo-Canada, such as in the Anglo-Saxondom of the Social Credit Party, it is significant that opposition to ethnic pluralism had a role to play.[56] In South Africa, English speakers were inclined to distance themselves from the excesses of the radical right, which challenged their cultural hegemony and opposed the allied war effort.

Sharing as they did a powerful ethnonationalism, it is no coincidence that French Canadians and Afrikaner South Africans were the most rabid and threatening anti-Semites. French-Canadian nationalists, supported by the Roman Catholic Church, saw the Jews (and other "foreigners") as an obstacle to their project. Calvinist Afrikaners similarly saw their lifestyle threatened by English speakers (among whom the Jew emerged as a convenient symbol) who dominated the urban centers. Everett Hughes's observation that Jews in Quebec "bore the brunt of attacks that the French Canadians would have liked to launch against their English Canadian dominator"[57] could well apply to South Africa.

THE POSTWAR ERA

Canada, America and South Africa all experienced a rapid decline in anti-Semitism after the war. This must be attributed in part to the erosion of cultural differences as second-generation immigrants merged into the dominant culture (although it should be noted that in 1980 one in three Canadian Jews were foreign-born),[58] and to the impact of the Holocaust on the popular consciousness. However, changes within the dominant culture itself cannot be ignored. In America, the war was "a great common experience," serving to undermine ethnic divisions and helping to shape a broader sense of national identity.[59] In addition, a new postwar consumerist culture meant, in the words of Higham, the "integration of rural America into an urbanised national culture" in which old "suspicions of the city as a place of alien intrigue" were eroded.[60] In Canada modernization, secularization and multiculturalism also modified attitudes toward the Jew, as did the erosion of clerical power and conservative national ideologies. Quebec, moreover, was integrated into the broader American economy and a primary value was placed on ethnic diversity.[61]

South Africa too witnessed fundamental changes. A new Afrikaner bourgeoisie—well educated, confident and more optimistic than their forebears—enjoyed the economic fruits of racist exploitation and political power. Like agrarian American populists and Quebecois nationalists, they developed a newfound respect for enterprise and material success. The very scaffolding that had underpinned their sense of inferiority was thus removed as they began to experience power and social mobility. A sense of competition with, and fear of, the Jew declined. Most significantly, however, the impetus of exclusivist Afrikaner nationalism waned. English speakers, including Jews, were necessary for the apartheid project. Color was the cardinal divide and, despite (early in the century) some observers equating Jews with the much-maligned Indians who similarly challenged the mercantile establishment, the white status of the Jew was never seriously questioned or threatened. Classic Jew-baiting in South Africa after the war, as in America and Canada, was restricted to a fringe ultraright element. With embourgeoisment these extremists became an endangered species. Significantly the majority black population, including Coloreds and Indians, has never focused specifically on the Jew when articulating grievances and aspirations. For them the issue has always been one of white oppression and domination. At most, distinctions were made between English and Afrikaans speakers.[62]

In terms of the discussion hitherto, it is important to note that resistance politics in South Africa has downplayed ethnicity, characterizing it as a construct utilized by the state to divide and rule. The reaction on the part of the newly liberated majority—at least at the ideological level—has been a nonracism devoid of ethnic categories.[63] The ANC espouses a brand of nationalism which is inclusive in orientation, nonracial in content and modernist in outlook. In this sense it differs fundamentally from the backward-looking and exclusivist Afrikaner nationalism of the 1930s and 1940s. Inclusivity takes the sharpness out of ethnic conflict and militates against anti-Semitism. An even greater palliative is the notion of "rainbowism" which celebrates cultural diversity and difference. Here comparisons with the Canadian "ethnic mosaic" are worth considering. In that country the insecurities of Francophone Canadians in an Anglophone country have generated a heightened sense of cultural identity among all ethnic groups. Pluralism is demonstrable in the Canadian census and Canadian identity is invariably hyphenated. Jews are an ethnic and a religious group, supported by a Charter of Rights and Freedoms which seeks to enhance multiculturalism and to promote diversity.[64] As such, the notion of nonconformity is absent and anti-Semitism minimized. This may well be the case in South Africa, as "rainbowism" transforms into a genuine celebration of cultural and ethnic diversity.

It is worthy of note that in America a variant of ethnonationalism has kept Jews on the public agenda. I am referring to African-American anti-Semitism, prevalent mostly among groups espousing a form of black consciousness. While Leonard Dinnerstein is surely correct when he accounts for this phenomenon primarily in terms of fundamentalist Christian teachings and the secularization of negative religious imagery in modern times,[65] his comments on the "nationalist" content of more recent anti-Jewish outbursts are important. Dinnerstein stresses a militancy associated specifically with "black power."[66] In this case, of course, black power has been juxtaposed by the Nation of Islam with religious hatred into an explosive mixture. Like their poor white counterparts of the 1930s in South Africa and Quebec, and their populist nativist forebears in late-nineteenth-century America, many African-Americans see the Jew as a symbol of the city and a cause of all hardships associated with the urban life. Ethnonationalism and, to a lesser extent, antimodernism are once again evident.

Quite clearly, explaining the ebb and flow of anti-Semitism is complicated and cannot be reduced to a single cause. The structural position of Jews and the timing of their entry into society cannot be discounted. Certainly one sees a significant increase in anti-Semitism during times of economic and social stress. The alien nature of Yiddish-speaking newcomers also had a major impact on perceptions of the Jews in all three settings. However, to account for anti-Semitism in terms of the conspicuousness of the victims is too simplistic. Prevailing discourses, as Cheyette argues, are inclined to construct the Jew within a particular frame and no account of anti-Semitism can ignore the historic evolution of an anti-Jewish discourse.[67] Ultimately, however, broader cultural patterns determine attitudes toward, and perceptions of, the Jew. As we have seen, nativism and ethnonationalism heightened and sharpened differences. Antimodernist ethnonationalism in the Quebecois and Afrikaner cases of the 1930s employed the "other" to enhance self definition and to deflect divisions within the group. Insular and backward-looking, it focused on the Jew, an exemplar of the modern. On the other hand, as Brym and Lenton demonstrate, ethnonationalism need not necessarily be anti-Semitic.[68] Thus, in more recent times, Quebecois nationalism has not generated hostility toward Jews as it did in the 1930s. The key variable appears to be that Quebecois nationalism in the 1980s has accommodated a modernist worldview.

In conclusion, it is important to deconstruct the particular nature of ethnonationalism. Ideologies are not static and changes can have important implications for ethnic relations. In the cases under consideration, accommodating a modernist worldview diluted hostility toward the Jew. Pluralism, multiculturalism and "rainbowism"—the very antithesis of ethnonationalism—provided further safeguards. Herein lies the most important antidote to ethnic conflict. Genuine respect for the "other" and the recognition of diversity must, in the long term, hinder chauvinism, undermine bigotry and protect minorities.

Notes

1. Todd M. Endelman, "Comparative Perspectives on Modern Anti-Semitism in the West," in *History and Hate: The Dimensions of Anti-Semitism,* ed. David Berger (Philadelphia: Jewish Publication Society, 1986), 96.

2. Ibid., 105.

3. He particularly takes issue with Jacob Katz, who sees nineteenth-century anti-Semitism primarily as a product of the failure of Jews to assimilate. See Jacob Katz, *From Prejudice to Destruction: Anti-Semitism, 1700–1933* (Cambridge, Mass.: Harvard University Press, 1980), 322.

4. For Endelman, "public" anti-Semitism refers to "the eruption of anti-Semitism in political life—the injection of anti-Semitism into matters of policy and the manipulation of anti-Semitism for partisan political ends." "Private" anti-Semitism, on the other hand, refers "to expressions of contempt and discrimination outside the realm of public life." See Endelman, "Comparative Perspectives," 104.

5. Colin Holmes, *Anti-Semitism in British Society, 1876–1939* (London: Holmes and Meier, 1979).

6. Albert S. Lindemann, *The Jew Accused: Three Anti-Semitic Affairs: Dreyfus, Beilis, Frank, 1894–1915* (Cambridge: Cambridge University Press, 1991).

7. Ibid., 9. On the role of the "minority group" itself as a cause of ethnic conflict, see also John Higham, *Send These to Me: Jews and Other Immigrants in Urban America* (New York: Atheneum, 1975), 124.

8. The title of a seminar given by Dan O'Meara to the Department of Political Studies at the University of Cape Town, Apr. 4, 1996.

9. Richard Menkis, "Antisemitism and Anti-Judaism in Preconfederation Canada," in *Antisemitism in Canada: History and Interpretation,* ed. Alan Davies (Waterloo, Ontario: Wilfred Laurier University Press, 1992), 17.

10. Jacob Rader Marcus, *The Colonial American Jew,* 3 vols. (New York: Jewish Publication Society, 1970), 3:1113.

11. John Barrow, *An Account of Travels into the Interior of Southern Africa in the Years 1797 and 1798,* 2 vols. (London: Cadell and Davies, 1801), 1:387.

12. Ira Katznelson, "Between Separation and Disappearance: Jews on the Margins of American Liberalism," in *Paths of Emancipation: Jews, States, and Citizenship,* ed. Pierre Birnbaum and Ira Katznelson (Princeton, N.J.: Princeton University Press, 1995), 164.

13. Menkis, "Antisemitism and Anti-Judaism," 23.

14. Michael Brown, "From Stereotype to Scapegoat: Anti-Jewish Sentiment in French Canada from Confederation to World War I," in *Antisemitism in Canada,* ed. Davies, 39.

15. See G. W. Eybers, *Select Constitutional Documents Illustrating South African History, 1795–1910* (London: Routledge, 1918), 28ff., 362ff. It should be noted that the marginalization of Jews in the Boer Republics and Quebec was not necessarily motivated by anti-Semitic intent. In the former it was the desire for sovereignty that generated Boer exclusivity and in the latter the desire of French Catholics to maintain a semblance of political control. These constitutions, to be sure, were drafted at a time when Jews were hardly a visible presence. Nevertheless, the implications for Jews were not, in the long term at least, insubstantial.

16. See Bertram Wallace Korn, "American Judeophobia: Confederate Version," in *Jews in the South,* ed. Leonard Dinnerstein and Mary Dale Paulson (Baton Rouge: Louisiana State University Press, 1973), 135.

17. See Hugh Brogan, *Longman History of the United States of America* (London: Longman, 1985), 312.

18. See Higham, *Send These to Me,* 129.

19. See Leonard Dinnerstein, *Anti-Semitism in America* (New York: Oxford University Press, 1994), 49–50.

20. Ibid.

21. Higham, *Send These to Me,* 182.

22. Brown,"From Stereotype to Scapegoat," 55.

23. See Menkis, "Antisemitism and Anti-Judaism," 24–26; and David A Gerber, "Cutting Out Shylock: Elite Anti-Semitism and the Quest for Moral Order in the Mid-Nineteenth-Century American Marketplace," in *Anti-Semitism in American History,* ed. David A Gerber (Urbana: University of Illinois Press, 1986), 217–20.

24. Milton Shain, *The Roots of Antisemitism in South Africa* (Charlottesville: University Press of Virginia, 1994), 24.

25. Michael Brown, *Jew or Juif?: Jews, French Canadians, and Anglo-Canadians, 1759–1914* (Philadelphia: Jewish Publication Society, 1986), 230–31.

26. Ibid., 231.

27. See, for example, *The Owl,* May 6, 1904; and Steven Hertzberg, *Strangers within the Gate City: The Jews of Atlanta, 1845–1915* (Philadelphia: Jewish Publication Society, 1978), 82. For anti-Jewish characterizations in all three settings, see Shain, *Roots of Antisemitism in South Africa,* chap. 3; Brown, "From Stereotype to Scapegoat"; and Michael N. Dobkowski, *The Tarnished Dream: The Basis of American Anti-Semitism* (Westport, Conn.: Greenwood, 1979), chaps. 1–4.

28. Leo Frank, a Yankee Jew, was convicted of murdering a thirteen-year-old girl in the pencil factory that he managed. When his death sentence was commuted to life imprisonment, a mob snatched him from prison and hanged him in the woods. See Leonard Dinnerstein, *The Leo Frank Case* (New York: Columbia University Press, 1968).

29. See Gerald Tulchinsky, "Goldwyn Smith: Victorian Antisemite," and Howard Palmer, "Politics, Religion, and Antisemitism in Alberta, 1880–1950," both in *Antisemitism in Canada,* ed. Davies.

30. John Atkinson Hobson, *The War in South Africa: Its Causes and Effects* (London: James Nisbet, 1900), 189.

31. Brown, "From Stereotype to Scapegoat," 46.

32. See Stephen Speisman, "Antisemitism in Ontario: The Twentieth Century," in *Antisemitism in Canada,* ed. Davies, 124.

33. See Henry L. Feingold, *A Midrash on American Jewish History* (Albany: SUNY Press, 1982), 179.

34. See Shain, *Roots of Antisemitism in South Africa,* chap. 5.

35. Feingold, *Midrash on American Jewish History,* 182–83.

36. Ibid., 183.

37. We know little about black attitudes. However, surveys of the African-language newspapers suggest immigration was not an issue.

38. See Shain, *Roots of Antisemitism in South Africa,* 137–41.

39. Speisman, "Antisemitism in Ontario," 117.

40. Ibid.

41. See Palmer, "Politics, Religion, and Antisemitism in Alberta."

42. Pierre Anctil, "Interlude of Hosility: Judeo-Christian Relations in Quebec in the Interwar Period, 1919–39," in *Antisemitism in Canada,* ed. Davies, 137.

43. Lita-Rose Betcherman, *The Swastika and the Maple Leaf: Fascist Movements in Canada in the Thirties* (Toronto: Fitzhenry and Whiteside, 1975); and Esther Delisle, *The Traitor and the Jew* (Toronto: Robert Davies, 1993).

44. See Delisle, *The Traitor and the Jew.*

45. Irving Abella, "Anti-Semitism in Canada in the Interwar Years," in *The Jews of North America,* ed. Moses Rischin (Detroit: Wayne State University Press, 1987), 240.

46. Anctil, "Interlude of Hostility," 149.

47. Abella, "Anti-Semitism in Canada in the Interwar Years," 244.

48. Anctil, "Interlude of Hostility," 153.

49. Patrick J. Furlong, *Between Crown and Swastika: The Impact of the Radical Right on the Afrikaner Nationalist Movement in the Fascist Era* (Johannesburg: University of Witwatersrand Press, 1991), 13.

50. See Edna Bradlow, "Immigration into the Union, 1910–1948: Politics and Attitudes" (Ph.D. diss., University of Cape Town, 1978), 275ff.

51. See Dunbar T. Moodie, *Rise of Afrikanerdom: Power, Apartheid, and the Afrikaner Civil Religion* (Berkeley: University of California Press, 1975), 21.

52. R. Miles, *Racism* (London: Routledge, 1989), 39.

53. Henry L. Feingold. *A Time for Searching: Entering the Mainstream, 1920–1945* (Baltimore: Johns Hopkins University Press, 1992), 252–53.

54. See Dinnerstein, *Antisemitism in America,* chap. 6.

55. Abella, "Anti-Semitism in Canada in the Interwar Years," 236–37.

56. See Alan Davies, "The Keegstra Affair," in *Antisemitism in Canada,* ed. Davies, 237–38.

57. Everett Hughes, *French Canada in Transition* (Chicago: University of Chicago Press, 1943), cited in Abella, "Anti-Semitism in Canada in the Interwar Years," 240.

58. See Morton Weinfeld, "Canadian Jews and Canadian Pluralism," in *American Pluralism and the Jewish Community*, ed. Seymour Martin Lipset (New Brunswick, N.J.: Transaction Publishers, 1990), 88.

59. "Phillip Gleason: American Identity and Americanization," in *Harvard Encyclopedia of American Ethnic Groups*, ed. Stephan Thernstrom (Cambridge, Mass.: Harvard University Press, 1980), 47.

60. Higham, *Send These to Me*, 193.

61. See Anctil, "Interlude of Hostility," 161.

62. Certainly an examination of the African-language press undertaken by the Kaplan Centre at the University of Cape Town reveals almost no concern with Jews.

63. There are, however, indications that this is changing and that ethnic politics is far from dead. See "Is Ethnicity in Vogue Again?" *Mail and Guardian*, May 24–30, 1996, 27.

64. See Weinfeld, "Canadian Jews and Canadian Pluralism."

65. Dinnerstein, *Antisemitism in America*, 197ff.

66. Ibid., 211.

67. Bryan Cheyette, "Hillaire Belloc and the 'Marconi Scandal,' 1900–1914: A Reassessment of the Interactionist Model of Racist Hatred," *Immigrants and Minorities* 8.1–2 (Mar. 1989).

68. See Robert J. Brym and Rhonda L. Lenton, "The Distribution of Anti-Semitism in Canada in 1984," in *The Jews in Canada*, ed. Robert J. Brym, William Shaffir, and Morton Weinfeld (Toronto: Oxford University Press, 1993).

15 Neither Maori nor Pakeha: Jewish Women's Cultural Identity

LIVIA KÄTHE WITTMANN

In his *History of the Jews in New Zealand* Lazarus Morris Goldman has a chapter called "The Maori Wars," which tells, among others, the story of two Jewish brothers, Samuel and Morris Levy, who lived in the 1860s in a small, mainly Maori settlement on the North Island called Opotiki. They owned a store there. One of the brothers, Morris Levy, also had a boat which he used for piloting warships between the Bay of Plenty and Auckland. At a time of intense warfare between Maori and white European colonizers in that area, the Levy brothers as Jews were safe because, as Goldman explains, the Maori associated with the Christian missionaries the beginning of their plight, that is, the confiscation of their land in the name of the Crown and the lack of respect regarding their laws and culture.[1] They saw similarities between the history of the Jews and their own, especially regarding the loss of land.[2]

The Levy brothers tried to rescue the life of two missionaries, Carl Sylvius Volkner and T. S. Grace, who were taken captive by the Maori in Opotiki, by offering their possessions, the boat and the store, in exchange. But Volkner was hanged, and Morris Levy succeeded only in saving Grace's life.[3]

It was fascinating for me to discover that Berta, one of the women who was interviewed for my research in 1994, spent the first five years upon her arrival in New Zealand in 1939 in Opotiki. She was fourteen years old at the time. Her family escaped from Germany and came to New Zealand via England. Berta recalls that her father had bought a small business in Opotiki, "which is the back of beyond" in her memory. She remembers:

> At school in Opotiki, I didn't have a German accent, I had a very English, upper-class or middle-class English accent and that of course was quite different from the Opotiki accent. We arrived in Opotiki in November and I started school in February. I liked school there; it was a District High School. We were the only Jews, the only Germans, not really a very healthy thing during the war. It was a bit hard in the beginning, but there was a very large Maori population and my father got on very well with the Maoris. I felt at home and my younger brother grew up there.

When asked how she fits into bicultural New Zealand, Berta has this to say:

> Oh I fit in quite well because I grew up with Maoris in Opotiki. At that time [1939–44] I didn't experience any nastiness from either side really. Although looking back there probably was. Strangely enough I have made contact with a Maori woman who was at school with me. This was when my father, who died at Shalom Court, celebrated his hundredth birthday. There was an article in the newspaper and this lady wrote from Opotiki to congratulate him. She said she had been at school with me in the first year, in the fourth form, and that my mother was the only Pakeha woman who had ever invited her to her home.

It is interesting that the Maori woman calls Berta's mother "Pakeha."[4] It is a term which for some means "of European descent," for others more specifically "New Zealanders of British descent." But "Pakeha" also implies white skin. Whereas a New Zealander of Indian-British or Pakistani-British descent would not qualify as "Pakeha" in the common usage, a New Zealand–born white person of Anglo-Saxon origin would. The official status of New Zealand as a bicultural society reduces the population into the categories of Maori or Pakeha. Everybody else is theoretically nonexistent. It is therefore not surprising that the Maori woman from Opotiki refers to Berta's mother as "Pakeha" although she was a German Jew, arriving as an adult to New Zealand. For the sociologist Paul Spoonley, who grew up in Hawke's Bay (not far from Opotiki) and who discusses the signifier "Pakeha" in a number of publications, "being Pakeha" means "being a product of New Zealand, not of Europe, not being English despite family connections with that country, also, not being Maori or one of the other ethnic groups that exist here."[5] He remembers:

> While the influences of my childhood created me as Pakeha, I was not conscious of it. It was a term that seldom appeared in the 1950s and 1960s, and provincial Hawke's Bay was not the place to understand what it meant. There was constant reference to things that occurred in a place called "Home," even

> by those who had never been to Britain nor had links with the country. In the twilight of the colonial empire, few saw any need to be sensitive to cultural groups other than British. The local Jewish pharmacist came in for the expected (and offensive) jokes. [6]

Marti, a young New Zealand–born Jewish woman, who was seventeen years old at the time she was interviewed in 1994, has this to say to the question "How do you see yourself fitting into bicultural New Zealand? Are you Maori or Pakeha?":

> I am not Maori. But I think I am not actually Pakeha—Jews don't come under the category of Pakeha. I can't remember how it is that Maori regard us but it's not as Pakeha. Maybe that has something to do with when Maori got into Christianity and got all those influences they started thinking they were one of the tribes of Israel—at least Ringatu?[7] Maybe technically I am Pakeha. I remember Mum telling me that they do regard Jews as something else. I feel outside that bicultural thing. I don't fit either of the definitions.

Toward the late 1980s, when I was involved in establishing Feminist Studies at a New Zealand university where I had taught German language and literature for eighteen years, the movement for Maori sovereignty was translated by a number of my feminist colleagues into an ethnocentrism which presented itself as progressive. Their aim was to have all feminists teaching at universities in New Zealand agree to an appointment-recommendation procedure whereby only Maori women and New Zealand–born white women, Pakehas, would be eligible for a new position. A colleague of mine, a Lebanese woman, and I, who was born in Germany and grew up in Hungary with a repressed Jewish heritage, started to feel very uncomfortable. We were made to feel invisible and unwanted. When I raised the issue that belonging to a specific land excludes Jewish people from any claim of equal rights within the discussed context, this was countered with a reference to the "imperialism" of Israel.[8]

Since then I pondered the exclusion of Others by the ideology of biculturalism which became official policy in New Zealand in 1984. One aspect of my study on how Jewish women living in this country perceive their Jewish identity was to find out how they see themselves fitting or not fitting into these binary categories.[9]

Aotearoa/New Zealand's official status is presently that of a "bicultural society." Andrew Sharp briefly summarizes the history of this signifier—which he calls an "ideal"—as applied in this country:

> The ideal of cultural (and genetic) melding or fusion of the Maori and European "races" had, in the 1960s and 1970s, been replaced by that of "multiculturalism," at least in official circles and among liberal reformers. The multicultural complex of ideas tended to translate the older—largely racial—denominators into cultural and ethnic ones, although the distinction between race and ethnicity was never strictly observed. There were now Maori and Pakeha, not Maori and European, and the ideal recognised and celebrated the wider array of other cultures (and races) in New Zealand: for instance, Chinese, Indians, Pacific Islanders and Europeans of various sorts. But during the 1980s, this ideal of a "multicultural society" yielded to that of a "bicultural society," and policy goals of "biculturalism" came to override—though not to extinguish—those of "multiculturalism."[10]

A bicultural society would mean, in my understanding, a society in which people of two distinct cultures live side by side. Although Maori *culture* is clearly distinct from so-called Pakeha cultures, the lived reality of its representatives is not. Nearly two centuries of having to negotiate for survival with the legal, political and economic system of a colonizing people, Maori also became acquainted with a different culture, the Anglo-Saxon Christian culture and its language. In order to "make it" in present-day New Zealand society and at the same time retain their own culture, Maori people need to be bicultural. Such biculturality, growing out of necessity, is shared to a greater or lesser degree by most immigrants to this country whose originary culture is different from the Anglo-Saxon Christian one.

Biculturalism as a "policy goal" remains prescriptive. As government policy it tries to redress historically specific injustices and promises to respect the Treaty of Waitangi signed in 1840. This prescriptive "biculturalism," in every day usage, became confused with "biculturality" and also resulted in a discursive denial of other cultures in Aotaroa/New Zealand. Eventually the social reality of these other cultures claimed visibility and resulted in the formation of The New Zealand Federation of Ethnic Councils in 1989. One of its objectives is: "To promote the recognition of New Zealand as a multiethnic society in order to remove the monocultural philosophies and structures that exist within New Zealand society." I imagine that the term "ethnic" has been employed to avoid any claim to equal political status with Maori as the *tangata whenua* (people of the land). Indeed in its manifesto the Federation states that it "has made a commitment in its Constitution to raise the consciousness among ethnic communities of the needs, aspirations and status of the Maori people." And it asserts that "New Zealand is a multi-ethnic society in which the Maori people have special status as *tangata whenua* and special rights under the Treaty of Waitangi." So what does "ethnic" mean in the understanding of the Federation of Ethnic Councils? In what way does it differ from "culture"? In the formulation of the Federation's manifesto, it refers quite clearly to a minority within the population at large: "'Ethnic' means pertaining to or relating to any segment of the population within New Zealand society sharing fundamental cultural values, customs, beliefs, languages, traditions and characteristics, that are different from those of the larger society."

It seems to me that "multi-ethnic" suggests a slightly different meaning from "multicultural" in the context of public debates. Perhaps it is a more accurate term for describing the social reality in this country because it refers only to differences in cultural values as they are understood in a narrower sense. However, the adjective "multicultural" applied to present-day New Zealand seems to be widely used. And more often than not it tends to add an -ism modeled on "biculturalism." The resulting "multiculturalism" becomes a prescriptive term, signifying a claim to equal political representation for all cultures. It is worthwhile noting that the Jewish women interviewed who referred to "multiculturalism" understood it descriptively, that is, describing an existent situation. My point is that such understanding of the signifier "multiculturalism" causes confusion. A multicultural situation, if one accepts this terminology as description at all, cannot be equated with multiculturalism as a prescriptive goal. The Federation of Ethnic Councils recognizes this matter clearly when it talks about the need to "remove the monocultural philosophies and structures that exist within New Zealand society."

It is the lived experience of Maori people and all *others* that the "philosophies and structures," which dominate the public discourses and the socio-economic, legal and political practices, are monocultural. This is one shared commonality between Maori and Jewish people, although it is complicated by the fact that most Maori people adhere to Christianity which has been one of the defining *cultural* features of "Pakeha" colonizers. On the other hand most Jewish people living in New Zealand have been assimilated or integrated into the above-mentioned dominant economic and political practices. However, their religious culture, with some related social practices, more or less sets them apart as a collectivity from the dominant "monocultural philosophies" of any country they lived in. Therefore it is also the awareness of their own history, from centuries-long pogroms to the Shoah, which generates Jewish women's affinity with the historical plight of Maori people. As referred to earlier, at times Maori people too established links between the history of the Jews and their own, like the uprising of Te Kooti in the second half of the nineteenth century, modeled on the biblical Exodus.

There are Maori Jews in the present too. Another point of connection is seen in the establishment of Maori language classes (Kohanga Reo) which served to strengthen Maori cultural identity, and the greater support for Jewish day schools. A study on Auckland Jewry claims that "the outstanding success of the Kohanga Reo movement and its continuation in Maori primary schools undoubtedly contributed to the new confidence expressed in Kadimah College."[11] The author notes that as an outcome of "the surge of pride within the Maori community and its overall renaissance" it became "gradually a lot more acceptable in New Zealand to be different and be proud of one's culture": "It was becoming somewhat easier to be open about being Jewish in New Zealand, a development greatly assisted by the appointment of a Jew to the position of Race Relations Conciliator."[12]

In 1994 and 1995, close to fifty Jewish women were approached in two main centers in the North and the South Island to participate in interviews on the research topic of Jewish identity. I was most interested to find out how these women define their Jewish identity, keeping in mind that their belonging to a small minority in a postmodern world would necessitate a greater fragmentation of identities, that is multiple identities, across collective and individual markers such as race, ethnicity, religion, language, class, gender and sexuality. I prepared thirty questions designed to seek the meaning/s the women gave to their Jewish identity from different angles. The questions included clusters regarding ancestry, community involvement, languages, definition of culture and customs, their reading of literature written by Jewish authors, their gender role expectations and their positioning within bicultural New Zealand.

In the analysis of the interviews I was guided by the recognition that the meaning of collective Jewish identity had always to be interactive with historically and geopolitically definable "host" environments and was therefore prone to changes.[13] The cultural identity of individuals is always linked to a collective understanding, but at the same time it is always in excess of it because of individuals' shifting subject positions due to their embrace of new discourses which are mostly grounded in lived experiences. Homi Bhabha succinctly formulates the complexity of individual and collective identities:

> The move away from the singularities of "class" or "gender" as primary conceptual and organizational categories, has resulted in an awareness of the subject positions—of race, gender, generation, institutional location, geopolitical locale, sexual orientation—that inhabit any claim to identity in the modern [or rather postmodern] world. What is theoretically innovative, and politically crucial, is the need to think beyond narratives of originary and

> initial subjectivities and to focus on those moments or processes that are produced in the articulation of cultural differences. These "in-between" spaces provide the terrain for elaborating strategies of selfhood—singular or communal—that initiate new signs of identity, and innovative sites of collaboration, and contestation, in the act of defining the idea of society itself.
>
> It is in the emergence of interstices—the overlap and displacement of domains of difference—that the intersubjective and collective experiences of *nationness,* community interest, or cultural value are negotiated. How are subjects formed "in-between," or in excess of, the sum of the "parts" of difference (usually intoned as race/class/gender, etc.)? How do strategies of representation or empowerment come to be formulated in the competing claims of communities where, despite shared histories of deprivation and discrimination, the exchange of values, meanings and priorities may not always be collaborative and dialogical, but may be profoundly antagonistic, conflictual and even incommensurable?[14]

The problem of how to position myself in the ever-changing discourses constituting my multiple identities, among them my Jewish one, is well captured by Sneja Gunew's elaboration of the following conception of identity offered by Stuart Hall: "Far from being grounded in a necessary recovery of the past, which is waiting to be found, and which, when found, will secure our sense of ourselves into eternity, identities are the names we give to the different ways we are positioned by, and position ourselves within, the narratives of the past."[15] Sneja Gunew asserts that "Hall argues for a new concept of identity as process rather than fact, and the need to position oneself both inside and outside certain systems of representation." She also claims that, according to Hall, "because positioning is always temporary, meanings are always provisional, and . . . the importance lies in always recognising the role of history and the prevailing circumstances of power."[16] This insight of course does not prevent the pain of having to deal with the "prevailing circumstances of power."[17] Indeed many of the Jewish women who participated in my research talk about the difficulties of trying to harmonize their multiple identities. These women are aware of the negotiation with or struggle within their subjectivities which takes place during identificatory processes seeking to belong to any one fixed identity frame, be it collective or individual. Whether one is inclined to see liberating values in this "negotiation" or "struggle," or whether one regrets the forever-lost security of former fixities, does not change the historical necessity of this process. Attempts to seek out supposedly unifying *collective* identities are always fraught with difficulties because of the complex interactions and affiliations with the many discursive practices outside of, or in excess of, those "primary" practices of identification. All representatives of any cultural or ethnic collectivity will experience the disruptive force of those new discourses which may serve as additional identity markers. This process, which leads to shifting identifications, or multiple affiliations with collective identities, will create new personal identity markers as well.

From the interviews conducted with Jewish women living in New Zealand I have chosen only a few to illustrate the thoughts and feelings of some of them on the topic of biculturalism. In order to capture a broader spectrum, I have selected some New Zealand–born women belonging to different generations who have lived in different parts of the country, as well as women who immigrated as children or as adults to New Zealand. They were all asked the same question relating to their understanding of culture, cultural affiliation and biculturalism.[18]

WOMEN BORN IN NEW ZEALAND

Dora, who is in her early seventies, responded to the question about culture with an awareness of the political connotations in the contemporary use of the term:

> I would have to say that I am first and foremost a New Zealander because I have lived my life amongst New Zealanders and participated in all the organizations that I have been involved with as a New Zealander. I suppose my Jewishness has taken second place if you like, at the same time all my friends know that I am Jewish. They are most helpful when it comes to banquets, parties, things like that. They all say "you won't want to eat this, let me find you something that is alright." Also, when I was travelling with the National Council of Women overseas they were most helpful to me and supportive of my preferences for kosher.

In connection with the establishment of the Ethnic Federation in 1989, which was formed by four Ethnic Councils, she says: "We had a great debate in the Jewish community throughout New Zealand as to whether we were ethnic and we decided that we certainly did fit the ethnic definition which is any peoples that have a tradition and a culture of their own." When asked how she sees herself fitting into bicultural New Zealand, Dora has this to say: "It's *multicultural* and I think the Ethnic Federation is endeavoring to ensure that New Zealanders realize that we are multicultural. By the same token, we pay tribute to the biculturalism of it, the *tangata whenua,* because they have a special place in New Zealand. We have always tried, in the Ethnic Federation, to emphasize this role but at the same time we are emphasizing the fact that in New Zealand today it is a multicultural society."

Pressed for a more personal response to the issue of biculturalism Dora reiterates her position: "We have two official languages in New Zealand and this has to be acknowledged. We have obligations to the Treaty of Waitangi and this has to be acknowledged. On the one hand you are talking about bilingual and bicultural, but it still has to be recognized that New Zealand is multicultural. I think any thinking Maoris are coming to that realization too. Probably in the South Island we don't have as many problems as they do in the far North where there are a lot more ethnic groups."

Kathryn belongs to a younger generation. She was fifty-three years old at the time of the interview. Although she was born in New Zealand, her parents came from Europe, escaping the Shoah. The question was blandly put to her: "Do you see yourself as a New Zealander?" Her answer reflects the complexity of her cultural belonging:

> It does apply. As a child growing up you never knew what was wrong. You knew you were different. You knew you were never accepted. The others wouldn't let you be part of them. You certainly did things the others didn't do, especially in rural Glen Eden. I mean Glen Eden fifty years ago was very rural. What you didn't understand until later was that you had a foot in both camps. Part of you was desperately trying to be a Kiwi, like everybody else, totally unsuccessfully, and part of you was in your parent-roots-world of middle-class, European, Jewish values. Like music lessons, like private French lessons, like going to concerts, like who gave a damn about sport? What the hell if you were good, or not good, at rugby, netball, soccer and what-have-you? So you were forever with a foot in two camps. So, yes in that sense you were neither New Zealander, nor were you part of the other world either. And you were torn inside, or I found myself torn inside out. I don't think my brothers had so much of a problem with it.

When asked why she felt torn, Kathryn's answer is straightforward: "Because I was never accepted." To the question "by whom?" she says:

> By anyone. I couldn't be this paragon of what my parents expected of a little girl because I had to try and be a Kiwi. They couldn't teach me how to be a Kiwi because they weren't. I couldn't break in, and Glen Eden being Glen Eden. . . . Particularly a problem for most rural kids. You were neither one thing nor another. And as a child I never knew why, I couldn't put my finger on it. As an adult I know why and the interesting thing is that I have had it confirmed since by classmates. As far as they were concerned it was a concerted [effort]

> to not allow me to be part of the group. They knew what they were doing, I was different, they were jealous.

Kathryn's childhood experience of being "different" obviously had a powerful effect on her. The interview generated a flow of memories which must have been painful and I don't quote them all. It was important to note how Kathryn, later in her life, dealt with the conflict between the two cultures in which she was supposed to feel at home. She talks about how she tried to "emulate" a classmate, hoping to develop identificatory features with collective Kiwi values and how she finally gained a feeling of self-acceptance, of being *intelligible* to her environment. She analyzes this most vividly herself:

> My parents kicked me overseas, to break up the great romance. And on that great OE [overseas experience] we all had, I ended up in Israel, and suddenly the whole world became clear. Like who the hell gave a damn. It was like putting on an old coat that had patches across the shoulders, it was a bit worn out around the elbows wasn't it but you knew, God, I am just like these bastards, what's new? Suddenly the whole thing then became quite a different picture because I knew who I was, I knew where I belonged, I knew who I was like. And that wasn't unusual, different, strange, weird. Whatever labels you want to put on it. And since then, I have comfortably been able to accept, OK I will never really be a New Zealander, in the IN way of being a New Zealander because of your middle-class-Jewish upbringing overrides that. The fact that you'll be in the middle of talking about something and you'll say "Bloody bullshit for God's sake don't you guys realize. . . ." Which is not the Kiwi way of doing things. I am probably more aware of international affairs and where things are going. You know, all those middle-class-European-awareness things, because they are the things that mean that in effect. . . . I used to get quite uptight when Kevin, my husband, would say "well, you are not a Kiwi, Kathryn." I am neither one nor the other. I can jump into either camp. That's how I see it anyway.

An ongoing negotiation between the differing cultural discourses positioning her emotionally and intellectually *within* and *without* seems to have remained. *Within* means that Kathryn is well aware that she has to continuously mediate between her culturally constructed Kiwi-self and her socio-historically constructed Jewish self. These differences in identification with collective values are only general ones which do not problematize the multiplicity of identificatory positions[19] within the discourses and practices of "Kiwiness" or "Jewishness." Her answer to the question "do you see yourself as a New Zealander first?" was: "If you are talking about locale, then New

Zealand is my home. I mean there is nowhere that can beat my favorite beach, there is nothing like the stillness of New Zealand, the greenness of New Zealand. If you are going to talk about locale, this is home, this place is part of my very soul and being. If you are going to talk on a more intellectual level, yes, I am a Kiwi so far as I can be a Kiwi. I am not particularly religiously Jewish but the Jewish thing is there and you know it is there. I just accept it now."

Living with the differences within, that is, accepting multiple discourses shaping one's subjectivity and giving meaning to one's multiple identities, is one thing, while living comfortably with socially inclusive or exclusive cultural representations defined by others is another. It is the idea of a homogeneous, clearly definable identity that is bothersome for Kathryn since her lived experience teaches her something else. Understandably she is outraged by the claim of biculturalism in New Zealand, which for her implies the existence of two, and only two, homogeneous cultures. If such homogeneous or pure cultures exist, Kathryn would not qualify as belonging to either of them despite having been born and brought up in New Zealand. She says: "Obviously I identify as Jewish, both culturally and ethnically. I get quite amused sometimes and every now and then on forms where it says race I carefully put in Semitic, to bugger up the system because we are not Caucasians dammit. I mean if you are going to talk race then Jews are Semites. Ethnically I see myself as Jewish."

At the same time that Kathryn makes her claim to a Jewish identity, she also maintains her affinity with Maori. For her the two are not exclusionary, on the contrary:

> One thing I haven't said perhaps, it means that I can identify with the Maori side of being a New Zealander very easily. I am often mistaken by Maori as Maori. I am totally comfortable on a marae. I am totally able to freefloat within a Maori context and not feel out of place. I have made it my business to be able to put several sentences together, to be able to call a mihi [ceremonial greeting] and a karanga [woman's ritual chant of encounter or mourning; call], so in that sense I am perhaps more New Zealandish than many New Zealanders. That Maori side is as natural as swimming for me. I don't have any problem in understanding problems about the Treaty. The inevitable thing about the Jew supporting the underdog perhaps. When I was in Teacher's College in 1958 I was already in the Maori Club. I already instinctively knew what was coming. I couldn't have put my finger on it at that stage but I knew you ought to know, and that's early.
>
> You have got to be careful when talking about New Zealand. Which New Zealand are we talking about? Because I am talking about a deeper New Zealand

than many New Zealanders even realize. I see in that sense I am even more a New Zealander in the sense that I think that what we are going through now is the beginnings of the creation of a New Zealand culture but, because we are right in it, we don't see it and we are threatened by it. The fact that we are learning to greet our visitors with a powhiri [ritual of encounter] and that's the way you do things. New third-formers are welcomed onto the school marae with a powhiri and too bad if they are bloody Pakehas, they'll sit there and they'll listen to it all in Maori. There is this Maori dimension, but because it is happening all around us a lot of New Zealanders are threatened by it all whereas I see it as the beginnings of the development of a culture. I have come to that realization.

Kathryn's understanding and vision of a New Zealand culture seems to be one of integration and not of separateness, a kind of integration which acknowledges all cultures in their distinctness and in their interaction within the country. She finds the concept of multiculturalism more appropriate when describing the social reality of New Zealand than the politically prescriptive term "biculturalism":

I think biculturalism is the gravest error that any country can fall into, because we aren't bicultural. You could only be bicultural if you have English and Maori. You can't because we don't. I worked in a school with a man who believed that you could not be multicultural until you were bicultural. He himself climbed on Maori backs to get where he wanted to be and, I maintain, used them. He would deny that vociferously. The reality is that as long as you don't rock the boat it is OK to be your own culture in New Zealand but thou shalt not rock the boat whether thou art Chinese, Maori, Pacific Island, or Yugoslav.

It is the old tall poppy syndrome, don't stand up, don't make a racket. Don't rock the boat. Yes, we are multicultural at that level but we are not multicultural and more than. . . . The most horrific example is Bosnia right now. Groups of people will never totally tolerate one another. Families can't get along, why the hell should groups of people within one country? So to say New Zealand is bicultural is an utter idiocy. We are not, we are multicultural but please don't rock the boat. Don't stand up and say "Oh, but this is the Samoan way. The Samoan way is we beat our kids. How else do you get discipline into the little buggers? That's what's wrong with the Pakeha kids isn't it?"

Or the Maori way, which is torn between the old and the new, and where do we fit? Let us not forget certain things about Maori society which they don't wish to publicize out loud. I think Alan Duff[20] is getting his hands chopped for that one right now.

The dynamics of Kathryn's thoughts on culture and biculturalism seem to bear witness to the fluidity possible in the interpretation of the two concepts. And also, of course, this highlights the interconnectedness of the two terms. This interconnectedness is partly the reason for the latent confusion when addressing culture and biculturalism. Or is what I call "confusion" simply a result of a confusing terminology?

Kathryn's understanding of "culture" seems to be a sum total of lived tradition; at least that is how she refers to Maori culture. She talks about her affinity with Maori customs on the marae: it is "as natural as swimming" to her. But this cultural affinity also contains a political aspect when she refers to the Treaty, and explains her affinity with "the inevitable thing about the Jew supporting the underdog." Cultural affiliation would then contain an awareness of belonging to a marginalized collectivity because belonging to a dominant cultural—and that mostly means also a dominant political—collectivity in any one country, hardly calls for an inventory of characteristics or any other justification of distinctness. (Except of course when it involves preparations for aggression against others.)

When Kathryn says that she is perhaps more "New Zealandish" than many New Zealanders, she refers to her knowledge of and affinity with Maori customs and history. When she is talking about the beginnings of the creation of a New Zealand culture then she refers to what is in her opinion a necessary integration of Maori culture with the dominant "Pakeha" one. But when she is asked about biculturalism she rejects the notion as phantom which has little to do with the lived reality of most people in New Zealand. The precondition for biculturalism means for Kathryn that all people living in the country are bilingual, speaking English and Maori. Since that is not the case, a bicultural claim is false. But beyond this argument there is again the sociopolitical critique of the term: Kathryn believes that only by calling the social reality of present day New Zealand "multicultural" would one do justice to a descriptive analysis. Biculturalism is then seen again as primarily a prescriptive political term.

Eleanor, who was born in New Zealand after World War II, responded to the question of cultural identification in a challenging way:

> The word "culture" is problematic because what on earth is it? You really don't recognize it while you are in it. You only recognize it from the outside. I don't know what New Zealand culture is. Is it those wooden buzzy bees? Is it Maori culture? Is it speaking an increasingly broad accent where vowel sounds are getting increasingly mangled? Is it the cultural swagger that replaces the cultural cringe? Is it actually learning more about this country and its history? I don't know what New Zealand culture is to some degree.

When asked in response what Jewish culture was, she had this to say: "Jewish culture is easier to define because it is exotic and because it is conducted in a foreign language you can pinpoint it more easily. But then again what is Jewish culture? Jewish culture is made up of practices, customs, ceremonies, a religion. And that is a whole issue in itself because the culture is determined by the religion and you can be rather steeped in the culture without being theistic. So again, it's a bit curious really." About how she sees herself fitting into "bicultural New Zealand," Eleanor had the following to say:

> Well I have always had a problem with bicultural New Zealand because I know it is a concept that one is supposed to subscribe to but to me it simply flies in the face of reality. There aren't two cultures. There is Maori. There is Pakeha. But there is Pacific Island, there is Asian, there is Jewish, there is Dutch and so many others. I don't feel that my empathy with the Maori struggle for their place in the sun—tino Rangatiratanga—is in any way diminished by my saying there are more than two cultures. So I have difficulty with that. Luckily I have never had to go to a course where I have to subscribe to this view. I have never been in a situation where I have been straitjacketed into saying something that goes against my sense of logic.

When she was asked again to respond to the question, "whereabouts do you fit?" she pondered:

> I don't know that I fit anywhere very easily. I remember an occasion when I felt this strongly. I was escorting an Israeli friend around the Auckland Museum feeling quite good about it. I took him to the big meetinghouse on the ground floor and I stood in there in the darkness listening to the Maori chant and I thought—this isn't mine. Much as I can appreciate it, it's not mine because I don't understand it and I am not part of it. He [the Israeli friend] and his people have their culture.
>
> It was a memorable moment because he being Jewish and being Israeli, but being Israeli is so different from being Jewish in the Diaspora. So he fully knew where he belonged. I felt quite bereft because I am not all one thing. But then since that time I have thought—well is that bad? Actually it is very nice. Just as in my life as a woman I am not all one thing. I am not only a mother. I am not only a person engaged in a career. I live a fragmented life. You can either look at that as a weakness and as a failing or you can look at it as a strength and I am now looking at it very much as a strength. In the same way having an identity which is a mosaic of New Zealandish and Jewish and so forth is nice. I think it's good so I am happy.

For some women the recognition that they can't define themselves by belonging only to one collectivity may be more difficult than for others. The reality of their historical situation, which they share with many non-Jewish people, is "that where once a subject might have been fully defined by a single membership, memberships now tend mostly to be multiple and identities accordingly complex."[21] Michael Krausz suggests that identities are constituted as intersections in specifically located human bodies of historically defined discourses.[22] It follows that, according to David Theo Goldberg and Michael Krausz:

> Social identities are not just givens, they are not simply established facts. What one is—the slipping tangle of what one takes oneself and is taken to be—is produced and reproduced against a complex of social, political, cultural, technological, and economic conditions. In being reproduced from one moment to the next, from one social setting to another, one's identity is often transformed by the push and pull of political economy and ideology, by the identities of others with whom one interacts, by what one does and says and reads. In short, whether one is Jew, Muslim, or Christian, Hindu or Buddhist, proletarian or capitalist, black or white or Arab, gay or straight is largely a product of the conditions in which social subjects find and in terms of which they make themselves. This production is, short of death, never complete, always in process (and after death is often carried on by others, in one's name).[23]

Marnie was born in 1946. Her mother escaped with her family as a child from Germany in 1932. Marnie's mother grew up in Israel, served in the army (the "ATS, part of the British army"), where she met her husband-to-be, a New Zealander. He was a tank commander in the New Zealand force (NZEF) and she served as his driver. She married him in Israel against the wish of her family and arrived in New Zealand in 1944, eighteen years of age, pregnant and on her own. After an initial time with her parents-in-law she settled with her husband in Invercargill. The cultural shock the mother suffered reverberated in the daughter. In fact, the whole interview revealed such a connectedness with the mother that I feel compelled to incorporate her "story" as well since it forms the historical, cultural and ethical framework for Marnie's social identity.

When her mother arrived in Invercargill, which was, with its "tiny population," even more remote and removed than Wellington, she was going "from one absurdity to another, from the Middle East where it was so war torn and so much strife to a very passive, quiet, backwater of the world."[24] From the mother's point of view, as remembered by the daughter, "Invercargill was in those days [the 1940s] absolutely extraordinary."

> My mother's account of arriving in Invercargill and being looked upon with great suspicion is something I have always thought I should write about be-

cause she had the real disadvantage of being a foreigner. Not only was she an import but she was a foreigner to boot. As the war drifted to a close and soldiers came back with their brides it was "OK," in quotation marks, if you brought a bride back from England, that was fine, the mother country, but oh god help you if you brought back a foreigner. This is really quite difficult. My mother was an extraordinarily attractive, lovely-looking woman and that also didn't aid her because women, with all respect to Invercargill, in those days were a pretty drab and dreary lot too, not exactly raving beauties, so that she very quickly established herself, had three children in three years, so we had this fabulous experience of growing up with a mother who was very young, really lovely, she just stood out I guess so significantly. And who had a culture and enrichment of life that was just remarkable. Very keen on drama and very quickly she got into the dramatic scene and our childhood was filled with that sense of learning. She went to the nuns to learn English properly and loved English literature, went on to study and complete her ATCL and LTCL, became a teacher of Speech and Drama, taught privately for years, taught at Southland Girls High School miming and deportment. Was the first woman member of the QE2 Arts Council of New Zealand. Went on then to enter local politics and then I think achieved such a significant first to be woman mayor of Invercargill. Eve Poole.

Marnie sees her Jewishness, as reflected in her childhood memories, as a marker of difference. However, as her narration unfolds, she acknowledges that the European cultural values her mother upheld must have added to the daughter's sense of her family's difference from the dominant social discourses and practices of her environment. Children's longing to be part of their contemporaries' seemingly homogeneous collectivity makes them especially sensitive to the "otherness" of their parents. Marnie's childhood memories betray this longing not to be different from "the crowd" when she reflects about her reaction to her mother's different way of self-representation. The daughter's appreciation and belated identification with the mother's difference gains momentum in her reflection on her adult life.

Marnie consciously and unconsciously identified with her mother's cultural values. This identification caused her to see herself also as different from the prevailing cultural practices of the small rural community in which she spent many years of her adult life. She acknowledges:

I always see myself as different and my kids, like me when I was small, wish to heaven that I was like the other mothers—because there was a huge difference. I think the parallels are very similar. Mummy had come from Palestine, from Israel, from a war zone, to Invercargill which was a huge shift. I have gone from Invercargill, but from a very enlightened home, into a small rural, ooooh

> Presbyterian farming backwater, can I put it any more bluntly than that—and people thought I was really odd. We lived in an appalling old house on the farm which we did up and I hung out for a toilet in the bathroom. Is this extraordinary or what? And we carpeted the bathroom. People actually came to our house and asked to have a look at the bathroom—and I remember one elderly woman coming in with my mother-in-law, who really thought I was very over the top—and this elderly lady came in, she was quite deaf and she plonked herself down in the living room and said "Oh well, the house isn't all that flash"—and I thought, "good heavens, what had she been told before she even arrived?" You see so I was sort of the unusual one who carpeted her bathroom and you know obviously had different views to the rest of them.
>
> The best thing we did was shift and very unfortunately we didn't shift early enough; we only moved in 1989. What I did notice was the change in our kids, whose development has been enormous. That's just going from a small rural community where they stood out because of me, because I was a writer and a journalist and my name was always in the paper, you know, and my mother who was the mayor, their grandmother, her name was always in the paper. They couldn't get away from it the poor blighters—and, coming to a city where the profile wasn't so high but we still did really lovely things and fun things and they found that actually we weren't that unusual. There were other kids' mothers and fathers who also worked, who held hands in the street and who did sort of fun things. They're far more comfortable with it.

Even if at the end of the quote the difference between Marnie's family and that of her environment seems to be reduced to the difference between urban and rural lifestyle—which one observes in most cultures—this would be a simplification, I believe. It is useful to remember that New Zealand went through significant changes in the last fifteen years, and these changes are prevalent mostly in the bigger cities. It is also in the cities where the majority of the population lives and where communities and subcommunities which are different from traditionally dominant discourses and social practices can exist.

So how does Marnie see New Zealand culture? She says: "We are not a country—I don't think—of great intellect and spiritualism and all those things, I don't think we are whereas Israel, because it is such a melting pot of many, many diverse races and cultures who all have that common religion—they bring with them, they enhance multiplicity and I mean they are truly multicultural, they must be." When asked about how she thinks she fits into the bicultural split in New Zealand, Marnie's response was surprisingly different from her critical view on the mainstream white New Zealand "culture." Again there is the association with the mother's attitude and her affinity with the Maori people. Indeed, it was for me one of the most impressive and moving responses to the question on biculturalism. And it certainly emphasized its political and historical pertinence.

I shall quote the relevant part of the interview at some length because it offers not only Marnie's interpretation but also an important concrete utopian dimension. I am referring here to the Maori community's gesture after the death of Marnie's mother. The appropriate part of the interview follows unedited. Marnie stated:

> I lean very heavily towards the Maori people and there are some reasons for that. They are personal associations as much as a recognition that they are part of a group that has suffered, and I think a lot of Jewish people actually appreciate that, recognize it. I certainly do and the contacts that I made up here in 1990 would reinforce that. I don't like prejudice of any kind, I don't like racism and I can't cope with fanaticism at all absolutely—and that's both sides as well. So I get very uncomfortable with strong fanatical views but at the same time I think that sometimes the pendulum has to swing really violently over to one side in order that it can come back to some kind of a balance and the Maori people, some of them have had that need to go way over the top in order to then come back and I actually see that as quite OK. My views are not shared by a lot of people so I tend to keep some of them to myself, particularly in Southland. Interestingly enough, Mummy identified very closely with the Maori community and the Pacific Island community, and when she died the Maori elders came to see us and they bestowed a great honor on us, they wanted to take Mummy's body to the marae but my father couldn't cope with that and we declined. So they said could they come and see her and say prayers for her and I took them and we did. I thought that was a tribute about the way they felt about her and the way she felt about them and it's something that I share. So yes, in terms of biculturalism I think that New Zealand is tiny yet, still developing, not learning from overseas experience and that's OK, I guess we have to make our own mistakes—but it's a pity that we do because it's just going around in a circle that's so unnecessary. I think that sometimes there are opportunities to do things and we don't grasp them.

From the four interviews, I have quoted only material as it relates to how the women understand their cultural identity vis-à-vis *others*. This process works with discursive constructions of identity as coming from two directions, collective and individual. One direction is to see the differences of others from what is familiar to oneself, and the other direction is to perceive the Other's view of oneself as different. These discursive constructs, coming from within and from without, interact with each other in space and time, and don't remain static as they do so.

Although in this essay I focus on how some Jewish women position themselves within or against a bicultural model in 1994–95, in the interviews a far greater complexity of self and other emerges from within the framework of telling the story of one's individual Jewish identity. There is, for example, the conflict within Orthodox communities of the gender-related restrictions women find alienating in contrast to the social roles they can play in white New Zealand society.[25] These women, whether they call themselves "feminist" or not, will define the meaning of their Jewish identity against a practice which excludes them from participating actively in the religious service or from being able to fill the main positions on the board of an Orthodox congregation. But it is the women, in my observation, who invest the most time and energy to keep the Jewish community alive.[26] It is often the young Jewish women who might leave the synagogue or community activities altogether and retain a sense of their Jewish identity mainly by respecting a Jewish religious-cultural tradition of their parents or grandparents and/or by identifying with aspects of Jewish history known to them.

I found remarkable differences in the understanding of Jewishness among women who came to New Zealand as children or young adults. Women who spent some years of their childhood or grew up in England, South Africa or the United States seem to have an easier relationship to their Jewishness than women who came from the former Soviet Union, Hungary or Poland. For the latter, confronting the meaning of their Jewishness entails dealing with a painful past, which can span from the experience of being an "alien" citizen with hardly any knowledge of her "obscure" religion or history, to a former concentration-camp survivor whose negative memories of Jewish Orthodoxy in her childhood are connected to years spent in a Jewish home after the war because her mother and older brother, who survived the concentration camp, were ill for years and not able to look after her.

Many of the women who immigrated to New Zealand from non-English-speaking countries might feel as Other not only vis-à-vis the majority and minority cultures with which they have to familiarize themselves in a foreign language, but also within the existing Jewish communities. There is often a differing understanding of a desired commonality of Jewishness. These differences, which are contingent on the dissimilarities of discourses constituting any of us, may create only a partial identification with local Jewish communities. For these women the latent request of official bicultural politics to identify themselves as either Pakeha or Maori makes even less sense than for those who grew up in New Zealand or immigrated from England.

WOMEN ARRIVING AS CHILDREN IN NEW ZEALAND, 1928–49

In the following section I shall refer more briefly to the relevant interviews conducted with some of the women who came as immigrants to this country. I believe that the New Zealand–born women have a different relationship to the intercultural, interethnic developments which took place in New Zealand over the last fifty years. For them, I imagine, the process of positioning themselves among the racial/ethnic tensions within the society at large, and the coming to terms with the often contradictory dynamics between their—mainly—European Jewish cultural heritage and the values and philosophies of their "Kiwi" environment, might have needed more effort and time. On the other hand the women who started to engage with the sociopolitical and cultural discourses of their new country of residence at a later age would have already had an understanding of their Jewish identity among other identities which may have shortcircuited the confirmation or questioning of their cultural/ethnic awareness.

Rivka, who came via England to New Zealand in 1928 as a child of seven, remembers "reading the *Merchant of Venice,* Rupert Brook, *Oliver Twist,* all the books we read at school were anti-Jewish. Even John Buchan whom we adored, but he talked about the greasy Jews and the Jewish swindlers." She recalls that she was "in the same class at school with girls who were refugees and although they were Jewish refugees, they were treated as aliens." Rivka believes that in the 1940s "one concealed an awful lot about one's background. This standing tall, being proud of yourself just didn't exist in the 40s."

When asked in 1994 whether she identifies partly with New Zealand culture and partly with Jewish culture, Rivka has this to say:

> If by New Zealand, you mean the total culture with Maori and Pacific Island, I am a very strong advocate. When you live in New Zealand, you must have a knowledge of Maori and Pacific Island cultures, an empathy with them. I am a strong advocate of Kadimah and this is why I am so delighted with the appointment of Wally Hirsh as the principal. To bring up Jewish children in isolation, particularly in Auckland, the largest city in Polynesia, you cannot have an idea of "we" and "they" and our culture superior and theirs as inferior. I believe that, as Jews, we can know what it is to be Jewish and I am a strong advocate that you can only stand tall when you know who you are but I think one has to go forward from that and encourage people from other cultures to discuss with you the differences and interact with them. It is only by knowing your own culture that you can do this. Too many of us Jews have not really known what it is to be Jewish. A strong Jewish identity.

Naomi and her family arrived around 1940 in New Zealand. She says:

> My family came from the part of Czechoslovakia that was occupied by the Poles. At the time of München, when the Germans took Sudetenland, the Poles, our "friendly neighbors," occupied part of Czechoslovakia. We were not delighted by that, apart from anything else the Poles were known to be grossly anti-Semitic.
>
> I came to New Zealand via England. We arrived one month before the Germans moved into Poland and war broke out. I went to an English boarding school and about a year after Paris fell it didn't look as if the lights were ever going to go on in Europe again. We had an entry permit to New Zealand and so we came.

Naomi attended high school in New Zealand in the early 1940s. She experienced her social environment as "homogeneous." She recalls that "apart from a very few of us every one else was of roughly Anglo-Saxon background. People were terribly similar in their outlook and their behavior and everything else and to them I seemed different. Which didn't actually bother me. I was reasonably happy about that and my friends made me feel good about it, made me feel I was interesting because I wasn't like everybody else. So that wasn't too bad. I had some experiences that weren't so good, when I wanted to do medicine suddenly an edict came out that nobody who was not a New Zealand citizen could go to medical school. This was in the 1940s."

WOMEN IMMIGRATING AS YOUNG ADULTS TO NEW ZEALAND, 1950S–70S

Gila came as a young married woman with children to New Zealand in 1954. When she was asked forty years later whether she sees herself as a New Zealander first of all, she says: "I would find it difficult to tell you what I see myself as. I have chosen to live in New Zealand. The least of my life I have spent in Czechoslovakia as I was fifteen when I left. I lived in England for eighteen years and then here. But I suppose I will always be Czech by birth." Regarding her cultural identity, Gila claims that she will always belong "partly to Czechoslovakia, partly to England, partly to New Zealand," but that she will be Jewish in all those part-identifications. She says: "Somehow my heart is divided, I can't say that it belongs wholeheartedly to anything. But in all those situations I am still Jewish."

Aviva came from England to New Zealand in 1958 as a young woman. She grew up in a Jewish orphanage where she learned to feel "lucky" that she was Jewish because Jewish people "had contributed so much to the world in thought." In 1994 she still thinks of herself as "lucky" to be Jewish because, as she says, "We know who we are." And she adds: "The odd thing is, when I came to New Zealand it was the first place in the world I'd ever come to where people actually envied me for being Jewish."[27]

Anya, who came in 1960 from England, has, like Aviva, a "strong sense of Jewish identity." Although she sees herself as a New Zealander, she was taken aback when asked whether she identifies with New Zealand culture. "I don't really know what New Zealand culture is," she said, "do you mean Maori culture?"

Anya doesn't see herself fitting into a bicultural New Zealand because the Maori-Pakeha division would not allow for it. She claims that there "has to be room for other cultures as well."

Hannah, who arrived in New Zealand with her husband and children in 1971, and who had lived before in South Africa, England, Zambia and Hong Kong, found among white New Zealanders "quite a bit of racism and anti-Semitism." She says: "Wherever I go I tell people I belong to an ethnic minority. Some people have very funny ideas about Jews. . . . Unconscious, like somebody at work, one of the young typists would say to me 'don't Jew me down.' I know this is the way they talk. I think I was the first Jew she'd ever met. They really know nothing."

Hannah's attitude toward Maori presents itself in an identificatory manner. When asked how she fits into bicultural New Zealand she claims:

> I feel very comfortable with Maoris. I feel Maoris and Jews have a tremendous amount in common. I have very close Maori friends. When they came to the Synagogue, for my kids' bar mitzvahs, they said they felt thoroughly at home in the Synagogue. They felt it familiar, whereas my English friends felt it bizarre, odd. They weren't comfortable, but my Maori friends were. I have gone onto marae [meeting house] several times and I have been part of the tangata whenua. I have a close friend who is one of the kuias [respected female elders] there and was alongside her so I felt quite comfortable. I was caught once. I was on a marae in Hawkes Bay for a conference. We went to visit another marae and there was a tangi [funeral] and I was head of the queue and I was expected to cope. I had no idea what to do but I just followed the Jewish thing of washing one's hands and that was the right thing. You know if you wash your hands when you go into the cemetery? Well they do the same when there is a tangi. I think it is a very close identification.

Neysa, who came from England with her husband and children in 1975, distinguishes between similarities and differences regarding Jews and Maoris. Although she claims that New Zealand is multicultural, when asked how she sees herself fitting into bicultural New Zealand, she talks about her affinity with the history of the Maori people but at the same time criticizes present-day Maori demands for restoring their right to the land they were deprived of by British colonizers in the nineteenth century. She says:

> While sympathizing with the Maoris, I do, I think its very like the Jews, they have been dispossessed and they are victims. I don't subscribe to what is going on in the name of the Treaty of Waitangi because I believe you can't ask Mr. and Mrs. Joe Bloggs of today to recompense the Maori for what Lord and Lady Bloggs did in the 19th century. You can't do that, it doesn't work that way. I think the difference is also, the Jews, no matter how dispossessed or victimized they have been they always have this inherent belief that they can make it back. If not them, their children, if not their children, their grandchildren.

Neysa, like the other Jewish women who grew up in England, has a clear sense of her Jewish identity. She asserts that she has "a sense of knowing who I am. A sense of being able to operate, to go out and say I am a Jewish woman and, when I say it, to know what being a Jewish woman is. It's part of victimization, it's part of immigration, it's part of that uncertainty, that you don't have material roots but I think that you certainly have spiritual roots."

Karoline came from Germany in 1985. She is married to a white New Zealander and has two children. When asked whether she identifies with any specific culture, she says: "I think my Jewish identity and culture is the area in the middle that keeps it all in balance. I don't feel terribly German anymore, I don't feel very New Zealand but my centerpoint is that I feel Jewish. That keeps it in balance. I can deal with both aspects knowing that there is a centerpoint. That's what my Jewish identity is doing and has done for me. It kept me centered. It doesn't matter, even if I lived in a different culture it would be fine because that centerpoint is there." Karoline claims that New Zealand is multicultural despite the bicultural naming. If the different groups would stand up and make a claim regarding their cultural distinctiveness it would enhance New Zealanders' awareness because "the majority of New Zealanders still think of themselves in terms of British heritage and forget that there are many others here, which need to be heard and seen."

Juliet came in 1991 to New Zealand. When asked about her cultural belonging, she is clear and brief: "New Zealand culture seems to be connected to rugby and beer which are two things I have no interest in. I am American, Jewish and an academic and those are my identities." Regarding the issue of biculturalism, she simply states that she is neither Maori nor Pakeha.

One of the most recent immigrants among the Jewish women, Justine, arrived in 1994 from the United States. Her answer to the question of cultural identity is thoughtful: "That's something I learned as a teacher in New York that every person in the room has, not only a visible cultural identity but an understood cultural identity and that's important to wait and allow that person to say, what that is or to signal in whatever way it is comfortable whatever that person is. Not to assume that because that person is black that person is black-identified." Justine also believes that New Zealand is multicultural but she finds that people's willingness to acknowledge difference is "very antithetical to the culture here. The willingness to say, 'oh I know I am different from you, so what?' It's like talking about something filthy or something and I am amused by that."

Finally I shall refer to Tamara who also came in 1994 to New Zealand and had before then been living in Latvia, Israel and South Africa. When asked how she sees herself fitting into bicultural New Zealand, she has this to say:

> Having South African experience behind me, and apartheid on one hand and knowing what belonging to an ethnic minority is like on the other hand I should clearly have feelings for other persecuted minorities. I believe, belief not founded on any knowledge, that Maoris should develop along the nonethnocentric path and I think that probably taking the Jewish example in Diaspora, Jews always managed to assimilate, to make a very important, significant contribution to the life of the states where they lived, at the same time preserving their national or ethnic or religious identity and belief systems. I don't see any kind of constructive movement trying blindly to adhere to some ethnicity, not quite understanding what it really means and where it leads one in terms of a social mobility in the contemporary world.

When asked what aspect of being Jewish is most significant for her, Tamara ponders:

> I think the sense of remembering, not forgetting, the sense of historical roots and to kind of see myself in that broad context of those forty centuries . . . I guess understanding that somehow I am part of that group of people, whether they are dead or alive, the enormous historical procession. Somehow I visualize being there. And of course one of the experiences . . . when I visited in Germany the former concentration camps and formed the ability to understand that it was part of me who was there forty years ago. I think that is somehow very strong in me. But that might be part of the generation I belong to, it might be part of the fact that I was part of the national awakening amongst Soviet Jewry in the 1970s. So putting oneself into that historical context of a nation that's been here for a long time, and it's good that we are still here and its good that there is a Jewish state and I would certainly like my son to marry a Jewish woman.

CONCLUSION

The women to whom I referred in this paper, as well as the fifty women who were interviewed for my study, conceive of their Jewishness as culturally or ethnically distinct from the two *cultures* given political representation in New Zealand: Maori and Pakeha. Many of the New Zealand–born Jewish women had to struggle in their youth to make their otherness acceptable to themselves *and* to their environment. This environment was perceived by some of them as homogeneous. Most of these women eventually understood their *self*[28] as consisting of multiple identities. Their affinity with Maori is based on aspects of commonalities in the history of Jews and Maori, acknowledged also by the latter, as referred to in my introduction. The women who came as immigrants to New Zealand from England, the United States or South Africa had a clearer sense of their Jewish identity at the time of their immigration, and have therefore formulated a more critical view on the discursively constructed Maori-Pakeha divide with its exclusionary practices.

The everyday reality of Maori and Pakeha does not adhere to any "pure" cultural framework. Their affiliations with a number of discursive practices also constructs multiple identities for Maori as much as it does for Jewish women. I therefore don't claim any additional, coherent collective or individual Jewish identity categories, but would like to see acknowledged the process of identity claims as being contingent on the discursive and material positioning of individuals. Therefore, instead of adhering to some fixity and timelessness regarding identities, my reading of how Jewish women give meaning to their cultural situatedness has to account for the temporality of any such articulation. As Sander Gilman puts it persuasively:

> Identity is a combination of internal and external, psychological and social qualities—you are always where you are, not who you are. Identity is always interactive, never separate from the world—either in a developmental or a cultural sense. Identity is a dynamic process—not a fixed point. Seen in this light, there is no such thing as a "purely" Jewish identity; from the prebiblical world to the Babylonian Diaspora to the world of Sepharad or Askenaz, Jews—like all people—have formed themselves within as well as against the world that they inhabited, that they defined, and that defined them.[29]

NOTES

1. Goldman writes: "The missionaries had brought the Bible. The trader had followed with his wares, and it all ended with the soldier with his guns and destruction. Converted to the teachings of Christianity to which they held with a simple faith, the

natives had *substituted* [see below] the new religion for their own paganism, and added the tales of virtue from the Old and New Testaments to their own heroic legends. They called a settlement in Wanganui, Hihuharama, the Maori for Jerusalem. With their hatred for the Europeans, especially missionaries, growing from day to day as the fortunes of war went against them, many of the Maoris discarded their Christianity and adopted a religion which, in their minds, opposed the faith which they had been taught by the European to believe. They embraced a form of Judaism which emanated from their imaginations and from perverted ideas about which they have read in the Bible." See Lazarus Morris Goldman, *The History of the Jews in New Zealand* (Wellington: A. H. and A. W. Reed, 1958), 85 (my emphasis).

The latest research suggests rather *dissent:* "Judaism is the Bible's obvious alternative religion, its obvious denomination of dissent, and Maori were quite capable of deducing this for themselves. Substantial chunks of the Old Testament did not become available in Maori until 1840. But snippets were translated and published before this; oral transmission of Old Testament stories must have occurred; and Jews are not absent from the New Testament. Maori biblicalism was shifted from Christ and towards Jehovah. This did not mean straight conversion to Judaism any more than to Christianity, but it did distance the new Maori religion from its European cousin." See James Belich, *Making Peoples: A History of the New Zealanders from Polynesian Settlement to the End of the Nineteenth Century* (Auckland: Penguin Books, 1996), 221. See also the very detailed account on the Ringatu religious movement in Judith Binney, *Redemption Songs: A Life of Te Kooti Arikirangi Te Turuki* (Auckland: Auckland University Press/Bridget Williams Books, 1995).

2. Another Jewish perspective on "Judaism and Maoridom" claims in 1990: "Maori-Jewish relationships throughout the period of contact, which date back well before 1840, [the year of the Treaty of Waitangi which was signed by Maori chiefs and representatives of the English Crown] have generally been sympathetic. Many Maori will have had little actual contact with Jews. From the beginning of missionary contact there has been close identification by the Maori with the Biblical Israelite. Attitudes based on hope for restoration of land, language and cultural identity have permeated each of the Maori religions that evolved subsequent to missionary contact. Each such religion includes the acceptance of Jehovah, the universal eternal Deity, as opposed to Jesus, the son of that Deity, and the identification of Maori leaders with Old Testament prophets" (Laurie Gluckman, "Judaism and Maoridom," in *Identity and Involvement,* ed. Ann Gluckman [Palmerston North: Dunmore Press, 1990], 225).

James Belich claims that the fact that a great part of the prophetic movements aligned themselves with Judaism by calling themselves "Hurai," or Jews, and by shifting the Sabbath to Saturday can be "overstated and over-Europeanised." He suggests that "Monogenist European missionaries quite often suggested that Maori were degenerate descendants of one of the lost tribes of Israel—[Samuel] Marsden's [a missionary who established the first mission station in New Zealand in 1814] evidence for 'Semitic Maori' included the fact that they were avid traders" (*Making Peoples,* 221).

3. Goldman discusses the events leading to Volkner's death and the brothers eventually leaving Opotiki in *History of the Jews in New Zealand,* 86–88.

4. "Pakeha" means "stranger" (that is, "other"), in contradistinction to "Maori," which means "normal, natural, usual." In everyday language use "Pakeha" means "Caucasian, of white or European descent."

5. Paul Spoonley, "Being Here and Being Pakeha," in *Pakeha: The Quest for Identity in New Zealand,* ed. Michael King (Auckland: Penguin Books, 1991), 146.

6. Ibid., 146–47 (my emphasis).

7. The Ringatu religion goes back to Te Kooti. Laurie Gluckman explains: "Te Kooti Rikirangi compared the suffering of the Maori with that of the Israelites. Te Kooti likened himself to Moses. He developed the theme of Te Ua [Te Ua Haumene claimed also to be a prophet to whom it was revealed by Kaperiere, or Gabriel, that he would develop a new faith and as a result the Maori would gain total supremacy over the Pakeha] that the Maori, like the Jew, was chosen of God. Like Te Ua before him he called his people Israelites. Te Kooti had been wrongly exiled to the Chatham Islands in 1867. He saw that as analogous to Egyptian captivity, his escape across the seas as his Exodus, his allying with the Hau Hau [the followers of Te Ua] as the beginning of a return to Canaan. His beliefs crystallised into the Ringatu religion. Ringatu means upraised hand. The hand was upraised in both Jewish priestly blessing and sacrifice. Exile, wandering in the wilderness and ultimate return to Canaan are core themes in Te Kooti's liturgy. On the second anniversary he decreed a Passover feast that commemorates both the Biblical and his personal exodus. . . . Ringatu became progressively Christianised and was constituted as a Christian church in 1938" ("Judaism and Maoridom," 233–34).

8. The reference was made by a white woman from South Africa who had become a New Zealand nationalist.

9. Norman Simms writes in 1990 in connection with Maori-Jewish relationships of the 1860s: "Today, several generations later, Maori written and oral testimony of witnesses to these past events is only through the filter of Christian identity; and much that was specific about relations between Maori and Jews has been assimilated to the dichotomy, often hostile, between Maori and Pakeha—the British, Christian 'other.' Today, on both sides of the bicultural relationship, there seems no room for the Jews as another case. Multiculturalism comes to mean, in such polemics, the argument against recognition of the Maori special status as *tangata whenua, am ha'aretz*" ("The Post-Colonialist Discourses of New Zealand/Aotearoa: A Chelmingtonian Perspective," in *Identity and Involvement,* ed. A. Gluckman, 269, also 270–72).

10. Andrew Sharp, "Why Be Bicultural," in *Justice and Identity,* ed. M. Wilson and A. Yeatman (Wellington: Bridget Williams Books, 1995), 116. Margaret Wilson explains the move to biculturalism: "The constitutional importance of the treaty has always been recognised and asserted by Maori. Although the treaty gave the Crown the authority and legitimacy to govern, it has not always been accorded such recognition by non-Maori. A renewed campaign for recognition of the status of the treaty emerged in the 1970s. It was led by young Maori, often women, but supported by some Pakeha (non-Maori). One of the expressions of this campaign was the emergence of the concept of biculturalism, which argued that Maori must be recognised as an independent sovereign people, and that all public decision making must specifically refer to and address their interests. The success of this campaign began to be seen after the election of the Labour government in 1984" ("Constitutional Recognition of the Treaty of Waitangi: Myth or Reality?" in *Justice and Identity,* ed. M. Wilson and A. Yeatman, 3–4).

11. Russell Jaffe, "The Ebb and Flow of Post-War Jewish Identity in Auckland," in *Identity and Involvement,* ed. A. Gluckman, 40–41. Another view attributes the greater

support for the Jewish day schools, Kadimah in Auckland and Moriah in Wellington, to the influence of new immigrants from America, but also to the impact of the 1967 war in Israel.

12. Ibid., 41. Wally Hirsh was the race relations conciliator from March 1986 to August 1989.

13. I will deal with the changes in interpretation of Jewish collective identity since the Age of Enlightenment in my book *Interactive Identities: Jewish Women in New Zealand* (Palmerston North: Dunmore Press, 1998).

14. Homi K. Bhabha, *The Location of Culture* (London: Routledge, 1995), 1–2.

15. Stuart Hall, "Cultural Identity and Diaspora," in *Identity: Community, Culture, Difference,* ed. J. Rutherford (London: Lawrence and Wishart, 1990), 225.

16. Sneja Gunew, *Framing Marginality* (Carlton: Melbourne University Press, 1994), 45.

17. Donna Matahaere deals with these issues for Maori women in her article "Maori, the 'Eternally Compromised Noun': Complicity, Contradictions, and Postcolonial Identities in the Age of Biculturalism," in *Aotearoa/New Zealand and their Others: Feminism and Postcoloniality.* Special issue of *Women's Studies Journal* 11.1–2.

18. I have changed their real names in order to assure their anonymity but I have not changed their words except to leave out identificatory passages. The interviews were conducted by my research assistant, who can claim among the multiplicity of her identities also a Jewish one. I know many of the women who generously participated in the interviews.

19. For example, the focus on gendered and sexual self had to be teased out by separate questions.

20. Duff is a New Zealand novelist and journalist of Maori and Pakeha descent who advocates the relevance of education for Maori and the necessity of a change in attitude on their part: instead of acting as eternal losers they should take control of their lives, claim responsibility for their actions. Duff refers to the high percentage of criminality, alcohol abuse and domestic violence among Maori.

21. David Theo Goldberg and Michael Krausz, "The Culture of Identity," in *Jewish Identity,* ed. by D. Th. Goldberg and M. Krausz (Philadelphia: Temple University Press, 1993), 8.

22. Ibid., 264–78.

23. Ibid., 1. I wonder why the authors left out the identity category of gender? Is it not as contingent and historically culture-specific as all the other identities? Laurence Silberstein includes results of feminist theorizing in a constructive way in his article, "Others within and Others Without: Rethinking Jewish Identity and Culture," in *The Other in Jewish Thought and History,* ed. Lawrence J. Siberstein and Robert I. Cohn. (New York: New York University Press, 1994), 1–34.

24. The mother later became Ivercargill's first woman mayor.

25. Such restrictions form another commonality with Maori women: on most *maraes* only men have speaking rights.

26. See the situation in the city in which I live: without the effort of women there would be no Jewish community-life to speak of.

27. Aviva adds: "People responded to me saying, 'You know, Aviva, it must be wonderful being Jewish,' and I said, 'Yes, it is terrific.' I knew why New Zealanders were envious of it because they have no identity. They were always looking and searching.

It's obvious to me and even now it happens that people are really quite envious that I am Jewish. Even my academic friends, I think, have a sort of envy because I am just so sure about who I am." Aviva is, of course, referring to white New Zealanders.

28. I am using "self" as understood by Leo Rangell: "The self . . . comprises the totality of the individual, somatic and psychic, body and mind. The self is what identifications lead to. Identity is what identifications cause one to believe about oneself. The self is actual, identity is a mental state" ("Identity and the Human Core: The View from Psychoanalytic Theory," in *Identity and Development,* ed. Harke A. Bosma, Tobi L. G. Graafsma, Harold D. Grotevant, and David J. de Levita (Thousand Oaks, Calif.: Sage Publications, 1994), 28.

29. Sander L. Gilman, "The Jewish Nose: Are Jews White? or, The History of the Nose Job," in *The Other in Jewish Thought and History,* ed. Siberstein and Cohn, 365.

16 Francophone Jewish Intellectuals in Present-Day Quebec

RÉGINE ROBIN

After the close race in the referendum of October 30, 1995, Prime Minister Jacques Parizeau, severely vexed by the results, said in effect that if the "Yes" side had lost by such a narrow margin, this was due to "money and the ethnic vote." And he went on to add that "we" had obtained 60 percent of the vote, that next time "we" would get 62 or 64 percent and that the "Yes" side would be victorious. Parizeau's comments caused such an uproar that he had to resign, even if the causes of his resignation are actually more complex than this one unfortunate statement. Thus a good number of foreign-born Quebecers who had become Canadian citizens and thereby acquired the right to vote (and these included Jewish intellectuals) were designated as "ethnic" and found themselves stigmatized and excluded from this "we"—which, in the circumstances, referred exclusively to French-Canadian Quebecers. This marked a new low in the complicated and difficult relationship between these intellectuals and the nationalist movement.

To understand the situation, one should know that more than 90 percent of these intellectuals had voted "no." Furthermore, we need to understand where the Quebec nationalist movement is at this point in time, and what the future holds in store for French-speaking Jewish intellectuals in Quebec.

With a lengthy history that goes back almost to the defeat of the Plains of Abraham and the subsequent Treaty of Paris of 1763 (in which France relinquished Canada to England, then the foremost marine power in Europe), the French-Canadian nationalist movement has long been a nationalism of survival, of collective withdrawal into roots and origins. And this has been supported and sustained by a clergy whose inspiration and intellectual leaders were provided by the Counterrevolution in France, by the advocates of legitimism, ultramontanism and extreme-right clericalism, and even by such champions of monarchism as the Action Française movement. (Of course, a more balanced profile of the situation would include other tendencies that also existed without holding sway.) This shadowy and exclusive nationalism was Catholic and xenophobic. Its more systematic side fought for the establishment of a North American French state defined by religion, ruralism (from this vantage point, industrial and urban America represented the Antichrist) and antidemocratic traditionalism. Under the French Ancien Régime, Jews did not have the right to settle in New France. After the establishment of the Canadian Federation in 1867, religious and linguistic divisions would play a key role in the distribution of immigrant manpower. The first large-scale immigrations of Jews to Canada took place between 1901 and 1931. Non-Catholic foreigners who came to Canada during the great waves of immigration in the late nineteenth century and the first half of the twentieth did not have access to the Catholic school system, which was, in any case, permeated by Catholic religious values and entirely focused on imparting them to others. All of the Jews from Central or Eastern Europe were obliged to choose English—in other words, Protestant—schools, since the latter more readily exempted their students from religious instruction and did not require a certificate of baptism. For these reasons, the Ashkenazi community is almost totally Anglophone and shares the political fate of Anglophones in the province. Overwhelmingly poor during the 1930s, it played a substantial role in the labor union movement, particularly in the textile industry, and had a significant political and cultural impact. In 1976, when the Parti Québécois came into power for the first time, many Jews (nearly 20,000) left Quebec, mainly for Toronto and Vancouver. They were spurred on by fear of the rising nationalist movement and the apprehension provoked by its ideological antecedents, even though the face of Quebec had changed in the interim. With the exception of a small minority of Ashkenazim who came from Paris, most of the Francophone Jews in Quebec are of North African, particularly Moroccan, origin.[1] Representing about 18,000 of the some 343,000 Jews in Canada (and the 100,000 in Quebec), they live mainly in Montreal. A part of this population, which essentially came to Canada in the late 1950s, spanned the linguistic divide and integrated with the Anglophone community. And this new community soon developed a distinctive ethnic character, creating its own institutions and associations on the margins of those dominated by Ashkenazi Jews, who tended to stigmatize the new arrivals. It was also encouraged to do so by cultural and linguistic pluralism, and by the interminable political infighting that saw the rise of a new brand of Québécois nationalism. Emphasizing its Sephardic character, it created Jewish schools and was somewhat religious—in fact, it was more observant than its counterpart in the United States. It was also able to combine the advantages of a "weak" state and the defense of multicultural democracy. Were its intellectuals sensitive to the official discourse, which attempted to dust off the image of nationalism? Before attempting a reply to this question, we must examine the complexity of the discourse of Quebec nationalism today.

What we are witnessing now are the remains of an ideology, a legacy of traditional ideology currently manifested as vestiges, slips of the tongue, abortive acts and out-of-context statements floated in letters to the editor, on talk shows, in bars and taverns and in political and intellectual circles—not to mention in the collective unconscious, as we see from the reaction of Jacques Parizeau on the evening of the referendum. And this always appears as somewhat strained, except in certain domains of social discourse, such as *Le Siècle de l'Abbé Groulx,*[2] which openly draws upon this heritage. Without putting them all in the same boat, we should also mention the statements of Pierre Trépanier in *Les Cahiers de Jeune Nation,*[3] or, in a completely different sector of social discourse, pronouncements by certain leaders of the Saint Jean-Baptiste Society, by certain hysterical defenders of the eternally threatened, eternally weakened French language in Quebec and, finally, by certain defenders of Québécois identity against immigrants. As for the rest, it is all just slips of the tongue, abortive attempts. Later on we shall see how these traces function within a highly instrumental and technocratic social discourse that hems in all sectors of social and intellectual life, a double discourse that makes it difficult to replace a culture-based concept of citizenship with one based on civic values. Is a pluralist Quebec possible? It will take more than the sheeplike solidarity massed behind the Bloc Québécois to dissuade me from the pessimism inscribed in the title. I would, however, very much like to be proven wrong.

What I have referred to as "abortive acts," as "slips of the tongue" and "gaffes," goes back to a discourse of homogeneity, to nostalgia for an imaginary *Gemeinschaft,* to fusion in the heat of prejudice (as Herder would have said), to everything reminiscent of French-Canadian society—at least as it is often imagined to have existed during the time of the French Canadians. These traces are filtered through the paradigm of roots and incorporated, along with the accompanying metaphors of trunk and branches, into a botanical concept of culture. A few examples of these slips and gaffes will suffice. How can we designate those people who live here and who are, at the same time, Canadian citizens—for the moment, in any case—or landed immigrants who have settled in Quebec? This problem of designation is in itself indicative of a certain uncertainty about identity. The French Canadians of yesteryear are now referred to as Québécois, while the appellation "French Canadian" is reserved for Francophones outside Quebec, or even used as an insult, as when Jacques Parizeau recently referred to Prime Minister Jean Chrétien as a "Canadien français de service" (servile French Canadian). To distinguish the old French-Canadian Québécois from Anglophones and everyone else, nationalists have resorted to terms such as *Québécois de souche* or *Québécois de vieille souche*—roughly, old-stock Quebecers. Since the 1980s, however, a new system of classification has been used to divide the population into three groups: Francophones, Anglophones and Allophones. Allophones are, apparently, those who speak neither French nor English. However, the tension between purely linguistic and ethnic denominations has never been resolved. Thus, depending on the light one sees me in, I am by turns a Francophone, or a Frenchwoman who has settled in Quebec—even though I have acquired Canadian nationality, everyone makes light of it. Or better still, I'm an Allophone, since the term "Francophone" refers not to a mastery of the French language—if it did, any bilingual Anglophone would also be a Francophone—nor even to the acquisition of French from birth—this does not apply to me—but to Quebec French. To go by the "old stock" paradigm, "Francophone" is synonymous with "old French Canadian." This is never openly stated nor inscribed in any official policy, but rises to the surface as traces. And it explains Jacques Parizeau's famous "gaffe" (prior to the one of October 30, 1995) to the effect that Anglophone and Allophone votes would not be required to achieve sovereignty. It is clear that, according to this line of reasoning, I am in every respect an Allophone. Parizeau has been reproached for saying out loud what could have been deduced from any survey. He assumed the air of a martyr of authenticity and frankness, whereas the only real political problem had to do not with accounting questions but with the type of society one should have. Do we want sovereignty acquired with the help of an ethnic vote, in other words, a culturally defined citizenship that would prolong ethnicity? Or do we want a civic citizenship founded not on origins but on a social project?

Curiously, the problem was never posed in this manner anywhere in the deluge of texts that followed Parizeau's gaffe. The concept of Allophone can include everything that is not French Canadian, but by a metonymic shift can also include all those who do not think or vote like the majority of French Canadians. There is a Québécois version of the "Unamerican" appellation favored by Senator Eugene McCarthy. Without going back over the historic and structural reasons that make Allophones potential and real federalists, note that one never asks if, in this desire for emancipation, there is not a measure of ambiguity, some unconscious or unconsidered traces of old 1930s ways of thinking—ways that were, of course, repressed during the Quiet Revolution but that were to come back with even greater force in the return of the repressed. Since I vote like the Allophones, I am, through metonymy, an Allophone all over again. Stephanos Constantinides stripped away the ambiguity in a piece published in the newspaper *Le Devoir:*

> Despite all the verbal precautions taken by the Parti Québécois since its inception, one would have to be blind not to see that it is concerned above all with "old stock" Francophones. "Old stock" Francophones are those who went from being French Canadians to Québécois and finally a nation in an evolutionary process dating back to the 1960s. The others, that is the "ethnics" and Anglophones, are, under the pressure of circumstances, barely beginning to define themselves as Québécois while identifying themselves above all as Canadians.[4]

At this point it is hard not to recall the comment made by Céline Dion when, at the entertainment industry's ADISQ gala in 1990, she refused the Felix Trophy for the year's best Anglophone artist. The problem was not that she said that she was not Anglophone but Francophone, even if she did sing in English for the occasion; for what she said was that she was not Anglophone but Québécois. This was, of course, a slip of the tongue, a trace that would not have been taken very seriously, if Jacques Parizeau had not hastened to congratulate her. "I thought she reacted very well," he confided to the *Montreal Gazette.* "I thought it was, for a girl like that, quite something to say. I was impressed and I wrote her a small note to say so."[5]

So we are back to the "old stock" paradigm, to the effects of unanimism, to the defense reflex, collective humiliation before every divergence of opinion and the impossibility of dissidence or debate. Many examples could be culled from the ocean of press produced in recent years. We will be content with the reception accorded Esther Delisle's thesis on Lionel Groulx and Mordecai Richler's *New Yorker* article of September 27, 1991 ("Inside, Outside"), which later came out in book form. Esther Delisle's thesis focuses on the discourse of the extreme right in Quebec during the 1930s, particularly as it appeared in *Le Devoir* and under the pen of Lionel Groulx. She explains the problems she came up against in trying to put together a jury for her thesis defense. Her book opens with a curious comment:

> Let's get the question of my ethnicity out of the way first. Many people with whom I discussed my research, people whose reactions covered the whole

> spectrum from the overtly hostile to the tentatively encouraging, asked me if I was Jewish. . . . My family genealogy was a favourite topic: Was my grandfather by any chance an important man in a Polish ghetto before the winds of chance deposited him at the foot of St. Lawrence Boulevard in Montreal? . . . Hidden beneath the skirts of these questions about my ethnic origins was the conviction that only a Jew could be *that* interested in anti-Semitism. It was highly improbable that a *real Québécoise* would develop an interest in this subject. Of course, this conclusion is postulated on the proposition that a person of the Jewish faith is not "Québécois," belonging instead to a vaguely defined constellation of "cultural communities."[6]

Delisle's defense of her thesis and the subsequent publication of her book led to a great hue and cry. Not everybody reacted like Jean Éthier-Blais; some responded with embarrassment, or with an oblique display of hostility. It was decided that the book, and hence the thesis, exhibited methodological weaknesses and that the candidate had not sorted through or read all the material. Others said that the mass of quotes was so damning that they must at least have been manipulated to create the impression that anti-Semitism was a general feature of social discourse in Quebec during the 1930s. The reply, in this case, was that anti-Semitism could be found practically everywhere and that, in any case, nobody could have foreseen the genocide perpetrated against the Jews. This is an odd, although almost unanimous, position. Meanwhile, intellectuals generally maintained an embarrassed silence. There was even greater unanimity in the case of Richler—although there were some exceptions, notably Gilles Marcottel's articles in *La Presse,* those of Dorval Brunelle in *Spirale,* and a powerful piece by Jean Barbe in *Voir.* The following is an excerpt from that article:

> If we do not wish to see the image reflected in Mordecai Richler's mirror (which is, it's true, a distorting mirror but a mirror nonetheless), it may be because we are ashamed of it.
>
> Quebec's glorious past (which we draw upon to explain why we constitute a people) contains, in fact, a number of dubious episodes. At one time the population of Quebec was more opposed to conscription and the war than it was to Hitler. . . . Our pacifism had an air of cowardice about it. Is it any wonder that, in the eyes of some, our ancestors were accomplices by virtue of their refusal to act? We have long been told (and we're hearing it again today) that the maturity of a people is measured by its capacity to take charge of its economy. This is not enough. Maturity comes when one is able to look at one's faults and begin rectifying them.[7]

Richler's tract was obviously provocative and occasionally excessive and one-sided; but it was also a call for debate, for a discussion of ideas and a critical look back at Quebec's past and the traditional obstinacy that has characterized relations between Francophones and Anglophones. It was, in short, an opportunity for a polemic on ideas and positions. But it was of no use! All of Quebec hid behind its fragility, its exclusion, humiliation and distinctness, its unfathomable specificity and its secular heroism. People's comments generally echoed Michel Bélanger's pronouncement (made in English) to the effect that he "does not belong."

This obsession with identity, which keeps cropping up everywhere, reminds me of what Claudio Magris said about the cultural price that Slovak nationalism paid (and still continues to pay) for the shrinking of its horizons and the one-sidedness of its vision.

> But a small people which has to shake off the disdain or indifference of the great—of those whose greatness may perhaps have only a little while to run—must also shake off its complex about being small, the feeling of having constantly to rectify or cancel this impression, or else totally reverse it, glorying in it as a sign of election. Those who have long been forced to put all their efforts into the determination and defence of their own identity tend to prolong this attitude even when it is no longer necessary. Turned inward on themselves, absorbed in the assertion of their own identity and intent on making sure that others give it its due recognition, they run the risk of devoting all their energies to this defence, thereby shrinking the horizons of their experience, of lacking magnanimity in their dealings with the world.[8]

Lukas Sosoe argues that the discourse of Quebec nationalism is still largely caught in a romantic logic of nationhood. For its idea of a nation is of an association of people bound together not by contractual ties but by the bonds of origin, ethnicity, language, culture and history. *One either is or is not a member of the collectivity.* The features of organic identity are clearly discernible here. Organic identity develops only by affirming its specificity, its distinctiveness and particularities. It is not a contractualist mode of thought, but one concerned with origins; it holds to an identity that is not constructed but given, inherited; a single, closed identity.[9]

COLLECTIVE RIGHTS VERSUS INDIVIDUAL RIGHTS: THE ENDLESS PUZZLE OF CANADA-QUEBEC PROBLEMS

The "old stock" paradigm has been taken up within a modernist, technocratic and instrumentalist discourse derived from the Quiet Revolution, which combined arguments from the left with a discourse of social control and normalization. This paradigm has been used to invert signs, making a touchy proletarian class with few aspirations into a people proud of its origins in the 60,000 *habitants* of time of the Conquest. In a recent work, Jocelyn Létourneau and Jacinthe Ruel analyze the uses of the past in the briefs submitted to the Commission sur l'avenir politique et constitutionnel du Québec, otherwise known as the Bélanger-Campeau Commission. They sum up the overall interpretation and line of reasoning as follows:

> From being submissive and oppressed, poorly educated and deeply religious, Quebec society, which had [until the Quiet Revolution] striven desperately for survival, began to make up for lost time; it acquired confidence, became more and more educated and secular and began to take charge of its economy and development; these reforms and this process of modernization gave rise to a feeling of pride and self-assurance. . . . A period of exemplary achievements and values, the Quiet Revolution was presented as the model for a new society.
>
> The vanquished figure of 1760, the submissive and poorly educated Catholic, the impoverished worker who had to learn English to overcome his background—in contrast, by the way, with the English conqueror imbued with his sense of superiority, the educated Protestant, the ruthless boss and the pampered minority taking advantage of the tolerance of the majority—was replaced [during the Quiet Revolution] by a new type of identity figure, the image of a proud, dynamic, free, open, pluralistic and generous society confident that its achievements since 1960 would guarantee those to come.[10]

The transition from *painful story* to *success story* was facilitated as much by state intervention as it was by a subsequent neoliberal ideology that retained only the nationalist (or *nous autres*) sense of solidarity. The latter went hand in hand with a powerful ideology of revenge and resentment and, in cobbling together its sense of identity, did not hesitate to blend the "old stock" paradigm with a very business- and performance-oriented ethic obsessed with optimization, calculation and communication. The model espoused was clearly that of the "winner." So the 1980s arrived under the sign of the dollar, and Quebec discovered that it had its own homegrown "golden boys."

Instrumentalization was the order of the day, extending as it did to social discourse, teaching institutions—where it occurred from the bottom up, as we see from the most recent college reforms and the attack on the teaching of philosophy—and, worse still, to Quebec literature, or at least a certain segment of it. By "instrumentalization" I mean not only performance-oriented procedures of social control, but also the tailoring of dreams to the possible, the disappearance of utopian vision, a utilitarian and calculating state of mind, conformism, facile consensus, the loss of critical thought, the impossibility of dissidence and the hegemony of the factual. At the same time, there developed a discourse of citizenship understood not in ethnocultural terms but as a "civic nationalism" purportedly espousing a universalist vision. In short, there has been a permanent refusal to recognize, through a plethora of ever fresh denials—the existence of a Quebec Charter of Human Rights apparently enables us to have a clear conscience while ignoring the Canadian Charter of Human Rights and Freedoms—that the concept of human rights has been painted with the brush of culture. This is no longer conceived as a universalist, intangible principle independent of political expediency, but as a highly relative concept that could conceivably take second place to the "necessary promotion" of collective rights. Thus it is possible to adhere to all discourses simultaneously: to the concept of human rights understood in both individualistic and collective terms; to "civic nationalism" (a contradiction in terms if ever there was one) and a nationalism based on culture; to a nationalism which holds that one must be a French Canadian to be a Quebecer, and one for whom residence in Quebec is a sufficient requirement; to a nationalism which reserves the appellation of "Francophone" for those who speak "Quebec French," and one that applies it to those who speak French or whose mother tongue is French (another potentially explosive confusion). Accompanying all this is a failure to see that all these discourses are full of aporias and mutually exclusive, that their potential for liberation is matched by their narrow focus on identity and withdrawal, depending on the meaning one gives to this confused hodgepodge of ideas. The simultaneous adherence to every discourse and its opposite is the source of a permanent confusion that prohibits all but the most rudimentary and emotional debates. It is, if you will pardon the expression, a real dog's dinner.

In such conditions, one is not surprised to learn that more than 90 percent of Francophone Jewish intellectuals are hostile to nationalism. Still, some of them have been drawn to Quebec;[11] what drew them was its fragility, the fact that French is spoken there, that they themselves could find good positions without having to change languages, that the political vision was, or aspired to be, social democratic and could, for a while at least, create the impression that its battles had something in common with the old third-world struggles against American imperialism. Other factors included a space in which they could "do intellectual work" and find a place for themselves without having to deal with the dehumanizing conditions found in the larger European cities, or in that contemporary monster, New York. All this explains why Jewish intellectuals not only came to Quebec, but chose to remain there. In an issue of *Tribune juive,* one of these intellectuals, a drama professor at the Université du Québec à Montréal, wrote the following:

> Why have the Québécois been unable to transmit their passion and their taste for life to all these minorities? Why is the finger pointed at the lamb when the fox cannot identify the illness afflicting it? The situation is complex. No nation can succeed in its struggle without the strength of a dream founded on a coherent policy and politics. And if this connection is not made, it is not because of ethnic groups or language, but simply because a project requires more than a race or language if it is to constitute a plan and vision for a society. As the illustrious and late Yeshayahu Leibowitz reminds us (speaking of Israel, but also about all the nations of the world), all nationalism degenerates into violence if it is not informed by an ethical intention.
>
> So there it is, the Quebec I dream about. A country consistent with history, one that would, through education, make the transition from politics to policy, in other words, to an ethical project affecting our common heritage, a creative and founding vision that would go beyond the survival of clan, blood, language, territory and race. Not a collage of ghettos but a transcendence of free subjects. Not a multiculturalism but a transculturalism that would leave plenty of room for the choice of a dominant language, since the language of the Other would be perceived not as an opacity but as a bridge to an ethics.
>
> A coming together of the national and the universal, one where everyone could know and feel that he or she has a legitimate place—this would require an enormous educational undertaking, one for which Quebec has been ill prepared.[12]

In this highly complex situation, French-speaking Jewish intellectuals could assume a constructive role, going beyond all the bitterness and resentment to build bridges and articulate, in books, newspapers and so on, a communal public discourse which would remind us that we must never lose sight of the universal. A good starting point for such a discourse can be found in Habermas, specifically in certain recent writings which go back to the 1980s debate on the quarrel of the historians, as well as in his reflections on German reunification after the fall of the Berlin Wall and on the choice of Bonn or Berlin as the future capital of Germany.

The polemic of the 1980s was sparked by the writings of certain historians who sought to restore a "normal" German national identity. Germany was to reestablish ties with its past, find a thread of continuity, put together a narrative that would incorporate those fateful years from 1933–45 into a history so that they would no longer mark an absolute rupture.

Habermas denounced such a project in the name of Auschwitz, an event that cannot be incorporated into the fabric of a history composed of platitudes. The historiographer must never assume the role of mouthpiece for the values of the community, must never become its hagiographer. Habermas opposes the notion of collective identity with that of a "problematized conscience of History." Going against current trends, he draws upon the example of the *Lumières* and their unrealized attempt to establish universalist values.

Of course, all nation-states represent unstable syntheses between the universalist principles derived from the French Revolution or elsewhere and policies centered around specific cultural heritages. In Germany, however, race madness knocked everything off balance; hence the danger of a return to a culture-based identity that would find it extremely difficult to conceive of cultural pluralism, especially since the large-scale migrations of peoples have completely transformed most of the big European countries.

These new communities, whose members constitute an increasing portion of the population, have great difficulty identifying with an identity built on ancestry and traditional ways. We must relativize the various modes of life. History itself, as a discipline and branch of knowledge, has evolved. It is much more critical than it was before, and much less disposed to play its traditional role of national conscience. It is as involved today with the "problematization of the conscience of history," as it is with "the constitution of an identity and the establishment of meaning."[13]

There are a great many collective identities and diverse cultural traditions currently in existence. Because of this, the various forms of integration must pass through channels other than those of the historic national traditions to which we have been accustomed. We must invent new ways of managing diversity, coexistence and heterogeneity, while remaining mindful of the inestimable importance of the universalist values of law, equality and the political and social contract. Hence the idea of a postnational collective identity and a constitutional patriotism.

Instead of building a patriotism on cultural (or prepolitical) factors such as language, culture and history, we must ensure that our postconventional identity is shaped by a political project intent on creating a *communal* space, a new public sphere informed by the universal principles of human rights and the concept of the just state. In my view, Francophone Jewish intellectuals can play a role in reaffirming these principles in Quebec.

Notes

This essay was translated from the French by Donald McGrath.

1. They also include writers from other countries, such as Nalm Kattan, an Iraqi Jew who writes exclusively in French.

2. Jean Éthier-Blais, *Le Siècle de l'Abbé Groulx* (Montreal: Lemdac, 1993).

3. Pierre Trépanier, "Une Doctrine pour la droite?" *Cahiers de Jeune Nation,* Apr. 1992.

4. Stephanos Constantinides, "L'Indépendence avec les purs réserves des lendemains amers," *Le Soleil,* Mar. 3, 1993.

5. *The Montreal Gazette,* Oct. 24, 1990.

6. Esther Delisle, *The Traitor and the Jew,* trans. Madeleine Hébert, Claire Rothman, and Käthe Roth (Montreal: Robert Davies Publishing, 1993).

7. Jean Barbe, "Les Uns et les autres," *Voir* 16 (Mar. 11, 1992): 4.

8. Claudio Magris, *Danube,* trans. Patrick Creagh (London: Collins Harvill, 1990), 225.

9. See Lukas Sosoe, "Le Contractualisme et la question des nationalités," in *Une nation peut-elle se donner la constitution de son choix?* 29–40. Special issue of *Philosophigues: Revue de la société de philosophié du Québec* 19.2 (Fall 1992).

10. Jocelyn Létourneau, *L'Historiographie comme miroir, écho et récit de "Nous Autres,"* CELAT document, Sept. 1993, 31.

11. It appears that Quebec nationalism is still capable of drawing a certain number of Francophone Jewish intellectuals into it ranks. As proof I need only cite the names of Salomon Cohen and Armand Elbaz, two *péquiste* candidates who ran for election in the riding of Outremont. Are these merely exceptions that confirm the rule, or are they manifestations of an enduring but slow and barely perceptible movement toward integration that is not merely political? It is too early to answer this question. I could, by the way, also mention Paul Nathan, who, with Ghila Sroka, founded the Rassemblement des Juifs pour l'indépendence du Québec. However, these found few followers in either the Sephardic or Ashkenazi communities. The Canadian Jewish Congress even made common cause with the Italian and Greek congresses when it appeared before the Commission sur l'Avenir du Québec, which held hearings prior to the 1995 referendum. In its brief to the commission, the CJC called upon the entire Jewish community to choose federalism over Quebec nationalism.

12. Serge Ouaknine, "Le Québec de mes reves," *Tribune juive,* Mar. 1994, 12–13.

13. Jürgen Habermas, *Écrits politiques* (Paris: Éditions du Cerf, 1990), 235.

CONTRIBUTORS

PAUL R. BARTROP is a research fellow in the School of Australian and International Studies at Deakin University and teaches in the Jewish studies department at Bialik College. The author of *Australia and the Holocaust, 1933–45* (1994) and the editor of *False Havens: The British Empire and the Holocaust* (1995), he has also published numerous scholarly articles in journals and books. He is an international authority on the response of British Commonwealth countries to the Holocaust and anti-Semitism and is working on a three-volume study of genocide and indigenous peoples and a series of essays on the Ten Commandments and the Holocaust.

CLAUDIA B. BRAUDE is a freelance writer and critic. She is editing the anthology *Jewish Writing in the Contemporary World: South Africa.*

SALLY FRANKENTAL, the first director of the Kaplan Centre for Jewish Studies at the University of Cape Town, now lectures in the Department of Social Anthropology at UCT and teaches a course in contemporary Jewry in the Department of Hebrew and Jewish Studies. Her early work focused on kinship among Tamil Indians in Cape Town and on urban (white) aging. Her current research examines the Jewish identity of Israeli migrants in South Africa.

SANDER L. GILMAN is Henry R. Luce Distinguished Service Professor of the Liberal Arts in Human Biology at the University of Chicago, where he also serves as chair of Germanic studies and a professor of psychiatry. A member of the Fishbein Center for the History of Science and the Committee on Jewish Studies, and a past president of the Modern Language Association, he is the author or editor of more than fifty books, including *Seeing the Insane* (1982), *Jewish Self-Hatred* (1986), *Picturing Health and Illness* (1995), and *Franz Kafka: The Jewish Patient* (1995).

HEIDI GRUNEBAUM-RALPH has completed a master's thesis entitled "Memory and the Auschwitz Experience: A Study of Shoah Narrative in French Literature" in the Department of French at the University of Cape Town and is a board member of the Holocaust Memorial Council of Cape Town. She has written and presented papers examining the works of an Auschwitz survivor, Charlotte Delbo, as well as Shoah survivor testimony as a narrative model for victims and survivors of human rights abuses in South Africa.

MICHAEL JOHN is an assistant professor in the Department of Social and Economic History at the University of Linz. The author of three monographs and more than sixty scientific articles, his main areas of interest are the history of housing, the history of everyday life, migration in Austria in the nineteenth and twentieth centuries, the history of minorities, and Jewish history in Austria.

JEFFREY LESSER is an associate professor of history and the associate director for research at the Center for International Studies and the Liberal Arts at Connecticut College. The author of *Welcoming the Undesirables: Brazil and the Jewish Question* (1994), which won the Best Book Prize from the New England Council on Latin American Studies, he is completing a book on the public negotiation of non-European immigrant ethnicity in Brazil.

MARCIA LEVESON, an associate professor in the Department of English at the University of the Witwatersrand, specializes in South African literature, nineteenth-century literature, and poetry. She is the author of *People of the Book: Images of the Jew in South African English Fiction, 1880–1992*, the editor of *Roy Campbell: Selected Poetry* and *Vincent Swart: Collected Poems*, and the coeditor of *Roy Campbell: Collected Works*. She founded Quartz Press and the arts magazine *Imprint*, serves on the editorial board of *Jewish Affairs*, and is president of the English Academy of Southern Africa.

ALBERT LICHTBLAU is an assistant professor in the Department of History at the University of Salzburg and, since 1992, a research fellow at the Institut fur Geschichte dur Juden in Osterreich, St. Polten. His publications include three monographs and thirty articles; he also coproduced an eighty-seven-minute documentary film, *Wien—New York* (1992), with Helga Embacher. His main areas of interest are the history of housing, migration in the Austro-Hungarian monarchy, the history of minorities, and the history of the Jews in Austria. He is working on a study of Austrian-Jewish exile in New York, focusing on language and acculturation.

BERNARD REISMAN is Klutznick Professor in Contemporary Jewish Studies at Brandeis University and founding director of the Hornstein Program in Jewish Communal Service, which provides graduate education to people preparing for professional careers in Jewish communities around the world. He and his wife, Elaine Reisman, have been involved for more than two years in a major action/research study of Jews living in Alaska.

RÉGINE ROBIN, a professor of sociology at the University of Quebec and a member of the Royal Society of Canada, is the author of more than a dozen books, including *Socialist Realism: An Impossible Aesthetics* (1993) and the novel *La Quebecoite.* She has published extensively in the field of Jewish identity as well as works on Freud, Canetti, Joseph Roth, and Kafka. She also has translated novels and short stories from Yiddish into French.

MILTON SHAIN is a professor of modern Jewish history in the Department of Hebrew and Jewish Studies at the University of Cape Town and director of the Isaac and Jessie Kaplan Centre for Jewish Studies and Research at UCT. He has published numerous scholarly articles, chapters in books, and encyclopedia entries and is the author of *Jewry and Cape Society: The Origins and Activities of the Jewish Board of Deputies for the Cape Colony* (1983), *The Roots of Antisemitism in South Africa* (1994), which was awarded the University of Cape Town Book Prize for 1996, and *Antisemitism* (1998).

GIDEON SHIMONI is Shlomo Argov Professor in Israel Diaspora Relations at the Hebrew University of Jerusalem and also lectures in the Department of Contemporary Jewry. He is the author of *Jews and Zionism: The South African Experience, 1910–1967* (1980) and, most recently, *The Zionist Ideology* (1995).

JOHN SIMON, chairman of the Jacob Gitlin Library in Cape Town, South Africa, and a member of the editorial board of *Jewish Affairs* and the management committee of the Kaplan Centre for Jewish Studies at the University of Cape Town, was actively involved in Jewish communal life for many years. He is a contributor to *Founders and Followers: Johannesburg Jewry, 1887–1915* (1991) and has published numerous papers in various journals.

JON STRATTON is a senior lecturer in cultural studies in the School of Communication and Cultural Studies, Curtin University of Technology, Perth. He has published widely in cultural studies, including books on postmodernity, Australian youth culture, and the body in later-modern European culture. In his recent work he has begun an examination of the relationship between multiculturalism and the nation-state and an investigation of the experience of postassimilation Jewishness.

LIVIA KÄTHE WITTMANN is an associate professor and head of the Department of Feminist Studies at Canterbury University, Christchurch. Her publications include books and articles on Alfred Andersch, Johannes R. Becher, Peter Huchel,

Gunter Eich, Bertolt Brecht, Marieluise Fleisser, Irmgard Keun, Irene Dische, Margit Kaffka, and the New Woman at the turn of the century. She has also written articles for *Comparative Literature* and *Feminist Literary Criticism* and is presently involved in research on Jewish women's identity in New Zealand.

SETH L. WOLITZ holds the Gale Chair of Jewish Studies at the University of Texas at Austin, where he is also head of the Jewish Studies Program and a professor of French, Slavic, and comparative literature. He has published books on Provençal literature and on Proust as well as many articles on Yiddish literature and Russian-Jewish art and Francophonic literature. An active translator of Antillian plays and Yiddish masters, he is on the editorial boards of various learned journals, including *Yiddishe Kultur* and *Jewish Affairs,* and is a charter member of the Board of Governors of the Texas Jewish Historical Society.

ZHOU XUN is a doctoral student at the School of Oriental and African Studies, University of London. She is completing a dissertation entitled "A History of Chinese Understanding of Judaism and the 'Jew'" and has published a chapter in *Racial Identity and Ethnicity in East Asia* (forthcoming) and an article in *Journal Vandkunsten: Konflikt, Politik I Histories* (1996).

INDEX

Typeset in 9.5/13 Stone Serif
with Stone Serif display
Designed by Paula Newcomb
Composed by Jim Proefrock
at the University of Illinois Press
Manufactured by Cushing-Malloy, Inc.

University of Illinois Press
1325 South Oak Street
Champaign, IL 61820-6903

www.press.uillinois.edu